THE UPPER ROOM

Disciplines

2019

UPPER ROOM BOOKS®
NASHVILLE

An Outline for Small-Group Use of *Disciplines*

Here is a simple plan for a one-hour, weekly group meeting based on reading *Disciplines*. One person may act as convener every week, or the role can rotate among group members. You may want to light a white Christ candle each week to signal the beginning of your time together.

Opening

Convener: Let us come into the presence of God.

Others: Lord Jesus Christ, thank you for being with us. Let us hear your word to us as we speak to one another.

Scripture

Convener reads the scripture suggested for that day in *Disciplines*. After a one- or two-minute silence, convener asks: What did you hear God saying to you in this passage? What response does this call for? (Group members respond in turn or as led.)

Reflection

- What scripture passage(s) and meditation(s) from this week was (were) particularly meaningful for you? Why? (Group members respond in turn or as led.)
- What actions were you nudged to take in response to the week's meditations? (Group members respond in turn or as led.)
- Where were you challenged in your discipleship this week? How did you respond to the challenge? (Group members respond in turn or as led.)

Praying together

Convener says: Based on today's discussion, what people and situations do you want us to pray for now and in the coming week? Convener or other volunteer then prays about the concerns named.

Departing

Convener says: Let us go in peace to serve God and our neighbors in all that we do.

THE UPPER ROOM DISCIPLINES 2019

The Upper Room Books website: books.upperroom.org

Cover design: Left Coast Design, Portland, Oregon

Cover photo: © Jacob_09 / Shutterstock.com

At the time of publication all websites referenced in this book were valid. However, due to the fluid nature of the internet some addresses may have changed, or the content may no longer be relevant.

Scripture quotations marked AP are the author's paraphrase.

Scripture quotations marked KJV are from the King James Version of the Bible.

Quotations marked UMH are taken from *The United Methodist Hymnal,* Nashville, TN: Abingdon Press, 1989.

The week of November 25—December 1 first appeared in The Upper Room Disciplines 2010. Reprinted and used by permission.

Writers of various books of the Bible may be disputed in certain circles; this volume uses the names of the biblically attributed authors.

ISBN: 978-0-8358-1742-4 (print, regular edition)

ISBN: 978-0-8358-1744-8 (mobi); ISBN: 978-0-8358-1745-5 (epub)

For quick access to the scriptures recommended in this book, visit
BibleGateway.com or Biblica.com

Printed in the United States of America

CONTENTS

FOREWORD

Recently, a friend reported to me that her husband, upon returning from a three-day retreat, had begun to get up early each morning to read the Bible and to pray. "Frankly," she admitted, "I worry that something may be wrong. Sometimes he even kneels!" The change my friend saw unfolding in her husband was only the first chapter in a beautiful story of inward and outward spiritual transformation.

Daily devotion can indeed be risky business—when it expresses, in the words of John Wesley, "a desire to know the whole will of God, and a fixed resolution to do it." In my own experience, however, even an experimental ten- or fifteen-minute practice as simple as reading scripture, journaling thoughts, and quietly listening can create an opening between us and God that changes our direction forever. How much more transforming then to live a life shaped by the Word!

Disciplines is an invitation to let your life be shaped by the Word. "The Word became flesh" (John 1:14) is one of the core convictions of Christian faith. The mystery of the Incarnation, however, doesn't begin and end with Jesus of Nazareth. As in my neighbor's experience, the Word that became flesh in Jesus can come alive in us as well. This is the whole idea and promise of Christian faith. As Athanasius put it, "[Christ] became what we are that we may become what he is."

Being shaped by the Word, becoming "what [Christ] is," manifests in a process of change from the inside out, not the other way around. Undergoing change from the inside out means learning to live from a listening heart rather than from my daily gush of good ideas, ideals, and moral judgments concerning God's will. Rather than promptly imposing these revelations on other persons or on the organization I lead before they've been sifted, living from a listening heart requires inner work and deepening self-awareness.

Over the years, one spiritual practice in particular has kept me moving on my stumbling walk with Christ. Praying the scripture helps me to listen deeply and consistently beyond my own reflections, "to be guided by the word of the scriptures," as Bonhoeffer put it, and "not become victims to our own emptiness." It's a process that the Benedictine tradition calls *lectio divina*. My perseverance in the daily practice is strengthened by my participation in a weekly class that studies the lectionary, with *Disciplines* as our daily guide.

The ancient pattern of *lectio* unfolds naturally in several movements. Robert Mulholland and Marjorie Thompson elaborate on the pattern and present the movements of *lectio* in a new way for our day in *The Way of Scripture,* a seven-week spiritual formation process for individuals and groups. The movements are *silencio,* preparing to read scripture; *lectio,* ingesting the Word; *meditatio,* wrestling with God; *oratio,* letting God know how we feel; *contemplatio,* abandoning ourselves to God in love; and *incarnatio,* the Word becoming flesh in us.

Working prayerfully with scripture in the practice of *lectio divina* guides us not only through reflection and identification with the text (the point at which we usually stop), but on to encounter with the living God who then returns us to the world in newness of life. Our center shifts from being in the world for God to being in God for the world, a subtle but critical distinction.

So, friends, I invite you to join me on the way of Christ with *Disciplines* as our guide to praying the scripture in 2019. May the Word that became flesh in Jesus become flesh in you in a life that grows from your intimacy with God.

—Stephen Bryant
Publisher, Upper Room Ministries

Following the Light, Being the Light

JANUARY 1–6, 2019 • J. MARSHALL JENKINS

SCRIPTURE OVERVIEW: As we approach Epiphany Sunday, we think of the coming of God into the world as the coming of a brilliant light—a light that shines into dark corners, a light that shines on people who dwell in darkness. The light of God brings with it the power of restoration to a people in exile. It shines transforming power on forgotten ones who will now arise and shine. God's presence brings light and well-being. At this time of year, we may desire God's light to shine upon us.

QUESTIONS AND SUGGESTIONS FOR REFLECTION

- Read Matthew 25:31-46. Where do you see darkness in your community? How can you shine Christ's light?
- Read Psalm 72:1-7, 10-14. Consider the differences between fairness, justice, and mercy. Who around you suffers when fairness wears the cloak of justice? How can you turn the situation toward mercy?
- Read Ephesians 3:1-12. Was there a time when you thought the gospel was not for you? What has changed?
- Read Matthew 2:1-12. We can decipher mystery through light, mercy, witness, and love. How is Christ revealed to you this Epiphany?

Author, spiritual director, and licensed psychologist, living in Rome, Georgia.

TUESDAY, JANUARY 1 ~ *Read Matthew 25:31-46*

New Year's Day

Jesus Christ is God's light in the darkness. Thus, we want nothing more than to see and know Christ. How shall we find him?

To find the light in the darkness, we must first find the darkness. It surrounds us. But we search clumsily because we instinctively avert our eyes from darkness as from a blinding light.

Jesus himself told us where to look: among the hungry, thirsty, alien, vulnerable, sick, and imprisoned. From their dark predicament, their faces will reveal the light. Seek the child born in a manger, not a resident of mansions and towers. Seek the servant, not a self-promoter. Seek the crucified, not one above it all.

But how shall we see the light of Christ in the lowly? Neither by passive spectatorship nor by armchair analysis; the light of Christ appears to those who step into the night with the lowly. We see by doing. When we give food, water, welcome, clothing, balm, and companionship, the giving opens our eyes, and we see Christ.

As for those who abide in the artificial light of worldly glory, cast a compassionate eye on them. See through the accoutrements of power to their spiritual nakedness, their vulnerability. Offer to them according to their need, and do not be discouraged if they refuse. The light of Christ will shine in God's time. The same goes for the poor but proud. It is easier with the poor in spirit, those who know their poverty and need. And the greatest challenge may come in front of the mirror.

Remove the mask you made to face a dark world. Cast a compassionate eye on yourself. Offer yourself food, drink, welcome, encouragement, strength, balm, and friendship. Allow yourself to receive the love God first gave you in Christ. Let the light shine. Not only you but the world will see.

Lord, give me a compassionate heart and eyes to see your light in myself and others. Amen.

WEDNESDAY, JANUARY 2 ~ *Read Psalm 72:1-4, 10-14*

Mercy is compassion in action. As discussed in yesterday's meditation, Jesus taught us to find him in merciful encounters. In doing so, he echoes the biblical sense of justice.

American iconography anthropomorphizes justice as a blindfolded woman holding a scale. We conceive of justice as no respecter of individuality where fairness is the bottom line. We deem mercy another matter altogether.

Biblical justice takes fairness into account, but fairness is not the bottom line. God, who wears no blindfold, insists on mercy in justice. The bottom line is a social order in which the hungry, thirsty, alien, vulnerable, sick, and imprisoned receive the care they need. Justice as fairness alone blindfolds us to human need. Justice infused with mercy shines light in the darkness, revealing the God who sees so attentively that no sparrow flies from divine care.

Today's reading beseeches God's justice for the king: to judge "people with righteousness, and [the] poor with justice." Specifically, the just king would "defend the cause of the poor of the people, give deliverance to the needy, and crush the oppressor."

In harmony with the prophets (see Isaiah 60:1-6), this justice beckons other kings to come, pay tribute, and bow down to the king who lights up the night with the glory of God. This king overwhelms them not with arms but with care and protection for "the weak and needy," for "precious is their blood in his sight."

This may seem idealistic and naïve. On the individual level, a life lived in kindness and mercy may work out, but to expect our leaders and our society to put mercy before fairness and to enact kindness before force may seem far-fetched. Yet, such are the ways of Christ. Such is the vocation to which God calls God's people. Such is the light in the darkness.

Lord, lead us from fear to faith so that we may see and be your light. Amen.

THURSDAY, JANUARY 3 ~ *Read Psalm 72:5-7*

Light and darkness offer rich metaphors for our life in Christ. Light is God's love that breaks through the darkness of cruelty and injustice. Light is Christ meeting us in the darkness of human poverty and need. Light is the glow we emit that illumines the road for all who walk near us.

But what about the sun that bathes us with day and the moon that allows us sight at night? Do they too reveal the divine? Do they show us the way on life's pilgrimage? What about all natural things? Do bird, hazelnut, and sea reveal the divine?

Of course they do. Sitting on a stump in the woods, walking along the shore, or standing atop a mountain, we sense expansive otherness, our smallness in a web of life, and the rich diversity and oneness of being. Nature evokes our praise.

Even when we narrow our focus to a tiny hazelnut, as Julian of Norwich teaches us, we find a source of revelation as rich as scripture. Even attending to our bodies, as the author of Psalm 139 sings, we sense the quiver in our Maker's fingers.

When we attend to our world with wonder, we can see what God is up to: Each created thing becomes a window, pointing beyond itself to the mystery of the Creator.

In today's verses, the psalmist wishes for the new king a reign as long as the life of the sun and moon. The psalmist wishes for the king fruitful subjects, like rain that nourishes vast fields of grass. Implicitly, just as sun, moon, rain, and flourishing fields point beyond themselves to their Creator, so the king brings to bear graces from above.

Sun, rain, and field as well as king and people, in their nourishing and flourishing, reveal the God who loves them.

Lord, as nature lights our vision of you, may we light the vision of others. Amen.

Paul argues that creation should suffice to reveal the Creator and prompt devotion. But the human heart's impatience for heavenly blessings leads us to worship idols and pursue cheap substitutes. In the frenzy, we miss the point of nature's sermon.

Paul never forgets how God wakes him. As Paul travels to Damascus to persecute Christians, Christ strikes him like lightning. The risen Christ convicts Paul and then calls him to a new ministry of love. Paul staggers around blind for three days until he comes to his senses in the care of those he came to persecute. (See Acts 9:1-19.) In today's passage, Paul refers to this experience as the revelation in which the mystery of Christ about which he preaches was made known to him.

Special revelation breaks through from outside the natural course of things, a divine intervention that disrupts the normal cycle of nature and the march of history. God is love, steadfast love to be exact, so God never gives up, even if it means knocking a self-righteous terrorist off a horse and commissioning him to a life of tireless telling about how that love raised a divine man from the dead. Such epiphany shakes things up. In Christ, God not only shakes up normal expectations of life and death. God blows down the walls that exclude anyone from the reach of God's love and the blessing of eternal life. Paul's commission from God is to bring understanding of this mystery to those who think it is not for them. But God insists through Paul that the mystery of Christ is for all of us.

Lord, when you shake up our lives, help us to discern your love at work and lead us to tell about it. Amen.

SATURDAY, JANUARY 5 ~ *Read Ephesians 3:5-12*

Biblical texts honor the power of words. Names matter. Stories transport the energy of plot and characters through the teller to the told. Whether we speak of God's light piercing the night through Christ or of faithful people, mercy, justice, or creation, our words illuminate God's creation. While the daily onslaught of words can numb us, God's words can warm those who listen.

Gospel means good news, and Paul serves that gospel. At all costs, he tells far and wide that this gospel was open to the Gentiles as well as the Jews and establishes gospel-sharing communities called "churches." Strictly speaking, the gospel refers to God's redemptive work in Jesus. But God so charges the gospel that Paul sees it in scripture and mysterious presence, in past, present, and future, in suffering and joy, in speakers and hearers transformed. It becomes Paul's force field, and everywhere he goes, things change: Gentiles begin to believe that the gospel is for them.

We find gospel truth in scripture. We do well to read the New Testament books called Gospels; yet, if we read them well, they point us to the gospel in the whole biblical library of history, legend, poetry, prophecy, and law. The stories of the Bible convey the unfailing gospel to those who read with the eyes of faith. "We have this treasure in clay jars, so that it may be made clear that this extraordinary power belongs to God and does not come from us" (2 Cor. 4:7), Paul writes of people like him who become gospels themselves by their telling of it.

Words and people who use them limit the truth they tell. Our words can only point to the ineffable mystery of God. Yet they grant us access to God. Through faith in Jesus Christ, we can approach God in freedom and confidence.

Lord, may our words illuminate the paths of others as we share the gospel. Amen.

Epiphany

The journey of three astrologers to the epiphany of Christ includes every means of revelation discussed this week. A peculiar star piques their interest. It prompts wonder to the point of fixation and a search for the truth to which it points. So they journey toward nature's beacon like children tracking down the rainbow's landing. They seek orientation in Jerusalem and listen to those who know scripture. Even paranoid Herod gives ear. Hearing prophetic references to Bethlehem as the anticipated birthplace of the Messiah, the astrologers take the clue, unlock the riddle, and draw a map. Yet, it leads them to an undecipherable mystery of love.

By the time they find the humble family with the small child, that love touches them. Having sensed Herod's intentions in commissioning them to report the child's whereabouts, they choose the way of mercy and justice for a family vulnerable to his power. They tear up the map and never share a word with Herod.

Touched by God, they prove faithful witnesses. They praise the child, honor him with gifts of gold, frankincense, and myrrh. In Matthew's telling, these outsiders worship the Messiah first. In their home country to which they return, they may bear witness there too. At personal risk, they put into action their trust in a wonder unseen. Such is faith. Faith lights the eye to glimpse the incomprehensible. They find something too wonderful to explain. Their journey leads to a revelation of divine love beyond natural or magical understanding.

A star lights their way, yes; but if they follow only literal light, they would see just a pitiful family on the edge, not the newborn Prince of Peace. God's gift of faith, scripture, and love lights their way and illumines the manger. The star is gone, but Jesus' eternal light remains.

Lord, light our way with love to truth that sets us free. Amen.

Befriending Baptism's Wildness

JANUARY 7–13, 2019 • DANIEL BENEDICT

SCRIPTURE OVERVIEW: Water is an important theme throughout the Bible. The authors of scripture use water as an image of transition and sometimes challenge and always tie it back to God's renewing work. Isaiah records the divine promise that God will not abandon Israel, even if they pass through trying waters—a reference to the deliverance of the Israelites from the Egyptians. The psalmist declares that God's voice covers all the waters, so nothing can come against us that is beyond God's reach. In Acts we see the connection between baptism—passing through the water—and the gift of the Holy Spirit. The emphasis is on the inclusion of the Samaritans, a group considered unclean by many but not by God. We see clearly the connection between water baptism and the Spirit in the baptism of Jesus himself.

QUESTIONS AND SUGGESTIONS FOR REFLECTION

- Read Isaiah 43:1-7. Isaiah presents an image of God's favor that is at once particular and universal. How do you experience God's love for you as part of the body of Christ as well as for all persons?
- Read Psalm 29. God's creation, in its wildness, incorporates destruction. In the face of disaster, how do you find a way to say, "Glory"?
- Read Acts 8:14-17. Our baptism is in the name of Jesus and the name of the Spirit. To what wildness does the Spirit prompt you?
- Read Luke 3:15-17, 21-22. Remember your baptism and listen for God's call out into the wildness of the world.

Writer; retired United Methodist pastor; former Director of Worship Resources for Discipleship Ministries; member of the Order of Saint Luke.

MONDAY, JANUARY 7 ~ *Read Luke 3:15-17, 21-22*

Heightened expectations unleash in and among us a palpable and playful wildness. Emotions stir. Our senses go on alert. We wonder and speculate. We ask questions: "What's the buzz? What does this all mean?" Throw "Messiah" into the river and the waters quiver. And John the Baptizer does not disappoint! His "wild" demeanor and preaching in the wilderness (see Luke 3:1-14) charge the atmosphere with expectancy and ethical upheaval. He points not to himself but beyond to the ultimate source of power and wildness: "the Holy Spirit and fire" with which his successor will baptize them.

Fire, spirit-wind, burning chaff, threshing: The prospects of an imminent and impending future promise to be fierce and undomesticated.

We Christians tend to resist the coming of power, change, the consumption of our "chaff," and the winnowing that brings us to our "true self." We tend to "remember our baptism" as a transaction that got us "in" where it is safe, rather than "sending us out" into the wildness of God's new creation. We prefer to think of our identity with the risen Christ, rather than to embrace our daily experience of dying and rising with him. (See Romans 6.)

So, we will spend this week expecting, contemplating, and befriending the wildness of creation and the new creation into which we have been and will be baptized. We cannot know fully the beauty of living on this planet apart from its wilderness and wildness. Its storms and floods, forest fires, earthquakes, hurricanes, tornadoes, rainbows, and our integral belonging to the food chain help us find language for our relationship with the divine Mystery. Isaiah and the psalmist employ images from the book of nature and geopolitics to form our vocabulary for baptism.

What expectancy stirs in you regarding baptism as a past event to be reclaimed in the present? In what ways have you or do you experience the wildness of Spirit-wind?

TUESDAY, JANUARY 8 ~ *Read Isaiah 43:1-7*

Redemption and wilderness experience go together. Isaiah's covenant people know God's love by going through literal and figurative flood and fire, by enduring exile and fear. God's covenant-making and -keeping engages us with powerful forces.

In Israel's experience, geopolitics are at stake: "I give . . . nations in exchange for your life." These lines in Isaiah 43 trouble us. Perhaps the sojourning God headed for the new creation will rearrange human structures and expectations with wild abandon for the sake of justice and love. God gives Egypt as ransom. Ethiopia? Rome? The Holy Roman Empire? The United States? The hegemony of oil, coal, and mineral extraction to suit the whims of humanity at the expense of other creatures? How wild are we willing for God to be to accomplish the divine purpose for creation? Will we risk this God being "with us"?

God does not promise life without crossing rivers and passing through flames, but God promises to protect us through water and fire. The unmistakable character of the relationship is one of redemption, endearment, love, and purposeful destiny. God's choosing us is dynamic, creative, and personal.

Baptism brings us from far away to make us sons and daughters formed for the glory of God. Birth and new birth are wildly creative. John the evangelist writes, "The wind blows where it chooses. . . . So it is with everyone who is born of the Spirit" (John 3:8).

God creates wildly, and we know God's love best on the edge of the river, in the eye of the storm, in the moral arc of the universe rising up in long-denied dignity and justice, in earth's ecosystems warning of human excess, and in contemplating the mystery of the many ways the Spirit-wind-breath descends and claims us.

God of the wilderness, when I step back from risk, bring me through the waters to your just and creative purpose. Amen.

WEDNESDAY, JANUARY 9 ~ *Read Psalm 29*

We could read today's psalm as a portrayal of a distant God separate from creation and thus capricious and rapacious. We could read it as God thrashing and trashing the trees, ravishing the wilderness, setting forests on fire, and flooding lands maliciously. (Perhaps a god like ourselves, careless with creation.)

Yet this is a psalm, a song for worship, a text with a liturgical context. When reciting or singing it, we encounter the numinous in our experience of nature. Thunder, lightning, wind, and storm, Lebanon skipping like a calf, and even an earthquake speak with God's voice. Without the natural world, we would have no images and no imagination with which to declare God's glory and power. The forces and realities of nature are a book we must read to know the glory of God in the other book: the Bible.

Disorder and destruction are so named because of our miscalculation of powers and cycles we cannot fully measure or control. What if we expanded our understanding of baptism to include yielding to such power and glory? Jesus speaks of it when he tells Peter, "When you grow old . . . someone else will fasten a belt around you and take you where you do not wish to go" (John 21:18).

How can we know the wonder and wildness of our baptism if we refuse to acknowledge that we are integral to the beauty and wildness of nature? How will we appreciate the force of the inbreathing Spirit if we have not stood in the gale and shuddered at thunder's intrusion? In our living and dying, baptism immerses us in nature. Our God, our creator, present in creation's order and wildness, comes to us, speaks to us, fills us with wind and fire, and evokes our declaration, "Glory!"

In this moment, be present to nature and its mediation of God's inbreathing presence.

THURSDAY, JANUARY 10 ~ *Read Acts 8:14-17*

We find parentheses in today's reading. Don't you love parentheses? I think of them as little Wikipedia entries within a story. They illuminate what we might not see otherwise. Christianity in its earliest days was a movement of wild men and women who had no handbooks, no instructions. All they knew was Jesus, who was crucified but somehow still alive, and they had to figure out or wait for the rest. So they performed baptism in Jesus' name.

Our parentheses tells us more of the story: "(. . . they had only been baptized in the name of the Lord Jesus)." But, according to the Jerusalem church, baptism in the name of Jesus was too tame. The apostles find the wildness of the Holy Spirit at Pentecost, as Jesus had promised. So Peter and John go to Samaria to install baptism version 2.0: "Holy Spirit Animated Discipleship." Peter and John do about the simplest thing you can imagine; they pray for the Samaritans and then lay hands on them. Then "they received the Holy Spirit." God's animating wildness comes upon them! The text gives us no more details about how this happens, but we know something of its effect. In the next verses, Simon, a magician, offers money to Peter and John to buy this power of bestowing the Spirit-breath (vv. 18-25). He wants the "big deal." So, what was the big deal? We don't know.

But trace through the Bible the Hebrew *ruach* and the Greek *pneuma*—words for wind, breath, and spirit—and the emerging litany will find you tingling with the stirrings of nature (human and otherwise).

Remember that you are baptized. How is the Spirit animating your discipleship?

How are we to understand the privileging of Israel here? It seems beyond our understanding of God's general justice. As Creator, God's love is for all creation. To the extent that there are tribes, peoples, and nations, God loves each and all. We might say that God delights in the rich diversity of cultures, languages, and ethnicities. Thomas Aquinas wrote, "[God] created the great diversity of things so that the perfection lacking to one would be supplied by the others."* Egypt, Ethiopia, Seba, the South Sudan, and the Crow nation serve to manifest the fullness of God!

But Isaiah writes out of his exilic context in which the people experience exile as a revocation of God's covenant. Before the Israelites can receive the good news of return, God must reaffirm their covenant. As with children baptized in infancy and later lost to addiction or self-justification, the people of Israel seek God's divine reestablishment of the covenant.

Here Isaiah gives voice to God's covenant love for a singular people. "I have called you by name, you are mine." This too reflects God's wildness. In the divine economy, covenant love for a people serves love's ecology for the whole. Devotionally, we can appropriate "you are mine" in personal ways. Yet we should not miss the original intent. God has elected Jacob and his descendants. Privilege? Exceptionalism? Yes and no. Isaiah later articulates God's universal vision: "It is too light a thing that you should be my servant to raise up the tribes of Jacob and to restore the survivors of Israel; I will give you as a light to the nations, that my salvation may reach to the end of the earth" (49:6). Before God, privilege is for service. Listen, church! Heed this, nations!

**Summa Theologica* I, q. 47, a. I.

What does the baptismal covenant mean to you in terms of privilege and vocation? Personally? Ecclesially? As a citizen?

SATURDAY, JANUARY 12 ~ *Read Psalm 29*

During the Sanctus at every Eucharist, we acclaim, "Heaven and earth are full of your glory." The psalmist proclaims the same throughout this psalm. The psalmist commands heavenly beings to declare God's splendor! But how shall they do so? With what language and imagery? With the earthly language and imagery we share! The psalmist declares God's glory in the wildness of floods, thunder, skipping calves, flames, earthquakes, and stripped forests. The psalmist even names particular places: Lebanon, Sirion, and Kadesh. We cannot get away from Earth. It is our home. As biological creatures, the planet is integral to our existence.

The hiccup in our understanding of redemption and the life of the "soul" is the extrapolation that we came from somewhere else and are going somewhere else. I do not mean that I deny our hope of everlasting life or of a new heaven and new earth. (See Revelation 21.) I wish to correct any notions of salvation that render earth, sky, and waters disposable or ultimately insignificant, because heaven and earth are full of God's glory. The "voice" of nature—the numinous Presence made manifest—is "powerful . . . full of majesty." God's "voice" is more than impressive; it wreaks destruction. And, with the psalmist, we stand amazed.

The victims of natural disasters are appalled, and rightly so. With some distance, the rest of us wonder at the sheer force of the planet and universe evolving. The universe is continually being born as it has been for nearly fourteen billion years. It is a wild and beautiful universe over which "the Lord sits enthroned as king forever." Befriending this is the great work of all religions, including all who are baptized. In our time, our great work of healing is to reconcile humanity's belonging to our earth and our earth's Creator.

Write or speak a psalm of wonder with words and images from your place on the planet.

SUNDAY, JANUARY 13 ~ *Read Luke 3:15-17, 21-22*

Baptism of the Lord

Weheia, the word used for "open" in the Hawaiian text of Luke, has an interesting range of meanings: open, untie, undo, loosen, unlock, take off (as clothes). So we can consider in myriad ways the heavens' opening for the Holy Spirit to descend. Maybe we get the sense that "the sky let loose" or "heaven became naked or exposed." In the Celtic sense, that time at the Jordan becomes a "thin place," where the vast distance between heaven and earth collapses and our experience of God becomes more immediate.

But God's immediacy may be at once reassuring and terrifying in Luke's narrative arc. Jesus may find the voice confirming his identity as Son of God much needed in the assault of temptation that follows. (See Luke 4.) Luke's genealogical interlude (3:23-37) interrupts the story, but his "story board" moves directly from the thin place at the Jordan to the wilderness thick with temptation. The gentle descent of the Holy Spirit gains ferocity in driving Jesus forward to confront the question, "If you are the son of God . . . ?" Baptism's conferral of identity leads to testing his resolve to reside in that identity in his life of ministry in the power of the Holy Spirit.

This juxtaposition should not be missed by those of us who again and again reaffirm our baptism. We who heed the invitation, "Remember that you are baptized," should brace ourselves for what may come. In the liturgy, baptism and reaffirmation always conclude with a dismissal to minister in the world, where the liturgical rubber hits the ethical and spiritual road. The water and the wilderness are never far from each other. Christian discipline reckons with the nearness of one and the other and relies on the strong animating breath present in both.

Wild Bird, come to us at the water's edge today, and be ever near us for the living of these days. Amen.

With You Is the Fountain of Life

JANUARY 14–20, 2019 • LINDA MCKINNISH BRIDGES

SCRIPTURE OVERVIEW: Popular conceptions of God sometimes mislead us. Messages coming even from within Christianity sometimes make us think that God is constantly angry, just waiting for us to slip up. This week's readings remind us of the truth. Isaiah teaches us that God delights in God's people just as a groom delights in his bride. This love, the psalmist proclaims, is steadfast and never-ending. The life of Jesus shows us that God even wants us to have a good time in this life. Jesus chooses a wedding as the place to perform his first sign. He multiplies the wine in order to multiply the enjoyment of the guests. Paul in First Corinthians speaks of spiritual gifts. These gifts are all given by God for the good of the entire community.

QUESTIONS AND SUGGESTIONS FOR REFLECTION

- Read Isaiah 62:1-5. Recall a time when you have flourished and a time when your life was far from peace and order. How did you feel God's delight in each situation?
- Read Psalm 36:5-10. When have you felt God's light, been quenched by the fountain of life, or taken refuge in the shadow of God's wings?
- Read 1 Corinthians 12:1-11. How can you use your God-given gifts to complement others' and to support the common good?
- Read John 2:1-11. How do Jesus' miracles help you to understand his identity as the Son of God?

President, Baptist Theological Seminary in Richmond, Virginia.

MONDAY, JANUARY 14 ~ *Read Isaiah 62:1-5*

Have you ever had one of those days when everything worked together? The kids ate their breakfast. The car started. You arrived to work early, *and* you remembered to pack your lunch. Your office mate spoke a kind word. You came home to a clean house and happy family. All just seemed right with the world.

The prophet Isaiah describes such a picture of God's relationship with Israel not because the days have been perfect but because Israel is a true delight to God. Isaiah uses the image of marriage as a symbol. The uniting of two into one promises flourishing. Israel, once without companion, desolate and forgotten, lost and rejected, is now "married," and the land flourishes just as the family of the young bride and groom is intended to flourish. No longer forsaken, "you shall be called, 'Sought Out, A City Not Forsaken'" (Isa. 62:12). In other words, God rejoices over you.

Hold that thought for a moment. God, the creator of the universe, the energy of the cosmos, delights in *you*. The creation story of Genesis tells us so. After the stars and moons, the birds and plants, the seas and the skies, all the critters, big and small, "God saw all that God had made, and behold, it was very good" (Gen. 1:31, AP). So what if you yelled at the kids this morning or your colleague made you so mad that you did not speak to her all week? Maybe you have just had the biggest fight of your married life over the most insignificant thing—socks on the bathroom floor or the shared, messy tube of toothpaste.

No matter how off the mark, how far from peace and order your life may be, your Creator God still rejoices in you! Not because of what you do or don't do. God delights in you because you are a child of God.

Just as a parent delights in a child on good days and bad, so does God rejoice in you.

TUESDAY, JANUARY 15 ~ *Read Psalm 36:5-10*

Read this passage again. And then once more, slower this time. Let these words sink into your bones. This is praise. If you need an attitude adjustment today, these verses can help you get there.

Sometimes we just need a lift. Looking at the details of the day, meeting the demands of our calendar and others' needs, we could benefit from a long breath and a look up to the sky. Sometimes the day seems dry and dusty, and our spiritual throats seem parched and dry. Compare that sensation with the words of this passage. God's love is the fountain of life. Have you ever experienced the physical respite that a cool drink of water can give? Perhaps you were walking a long trail in the mountains and discovered a natural spring of water, spraying out from the ancient rocks and tender spring flowers. Imagine walking across a hot, burning desert and seeing over the next hill a beautiful green oasis complete with towering palm trees and a flowing fountain of water.

My great-grandparents' North Carolina mountain farm had a natural spring with the coldest water I have ever tasted. My dad once told me of the exquisite taste of drinking water drawn from that spring with a crude cup made of natural gourd on a hot summer afternoon while he played with his cousins around the stream. I remember playing with my cousins, another generation later, around that same spring. We stored the watermelon that we would cut later in the evening and drank from the cold pitcher of tea that had been submerged in the water all morning. That pitcher of tea needed no ice because of the cold temperature of the subterranean water. Refreshing, tasteful, welcomed. Such is the love of God.

May you experience God's love today like a fountain of refreshing water that can bring rejuvenation to your tired and thirsty soul.

WEDNESDAY, JANUARY 16 ~ *Read Psalm 36:5-10*

We welcome the light. In 1974, a scientist discovered an ancient burial chamber in Newgrange, Ireland, that has a particular attachment to the Winter Solstice, the day after the longest night of the year. On the morning of December 21 (and a few days before and after), if there are no clouds, light streams in through a tiny hole above the door's lintel for a few moments as the small porthole and the sun align. All other days, the cave-like structure remains dark.

From December to the middle of February, most of us in the northern hemisphere become weary of the winter dark, knowing that we come home from work in the dark and leave the next morning in the same darkness. Our sleep patterns change. We go to bed early and want to sleep later. We become more lethargic. We sometimes need more food. Our bodies are unaccustomed to the constant darkness. Then about early February, life seems to become normal again. We don't have to turn on the car lights to drive to work in the morning, and we don't start readying for bed the moment we return home from the workday. Our steps lighten, and we have more energy and zest.

Thank goodness for seasons of light and our body's flexibility to adjust to both light and dark. But just as the weary international traveler knows the best way to recover from jet lag is to sit out in the sun, so do we know that this light of God has the power to provide the same kind of spiritual recovery.

May you walk into the light this week—the light of the sunshine on your face and the light of God's love in your heart. May you find deep refreshment in both!

THURSDAY, JANUARY 17 ~ *Read 1 Corinthians 12:1-11*

The language of "common good" seems missing these days. Public servants, servant leaders, and persons working for the good of the whole seem to be in short supply. Paul uses an interesting Greek word with two parts to describe this concept of common good—sum + gifts. The summation of all gifts—the common good—comes when we all bring our individual gifts to create the whole.

I like to think of this in terms of a potluck: Susie bakes wonderful coconut cakes, so she should not bring macaroni—just her grand cake. John grills out-of-this-world ribs, so he should not bring a cake—just his ribs. Jane does not cook at all, but she sets a beautiful table. Because they all bring to the table their best gifts, the sum of those gifts becomes a lovely lunch all can enjoy.

We are members of something much larger than ourselves. Poet John Donne said it this way, "No [person] is an island." The feeling that we can do everything on our own leads to failure. The early church, in their early hours, quickly determined that if the gospel were to be preached from Judea to Jerusalem, the work would take a lot of people. Oh yes, there would be squabbles with one group wanting the credit and one seeking to triumph over another. (See 1 Corinthians 1.) Paul's teachings in today's reading help reestablish such independent ventures. In other words, my special coconut cake is good, but when it is paired with your ribs and Jane's corn casserole, the meal is out-of-this-world good. So it can be in the church and in the world when our God-given gifts are brought, used, and shared to bring unity among all God's people.

On this day may you recognize your gifts and then match them up with another and enjoy watching God's world grow.

FRIDAY, JANUARY 18 ~ *Read John 2:1-11*

"They have no wine." I smile when I read this verse in John's story of Jesus and his mother at a wedding. In a very motherly voice, Mary tells her son, Jesus, that the wine supply has been depleted. She does not tell him what to do; she just states the obvious—the wine is gone.

What parent among us has not made a request to our child in such a way? A mother walks into a messy bedroom and, rather than asking her child to clean up the room, declares, "This room is a mess." A father finds the gas tank empty after his teenager borrowed the car and tells the teenager, "The tank is empty." These declarative sentences are not meant simply to describe the situation. Rather, the parent's tone implies the child should interpret the sentence as an imperative. Something needs to be done—and soon. The honored guests are out of wine. "Do something," a mother tells her son.

Sometimes our lives are so mangled and confused that we do not know how to ask for help. The situation is messy, our emotions are on empty, and we can only say, "I hurt."

Yet God hears our feeble attempts to ask for help even when all we can do is name our pain. "My marriage is falling apart; (repair it)." "My job is insecure; (provide financial support)." "My best friend is dying; (heal her)."

The intimacy of mother and son, of God and believer, allows for clarity. We do not have to make detailed requests for the God of the universe to understand our needs. The water jars become filled with good wine. God knows even when we cannot ask.

May you walk in the confidence that God knows your needs even before you speak them.

SATURDAY, JANUARY 19 ~ *Read John 2:6-11*

The guests are present. The wine supply has been depleted. After a mother-and-son conversation, the six water jars, standing empty and ready for religious rituals, are filled with water. When they have been filled with water at Jesus' request, a sample is drawn to give to the party planner, the steward. The water is no longer just water; the water has been turned into the most expensive wine available for consumption. It is a miracle!

Jesus says, "Fill those jars to the very brim" (AP). Jesus knows that this moment will be special. The ordinary water is about to become extraordinary wine. Expect abundance. Prepare well, for the best is yet to come.

We have come to expect just the ordinary. "Oh, today is just a regular day," we say. "Nothing special happening this day—just routine, hum-drum." We expect a dull routine of life—a wake up, go to sleep, live-until-we-die kind of daily existence.

The miracle of this story is on multiple levels. Yes, there is the miracle of water turning into wine. That is supernatural, and I cannot explain it. In many ways, however, the greater miracle is the expectation of a miracle. Jesus, anticipating that something good is about to happen, says, "Fill those jars to the very brim."

In the midst of scarcity, our faith can be so strong that we go ahead with preparation for God's work to be seen. The high school student who cannot possibly afford to go to college completes a college application anyway—"fill it to the brim." The unemployed worker before the job search buys a new interview suit—"fill it to the brim." The miracle of faith is simply this—"the assurance of things hoped for, the conviction of things not seen" (Heb. 11:1).

On this day expect God to work in your life. And God will in both ordinary and extraordinary ways. Be prepared to "fill it to the brim."

SUNDAY, JANUARY 20 ~ *Read John 2:11*

The Gospel of John is more interested in revealing the identity of Jesus than in telling miracle stories. While extraordinary events occur in John's telling of Jesus' story, the primary focus is on the clear presentation of Jesus as the Son of God. The signs tell the story and identify the primary character, Jesus.

Seven signs, or miracles, dot this powerful story. Jesus turns water into wine (1:11), heals a royal official's son (4:46-54), heals a paralytic (5:1-5), feeds five thousand people (6:5-14), walks on water (6:16-24), heals a man blind from birth (9:1-12), and raises Lazarus from the dead (11:1-45). Powerful stories of a powerful leader. In Mark's Gospel, Jesus incurs resistance for performing such wonders and miracles. In John's Gospel, the primary emphasis is not on the elements of the stupendous feats or miraculous spectacles. Its singular focus is to reveal the Christ, who is the Light of the world. The clearer the revelation of Jesus' identity, the more resistance incurred. The more resistance, the closer Jesus comes to his own death and resurrection.

Turning water into wine is just the "beginning of the signs" (KJV)—just the beginning of understanding who Jesus is. Where do you begin to understand Jesus Christ? We all have a starting point. Maybe in the Sunday school room as a child, maybe in an evangelistic meeting, maybe in your own study or place of prayer, maybe in the woods or a special place in nature. Wherever you see Christ for the first time, for the fifty-first time, or even for the one thousandth time, God is revealing God's self to you.

Be on the lookout today. For God will be showing something to you. Listen for God.

The Harmony of One

JANUARY 21–27, 2019 • BRADFORD BOSWORTH

SCRIPTURE OVERVIEW: How do we feel when we read the Word of God? The Israelites rejoice in God's law. At the time of the restoration of Jerusalem after the return from exile, Ezra reads from the Law and explains its meaning to the people. They respond by holding a feast because understanding God's teachings is a source of joy. The psalmist says that God's law revives the soul, causes the heart to rejoice, and helps us to see clearly. Paul continues with his teaching on spiritual gifts, emphasizing that all members of the body of Christ have an important role. No one can claim to be any more important than anyone else. In Luke, Jesus reads from Isaiah and declares that his messianic ministry will focus on justice, mercy, and healing.

QUESTIONS AND SUGGESTIONS FOR REFLECTION

- Read Nehemiah 8:1-3, 5-6, 8-10. When has God's word overwhelmed you? How did you react?
- Read Psalm 19. How do you seek to speak or sing words acceptable to God? How does this shape your life?
- Read 1 Corinthians 12:12-31a. Within the body of Christ, as within our human bodies, parts compensate for one another. How do you take on more to support the body of Christ when others struggle? How do you allow others to take on your roles when you struggle?
- Read Luke 4:14-21. In what ways have you rejected Jesus?

Writer; worships and serves at St. Andrew UMC, Marietta, Georgia, and Smyrna First UMC, Smyrna, Georgia.

MONDAY, JANUARY 21 ~ *Read Psalm 19:14*

If you, like me, dedicate your early morning to prayer and meditation, then you are reading this less than twenty-four hours after exiting your place of Sunday sabbath worship. I often walk out of our sanctuary with the Holy Spirit's light shining brightly. Yet long-lamented Monday comes quickly, and I go back into a stormy world full throttle. My forgetfulness is the Light's dimmer switch. I begin to wander into the awaiting wilderness willfully captive to material distractions, and I distance myself from God's presence. If you are like me, we are like the Israelites. By midweek, we've hit the forget switch and—bam—we find ourselves in a figurative Babylon, exiled in a foreign culture.

One of my prayer and meditation practices has been to write on index cards selections of scripture that seem to speak to me personally. I keep a stack of them on the end table next to where I write devotions. Today's verse is on a card in that stack. It has served me well, especially when I am writing for a deadline. My words drip onto the page at a trickle rate when I am not in concert with God's will. When the words of my mouth and the meditation of my heart are in sync with the gospel of Christ, the flood gates open and my words pour out.

In the rooms of Alcoholics Anonymous, we hear at every meeting a reading of the 12 Steps. The eleventh step is this: "Sought through prayer and meditation to improve our conscious contact with God, as we understood him [*sic*], praying only for knowledge of his [*sic*] will for us and the power to carry that out." This final verse of Psalm 19 is such a prayer. It is our supplication only to align with God's will, for when we do it is pleasing in God's sight.

God, may we go into this week with your light shining in our hearts. Amen.

TUESDAY, JANUARY 22 ~ *Read Nehemiah 8:1-3, 5-6, 8-10*

What would make God happy? What would cause our Creator to be supremely contented with a big smile, folded arms, nodding head, and misty eyes gazing on those created in God's likeness? We find one answer in the first verse of today's scripture: "All the people came together as one" (NIV). Why does it always require a 9/11, a World War, or the exile of a people like the one the Israelites experience in Babylon to bring a nation, a people, back together? We forget from whence we come—our Jerusalem. We turn away and step outside of God's all-encompassing love for us. Yet God wishes for us to desire to remain in God's love as one people; God calls us to come home and rebuild the relationship.

Ezra and Nehemiah know the Law serves as the people's spiritual divining rod. God's chosen ones have turned away from the law brought down by Moses. As the people gather as one in the square before the Water Gate, God's word washes over them like a river of life bringing them home. Have you ever held up your hands waiting for God's love to pick you up?

I came late to the understanding of grace. I recognize it now. Sometimes it comes in glimpses; other times in torrents. Occasionally it arrives in unexpected locales. Frequently it covers me in most familiar surroundings, like a church sanctuary. I know when I am experiencing this unmerited love of God because I become weepy in my feeling of unworthiness. As the Israelites in front of Ezra and Nehemiah, I want to fall on my knees with my face to the ground as I feel complete and at home again in the presence of God, who stands smiling before me.

God, we long to hear your voice and to turn from weeping to sharing in your joy when we do. Amen.

WEDNESDAY, JANUARY 23 ~ *Read Psalm 19*

My church in Smyrna, Georgia, has an exceptionally vibrant music ministry. The church's half dozen choirs include a nationally traveled youth choir. The church's journey through Advent 2017 was uniquely special because Christmas Eve dawned on the sabbath. The singers were active in five distinct worship services, concluding with a midnight candlelight service. The Lord's day was made complete with all as one singing "Silent Night." Our "voice [went] out through all the earth, and [our] words to the end of the world."

This grand musical experience helped me to grasp the role of the psalms in Israel's experience of God's grandeur. Psalm 19 was likely part of the music of Israel's return from exile. We can easily imagine Psalm 19 as part of the ceremony of the events that unfold in the Nehemiah story. Nehemiah records a monumental rebuilding effort being undertaken in Jerusalem. This recovery is more than reconstruction of the wall or rebuilding of the Temple. It is expiation for a wayward people. It begs for a consistent presence of worshipful song. Four times in the preceding chapter, Nehemiah speaks of the singers who have returned from exile (7:1, 44, 67, 73).

Imagine the moment in the Water Gate square as Ezra and Nehemiah stand before the people to reestablish the covenant, and the words of Psalm 19 wash over all that is happening, "The law of the LORD is perfect. . . . The precepts of the LORD are right." We can sense God's awareness of our human propensities as the singers repeat the words of verse 13, "Keep your servant also from willful sins; may they not rule over me" (NIV). In the economy of God's creation, all is sufficiently efficient until humanity begins to obstruct the way. When we seek words acceptable in God's sight, we can experience the glory of God.

God, as we worship you in our return, may our words be acceptable to you. Amen.

THURSDAY, JANUARY 24 ~ *Read 1 Corinthians 12:12-31a*

I am a recovering alcoholic. My recovery has been a decade-long awakening. After sharing my story with my senior pastor, he declared to me, "We are all in recovery." Isolation is a symptomatic behavior of my alcoholism that can telegraph for me a potential relapse. Turning off the phone, closing the blinds, and pulling the covers over my head can be cozy. In my inactivity I experience the illusion of being comfortably in control. But our Creator did not make us to go it alone. I cannot sustain my recovery on my own.

Paul's message today addresses this truth: We need each other, and the church needs us to be the body of Christ. We are meant to be in fellowship. The healing redemptive love of Jesus is present where two or more gather. (See Matthew 18:20.) In God's economy, if one of us suffers we all ache. If one of us succeeds, we all celebrate. We drink from one and the same water fountain—the fount of the Holy Spirit that baptizes us into the body of Christ. The word *one* appears a dozen times in the New International Version (NIV) translation of this scripture, six times in the first three verses. It exemplifies God's economy's divine paradoxical nature: one is many, last is first, we receive by giving.

I lament the dawning of the digital age. Digital publications of God's word conveniently viewed on phones can thwart fortuitous learning experiences. On many occasions I have opened a Bible to search for specific scripture and, while thumbing through the pages, have stumbled on other verses pertinent to the moment. First Corinthians 12 gives little context to the last verse of today's reading. But reading forward, I notice Paul's amazing treatise on love. In chapter 13, it all makes sense. Love ties it all—ties us all—together. Love completes us as one.

Savior, may we, as one, always desire the greater gifts of your love. Amen.

FRIDAY, JANUARY 25 ~ *Read Luke 4:14-21*

Aloneness is a persistent thread running through the story of Jesus' life. It resonates with us through the human condition we share with our Savior. In today's reading Jesus has emerged from forty days in the desert alone. His experience is magnified because the devil barks at him the entire time. Fresh from baptism, the Messiah is beginning initiation into the fallen world of humanity. Having shunned the devil, Christ is primed ("filled with the power of the Spirit") to begin his mission of salvation and redemption. The journey goes smoothly and the countryside is abuzz for this new ministry—until he arrives in his hometown of Nazareth.

If you have spoken to a roomful of people, then you have experienced a twinge of aloneness. The message you impart will be well received, or it will not. In the NIV translation the section subheading of these verses reads, "Jesus Rejected at Nazareth." If Jesus does not feel alone when he starts reading from Isaiah, he certainly feels so when leaving town.

We might ask ourselves several questions about this scene in the synagogue: Why is Jesus given the Isaiah scripture to read? How does Jesus come to choose the specific section (Isa. 61:1-2)? Why does he stop reciting Isaiah's prophecy at "to proclaim the year of the Lord's favor"? Why does Jesus sit down before concluding with, "Today this scripture is fulfilled in your hearing"? These last words get him run out of town. Rejection remains the story of Immanuel. Although Jesus is often alone, either of his own choosing or by others' spurning, he is seldom lonely. For he is one in the Father as the Father is one in him. (See John 14:10.) Jesus was often alone but never isolated because the Spirit of the Lord was on him.

Come, Holy Spirit. Lead us out of isolation into the refuge of Immanuel. Amen.

SATURDAY, JANUARY 26 ~ *Read 1 Corinthians 12:17-20*

I was ten years old and was fishing in a canal running through a Miami park. I had cast a lead lure too far and it had snagged in the mangrove on the far bank. I jerked the pole so hard the lure came back and struck my closed right eye. The impact caused blindness in that eye for a few hours. Later on, when I was in my forties, I was diagnosed with a cataract in that eye. For years, my left eye had been doing the work for my right eye. It was not a conscious decision for me to let my left eye compensate for my failing right eye. Yet in God's economy of creation, this was the natural progression of the parts placed in my body.

Our segmented world engenders a self-concept that is tied frivolously to ever-changing status symbols. We define ourselves by identifying with groups we belong to, teams we cheer for, cars we drive, or uniforms we wear. Our identities become driven by material sensibilities. Such worldly comparison is born of the ego's need to place us either above or below all else. But Paul invites us to turn our attention to the One who touches us in the eternal place of our soul, transcends our bodily senses, and connects us to the Spirit in which we are baptized and given life.

What do the new Christians in Corinth think of Paul's "body of Christ" idea? Still, after thousands of years, we struggle to grasp its full meaning. Paul's analogy comparing the church's body of Christ to our body parts is visionary. When we wholly become one as the body of Christ, our actions meld into one harmonious purpose in perfect alignment with God's will for humanity. When one member stumbles, others in the body compensate effortlessly. Creation adapts as one in God's economy.

Lord Jesus, we long to live as one in the harmony of your eternal love. Amen.

SUNDAY, JANUARY 27 ~ *Read Luke 4:14-21*

New Testament writers reference the words of Isaiah more than any other Hebrew scripture except the Psalms. Isaiah speaks a truth that is as yeast in leavened bread. Jesus of Nazareth's reading taps into the prophecy's mother lode. When we look at the scene in the synagogue, we apply this premise to answer the first question posed in our Friday devotion: Jesus is given the scroll of Isaiah to read for it contains the truth. The answer to the second question thus becomes self-evident: Jesus reads the prophecy about the coming messiah because it describes him and his ministry.

In the late 1980s, southern blues legend B. B. King asked Irish rock group U2 front man Bono to write a song for him. Bono penned the blues classic, "When Love Comes to Town." In a graceful example of respect and love for their musical hero, the band's musicians came all the way from Ireland to record the song with King in his hometown: Memphis, Tennessee. U2 then included this version of the song on their 1988 album, *Rattle and Hum*.

Back in Nazareth, we know why Jesus stops reading at "the year of the Lord's favor." It is the year of the Lord's favor because love has come to town. The Nazarenes cannot see it. We continue to struggle to see that it is, even now, the year of the Lord's favor. Love still comes to town. The redemption of Israel, of you and me, of God's people, culminates with the arrival of our suffering servant. The scripture is fulfilled in our hearing. Jesus, the truth of our salvation, lives. The question remains, When Truth stands before us, will we recognize and accept him or, like our brothers and sisters in Nazareth, will we reject him and the love that comes to town?

God, open our hearts so we will recognize your Son standing before us and will become the harmony of One. Amen.

Living Out Our Calling

JANUARY 28–FEBRUARY 3, 2019 • LEIGH HITCHCOCK

SCRIPTURE OVERVIEW: The readings from the Hebrew scriptures share a common theme of calling. Jeremiah is called at a young age to be a prophet. God knew and set apart Jeremiah even in the womb. The psalmist also expresses confidence in God's call, because God knew him even before he was born. In the same way, God knows each one of us and has a plan for our lives that is not an afterthought. In this First Corinthians passage (often read at weddings), Paul speaks of love. But this love is not infatuation and is not based on emotion. It is intentional, strong, gritty, and unselfish. In Luke we see that many struggle with the fact that Jesus' calling is also to serve the marginalized. Jesus reveals that God has a missional heart.

QUESTIONS AND SUGGESTIONS FOR REFLECTION

- Read Jeremiah 1:4-10. What is God calling you to do? What excuses are you making to ignore your vocation?
- Read Psalm 71:1-6. God promises not to make our lives easy or perfectly safe but to be with us when we face challenges and violence. In a world that seems increasingly violent, how do you find assurance of God's continuous presence?
- Read 1 Corinthians 13. God calls us to a vocation of love. How can you be more loving in your daily work or activities?
- Read Luke 4:21-30. How do you see God's call in those you know best? Do you accept or reject the call God has placed on their lives?

Member of Nashville First Baptist Church, Nashville, Tennessee; works at Belmont University; married to Shane and mother to two teenage daughters.

MONDAY, JANUARY 28 ~ *Read Jeremiah 1:4-10*

What does it mean to be called by God? Usually, we think only of ministers as having a calling. Occasionally, professionals such as doctors and teachers will speak about their careers as their callings. But when we think of all lifelong careers, we often call them vocations. The Latin root for vocation is *vocare,* which is also the root of words like *voice, vocal,* and *invoke.*

Jeremiah's calling from God doesn't begin with an aptitude test for a career match. It begins with hearing the voice of the Lord and then being the voice of God's message. In this same way, God calls us all, no matter our vocation.

The occasion of our call may not be as dramatic as Jeremiah's, but God calls us to share the good news to our hurting world and to be God's hands and feet as we answer the call. Perhaps instead of thinking of a calling only as a career, we can consider our shared vocation: listening for God's voice and finding the courage to use our voice for God. In the final verse of today's scripture passage, the Lord says, "Look, I am putting my words in your mouth. This day I appoint you over nations and territories, to uproot and to tear down, to destroy and to overthrow, to build and to plant" (TIB). God's word through us has tremendous power. God's word has the power to save.

God, help me to hear your voice when you speak to me. Give me the courage to use my voice to share your message to a hurting world. Amen.

TUESDAY, JANUARY 29 ~ *Read Jeremiah 1:4-10*

Like most teenagers, my children make excuses, particularly when they have to do an unpleasant task. Their excuses involve reasons for not doing chores or for why they argue with each other. And like most parents, I do not put a lot of stock in their excuses. I see them for what they are: attempts to get out of what needs to be done.

When God calls Jeremiah, Jeremiah also makes excuses. But God seems prepared for it. Before Jeremiah utters a word, God starts with a reminder that God appointed Jeremiah before he was born. "Before you were born, I dedicated you. I appointed you as a prophet to the nations" (TIB). In other words, I know what you're going to say, and in case you were thinking about bowing out, remember who made you and to whom you belong.

Most days, we aren't much better than Jeremiah. Like my kids making excuses for not doing chores, we try to find reasons for not doing the things that God has called us to do. I don't have enough time. I don't have enough money. I'm not good enough, smart enough, old enough, eloquent enough. Do any of these sound familiar? To some degree, we're right. We aren't enough; but God is. God is more than enough. When the Creator of the universe calls us, we can be sure God will go with us. We have nothing to fear. Our flimsy excuses don't stand a chance against the power of the Almighty.

Almighty God, calm my fear. Help me to know that when you call me, you call me to walk alongside you to accomplish your work. Amen.

WEDNESDAY, JANUARY 30 ~ *Read Luke 4:21-30*

Recently I took a class centered around the theme of "home." We discussed questions like, What is home? What happens when you lose your home? How do you find your place within a home? In today's passage, Jesus finds it hard to be at home again. The community cannot resolve the tension between the carpenter's son they thought they knew and the prophet who works miracles. Surely this isn't Mary and Joseph's son! How can this hometown boy be so eloquent? How can he speak with such authority? Remember all those rumors about his birth?

A veil covers our eyes when we consider a hometown prophet. We do not see clearly. One of two things happens: We either overrate the hometown prophet's achievements or dismiss them as impossible. The crowd wants Jesus to prove himself with signs and wonders. Why do they need signs and wonders to believe him? For Jesus, this could be a temptation just like in the wilderness. You can almost hear the devil whispering, "Show them what you can do so that they can be proud of you. They want to claim you and say that you belong to them. You will be adored." But Jesus belongs to God. He never belonged to them.

Sometimes when we live out our calling, we meet the most resistance from the people who know us best. It's tempting to fall back into familiar roles we once played, like slipping on an old comfortable coat, but God rarely call us to be comfortable. On the contrary, God usually calls us to stretch beyond what we know and what others think they know about us. Our God makes all things new.

Creator God, help me to step out in faith when you call me to unfamiliar territory. When others want to mold me into something other than what you have planned, remind me that you are the one true Creator. Amen.

THURSDAY, JANUARY 31 ~ *Read Psalm 71:1-4*

Raw emotion and striking honesty with God fill many of the psalms, and Psalm 71 is no different. Save me! Deliver me! Today's passage is a desperate cry for help. The psalmist isn't afraid to bare his soul and be completely open with God about his need for deliverance. For many adults though, asking for help isn't easy. Sometimes one of the hardest things to admit is that we can't do everything on our own. We so badly want to prove to others that we are capable, independent people who can manage everything quite nicely, thank you very much. We think someone will give us a medal for Most Independent or Juggled Everything Singlehandedly.

Children, however, ask for help much more willingly. My kids never hesitate to ask for assitance with homework or difficult projects. Most children know that they will receive help from a parent when they ask. There is an implicit trust. The psalmist in today's passage cries out with a childlike faith for God to rescue him. When we follow God's call, we will face obstacles. Just as in Jeremiah's day, God's message isn't always popular. We will encounter hard times. But just like the psalmist, we can cry out to God to deliver us.

Heavenly Father, help me come to you with the childlike faith that you will help when I ask. Amen.

FRIDAY, FEBRUARY 1 ~ *Read 1 Corinthians 13:1-8*

What are you called to do? Teach, heal, protect, preach? Whatever it is, Paul says it is nothing without love. You may be the best algebra teacher in your state, but if your students don't know that you love them, their ability to solve linear equations means little when they face the pressures of adolescence. You may be a gifted doctor, revered in your field across the world; but if you don't have love, your patients will not be completely healed. Doctors who show love to their patients provide healing even when medicine fails.

No matter what else God calls us to do or say, God calls us to love. Paul makes it pretty clear that nothing matters without love. But the love described in First Corinthians is not an easy kind of love; it is a radical love that puts others first, rejoices in the truth, always hopes, and always trusts. Sometimes love requires us to tell the truth when the truth is hard to hear. Jeremiah's message to Israel isn't popular, but his love for Israel and God lead him to share God's message no matter how unpopular it may be. He becomes known as the weeping prophet because of his sorrow over Israel's disobedience and the consequences that follow. It reminds me of the saying, "No one cares how much you know until they know how much you care." But radical love is patient and kind even in the face of resistance. Radical God-like love never fails. When we live out God's call, we will face obstacles and resistance; but if we live in love, we cannot fail.

Loving God, help me to love the way you love: with kindness and patience and always seeking the truth. Amen.

SATURDAY, FEBRUARY 2 ~ *Read 1 Corinthians 13:9-13*

When I was in junior high school, I had the opportunity to take photography classes. Long before the days of digital photography, we had to develop film to produce an image on paper. Once we developed the film, we then transferred the images onto photo paper, which also had to be developed in special solutions. My favorite part of the whole process was putting the paper in the first tray, the developing solution, and watching the image form on a blank piece of photo paper. While I stood in the dark room over the tray of developing solution, the image would gradually take shape. It was like magic to me. Paul says at the end of this passage, "Now we see indistinctly, as in a mirror; then we will see face to face" (TIB). It's as if we wait in the dark room for the image to appear. It isn't completely clear yet; but the longer we stay immersed in God's love, the clearer the image becomes.

Our response to God's call changes us. Several of the passages this week speak of God's presence from our birth. Paul brings it full circle by reminding us that we move toward maturity in God and with God. As we live out God's call to love without ceasing, we better reflect the image of God. We emerge from the developing solution no longer an image of our imperfect selves but a perfect image of God.

Perfect and holy God, help me to reflect your image more and more each day as I seek to live out your calling in my life. Amen.

SUNDAY, FEBRUARY 3 ~ *Read Psalm 71:1-6*

What does shelter mean? At its most basic, shelter is a physical need for all humans. It is almost as essential as food, water, and air. Without shelter we are physically vulnerable. We may also think of shelter as the command to "shelter in place." The news is filled with stories of violence in our workplaces, schools, and even churches. If we haven't been personally affected by one of these tragedies, we probably know someone who has. Additionally, Christians all over the world are persecuted for their faith in various ways. We enjoy some freedom from that kind of persecution here in America, but stories of violence in our churches remind us that God does not promise physical safety when we choose to follow God's call. On the contrary, we may even create enemies when we live out our faith.

When Jesus refused to show the crowd the miracles they were looking for, they tried to throw him over a cliff. But we say with the psalmist, "You are my rock, my fortress! . . . You alone are my hope" (TIB). We have a reason to hope in the Lord. Our hope is a confident expectation, not a fruitless waiting with doubt. We build our hope on a solid foundation, our rock and our fortress. The Lord God Almighty who fashioned us in the womb and knows the hairs on our head will never forsake us. We need never despair. We are treasured and loved. Following God's call is not an easy journey, but it is never a solitary one. For that I praise God.

God, I know you've taken care of me in the past, you've given me today, and I can trust you to take care of tomorrow, no matter what happens. Help me never forget that I can place my hope in you with confidence. Amen.

We Are Not Alone; God Is with Us

FEBRUARY 4–10, 2019 • ROLAND RINK

SCRIPTURE OVERVIEW: The theme of calling is continued in this week's readings. Isaiah has a vision of God on the throne and is terrified because he knows that he is unworthy; yet he is being called by God. The psalmist, traditionally David, praises God for having a purpose for his life and bringing it to completion. Paul echoes Isaiah's sentiments of his own unworthiness to the Corinthians. While assuring his readers of the reality of Christ's bodily resurrection, Paul recognizes that he preaches only by the grace of God. When Jesus is calling his disciples, Simon Peter recognizes him as the Lord and cowers because he feels unworthy—much like the prophet Isaiah had done. These readings teach us that God's call is based not on our worthiness but on our willingness.

QUESTIONS AND SUGGESTIONS FOR REFLECTION

- Read Isaiah 6:1-13. When have you heard a difficult call from God? How did you come to finally say, "Here I am; send me"?
- Read Psalm 138. How have you seen God uplift the lowly and the humble? How have these experiences changed the way you live out your faith?
- Read 1 Corinthians 15:1-11. How does your life witness to Christ's resurrection?
- Read Luke 5:1-11. How has Christ called you? Whether or not you feel worthy to the call, Christ wants you to follow.

Born and raised in Johannesburg, South Africa; enjoys family, music, sports, and attending rock concerts; works for Africa Upper Room Ministries.

MONDAY, FEBRUARY 4 ~ *Read Isaiah 6:1-8*

This wonderfully descriptive opening passage of Isaiah 6 vividly illustrates Isaiah's breathtaking vision of the sanctity of God whose glory fills the whole of the earth.

In the face of this glory, Isaiah's vision quickly dissolves into serious reflection and personal confession. He is humbled by the grandeur of God and feels wholly unqualified to speak of the glory he has witnessed. God senses this guilt and forgives Isaiah his sins. This act of loving forgiveness enables Isaiah to hear God clearly asking "Whom shall I send, and who will go for us?"

His response is both dramatic and spontaneous: "Here I am; send me."

Today we experience God's grandeur through the natural world. We hike, camp, climb, and explore nature reserves, and urban areas have begun to make space for God's natural growth in parks and rooftop gardens. It is little wonder in the noisy, polluted, electronically impersonal world we inhabit that we should seek out ways to experience the majestic work of our Creator.

When we experience God's majesty in the vastness of nature reserves or the wonder of green life surrounded by concrete, we are overwhelmed. For many of us, experiencing the glory of creation has become so rare that even a hint of it convicts us: How have we sinned that we do not recognize God's overwhelming majesty everyday? How have we sinned that our neighbors must grow food on the roof in order to have access to it?

When we recognize our sin, we may hear God's call to make a change—to be changed by God and to advocate for change for others. The abiding question remains: Will you say, "Here I am; send me"?

Loving God, open my eyes, my ears, and my heart this day so that I may be renewed to answer your call. Amen.

TUESDAY, FEBRUARY 5 ~ *Read Isaiah 6:9-13*

God tells Isaiah precisely what his calling is and of the effect his words will have on Judah.

God anticipates that the outcome of Isaiah's work will be frustrating and tedious. No doubt, the road ahead is strewn with seemingly immovable obstacles for Isaiah. One can marvel at Isaiah's courage and fortitude in confronting the perceived outcomes of honoring his calling.

Seeing, hearing, and perceiving are basic human functions, but unless the people earnestly repent, these faculties will be denied and the prophetic words of Isaiah will be lost on the majority of the population. This is not a hopeful outcome from Isaiah's perspective, but it is his calling nevertheless.

One can almost sense Isaiah's heart sinking as he asks, "How long, O Lord?" Perhaps more significantly—though Isaiah has no way of knowing this—his words will become seeds of hope for the people in the future.

Many of us understand God's call as a broad, non-specific call to humankind in general. Responding positively to a specific, personal call seems to be where matters become more complicated. We spend days, months, even years creating reasons for ignoring our personal call. Perhaps one of the biggest challenges we face is the fact that our call often grows far bigger than we ever imagined—more than we can manage ourselves. Perhaps such size marks a real calling; we have no option but to rely on the One who calls us rather than on our own devices.

How much longer will you delay saying "yes, send me" to our loving God in response to your calling?

Lord, thank you for your patience. Please send the Holy Spirit to help me make brave decisions regarding your consistent call on my life. Amen.

WEDNESDAY, FEBRUARY 6 ~ *Read Psalm 138:1-3*

I will praise you, LORD, with all my heart" (NIV). The opening words of this psalm of thanksgiving are a timely reminder of what Jesus calls the greatest commandment of all: to love God with heart and soul and mind.

In the times of the psalmist, Jerusalem is regarded as the one place where heaven and earth meet. It was where God chooses to dwell on the ark of the covenant. For this reason, wherever they are, the Israelites pray facing Jerusalem.

A habit of total dedication—continual faith and repentance—leads us toward true discipleship. Our own personal relationship with God is of paramount importance. The psalmist's sobering words remind us that our relationship with God has little or nothing to do with just our works or our efforts.

This psalm of thanksgiving reminds me that my regular attendance at worship on Sundays is often more out of habit than for the joyful worship of God. Too often I come to worship preoccupied by the troubles of the world and the workweek. I am adept at disconnecting from the passages of scripture we hear and many of the hymns and choruses we sing as I merely go through the motions of worship. My heart is not in the service. Sadly sometimes, even just ten minutes after a service, I cannot recall the message from the sermon.

Worshiping God, not only on Sundays but every day, requires our undivided attention. I need to be far more prepared and eager to worship. I need to expect that God will speak to me through one or more of the methods of worship. I need to listen to my heart. The well-worn cliché resonates in this scenario: "What you put in is what you get out."

What real action do you have to take to make your worship experience more personally meaningful?

Loving God, thank you for your continual patience with me. Help me to worship you with a joyful, undivided heart. Amen.

THURSDAY, FEBRUARY 7 ~ *Read Psalm 138:4-8*

The psalmist's reminder that God regards the lowly and is removed from the haughty echoes throughout the Bible. Micah's oft-quoted words render the psalmist's words as a prescription for action: "What does the LORD require of you? To act justly and to love mercy and to walk humbly with your God" (6:8, NIV). Jesus makes it personal: "All who exalt themselves will be humbled, and all who humble themselves will be exalted" (Matt. 23:12). Mary's song remembers when leaders have experienced the truth of the psalmist's words: "He has brought down rulers from their thrones but has lifted up the humble" (Luke 1:52, NIV).

These words can serve as a warning to those in elected, nominated, or even self-proclaimed leadership roles today. When we look at the global leadership stage, we can sense that God is far away from leaders haughty about their high positions.

The psalmist believes in the Lord's promise to support the lowly. The Lord will be with all who seek God's purpose. When we lead out of a sense of our lowliness, we call this model "servant leadership." Leader-as-servant is often the only way for a leader to achieve respect or lasting results. We show that we have in mind the best interests of those whom we lead when we humbly seek to serve them.

As Christians, we have a perennial model of servant leadership in Jesus who simply, deliberately, and effectively turns the image of leadership upside down with common utensils—a basin and a towel—to serve his followers.

Where have you seen or experienced signs of servant leadership?

Loving Lord, clothe us in humility that we may more closely resemble you. Amen.

FRIDAY, FEBRUARY 8 ~ *Read 1 Corinthians 15:1-11*

It appears that Paul intends to use the testimony of many eyewitnesses to prove the historical truth of the Resurrection. Amongst these witnesses he names Peter, the disciples, and more than 500 other followers of Christ. Despite his previous persecution of Christians, Paul includes himself in the list of witnesses who were blessed to see the resurrected Lord. Resurrection from the dead is not easy to believe for many people, hence the need for eyewitnesses to corroborate the facts. Our loving God, knowing our doubts, supplies hundreds of witnesses.

Belief in the resurrection of Jesus is a central pillar of Christian faith. Each time we recite the words of the Nicene Creed, we acknowledge our belief that "on the third day he rose again in accordance with the scriptures."* During the celebration of Holy Communion, we repeat the words "Christ has died, Christ is risen, Christ will come again."** As Christians, we live in the hope and belief that we, like Christ, will be resurrected into the kingdom of God because God has promised that we will.

Today's passage reminds us of the sacred moment in time when we accept Jesus Christ as our Lord and Savior, that crucial moment when we decide to become followers of Jesus and we promise to "hold firmly to the word" (NIV). In our everyday lives, how do we transmit these sacred words of life? How comfortable are we in telling our family, our work colleagues, or our friends the good news that Jesus lives, is crucified, dies for our sins, and is raised from the grave after three days?

What evangelism program has your congregation undertaken in the last five years?

---

*UMH, 880.

**"A Service of Word and Table I," UMH, 10.

Loving God, give me the courage and the words to be your witness this day. Amen.

SATURDAY, FEBRUARY 9 ~ *Read Luke 5:1-7*

Too often we observe serious competition among local churches or denominations to attract new members to their communities when a joint communal, inclusive approach to evangelism and outreach would be far more effective and beneficial to all. We can be rightly disturbed by the individual need for prestige and honor in these circumstances. Yet they seem to occur with increasing regularity while quietly eroding the powerful construct of community.

Notice that today's scripture mentions two boats. From my African perspective, this reminds me of the Zulu word *ubuntu,* which means "I am because we are." I am enabled and empowered, made fully human, because I am part of a family, a tribe, and a community. It appears that fishing is a communal activity in biblical times. To have one boat at one end of the net and another boat at the other end surely allows the team to catch more fish. The boats have a common goal and rely on each other to jointly harvest the catch. They embody the concept of *ubuntu.*

But the disciples have toiled all night and have caught nothing! We can sense their feelings of failure, disillusion, and disappointment. Few people enjoy working with no reward, and in this regard, the disciples are most certainly human.

Jesus recognizes their plight and gently emphasizes the need for community: Simon Peter catches so many fish he has to call for his partners in the other boat to help him. Jesus understands their real need and, as with all of us in times of despair and darkness, reveals his amazing power to overcome all difficulties.

What new project can your faith community initiate to invite more people to begin a relationship with Jesus Christ?

Father, forgive me for not recognizing and responding to the cry of those around me who long for a deeper relationship with you. Amen.

SUNDAY, FEBRUARY 10 ~ *Read Luke 5:8-11*

Peter, James, and John are working their "day jobs," seemingly unaware of God's persistent call on their lives to become three of the apostles. When Peter realizes that he is in the presence of the Divine, he falls on his knees—not in worship but in confession of his sinful human condition. Peter asks Jesus to leave him because he is not worthy of being in the presence of the Divine.

Despite Peter's feeling of unworthiness, Jesus calls Peter to serve. And Jesus gives Peter a task with which he is familiar: "From now on you will be catching people." Peter and his companions leave everything to follow the man who has made them miraculously successful at what they have done their entire lives.

I can identify with the disciples. In April of 1991, I participated in a Walk to Emmaus retreat. At the end of my Walk, I remember saying three words: "Lord, I'm available." God took those words seriously! Over the next nine years, while continuing to fulfill my role as an executive for a global telecommunications company, a vision emerged to set up an office in South Africa that locally would publish and print Upper Room Ministries resources. I felt a calling to provide Africans with quality, low-cost resources to nourish and feed our spirits and assist us in keeping our daily appointment with God.

Like the disciples, I needed God's help to make me successful. I was familiar with the task of reaching many people, but I knew absolutely nothing about printing or publishing. All I could do was trust God and allow the Holy Spirit to guide me. Now, Africa Upper Room Ministries has been providing spiritual resources for eighteen years. God called me to follow, and I have a strong sense of peace that the work is exactly what God had planned for my life.

Leading God, help me to follow when you call, knowing that you will help me to serve. Amen.

The Bible in One Hand and Ojibway Fiction in the Other

FEBRUARY 11–17, 2019 • PAMELA COUTURE

SCRIPTURE OVERVIEW: God wants us to be rooted firmly in our faith. Jeremiah contrasts those who put their trust in themselves with those who trust in God. The latter are like healthy trees with deep roots and a constant water supply, never in danger of drying up or dying. The psalmist uses the same image to describe those who meditate on God's teachings. Thus, as you do these daily readings and reflect on them, you are sinking deep roots into fertile soil. Agricultural imagery is continued in Paul's letter. Paul describes Jesus Christ risen in the flesh as the first fruit, meaning that he is the first of many who will be resurrected. In Luke's version of the Beatitudes, worldly success is not necessarily an indication of God's blessing.

QUESTIONS AND SUGGESTIONS FOR REFLECTION

- Read Jeremiah 17:5-10. Examine your heart. Do you place your trust in "mere mortals" or in the Lord?
- Read Psalm 1. How do you seek to meditate on God's word day and night?
- Read 1 Corinthians 15:12-20. How has your understanding of the resurrection of the dead changed your living?
- Read Luke 6:17-26. How do you hold together the paradoxes of Jesus' blessings and woes?

Jane and Geoffrey Martin Chair of Church and Community at Emmanuel College of Victoria University, University of Toronto; author of *We Are Not All Victims*.

MONDAY, FEBRUARY 11 ~ *Read Luke 6:17-26*

This week's scriptures are rife with uncomfortable contrasts. Scriptural formulas like "Blessed are you" and "Woe to you" vault me first into a childish form of works righteousness: What must I do to be on the blessed side of the contrast? Then I relax. The world is filled with wickedness, to be sure, but curses and woes? Don't such ideas reflect a magical worldview that modern Christians like me have long discarded?

When I researched *We Are Not All Victims: Local Peacebuilding in the Democratic Republic of Congo,** I felt myself living in a world where biblical ideas that I might disdain in North America came alive. For example, while interviewing the Pentecostal prophet Meshac, I experienced a Z-shaped streak of blood across my vision. I impulsively explained the phenomenon spiritually: The *megwishi* (evil spirit) is messing with me. *You are with the prophet Meshac, so ask him to pray for you.* When the same thing happened a few months later as I stood on my dog sitter's back porch in Wisconsin, I explained the phenomenon medically: I'm having another vitreous detachment.

Are these contrasts opposites or paradoxes held together by a hidden thread? Ojibway writer Richard Wagamese teaches me the connection. In *Keeper'n Me,*** Keeper describes two worlds: one peopled by storytellers and their teachings; the other by rich American fishermen and their photographs. It seems that one cannot traverse these incompatible worlds without becoming lost. But then he offers the connecting thread: All people are tourists, lost in need of a guide. All are the blessed, the cursed, the woed, the righteous, and the wicked. This week, we'll let Ojibway fiction lend insight to the uncomfortable contrasts in our biblical texts. With God as our guide, we may find a hidden thread.

---

*Berlin: LIT Verlag, 2016.

**Doubleday: Canada Ltd, 1994.

May I find the Guide who can lead me to true happiness.

TUESDAY, FEBRUARY 12 ~ *Read Jeremiah 17:7-8; Psalm 1:1-3*

I can lose myself easily in Richard Wagamese's descriptions of Ontario lake country—the pines, the cliffs, the water. I imagine paddling the lakes or driving through the forest to White Dog reserve.

His town, Kenora, Ontario, lies across the border and northwest of Minnesota's Voyageurs National Park, where my family formerly vacationed on a wooded island, Nokomis. A lodge on the island allowed us to take our whole family, from infants to elders, into the lake country we treasured. At the end of summer 2003, Nokomis was scheduled to revert to wilderness as part of Voyageurs. One sunny August day, a few weeks before the park service burned to the ground the lodge on the island, my brother stood on the pier gazing at the lake, mourning. I vowed to find a cabin in a similar setting where we could continue to create intergenerational memories.

A decade later I sat at my desk in the second-story window of this new cabin contemplating the trunks of the tall white pines with new eyes. I wondered for the first time, *How is it possible that a collection of biological cells, one built upon another in a narrow, round cylinder, can be strong enough to grow to fifty feet and support the graceful, sweeping arms of the white pine's branches and needles?* I'd taken these trees for granted. As I marveled at this miracle, I felt equally blessed and naïve. Richard Wagamese captured this gratitude in his description of lake country from his native perspective, and Jeremiah and the psalmist offer the image of a tree's flourishing near water as a basic description of those who trust and delight in the Lord. A flourishing tree seems like a miracle; what miracles might we experience in our lives when we trust in the Lord?

Blessed are those who know the miracle of the tree, its strength and its grandeur.

WEDNESDAY, FEBRUARY 13 ~ *Read Jeremiah 17:5-10*

In this passage, Jeremiah presents us with a series of potent metaphors for the person who places trust in mere mortals rather than in God, concluding with the shocking image of the devious heart. We think of the heart as the place that unites passion and goodness. In Richard Wagamese's imagery, the full moon reflects the drum which echoes the heartbeat we heard in our mother's womb—and this heartbeat is a source of healing. How can the heart betray such goodness? What if passion and good intentions—zeal—cannot see the heart's tragic effects?

Wagamese's fiction is based on the truth of what happened to native children who were removed from their families by government social workers and placed in foster care or residential schools. These placements, guided by Canadian government policy, sought to eradicate any native identity from the children. Churches partnered with the government in this effort. These social workers passionately believed they were doing a good thing, yet they were perpetrating a great evil. If they did this today, they would be guilty of kidnapping. Such is the nature of what Dietrich Bonhoeffer called "folly," or good, well-intentioned people led to cooperate with evil.

Again, Wagamese's metaphors instruct us: What Jeremiah calls the "devious heart" may be healed by syncing our heartbeat to the heartbeat of the mother who gave us life, who takes us to the depth of our being, who reveals the Creator to us. These meanings of heart recall John Wesley's famous metaphor of "the circumcision of the heart," or the heart that is purified by turning toward God. Some people will identify with a metaphor of aligning our heart, others with the idea of removing imperfections. Regardless of our method, examining our heart in the spiritual realm is as important as caring for our heart in the medical realm.

Realign and purify my devious heart, O God. Amen.

THURSDAY, FEBRUARY 14 ~ *Read Luke 6:17-19*

Richard Wagamese's books record the difficult, diverse, and complex paths of human beings toward healing from deep emotional wounds. In *Keeper'n Me,* Garnet Raven seeks his Ojibway identity, learns the teachings of his people, figures out the place and meaning of ritual in his life, and finds the power available to him in symbols, dreams, and metaphors. Garnet's story incorporates wild moments; but once he establishes his journey with Keeper as his guide, he progresses.

In *Indian Horse,** Saul quests for the power that heals the trauma of sexual abuse. He is desperate. His search has stalled. He has no guide. In his distress, Saul wanders into the bush behind his alcoholism treatment center, watches the beavers and the stars, and falls asleep. Sometime in the night when he is half dreaming and half awake, his grandfather and then other figures of his deceased Ojibway family appear to him. By morning, he knows exactly where his search must take him.

In Luke, healing is bound up with teachings—as it is for Garnet Raven—and healing power comes from another person—as it does for Saul. Healing occurs in encounter; the power to heal shared through relationship. Jesus teaches the disciples and all who listen in the midst of his healing. It may seem like healing happens in the moment, but Wagamese reminds us to ask: What kind of difficult, diverse, and complex paths might the sufferers have taken to come to the "level place" where they found healing in the power Jesus had to offer? How might we honor the complex paths toward the healing of our relationship with God?

---

*Vancouver: Douglas and McIntyre, 2012.

How may I honor the duration and sometimes circuitous path of my own healing? In what context might I bring my diseases and unclean spirits to the power of Jesus' presence?

FRIDAY, FEBRUARY 15 ~ *Read 1 Corinthians 15:12-20*

Resurrection of the dead is one of the most difficult Christian doctrines to understand. It is easier to find imagery that allows us to glimpse resurrection than to define it.

When religious leaders in the first century die, their followers usually return to their homes or find a new prophet to follow. Yet after Jesus' crucifixion, something happens that changes the common pattern; communities coalesce with a witness to Jesus' life and teachings even stronger than during his lifetime—to the point that they are willing to give their lives. That *something,* we believe, is Jesus' resurrection—particularly his resurrection appearances. In today's passage, Paul calls this change-making difference the resurrection of the dead. And it has the power to change the direction of the living.

In Wagamese's writings, appearances of deceased relatives play a direct role in the characters' journey toward healing. In *Indian Horse,* Saul receives strength and support through a vision of his ancestors. Saul returns to the residential school where he was taken as a child and remembers for the first time that he experienced sexual abuse by a favorite priest. Then Saul returns to his family's original home, God's Lake. There he has another powerful vision of a gathering of his ancestors—a vision of the resurrection of the dead. And with this vision, his healing occurs. He reenters society and lives for others rather than for himself. In this he is much like all those whose lives are radically rearranged by the resurrection of Jesus.

Ojibway fiction draws us into a deeper understanding of the resurrection of the dead. Beyond Christ's provision of hope for a future beyond death, the resurrection of the dead may offer us healing through which we can reestablish a new relationship that brings us closer to Christ in this life.

Connect me, God, with my benevolent ancestors, the communion of saints. Amen.

SATURDAY, FEBRUARY 16 ~ *Read Psalm 1; Luke 6:22, 26*

Happy are those . . ." Garnet Raven shows us that happiness is a complex state not easily achieved. The kind of happiness referred to in Psalm 1 is partially captured in Wagamese's slang term "Lookin' Jake." Lookin' Jake means getting right on the inside, learning and following the teachings of tradition and using ceremony and ritual to go deeper, to the point that others might notice a change on the outside. Happiness comes when we can heal the wounds of the tragedies for which we are not responsible and resolve the sins that result from those wounds. Lookin' Jake is the true way to happiness.

In Wagamese's writing, the tragedies that leave his characters wounded—tragedies enacted by government, culture, society, community, and even family—also leave the characters lost. The condition of being lost can lead to what Christians call sin. In his profundity, Wagamese weaves a complex web that links tragedy, sorrow, helpful and problematic behavior, and happiness.

Psalm 1 and Luke 6:22, 26 encourage us to stop relying on our façades, our reputation, or our achievements to hide from our wounds. The psalmist encourages us to meditate on the teachings of God day and night to make ourselves right. Knowing God reveals the way of blessedness. In Luke, Jesus teaches that notoriety for personal works leads to wickedness; it is better to be defamed "on account of the Son of Man"—to be reviled for being right on the inside. Right living will bring prosperity—not *external* but *eternal* prosperity. The wicked ultimately will not judge us. Rather, that act lies with the God to whom we have turned, our God of goodness and mercy. Psalm 1 reassures us that God watches over the way of the righteous.

Let your reassurance sink into my heart, O God. Amen.

SUNDAY, FEBRUARY 17 ~ *Read 1 Corinthians 15:12-20*

Our greatest reassurance lies in our faith and confidence in the resurrection of the dead and, specifically, the resurrection of Christ Jesus. Resurrection overpowers all the negativity that weaves through this week's scriptures—woes, curses, wickedness, perversity, deviousness, sinfulness, scoffing, diseases, unclean spirits—and what I've called tragedies, wounds, and the sins that arise from them. The Resurrection promises that we can be redeemed, that we can be made righteous, that we can delight in God.

What are we to do with the promise that we can be redeemed? Reading these scriptures together with the teachings in two of Wagamese's many books of Ojibway fiction, we find some answers. *Keeper'n Me* ends with a feast to celebrate Garnet Raven. Ninety-four-year-old Old Lazarus, one of the last of the medicine men from a nearby reserve, arrives. When he shakes hands with Garnet, Garnet feels power go out from Old Lazarus. Old Lazarus truly is a spiritual man. The book ends with Keeper deepening his search by apprenticing himself to Old Lazarus. Through Keeper, Old Lazarus will also be Garnet Raven's guide. At the end of *Indian Horse,* Saul, who could have been and could still be a great hockey player, chooses to settle with his adoptive family and to coach younger boys, who, like himself, need a role model. One book shows us a response to healing as a search for further piety; the other, a call to offer mercy.

The promise of resurrection and redemption turns an ending into a beginning. It becomes the ground from which our actions of piety and mercy spring. The promise provides a moment of rest from struggle on our journey, a moment of happiness in which we can revel. But before we become self-righteous, these scriptures return, calling us again to self-examination.

Thank you, God, for moments of peace and reassurance. May they inspire my relationship with you and humankind. Amen.

Looking for the Bigger Picture

FEBRUARY 18–24, 2019 • CHEBON KERNELL

SCRIPTURE OVERVIEW: Joseph had experienced betrayal by his brothers and then had been sold into slavery. At the time, he no doubt had felt abandoned by God. However, after God raises up Joseph in Egypt, Joseph is able to provide for his family in a time of drought. Although others have acted with evil intentions, God uses it for good. The psalmist offers a similar encouragement. We struggle in the real challenges that face us, but we believe in a God who can carry us through them. In First Corinthians, Paul explains that God carries us even through death to resurrection glory on the other side. Jesus teaches us to respond to evil with mercy. Because we believe in a God who will ultimately bring justice, we do not need to serve as judge and executioner.

QUESTIONS AND SUGGESTIONS FOR REFLECTION

- Read Genesis 45:3-11, 15. How would considering your children's children to seven generations change the way you make decisions?
- Read Psalm 37:1-11, 39-40. What is your relationship to the land on which you live now and the land on which you lived as you grew up?
- Read 1 Corinthians 15:35-38, 42-50. How do you live out the characteristics of God's imperishable realm?
- Read Luke 6:27-38. How do you respond to Jesus' call to love your enemies as an individual? How does your community of faith follow this gospel requirement?

Executive Secretary, Native American and Indigenous Ministries, UMC Global Ministries; member of the Seminole Nation of Oklahoma.

MONDAY, FEBRUARY 18 ~ *Read Genesis 45:3-7*

The story of Joseph in the book of Genesis is a fairly well-known saga, possibly one of the best-known texts of the Hebrew scriptures. The story is full of controversy, betrayal, wonder, and even forgiveness and reconciliation.

Our reading for today projects us into the moment Joseph reveals to his brothers his identity. This moment, we assume, has haunted Joseph for many a year, as would be the case for most human beings, especially in the ancient world where vengeance was a pursuit of gratification as it is today. But the story takes a turn that may surprise those reading the story from start to finish or perhaps listening to it being told orally. As opposed to retribution, Joseph offers forgiveness and interpretation for the events that have transpired: "God sent me before you to preserve life." By not focusing on understanding the outcome but looking at the bigger picture, Joseph now has the ability to preserve life and to limit suffering.

Today the actions of others bombard us with the same debate of whether to continue harm and violence or to preserve life and peace.

Native American cultures have an unwritten understanding that the decisions we make have the ability to impact those yet to be born seven generations forward. As we live and make decisions in this life, we must consider whether our decisions will harm those around us and those who have not yet had a chance to make decisions of their own—those who have yet to be born.

Just as Joseph realized God's bigger picture of provision for Joseph's family, so must we realize that even the most difficult of circumstances can bring blessings and harmony.

Creator, in all that life has to offer, help me to choose the essence of life, which is love and harmony. Amen.

TUESDAY, FEBRUARY 19 ~ *Read Genesis 45:8-11, 15*

Children have always held a special place in the lives of Native American and indigenous communities across the world. Many in North America believe that the innocence and purity these little ones possess is the closest we can get to the spirit world or to the realm of God our Creator. Special moments are provided for various events in the lives of these children as they begin to make their mark in life. These cultures believe that children have not been marred by the trauma of life that often causes us to lose our focus as we get older. Native American tribal communities are mindful of the presence of children when speaking about the importance of maintaining tribal languages and even when performing certain spiritual ceremonies. The hope that the children will have something to carry on becomes the purpose of all activities in life. In most cases this *something* they carry on is their culture and identity.

In a world often harsh to the reality and needs of children, Joseph makes special mention of the children: "You shall be near me, you and your children and your children's children." The environment of the part of the ancient world where Joseph's family dwells does not provide an easy life for anyone. Minimal access to food and water, and manual labor to bring in a harvest make life challenging. If a family is not large enough to tend what they own, hired hands create another expense. In Joseph's time, families look upon having many children and grandchildren as a blessing from God. If one is poor or forced into slavery, life is unbearable.

Joseph's instruction to bring not just his father but the children as well displays an act of compassion that at times is absent in this ancient environment.

Creator, protect the children of the world. May they laugh and enjoy life as young people should. May your Spirit surround children of all faiths, countries, and communities. Amen.

WEDNESDAY, FEBRUARY 20 ~ *Read Psalm 37:1-6*

When we encounter the words of the Psalms, we find language of loving God and being loved by God that is becoming more foreign to our day and time. In this age we encounter only on rare occasions a poet or orator who can use the words of written or spoken language to capture the feelings of one's innermost spirit. Yet we find language that demonstrates human adoration for the divine not only throughout the Psalms but also in Song of Solomon and early Christian writings such as the Odes of Solomon and the Gospel of Truth. Some early prayers attributed to Paul also capture an intimacy that we often lack in communication with God in this digital world.

In today's psalm we witness this intimate language and the comfort the psalmist offers the audience: "He will make your vindication shine like the light, and the justice of your cause like the noonday." So, while the text captures the call to be faithful to God, it also captures the promises of God for the psalmist's audience. Quickly, one notices the psalmist addressing the plight of those who seek justice. Perhaps those persons who thirst for righteousness in the world and have become weary will now have their cries heard. Those who have had injustice inflicted upon them are now on the brink of their plight being known, which will lead to resolution and reconciliation.

Today, as we meditate upon these words, may we be mindful of those worthy movements across the world whose call for justice remains unheard.

Mighty One, who has created all, may our ears hear and our eyes see those who search for justice. We pray today for those Missing and Murdered Indigenous Women (MMIW) from across North America and the world, whose stories are just now coming to the light of the noonday. May violence, harm, and exploitation cease in the world we live in. Amen.

THURSDAY, FEBRUARY 21 ~ *Read Psalm 37:7-11, 39-40*

Who owns this land? This question was foreign to many Native American tribes as they encountered European explorers. They often responded, "How does one own the land?" Or, "How does one own the air of the sky or the water that surrounds us?" Ownership of the natural world was a foreign concept to the Indigenous People's cosmology, which maintained an undergirding belief that all of creation—the air, the earth and all that dwells on it—belongs to the One who crafted it. All, including plants, animals, and human beings, stood in equality as they each lived life accordingly.

This concept of ownership plagues us even to this day. In a world and time when land and its natural resources become more scarce as the decades go by, the pursuit to protect our resources that we cannot live without—such as our water—has become a growing crisis. This planet could very possibly come to war over access to clean water as sources become more contaminated.

Many Native American cultures and traditions believe that the true ownership of the land or earth belongs to the women of the culture. Just as women bring life into this world, so too the earth that we live on gives us life with food and water.

Psalm 37:11 captures this life-giving notion. Who shall inherit the earth but the meek? Not those who will harm or exploit. The earth will be inherited by someone who protects the life of all members of creation. Jesus says, "Blessed are the meek, for they will inherit the earth" (Matt. 5:5, NIV). While the Psalms offer us a vocabulary to use in speaking of the divine, they also remind us of the values we must possess as we live in the Creator's world.

You who has given us the breath of life, walk with us as we remember those characteristics of this journey that respect all members of creation. Help us to be meek and humble and to resist anger and violence. Amen.

FRIDAY, FEBRUARY 22 ~ *Read 1 Corinthians 15:35-38, 42-50*

Flesh and blood cannot inherit the kingdom of God, nor does the perishable inherit the imperishable," states Paul in his letter to the church of Corinth after a lengthy discussion on death and resurrection. Paul's discussion parallels other Pauline texts as he lays out in different contexts the wrestling between the will of humanity and the will of God. Paul minces words little in this letter to the church.

We can only imagine the temptations for distraction that existed in the ancient world in general. Marriage is different then than in the world we live in today. Spousal expectations are different. Even basic rules of society would be foreign to our understanding now. But we can relate to the difficulties of trying to live a life full of imperishable characteristics in a society that revolves around the perishable. Corinth, whose patron goddess is Aphrodite, is a port city with much traffic and trade. We can understand easily the admonitions Paul gives to the church about what is perishable (bad) and what is imperishable (good). In a bustling port city dependent on the patronage of Aphrodite, it would be easy for anyone to lose focus and to begin to participate in habits that do not represent the realm of God.

While our world today differs from the city of Corinth in some ways, we can pull the basic tenets of inspiration from Paul's writing. Paul calls us to surround ourselves with those things that represent another realm, those things that represent the kingdom of God. Hate, jealousy, and exploitation cause suffering and harm to our neighbors in our time just as in Paul's. Paul invites us to surround ourselves with the characteristics of an imperishable society that represents God: love, peace, forgiveness, and justice. We will find these characteristics when we walk closer to the realm of God.

God of all, help us to work to build a world that represents your full presence. Amen.

SATURDAY, FEBRUARY 23 ~ *Read Luke 6:27-31*

In a world familiar with occupation and military control by the Roman empire, the words of the Gospel of Luke are quite striking, even revolutionary. Roman authorities demand obedience and order. The concept of *Pax Romana* (Roman Peace) is not attained through spiritual pleadings of clergy but most often through violence. Those who dissent with the rulers of this world are eliminated. After all, this is the world that develops the technique of crucifixion, which serves not just to extinguish an individual threat but to intimidate all who witnessed the execution. Crucifixion demands obedience and demands notice of any revolt.

Luke captures the essence of Jesus in his clear instructions for those who wish to proclaim another world or another empire. Today's reading demonstrates an alternative to the harsh reality of living under occupation. Rather than entering into a mode of warring violence, which surely would bring one's death from Roman legions, do the opposite. "Love your enemies, do good to those who hate you," the Gospel pleads. Not only will this preserve our physical life but it also will demonstrate the true revolution of the movement whose foundation is the One that we have come to call the Son of God, Jesus. By following this way of nonviolence and true peace, we continue to build the new world ruled by the values of a holy and loving God, not by the sword. The movement that surrounds Jesus is about this kind of love, and it is a threat to those who control their world by force.

O God, we pray for those across the world searching for peace. We pray for the innocent who have suffered and for the refugees who have sought shelter. May we assist in making the world a place where violence in all its forms ends. Amen.

SUNDAY, FEBRUARY 24 ~ *Read Luke 6:32-38*

In this section of Luke, we continue to see the subversive movement that is meant to undermine the dominant thinking of the day. What value is it to bless only those who have blessed us? Luke has caught on to a characteristic that was present in the movement of the day but also in the everyday lives of those of us in the church today.

Since the time of my youth I have been asked to be a part of design teams, consultations, dialogues on inclusivity, and other such movements of revitalization. In more circumstances than I can count, the conversations have contained comments such as this: "If we take a field trip with young people, whom shall we allow to go? Will it be for church members only?" or other comments with similar mentalities. In our modern society it is easy to reserve our hospitality, our love, and our generosity for those persons who "deserve" it or with whom we are comfortable.

What if God used the same judgment with us: "You shall not have water for you are not really thirsty," or "You shouldn't have exerted yourself that much; you should have known you would get thirsty," or "You shall not have food today, for you do not know hunger."

It is easy to love only those who love us or to pray only for those whom we care about. Anyone can show such acts of piety. The gospel of the movement of Jesus demands that we lose our self-absorption to focus on the needs of our neighbors. And our neighbors may be those who do not look like us, those who speak other languages, those on the opposite side of the political spectrum, or even those in other countries and regions. This is what the gospel requires of us.

God, may we love as you have loved us. Help us to take care of those in need, wherever they may be in your world. Amen.

A Noticeable Difference

FEBRUARY 25–MARCH 3, 2019 • TRAVIS COLLINS

SCRIPTURE OVERVIEW: God's glory is always revealed, even if never completely. When Moses encounters God on the mountain, his face undergoes a physical transformation as a reflection of God's greater glory. The psalmist reminds us of how great God is and how even Moses and Aaron bow before God's throne. Paul refers to the story of Moses, but because of Christ, God's glory is now more openly revealed. There is no need to wear a covering as Moses did, for Christ reflects openly the divine radiance. Luke recounts the Transfiguration, when the face of Jesus, like that of Moses, begins to shine. God's voice reinforces the revelation of the Transfiguration, declaring Jesus to be God's Son and the revelation of God's glory.

QUESTIONS AND SUGGESTIONS FOR REFLECTION

- Read Exodus 34:29-35. Consider the ways you provide evidence of your faith. Do you display it for your glory or for God's?
- Read Psalm 99. How do you seek a healthy balance of awe and intimacy in your relationship with God?
- Read 2 Corinthians 3:12–4:2. What "veil" separates you from God—a sense of unworthiness, a hardened heart, a lack of understanding?
- Read Luke 9:28-43a. Jesus shines with God's glory, but then he gets back to his work of healing. Consider how God might transform you to do better the work you are already doing for God.

Former missionary; pastor of First Baptist Church, Huntsville, Alabama.

MONDAY, FEBRUARY 25 ~ *Read Exodus 34:29-35*

Moses' face is glowing. Not the glow one gets after too much sun. Or when one is embarrassed or in love. But mysteriously radiant.

We shouldn't be surprised. After all, Moses has been as close to God as a human can get on this earth. The conspicuous radiance of Moses' face reflects the mysterious transformation of an up-close-and-personal meeting with Yahweh.

Moses' spectacular encounter with God makes a difference. The kind of difference that makes people sit up and take notice. The difference in Moses lends credence to his words and points beyond his imperfections to One who is mysteriously and infinitely more wonderful than any human. I can hear parents telling this story to their children who weren't around during Moses' day: "You should have seen his face!"

Moses isn't the only person changed by Divine Presence. Acts 4:13 describes a similar effect on Peter and John. People around them "took note that these men had been with Jesus" (NIV).

Can others tell where we've been after we've been to worship?

Do people see us as those who walk closely with the Lord?

Does something about us make those around us believe that they have been in the presence of one who follows Jesus closely?

You've probably heard about the Christian who was arrested for his faith but was found not guilty for lack of evidence. May there always be conspicuous evidence of our faith!

God, transform me such that people see you in me. Make your presence visible in my life so that others look beyond my frailties to see your powerful perfection. May the afterglow of our visit be obvious to those around me. Amen.

TUESDAY, FEBRUARY 26 ~ *Read Exodus 34:29-35*

Moses glows. Not like someone on his or her wedding day. Not like someone who just won *America's Got Talent*. But like someone who has just been with the All-Powerful Master of the Universe. Moses' physical appearance has taken on some of the holiness and glory of God, just for having been close to God.

Then Moses places a veil over his face.

Why the veil? There has been a lot of speculation about that. Perhaps Moses is simply trying to calm people's nerves. (The text says people "were afraid to come near him.") Or, as some have suggested, maybe the veil signals when Moses is offering his own perspective rather than quoting God.

I fear that if I were Moses, I would ditch the veil and enjoy the glow. I'm afraid I would want to show off my religious credentials.

Moses' shining countenance gives us a visual representation of the change that happens within us when we are in close proximity to God. God's holiness and righteousness rub off on us. We face the temptation to show off our glow when we do God's work. The danger is that we morph God's holiness within us into a holier-than-thou posture and God's righteousness into self-righteousness.

Perhaps Moses wears a veil to remind himself that his authority is not his own. So what can we do as we seek to serve others out of God's blessings? We can pray that we stay focused on displaying God's glory. We can be honest about our frailties. We can serve through anonymous acts so that we break the hold on our human desire for recognition.

God, I confess that I seek recognition as I work for you. Help me to tame my ego as you transform me to act for your glory. Amen.

WEDNESDAY, FEBRUARY 27 ~ *Read Psalm 99*

The night I rode out Hurricane Isabel I felt the earth shake. Historic, majestic, seemingly indestructible trees bowed before their Creator, and the wind declared a power far greater than its own.

Anyone who has been through a fierce storm understands why one of the many adjectives that describe God is "fearsome."

I'm not suggesting we should be terrorized at the thought of God. Yet God is the holy Creator of the universe, and trembling before God is not uncalled for. A good dose of trepidation before the Almighty is good for us. Proverbs 1:7 tells us that fear of God is the very beginning of wisdom!

This week we look afresh at mysterious, life-altering encounters with the Creator. We remember that communion with God is infinitely different than coffee and casual conversation at Starbucks with a pal. After all, after encountering Yahweh, Moses begins glowing! To meet with God is no commonplace encounter.

When my family lived in Ogbomoso, Nigeria, we would visit the Soun, the local king, in his palace from time to time. When we went, our sons and I would bow and our little preschool daughter would curtsy.

When we greeted the Soun we would say, "Kabiyesi." And we really drew out the "Kaaaaaa," for that was a way of signaling respect. The Soun was kind and gracious, but we never forgot he was the king.

God is our loving Father, but worship takes on new depth and richness when we remember that we worship in the presence of the King of the Universe.

God, forgive us for any inappropriate familiarity we have assumed in our relationship with you. Remind us of the need to maintain a healthy respect for you even as we enjoy the tenderness of your grace. Amen.

THURSDAY, FEBRUARY 28 ~ *Read 2 Corinthians 4:1-2*

God invites us to join in God's mission to the world. For some, that invitation is to vocational ministry. For most, it is an invitation to ministries for which they are not paid but are nonetheless vital to the fulfillment of God's mission.

So what kind of people does God call to these places of service? One thing we know for sure: God requires neither past nor present perfection. Paul would offer himself as the first example of this. He lives with his own amazing story of transformation—from a life of persecuting the church to propagating the church.

Remember Moses, the glowing deliverer of God's laws? Moses is not perfect. He kills a man in an act of ethnocentric passion. Yet God calls Moses to a place in God's plan.

Surely someone reading this is thinking, *God couldn't call me. Not with my limitations and imperfections.* That would be wrong. I know God calls unworthy people, for I am one. I am both skillfully inadequate and personally unworthy to join in God's amazing plan for the world. Yet one of today's verses reminds me that the calling God gave me is purely a gift of mercy: "Therefore, since through God's mercy we have this ministry, we do not lose heart" (NIV).

Someone suggested that beautiful flowers should be displayed in plain pots, so that the pots will not detract from the flowers' splendor. Perhaps that is why God invites imperfect people like you and me to serve in God's plan for the world.

God, thank you for your invitation to join you in your mission despite my imperfection. Remind me that this invitation is a gift and not based on my merit. Amen.

If the mountain in this story is Mount Hermon, as many believe, it requires a long climb, probably high enough to where there may be snow on the ground. When they reach the top, Jesus begins to pray intensely. His friends are exhausted, perhaps as a result of the climb or simply the altitude.

Then the three are made fully awake by a dazzling light. Jesus is literally glowing. And it is not just his face, as it was with Moses. Even Jesus' clothes become "as bright as a flash of lightning" (NIV).

Two men are with Jesus—Moses and Elijah. Why these two? Often in the New Testament you will hear the Old Testament referred to as "the Law and the Prophets." Moses represents the Law and Elijah represents the Prophets. Their presence symbolizes Jesus' continuity with the ancient traditions and his fulfillment of their prophecies.

Moses and Elijah speak with Jesus "about his departure, which he was about to bring to fulfillment at Jerusalem" (NIV). They speak of his soon and certain death. Then God's voice resounds, "This is my Son, my Chosen; listen to him!" At the risk of assuming too much about the mind of Jesus, perhaps our Lord will remember these words, an echo of the words from heaven at his baptism, during his imminent suffering. The pleasure of the Father might encourage the Son.

That experience on the mountaintop means a great deal to Peter for the rest of his life. He later recalls: "We ourselves heard this voice come from heaven, while we were with him on the holy mountain" (2 Pet. 1:18). Perhaps, during times of intense persecution, Peter remembers that night on a mountain when his Lord shone like the sun.

God, remind me that you take pleasure in me as your child. Help me to experience your grace so deeply that my heart may be strengthened when I am tested. Amen.

SATURDAY, MARCH 2 ~ *Read Luke 9:28-43a*

As a little boy walking with my mom and dad through the county fair, I'd see men standing at the entrance to tents trying to entice people to enter. It might have been a museum exhibit, what we called then a "freak show," or even something less than wholesome. Whatever was inside, they'd hold the tent door open just enough for a glimpse of what was inside with the hope that we'd buy a ticket.

From time to time God seems to pull back the curtain to give us a brief look into the unseen world.

Jesus' transfiguration is one of those rare glimpses.

Jesus' face changes, and his very clothes glow. Elijah and Moses also "[appear] in glorious splendor" (NIV). The shining features of the three indicate for us a glimpse into life beyond this world. There is, indeed, a world we cannot see with our natural eyes where God works in mysterious ways to perform wonders. The disciples with Jesus see into this world, yet they do not understand. Peter ignorantly suggests he build dwellings at the top of the mountain. But Jesus knows he has been transformed for another purpose. Jesus and the disciples go back down the mountain and the disciples prove they still do not understand: They rely on Jesus to heal the boy.

Jesus' transfiguration signals not a change in his work but that it is about to be fulfilled. After his transformation, he goes back to serving the people and healing them. God transforms us not to be set apart on a mountaintop but to go out into the world to serve others. This too is a glimpse of the kingdom of heaven.

Remind me, Lord, that as I pray I glimpse the unseen world. Transform me to bring your glory into this world. Amen.

Transfiguration

In today's text Paul uses Moses' veil as a metaphor for the lack of spiritual understanding outside of a relationship with God through Jesus. Paul writes that the purpose of Moses' veil was "to prevent the Israelites from seeing the end of what was passing away" (apparently a reference to the fading glow of Moses' face). We don't find that interpretation in Exodus 34, but Paul looks back from a Christian perspective. He believes the old covenant has faded in the new light of God's plan revealed in Jesus.

For those who do not yet trust Jesus, Paul writes, "That same veil is still there." Christ removes the veil, and "when one turns to the Lord, the veil is removed." When the Spirit comes to live in us, we gain new understanding of our relationship with God. The Holy Spirit lives within those whose hope is in Jesus. Our insights are imperfect, for we are fallible creatures. Nevertheless, the Spirit illumines our thoughts and sheds light on spiritual mysteries.

In Paul's first letter to the Corinthians, he writes: "The person without the Spirit does not accept the things that come from the Spirit of God but considers them foolishness, and cannot understand them because they are discerned only through the Spirit" (2:14, NIV).

Warning: The Christian family is not the exclusive Fraternity of the Enlightened. Let's not congratulate ourselves as the "well-versed ones" and dismiss those who have not turned to Jesus as "boorish." You and I have a lot to learn too! Yet, those whose faith is in Jesus can pray for God's Spirit to enlighten us, to teach us, and to unlock mysteries as we study God's word. And through our faith, God promises to transform us "from one degree of glory to another."

Lord, illumine my thoughts by your Spirit. Give me clarity and lead me into truth. Amen.

God's Unwavering Presence

MARCH 4–10, 2019 • NORA E. COLMENARES

SCRIPTURE OVERVIEW: As we begin the season of Lent, the readings provide several images of how we might prepare our hearts. Deuteronomy focuses on gratitude with a recitation of the history of God's faithfulness. The people are instructed to offer their gifts to God as a response to God's generosity. The psalmist focuses on faithfulness. If we put our confidence in God, God will protect and sustain us. In Romans, Paul emphasizes faith. Our confession of faith from the mouth should come from the heart, and this heart confession saves us. The story of the temptation of Jesus admonishes us to know biblical truth. The devil tempts Jesus with half-truths—even scriptural quotes—but Jesus counters with correct understanding of God's word and God's character.

QUESTIONS AND SUGGESTIONS FOR REFLECTION

- Read Deuteronomy 26:1-11. We no longer offer physical sacrifices to God. How do you give the "first fruits" of your labor to God in thanksgiving?
- Read Psalm 91:2, 9-16. Recall a time you have felt abandoned or insecure. How did God respond to your call?
- Read Romans 10:8b-13. Paul learned to see those he once despised as his equals in Christ. Whom does God call you to learn to love?
- Read Luke 4:1-13. How do you follow Jesus' example to use scripture to resist temptation?

Ordained Deacon of the United Methodist Church; Senior Manager, General Board of Global Ministries; passionate about the church embracing its multicultural identity and crossing boundaries to fulfill God's vision.

MONDAY, MARCH 4 ~ *Read Deuteronomy 26:1-11*

In the book of Deuteronomy, we read over and over again about the land God promises to God's people. Trusting that promise, they leave the nation where they have been foreigners and have been enslaved to set out on a journey to settle in that promised land. But they complain and drift away from God and into worshiping idols, so a journey that should take them about eleven days (Deut. 1:2) takes them forty years. To provide them with direction, God gives commandments for them to follow in love and obedience to God.

After forty years in the desert, God's people arrive at the promised land where God commands them to show gratitude for the fulfilled promise. Today gratitude can be a shallow expression; saying "thanks" will do, sending a "thank-you card" will suffice. But that is not what God wants from Israel. God instructs the people to remember the journey, to remember the darkest times, to remember God's continuous presence with them, and to express their gratitude by offering publicly the best of what they have—the first fruits of their labor. God calls them to do this not only before those who are important in society but also before those who are less important so that all people will rejoice and share in this moment of gratitude.

This story reminds us of God's presence with us during difficult times and during joyous times, and of how important it is to show gratitude to God by publicly acknowledging God's unwavering love toward even the most unfaithful of us. This witness and joy can be experienced by all, those in high places and those who live at the margins of society.

Creator God, I remember the many times you have walked with me, even when I went astray. With all of my heart I give you thanks for everything you have given me. I rejoice in your presence and in your grace. Amen.

TUESDAY, MARCH 5 ~ *Read Psalm 91:2, 9-16*

You who live in the shelter of the Most High, who abide in the shadow of the Almighty, will say to the LORD, 'My refuge and my fortress; my God, in whom I trust'" (Ps. 91:1-2).

These powerful words remind us of God's unwavering presence in our lives.

We all go through dark times when our faith is tested, when our determination to follow Jesus wavers. We face illnesses or financial difficulties; we experience the loss of a loved one; we find ourselves in a damaging relationship and we need to make a tough decision.

Often during those times we feel lost, confused, and consumed. We might even feel as though God has abandoned us. But God understands these feelings. Jesus understands our pain because he also goes through it. Before he was arrested, Jesus goes aside to pray and feels the weight of what is about to happen. At that time Jesus felt overwhelmed and abandoned, and he cries out, "My God, my God, why have you forsaken me?" (Matt. 27:46, NIV).

When we go through difficult times, prayer is the key. When we feel abandoned and persecuted, God is our refuge and our fortress. With God we can feel secure and safe, remembering that nothing can separate us from God. God will protect those who know God's name. All we need to do is call to God.

Whatever happens, whatever life throws on our path, God's love is ours today and tomorrow. We are God's beloved.

Loving God, thank you for your unwavering love for me. Even when I waver, your love is steadfast. Give me courage to live in the certainty that your love surrounds me and to share that love with others. Amen.

Ash Wednesday

Ash Wednesday marks the beginning of the season of Lent when we focus on reflection, fasting, and prayer.

Many Christians choose to fast during Lent. It has also been a custom to give up a favorite food or a luxury to dedicate this personal sacrifice to God. This is not necessarily wrong unless this act reflects the shallowness of our understanding of what fasting is.

In Isaiah 58 the prophet highlights shallow ways in which people pray and fast to seek God's favor and justice. The prophet denounces those who fast but at the same time exploit their workers, fight, and even physically attack others.

A believer may fast for days on end, dress in clothes of mourning, bow his or her head, and lie in ashes for all to see; but these pious activities are worthless if they are not accompanied by acts of compassion.

The fasting God seeks is not a religious performance. God seeks fasting that works for justice, sets free the oppressed, shares our own food with the hungry, opens our home to the poor, and not only clothes the naked but acknowledges them and treats them as we treat our own.

Notice this is not a call to give handouts to nameless people. God calls us to be in relationship with those who live a life different than ours, to welcome them into our lives, and to be with those society rejects and marginalizes.

It is then, when we pour out our lives for the outsider, that our prayers and our fasting reach God and our lives become light in the darkness.

Loving God, forgive our shallow activities, and give us the courage to live our faith through actions that are instruments of liberation so that we may be in community with our neighbors who suffer and feel rejected. Amen.

THURSDAY, MARCH 7 ~ *Read Romans 10:8b-13*

The apostle Paul writes this letter to an emerging Christian congregation in the capital of the Roman Empire. This congregation probably meets in someone's home and is composed not only of Gentiles but also of Jews. Paul never visits this congregation; but since they are new in the faith, he writes this letter to introduce himself as a leader of the movement and to explain carefully the gospel from beginning to end.

Paul explains to this faith community that salvation cannot be earned by obeying the law. We are made just before God by believing in our hearts in the resurrected Jesus. Our salvation comes by proclaiming with our mouths that Jesus is Lord.

Notice that Paul highlights the resurrection of Jesus as a crucial component of the Christian faith. It is not enough to believe in Jesus as a prophet or as a great teacher. We must believe in the core of the gospel: God conquered death by raising Jesus from the dead.

This faith is not a mere concept; it goes from the heart to the mouth to proclaim that Jesus is Lord. For believers in Paul's time, proclaiming Jesus as Lord could be considered a treasonous act, as this kind of declaration stood against the authority of the government.

Paul wants to make clear that Jesus did everything necessary to attain our salvation. There are no sacrifices left to be made, no works to be completed. God invites us to respond in faith and in action.

Loving God, I commit myself to follow Jesus and to live this faith in a way that gives witness to the Lord I follow. Amen.

FRIDAY, MARCH 8 ~ *Read Romans 10:8b-13*

Today we continue reflecting on this passage from the letter to the Romans. The apostle Paul, the author of this letter, is an expert in Jewish law and had lived his life obeying it. He was part of the Pharisees, an important religious group. Because of this religious and social context, Paul had followed carefully the rules that separated Jews from Gentiles and did not relate to anybody who was a Gentile. Paul's zeal to obey God's law had gone so far that before believing in Jesus he mercilessly had persecuted, punished, and killed Christians.

But when Paul encounters Jesus, the experience completely transforms his life. God chooses him to share the gospel of Jesus with the Gentiles, those he had once despised.

With this background in mind, we recognize further depth in Paul's statement that there is no difference between Jew and Greek, or Jews and Gentiles. These words go against everything Paul once believed. Paul recognizes that God has torn down the wall of separation to bring salvation for all, not just for a chosen few.

In our own communities we too have been taught to despise certain people who society deems less worthy and to exclude them from our circles and even from the church. As followers of Jesus we are called to challenge those beliefs and practices and to include the excluded. The transforming message of the gospel is for all, and all who believe belong in the body of Christ; for "everyone who calls on the name of the Lord will be saved."

God of grace, thank you for reminding us once more that through your loving grace you became one of us to offer us salvation by faith in Christ. Continue reminding us to share that salvation even with those who have been excluded in our communities. Amen.

SATURDAY, MARCH 9 ~ *Read Isaiah 58:1-12*

When we read these verses of the book of Isaiah and reflect on our world today, we have no choice but to conclude that these words are as relevant today as they were when they were written. They are an indictment on the hypocrisy of people of faith.

God, speaking through the prophet, bluntly makes the case that many who want to appear devout go through religious motions just for show. God sees right through their phony acts and their empty prayers. God sees that their lives show no proof of transformation. They beseech God and seem penitent, but they quickly turn around and go back to their daily lives of oppressing their own employees and hurting their own friends.

We do that too. We go to God. We pray and fast. We aim to devote our lives to God. But we go back to our sinful ways and treat our workers unfairly and do violence to our friends.

These verses are a compelling reminder that "faith without deeds is useless" (James 2:20, NIV); faith must be lived out, not only through charity but through crossing the boundaries that separate us from one another.

God's call is not for a faith for show. God's call is for a revolutionary faith that inevitably makes us take the steps to be involved in the liberation of those who are oppressed; a faith that makes us see the poor, feed the hungry, clothe the naked, and welcome them as family, as our own.

Forgiving God, we repent from being worried about showing how religious we are and ignoring those you put in our path for us to befriend. We repent from this sin. We vow before you that we will get involved in their struggle and welcome them into our lives as family. Amen.

FIRST SUNDAY IN LENT

Reflecting on the temptations of Jesus can be difficult. They touch on our human desires to eat, to have power, and to be immortal. We all feel these desires at one time or another. We certainly wish to eat regularly, and we often overeat to be comforted by food when we feel bad. From childhood we wish to become superheroes who can do good things with our powers and learn how villains use their powers to hurt others. Our mortality constantly gnaws at us. We learn to fear death, and we often struggle to accept our fate as mortal; we even go so far as to make deals with God to stop the inevitable.

Now notice how Jesus responds to the temptations. He uses one powerful tool to stay focused on God: scripture.

Even though Jesus is terribly hungry and would have welcomed a piece of bread, he remembers how God provided food for the people of Israel in the desert to teach them to depend solely on God.

Jesus is tempted with having power over the world in exchange for worshiping the devil. While some power can be used for good, power has unbreakable links to egoism and self-centeredness, which move our focus from God. Jesus remembers the scriptures and tells the devil: "Worship the Lord your God, and serve only him."

Then the devil gets tricky. The third temptation challenges Jesus to test God to save him from certain death using God's own words from this week's psalm. From Jesus' response we learn that we should not make deals to demand God to do our will but should seek God's will instead.

Almighty Creator, thank you for your word that feeds and empowers us in our journey with you. We renew our commitment to depend wholly on you, to worship you, and to do your will and not ours. Amen.

The Paradoxical Ways of God

MARCH 11–17, 2019 • GWENDOLYNN PURUSHOTHAM

SCRIPTURE OVERVIEW: This week's readings give witness to the ways of God and provide confidence and hope in our faith. In Genesis we read of God's promise to Abram, a promise that seems very unlikely to a man with no children. But God seals the covenant, and the story later shows that God never breaks God's promises. The psalmist even while mired in conflict praises God for being his light, his salvation, his stronghold. The psalmist longs to be in God's presence forever, a desire that can inspire all of us as believers. Paul says that in the future reality, we will no longer experience resistance from those who oppose God. One day Christ will fully transform us to our citizenship in heaven. Jesus himself experienced resistance even in Jerusalem, yet he ultimately triumphs, as will all those who trust in God.

QUESTIONS AND SUGGESTIONS FOR REFLECTION

- Read Genesis 15:1-12, 17-18. How can you take a step forward in the dark toward God's seemingly impossible promises for the future?
- Read Psalm 27. Recall a time when you waited in the shadows of your life. What did you learn about God's provision during this time?
- Read Philippians 3:17–4:1. How do you live in the paradox of standing firm in faith by being vulnerable?
- Read Luke 13:31-35. When have you been unwilling to accept love? How can you comprehend the depth and yearning of God's love for you?

Retired Elder, New England Conference, United Methodist Church; former pastor, district superintendent, and staff of the General Board of Higher Education and Ministry; author of *Watching Over One Another in Love*.

MONDAY, MARCH 11 ~ *Read Genesis 15:1-12, 17-18*

The Lord comes to Abram "after these things." After what things? The verses immediately preceding tell us that Abram has come from battle with those who captured his nephew. The Lord comes to Abram when he is weary from war, old, and childless; when his world is shrinking along with his hope; when his body is tired and his mind will not let him rest in peace.

The Lord comes with this message: "Do not be afraid, Abram, I am your shield; your reward shall be very great." From Abram's perspective, God's promises—that Abram's descendants will be more than the stars in the heavens and his heirs will possess the land—seem pretty far-fetched.

The story does not say that Abram suddenly "gets it," makes an agreement with God, pulls down the shades, and nods off to sleep. Instead Abram falls into a deep sleep as a terrifying darkness descends on him. While he sleeps, while it is pitch dark, and while he cannot reciprocate even if he wants to, God makes a covenant with him. Only when Abram cannot see a thing does God speak to him.

Have you known weariness, sorrow, and desolation? Have the circumstances of your life robbed you of hope for the future? Have you ever been terrified by the darkness? The Lord speaks to you and to me: "Do not be afraid." Remember that "when the sun goes down," God will speak.

O God, help me to see you when you come in my hour of darkness. Amen.

TUESDAY, MARCH 12 ~ *Read Genesis 15:1-12, 17-18*

Abram is old and childless; his wife, Sarai, is well beyond childbearing age. Abram cannot believe that his own child will be his heir and that his descendants will outnumber the stars. Everything Abram knows—about himself, about his circumstances, and about the way things work—makes God's promise seem utterly impossible. Yet Abram believes God so, no matter how skeptically, he can take the next step forward into a future that he cannot envision.

Virginia McLaurin was born in South Carolina in 1909 when Howard Taft was the twenty-seventh president of the United States. She lived through decades of segregation, the terror of lynchings, and other kinds of racial violence. She was not granted the right to vote until 1965 at the age of fifty-six. Virginia experienced and witnessed the effects of individual and institutional racism.

In 2016, seventeen presidents later, at the age of 106, something occurred that Virginia had every reason to believe was impossible. She received a special invitation from the White House to meet privately with Barack Obama, the first African-American to be elected president of the United States, and with First Lady Michelle Obama. The images of that joyful encounter—of Virginia's exuberance and of Virginia dancing with the Obamas—are unforgettable.

Do current realities in your life and in the world cause you to question the possibility of a peaceful and sustainable planet and world order? Can you take one small, perhaps skeptical, hopeful step forward toward a future that seems impossible?

God of Abram and Virginia, help us! Help us to move forward with faith toward a future that we cannot yet envision. Amen.

WEDNESDAY, MARCH 13 ~ *Read Psalm 27*

When my sister was dying, her son asked her, "Mom, if you were granted one wish, what would that be?" With the small voice she had left after undergoing three surgeries and radiation to her head for the aggressive cancer that eventually took her life, she replied, "I wish everyone would have good health."

Her reply to my nephew's question is remarkable not as much for what she said as for what she did not say. She did not say she wished God would take away her unbearable and excruciating pain. She did not say she wished God would add years to her life, though I am sure she wanted to live. She did not say she wanted to know why this was happening to her. Her wish struck me as simple, surprising, and pure.

Psalm 27 reflects a similar response to suffering. In the midst of troubles and desperation, the psalmist names the one thing he seeks. He does not ask for fortress against his enemies. He does not ask for more troops and armaments to overcome his adversaries. He does not ask for more power to overcome evil. The one thing he seeks to behold is the beauty of the Lord. The psalmist, beaten down by forces within and without, desires beauty more than anything else. He seeks God's beauty—not God's power, not God's might, not God's vengeance—only God's beauty. What a remarkable wish for one who knows suffering and adversity!

What do you seek after? Do you long for beauty? Where and in what circumstances have you encountered beauty? How does beauty transform you? How have you witnessed beauty that transforms the world? What is the power of beauty? What would it mean for you to seek after God's beauty?

God, let me seek, behold, and reflect your beauty. Amen.

THURSDAY, MARCH 14 ~ *Read Psalm 27*

The psalmist's life has been anything but a bed of roses. He has been beset by trouble, ravaged by war, pursued by enemies, and victimized by violence and false testimony. Even as the psalmist affirms that God has upheld him through times of trouble and has protected him from that which has sought to destroy him, he pleads with God not to hide from him. Though he claims to be confident and unafraid, he begs God not to forsake him, not to turn him away. In one breath the psalmist eloquently affirms his faith; in the next he confesses his uncertainty that God will be with him in the future.

Fear and hope, faith and doubt, belief and lament, light and darkness live side by side in all of us. Our experiences and emotions waver wildly. Our prayers sound like the psalmist's. In one moment we confidently confess, "The LORD is my light and salvation." In the next, we cry out from a place of forsakenness for God to answer us. In one moment we sing and shout for joy. In the next, we plead with God not to hide from us.

Have you ever wished you could erase all doubt and fear from your life? Have you had a mountaintop experience and then found yourself wandering in a wilderness? Have you ever wanted to cast away the shadows from your life only to discover that they linger and follow you? Have you ever wondered what you really believe? If so, Psalm 27 can be your prayer.

After pouring out his faith and doubt, fear and courage, the psalmist concludes, "Wait for the LORD." We cannot and need not run from the shadows of our lives. Light and darkness exist side by side within each of us, and God is in it all.

God, help me to wait upon you whether in the light or in the shadows. Amen.

FRIDAY, MARCH 15 ~ *Read Philippians 3:17–4:1*

Paul encourages his sisters and brothers "to stand firm in the Lord in this way." What way does he mean?

First Paul advises them to imitate him. But wait; Paul's conversion experience literally knocks him to the ground, strikes him blind, forces him to leave behind his old beliefs and practices, makes him extremely unpopular, and lands him in prison, the place from which he writes this letter. Further, he instructs these Christians to observe those who "live according to the example you have in us." That is to say, not according to those who are enemies of the cross because "their end is destruction."

How can this be the description of the best way to stand firm? Paul's instructions seem questionable at best. If we read carefully Paul's words, we cannot help but ask, Was not the cross the way to suffering and death? How does choosing the way of the cross provide firm ground upon which to stand? How can these seeming opposites (vulnerability and standing firm) be held together?

If you are asking such questions, you have likely begun to grasp the paradox that expresses the truth Paul wants to convey and that lies at the heart of the gospel message. The way of vulnerability, the way of the cross, is the way of Jesus. It is folly to the Gentiles and a stumbling block to the Jews. The way of the cross still confounds us to this day.

How has loving made you vulnerable? Have you ever experienced failure or falling? When have you been vulnerable to pain and suffering? Did those experiences enlarge your heart? Did they open a way forward? Did they cause you to see and love yourself and others in a new way? The changes within us that result from pain and suffering for love can give us firm ground upon which to stand.

God, help us to stand firm by following your way of vulnerable love. Amen.

SATURDAY, MARCH 16 ~ *Read Luke 13:31-35*

The first verse of this text says, "At that very hour." What hour? The hour when Jesus, while making his way to Jerusalem, is casting out demons and curing the sick. It is the hour when he is telling the townsfolk that the arrangements in the kingdom of God will be radically different from the present order of things. "Some who are last will be first, and some are first who will be last," Jesus says. This message does not sit well with those who hold power and see themselves as deserving first place. Jesus' message sounds like anything but good news to religious and political authorities. "At that very hour" some Pharisees come with their own message and say to him, "Get away from here, for Herod wants to kill you."

"That very hour" is not relegated to biblical times. "That very hour" is now. The news of God's radical reversal of power still threatens those who work hard to maintain arrangements that benefit themselves at the expense of others. Greed and lust for domination and power continue to wreak havoc on the planet, the poor, the most vulnerable in our society, the church, and our own spirits. Jesus clearly sees right through the Pharisees' pretense and Herod's scheming, and he will have none of it. He must be on his way to fulfill his purpose.

Our faithful and hopeful response to God's call includes examining ourselves to see how we contribute to or benefit from arrangements that harm others. It requires our participation in dismantling systems and structures that oppress peoples and harm the earth. Our faithful response involves taking our proper place at the table in God's kingdom.

Loving God, show us how to see ourselves and others within your beautiful upside-down order of things. Amen.

SUNDAY, MARCH 17 ~ *Read Luke 13:31-35*

Second Sunday in Lent

How often have I desired to gather your children together as a hen gathers her brood under her wings, and you were not willing!" What a tender and helpless image! What a soulful lament. God understands the depth of our yearning and sorrow.

Jesus' heart is broken. It has been broken by persons' inability to understand the depth of his love for them. Their hearts are hardened and their minds are made up. They cling tenaciously to their false beliefs about God and to their flawed and destructive notions of security and power. In their ignorance, they reject the one who longs to care for them. For one who comes as love and lives as love and will die for love, this reality is cause for deep sorrow.

Jesus' lament is perceptible in our time. We who were created out of love and for love seem unable or unwilling to embrace Jesus as the way, the truth, and the life. We can witness the evidence of our inability to accept love everywhere: in our judgment and scapegoating of others, in our rigid notions of right and wrong, in the ways we execute justice, in our rejection of those whom God loves, in our presumption of superiority over the earth and other living things, and in our insistence that our group, race, or religion possesses the whole truth. Our rejection of love and mercy breaks God's heart. Yet God, like the hen who would gather her brood under her wings, longs to gather us together in safety and love. And so Jesus continues his journey toward Jerusalem and his journey toward us.

O God, who came as love in Jesus, continue to pursue us with your unstoppable love and mercy until we finally allow you to enfold us beneath your wings. Amen.

Thirsting for God

MARCH 18–24, 2019 • JAMES C. HOWELL

SCRIPTURE OVERVIEW: In the midst of Lent, when many might be giving up a certain food that they love, we read about feasting. The focus is not on physical feasting, but on feasting as a metaphor for communing with God. Isaiah describes food and drink that one cannot buy with money, for it comes freely from the Lord. The psalmist describes the state of his soul as being hungry and thirsty. Only meditating on God's faithfulness nourishes his soul at the deepest level. Physical food is momentary, but spiritual nourishment endures. In First Corinthians, Paul appeals to this imagery. Although the ancients experience this spiritual nourishment, some pursue physical pleasure and stray into idolatry and immorality. Partaking in this nourishment should cause us in turn to produce spiritual fruit, as Jesus admonishes his listeners.

QUESTIONS AND SUGGESTIONS FOR REFLECTION

- Read Isaiah 55:1-9. When has God's grace inverted your expectations?
- Read Psalm 63:1-8. As you mature in faith, what new questions about God do you ask?
- Read 1 Corinthians 10:1-13. Think of a time you have faced great temptation. How did God help you endure it?
- Read Luke 13:1-9. For what do you need to repent?

Senior pastor, Myers Park UMC; author of seventeen books, including *Worshipful: Living Sunday Morning All Week* and *Weak Enough to Lead*.

MONDAY, MARCH 18 ~ *Read Isaiah 55:1-5*

The Israelites who hear the prophet's ringing, joyful proclamation must scoff. The city is in ruins; the possibility of rebuilding the nation must seem ridiculous. To such demoralized people, needing a fortune to rebuild but nearly broke, Isaiah sounds like a street peddler hawking his wares. Come! Buy! But instead of gouging them, he says it's all free.

God always does the same. When we find ourselves expending our very lives trying to secure what we need or crave, we overhear God offering us the only goods that will ever satisfy us; and surprise of all surprises, they are free. We call this grace.

For God's offer of life to work, we need two revolutions in the soul. The first is to recognize the upside-downness of what is valuable and what isn't. William Temple said the world is like a shop window into which someone has sneaked in the middle of the night and switched around all the price tags. We gawk over what has a high price, fooled into thinking it must be cool. But then the affordable and free (life, mercy, salvation, and hope) we take for granted or don't invest much of ourselves in. Believe it: The precious gifts of God really are precious.

The second revolution is that what seems impossible, God can make possible. Israel's great ancestor, Abraham, while chuckling over the notion that he and Sarah would have a child, is told that with God, all things are possible. Isaiah's listeners just can't believe this anymore. Oswald Chambers wrote: "We won't believe . . . we prefer to worry on." God invites us to purchase the free gift by our trust: "If it is an impossibility, it is the thing we have to ask."*

---

*Oswald Chambers, *My Utmost for His Highest* (Grand Rapids: Discovery House, 1927), February 29.

Lord, here is the impossible thing I need. I ask trusting your power and love will sustain my life. Amen.

TUESDAY, MARCH 19 ~ *Read Isaiah 55:6-9*

Seek the LORD while he may be found." When would that be? Now! Claus Westermann translates it, "Seek Yahweh *since* he may be found."* God does not hide in some distant location. God is as close as the breath you just took, the beating of your heart. We like to think of ourselves as "seekers," as if we are the jockeys setting the agenda. But if we "seek and find" God, it's only because God has sought and found us; our role is to notice, to realize, and to stop our foolish flight away.

But are there times in which we can more readily find God? In worship or prayer? In pain and sorrow? There was a window in time when God was easy to find: during the earthly life of Jesus. And so we rely on the Gospel stories as we seek to realize God's presence today.

Jesus shows us the mind and heart of God. Isaiah hears God say, "My thoughts are not your thoughts . . . my ways are higher than your ways" (55:8, AP). As Colossians 3:2 puts it, "Set your minds on things that are above." The wonder of God's very "high" way is that it is really very low, humble, earthly. Jesus goes low. Jesus "emptied himself" by being born human (Phil. 2:6). We need not soar or stretch upward to reach God. God has come down to us, in humility, kneeling so low as to wash our feet.

God's will is not what we want with God giving us a boost. God's will is surprising, out of sync, yet alluring. We can know the high and low mind of God. God requires us to seek God's will, but God has left a well-lit trail for us to find and to know God's mind and heart.

---

*Claus Westermann, *Isaiah 40-66: A Commentary* (Philadelphia: The Westminster Press, 1969), 286.

Lord, thank you for being so easy to find. Show me your mind and heart so that I may follow you. Amen.

WEDNESDAY, MARCH 20 ~ *Read Psalm 63:1-5*

G*ot Jesus?* is a question, almost a dare, I've seen posed by posters and sweatshirts. I want to respond by saying, "I hope he's got me." But a better answer might be, "Not yet." Psalm 63 epitomizes what the spiritual life is all about. "I seek you, my soul thirsts for you; my flesh faints for you." Prayer is about seeking, not possession; about being thirsty, not quenched. Jesus says, "Blessed are those who hunger and thirst for righteousness" (Matt. 5:6). Not, "Blessed are those who are righteous."

Our culture demands that we satisfy every desire. But God asks for unquenched desire. God has made us so that as we reach out for God and grasp some truth about God—as we have a question answered—we stumble upon new questions we didn't have before. God is still just out of reach, but lures us more urgently forward. As we make progress toward knowing God, we become a bit holier, only to notice unholy debris in our souls we had not noticed before.

Recently, I visited a women's Bible study that has been meeting weekly for fifteen years. When I asked how much they had grown over the years, they laughed: "We have more questions and are more confused than when we started." This was their testimony to deep joy, not frustration or failure. Learning what we don't know, a craving for union with God, and a yearning to be holier; these are the delights of prayer.

Lord, I get mixed up thinking of my cloudy vision of you and my ongoing yearning for more as problems. Teach me to delight in my quest for you, to find pleasure in having more questions, and to know it is a privilege to be thirsty for you. Amen.

THURSDAY, MARCH 21 ~ *Read Psalm 63:6-8*

Psalm 63 takes a surprising turn in verse 6. Verse 5 begins, "My soul is satisfied . . . my mouth praises"—but when? "When I think of you on my bed, and meditate on you in the watches of the night." If the word *insomnia* makes you shudder, if you battle depression or worry, if a rough patch in life keeps you awake, you know the darkness can be terrifying, the soft bed no comfort at all.

We each have our ways of ensuring sleep: pills or alcohol or the proverbial counting of sheep. What if we learned a new habit of counting? Alone in the dark, try to replace the obsessiveness of anxiety, guilt, loneliness, or plotting what to try next with a focus on God—God's beauty and wisdom, God's care and compassion, the stories of Jesus. Count! Not sheep, but instances of God's goodness from the past day or your whole life you can recall.

God is counting too. How many times have you rolled over since 3:00 a.m.? God knows. God loves. God cares. God is there in the dark; it was in the dark that God created light. Jesus was born on one of the longest nights; you came to be in the darkness of your mother's womb.

Psalm 63, after the idea of meditating on God in bed, adds "in the shadow of your wings I sing for joy." Can we envision the dark shadows not as peril but as the protective shadow of God's presence?

Lord, as I fall asleep tonight, I will look for your shadow in the dark; if I waken prematurely, I will ponder your loving heart. Amen.

FRIDAY, MARCH 22 ~ *Read 1 Corinthians 10:1-13*

I once heard a comedian say, "The problem with the lessons of history is we never learn the lessons of history." These primal days of Israel's history as a nation liberated from bondage are far from glorious. Murmuring, doubting, hollering, "Back to Egypt!" The popular saying holds: "It is easier to take the people out of Egypt than to take Egypt out of the people."

Looking back on the Exodus, Paul says, "God was not pleased." How fantastic are we? We have the ability to please or to displease God. We matter to God that much.

Paul, living in cities, points to the wilderness—a real place also symbolic of the parched soul, the dryness of the spirit. Paul tries to comfort his readers: "No testing has overtaken you that is not common." But the commonality is still tough. The powers of the world lure us away from God. Yet God trusts us enough to place us in tough spots believing we might trust in God to provide our way of escape.

Jesus, who overcomes temptations that would undo any of us, buttresses us with the grace and strength required to stand and not be undone. We should not think of temptation as garden-variety attractions in the world. Oswald Chambers suggested that "Temptation . . . is the thing we are bound to meet if we are [human]. Many of us suffer from temptations from which we have no business to suffer, simply because we have refused to let God lift us to a higher plane where we would face temptations of another order. . . . [Our] disposition on the inside . . . determines what [we are] tempted by on the outside."* Despite the inevitability of temptation, Paul assures us that God provides the way for us to overcome it.

---

*Oswald Chambers, *My Utmost for His Highest* (Grand Rapids: Discovery House, 1927), September 17.

Lord, my temptations reveal how thin my soul is. Forgive me; empower me to please you. Amen.

SATURDAY, MARCH 23 ~ *Read Luke 13:1-9*

Pilate reportedly ordered the execution of some Galileans just as they were offering sacrifices in the Temple. Hearing this news, Jesus reminds his listeners of the eighteen people who died when a tall stone structure near the pool of Siloam crumbled. Pilate's bloodletting is a grave political injustice, while the collapse of the wall is a tragic accident. Jesus might score popularity points by judging the wicked Romans. Instead, he instructs the fuming disciples to repent. When there is suffering, we can blame the perpetrators, bad luck, or even God. But Jesus says that everyone, the innocent victims as well as the doers of evil, needs to repent.

Why do bad things happen? There are many reasons, and repentance is always in order. Repentance isn't merely apologizing for sin. Biblical repentance is turning toward God and changing our thinking to see everything through God's eyes. Dietrich Bonhoeffer taught us that repentance is "not in the first place thinking about one's own needs, problems, sins, and fears, but allowing oneself to be caught up into the way of Jesus Christ."*

We can repent with trust in the love of God. God does no evil. In Jesus, we see how God redeems evil and suffering. God bears it for us. Instead of raging against Pilate, Jesus stands before him humbly, with compassion Pilate never before has witnessed. Jesus absorbs every tragedy, all injustice, into his body. Pilate's last cruel act, sealing Jesus in the tomb, fails. Jesus, the fully repentant one, turns toward God, and God raises him up to redeem him and all of us. Before such wondrous love, we can only repent.

---

*Dietrich Bonhoeffer, *Letters and Papers from Prison* (New York: SCM, 1974), 361.

Lord, whatever I've suffered and whatever suffering I've caused, I repent. I turn to you. Amen.

SUNDAY, MARCH 24 ~ *Read Luke 13:1-9*

THIRD SUNDAY IN LENT

Jesus knew trees. As a carpenter, he understands how even the chopped-down tree has its uses. Like everyone else in ancient times, he eats directly from trees along the way.

Thomas Merton said, "A tree gives glory to God by being a tree. . . . It 'consents' . . . to [God's] creative love. It is expressing an idea which is in God . . . and therefore a tree imitates God by being a tree. The more a tree is like itself, the more it is like [God]. If it tried to be like something else which it was never intended to be, it would be less like God and therefore it would give [God] less glory."*

The tree in Jesus' parable isn't being itself; it has produced no fruit. So the owner says, "Cut it down!" But the patient vine-dresser pleads for care, more manure! Give it one more year.

God's greatest gift to us is time. And what is our time for? To become ourselves, to produce fruit. Like a tree, which requires sun, rain, and soil, I am not my own; I need God's creative energy, word, and mercy. What matters in me is what goes down deep, my roots, the unseen.

Jesus looks for fruit in me. My true self emerges not when I grit my teeth and try hard, but when God works in and through me. No matter how humble, faithful, and holy my life might be, sometimes I don't produce the fruit I'd like or that God needs. What is Jesus' response? Time, yes, but also this: Not long after this parable, someone cuts down another tree which becomes Jesus' cross. Gnarled, sweat- and blood-stained, a wondrous cross.

---

*Thomas Merton, *New Seeds of Contemplation* (New York: New Directions, 1962), 29.

Lord, I am yours; bear your fruit in me so I may glorify you. Amen.

The God of New Beginnings

MARCH 25–31, 2019 • CAROL CAVIN-DILLON

SCRIPTURE OVERVIEW: Lent is a time for focusing on our need for God and for remembering God's abundant resources for filling that need. When the Israelites finally pass into Canaan, they observe the Passover as a reminder of God's deliverance of them from Egypt. The psalmist, traditionally David, rejoices in the fact that God does not count his sins against him. Paul declares that through Christ, God has made everything new. God no longer holds our sins against us, and we in turn appeal to others to accept this free gift. Jesus eats with sinners and tells the story of the prodigal son to demonstrate that no matter how far we stray, God will always welcome us home with open arms. God never stops pursuing us, even if we feel unloved or unworthy.

QUESTIONS AND SUGGESTIONS FOR REFLECTION

- Read Joshua 5:9-12. What stories do you tell about your faith? What do these stories help you remember?
- Read Psalm 32. When have you hidden from God? When has God been your hiding place?
- Read 2 Corinthians 5:16-21. We are ambassadors for Christ. How does your life display for others that life in Christ eliminates worldly identity labels?
- Read Luke 15:1-3, 11b-32. Do you identify with the prodigal son, the elder son, or the father in the parable? Are you ready to rejoin God's household on God's terms? Are you ready to welcome everyone home?

Senior Pastor at West End United Methodist Church in Nashville, Tennessee.

MONDAY, MARCH 25 ~ *Read Joshua 5:9-12*

The Israelites finally have arrived. After forty years of wandering in the wilderness, God has brought them into the Promised Land. The long and difficult journey has lasted for a generation, but now it is over. They have a new beginning.

After the people cross the Jordan and enter into the land, they make camp at a place called Gilgal, from the Hebrew word *galal*, which means "to roll." God declares that God has "rolled away from [them] the disgrace of Egypt," where their ancestors were enslaved, oppressed, and treated as less than human. God clears away all of that pain and suffering and gives the people freedom.

In this moment, God not only rolls away the yoke of slavery; God also washes away the people's sin. They would have arrived forty years sooner if they had trusted in God's power to deliver them. When God first brought their ancestors to the edge of the Promised Land, they gave in to fear and couldn't believe that God would help them. But now, in spite of their wavering faith along the way, God has delivered them.

This story of new beginnings plays out again and again in the lives of God's people. God is always ready to roll away our past and give us a new beginning. Whether we suffer at the hands of others who oppress us or from our own fear and doubt—or both—we proclaim a God who frees us from what binds us and, with each new day, gives us a fresh start.

Liberating and forgiving God, thank you for giving us a new beginning with each new day. Help us to trust in your power to roll away all that binds us. Guide us through our seasons of wilderness, and bring us into the fullness of your love and hope. Amen.

TUESDAY, MARCH 26 ~ *Read Joshua 5:9-12*

The moment the Israelites cross over the Jordan River into the Promised Land is momentous and powerful. But it is not the Israelites' achievement. It is God's.

Even though they have lost trust in God at times, God is faithful. Even though they have doubted God's power, God delivers them. Even though they have whined and complained along the way, God never leaves them. God repeatedly shows them mercy and unconditional love.

Now it is time for the people to respond. After they cross the river Jordan, they celebrate the Passover. They remember all that God has done for them. They reenact their liberation from slavery and recount their escape from Egypt. They retell the powerful deeds of God. Celebrating the Passover reminds them of God's power and helps them remember who saved them.

As the people of God, we are called to remember, to reenact, to recount, and to retell the stories of God's faithfulness. We do this every week in worship. We do it when we celebrate the Eucharist. We do it when we share the stories of times when God helped us, when a prayer was answered, when we felt God's presence. As the Israelites well know, remembering what God has done for us in the past can sustain us in seasons of doubt and suffering in the present and in the future.

What helps you remember and recount God's goodness? Take a few moments today to write down some of the ways you have experienced God's power and love in your life. Then give all the thanks and all the credit to God.

Gracious God, you are always with me. You never stop working for good in me and in your world. Thank you for your faithfulness and the many ways you have helped me in the past. Hear me now as I remember and recount your works . . . Amen.

Humanity knows how to play hide-and-seek with God. It all starts with Adam and Eve. As soon as they bite into the forbidden fruit, they hide from God. They hear God's voice calling them in the garden, but they stay hidden in shame and fear. And we have been hiding ever since.

The whole story of the scriptures can be described as a game of hide-and-seek. We hide and God seeks. We break from God and go our own way: the Tower of Babel, the golden calf, the adultery of David, and the desertion of the disciples. But God never stops seeking us and trying to bring us out of hiding.

The psalmist confesses that he has been avoiding God. We don't know the nature of his sin, only that he feels he has broken his relationship with God. In shame and fear, he has kept silent. In time, however, he comes out of hiding, and instead of judgment and shame, he finds forgiveness and love. He declares in joy that God is now his hiding place!

Throughout the scriptures many people come out of hiding to respond to God. When God calls, they say, "Here I am." Moses, Samuel, Isaiah, Mary—all of these step forward and allow God to see them and to use them.

Like the psalmist, we have many ways of hiding our true selves. We hide from God, we hide from others, and we even hide from ourselves. But the time comes when we can say, "Here I am." When we come out of hiding to acknowledge our sin and accept our identity, God receives us with love and acceptance. We find our true home in God.

O God, help me to come out of hiding and step into the light of your love. Here I am, Lord. You are my true hiding place. Amen.

THURSDAY, MARCH 28 ~ *Read 2 Corinthians 5:16-21*

The Corinthian church is a mixed bag of folks. They are rich and poor, men and women, enslaved persons and slave owners. Through the power of the Holy Spirit they have all come to believe in Jesus Christ, and now they are trying to figure out how to live together as the church. How can an enslaved person and a slave-owner be one in Christ? How can a poor person be as worthy of honor as a rich person?

As they struggle to form a new kind of community, Paul reminds them that life in Christ gives each of them a new identity. All their worldly labels have been washed away, and they now belong to Christ. They are a new creation!

Now they have a responsibility to live differently in the world. They can no longer live by the old rules. They cannot allow the lines of rich and poor, male and female, enslaved and free to divide them. Paul tells them that they are now ambassadors for Christ, and it is their ministry to bring reconciliation where there has been division.

The world today is just as divided as it was in Paul's day. Like the people of Corinth, we experience deep lines of division based on class, sex, race, ethnicity, political party, and the list goes on. But our identity in Christ washes away all our worldly labels. We are a new creation! Our faith and identity in Christ call us to a ministry of reconciliation that breaks down the walls that divide people from one another.

How can you be an ambassador for Christ in your life today? Can you reach across a dividing line and offer friendship and reconciliation?

God of all, help me to let go of worldly labels for myself and others. Help me to recognize the oneness of your people and to serve as an ambassador of your love. Amen.

FRIDAY, MARCH 29 ~ *Read Luke 15:1-3, 11b-32*

Even though we call this story "The Parable of the Prodigal Son," it's really all about the father—that father who goes running down the street to embrace his no-account son; that father who goes out and begs his angry son to come inside to the party. God's love and grace shines through this parable.

The parable reveals a lot about human nature too. When we look at these sons, we realize that neither of them loves his father. The younger son regards him as a "moneybag" to finance him in the lifestyle to which he would like to become accustomed. He is selfish and mercenary. The older son sees his father more as a boss than a loving parent. He is obedient but becomes resentful. In both cases, their relationship with their father is transactional: "Give me what I am due."

The father, however, offers unconditional love and mutuality. He offers himself completely to his sons (the Greek word translated as "property" in the New Revised Standard Version literally means "life") not based on their deserving or any transaction, but based on the father's very nature.

The sons struggle to believe in their father's complete and unconditional love. How much do we struggle to accept God's? Whether we are weighed down by the shame of our past or by the self-righteousness of our deserving, we find it hard to accept that God loves us completely and unconditionally because of who God is, not because of anything we have done.

As we move toward Good Friday and Easter, we once again come face-to-face with the raw truth of God's love. We do not deserve it. We have not earned it as reward for good behavior. God's offer of love comes only through the nature of God's grace.

Loving and merciful God, help me to see you running toward me with open arms and offering me all that is yours. Lead me into your loving embrace. Amen.

SATURDAY, MARCH 30 ~ *Read Luke 15:1-3, 11b-32*

When Jesus finishes telling the Parable of the Prodigal Son, we wonder what will happen next. What will the younger son do after the party is over? Will he wake up early the next morning and start pitching in? Will he find ways to express his gratitude to his father? Has his father's grace changed him?

What about the elder son? Will he go in to the party? Will he have a change of heart, raise a glass to his brother's life, and step out onto the dance floor? Can he welcome his brother back into the family and work side-by-side with him? Has his father's grace changed him?

Jesus leaves us with these questions to get us thinking about our own response to God's grace. Have we experienced the deep forgiveness of God, like the younger son? If so, has it changed us? Are we ready to rejoin the household of God and do our part?

Are we resentful about the disparity of work like the elder brother? Are we willing to accept that God loves everybody unconditionally? Can we let go of what we think we deserve and accept the unearned, radical grace of God for us and for all? Are we willing to rejoin the household of God on God's terms?

This parable confronts us with the radical grace of God and invites us to respond.

God of radical and unconditional love, you never stop pursuing us and inviting us into a loving relationship with you. Thank you. Today, may every word I say and every action I take be a grateful response to your love. May I embody your grace toward all people. Amen.

SUNDAY, MARCH 31 ~ *Read 2 Corinthians 5:16-21*

FOURTH SUNDAY IN LENT

Around this time of year, we see a lot of people wearing college gear in every color and with every school logo. When March Madness comes around, we see fans proudly announcing to the world that they are loyal to their team. We gather from their clothing that they are basketball fans, and we know where their loyalties lie. What's more, we often judge their school by their behavior. If we see them misbehaving, we're tempted to judge all fans and students of their school.

Paul reminds the Christians in Corinth that they now belong to Christ. They bear the name of Christ in the world like a new white robe—or maybe a shirt that reads "Christ." Wherever you go, Paul says, you represent Christ. You are an ambassador for Christ, a messenger of God.

What message from God do we convey to the world? The message we should send, says Paul, is this: God has reconciled the world to Godself. God has not counted our sins against us. God has washed away our past. (See Joshua 5.) God has come looking for us. (See Psalm 32.) God runs out to meet us. (See Luke 15.)

Do we live in such a way that others get the message? Every day we encounter persons who feel unlovable. We look into the eyes of folks who feel unworthy of God's love. We see persons weighed down by their past. We encounter those who are hiding themselves out of fear or shame. What a glorious privilege it is to carry the message of God's reconciling love for all people! How can you be an ambassador for Christ today?

God of love, sometimes I forget that I bear your name. I act in ways that divide rather than reconcile. Forgive me, and help me joyfully proclaim your love in how I act, what I say, and how I think about others. Amen.

A New Thing

APRIL 1–7, 2019 • TODD OUTCALT

SCRIPTURE OVERVIEW: God is constantly performing works of renewal. Isaiah had warned Israel of judgment, yet here the prophet turns his attention to the other part of God's message, that of restoration. God will breathe new life into the people, like sending rivers into the desert. The psalmist celebrates a communal festival in honor of the renewing deeds of God, who has turned their weeping into joy. Paul also experiences this work of renewal. He previously had boasted of his privileged position in society, but God has changed his thinking so that he considers his knowledge of Christ his greatest possession. In John a woman named Mary begins to point our attention to Christ's coming passion by anointing Jesus' feet. Crowds begin to gather, and the stage is set for the impending conflict.

QUESTIONS AND SUGGESTIONS FOR REFLECTION

- Read Isaiah 43:16-21. When have you seen God make a way for a new thing in your life?
- Read Psalm 126. Consider how your joy and laughter might heal others.
- Read Philippians 3:4b-14. When has God's strength helped you finish a race, literally or metaphorically?
- Read John 12:1-8. God gives gifts to all of us. How do you share your gift from God with others?

United Methodist pastor; author of over thirty books, including *Praying through Cancer* and *Blue Christmas.*

MONDAY, APRIL 1 ~ *Read Isaiah 43:16-19a*

Some years ago a noted scholar from Harvard created a list of the three greatest poets in human history. Homer was there. And Shakespeare. The third was the prophet Isaiah.

Isaiah is no surprise, really—not when one considers how the words of the prophet have impacted musicians and mystics, lyricists and orators, and other voices as far-ranging as poets and politicians. Isaiah speaks words of challenge and comfort, words that are equally accessible and metaphorical.

Although we don't know much about Isaiah, his poetry has certainly echoed through the centuries in the church—through music and message, lyrics and liturgy. Isaiah holds a special place among the prophets but is unrivaled as a poet.

Time and time again, Isaiah visits the theme that while we are often dismayed and distressed by our current circumstances, God does not leave us to our own devices. Rather, God can transform the former things. God can make creation new. The violence, the hatred, the hungers of our world will be transformed into new ways, new attitudes—new creation. "Do not remember the former things," God says through Isaiah. "I am about to do a new thing."

Most people can identify with these ideas, especially in times of hardship. We crave the new; we long for what is fresh and vital. We rarely enjoy living in the humdrum routines of existence. We all crave familiarity and find comfort in the routine and the dependable, and yet we realize that change is inevitable. God is always creating the new in and through us.

New things! Yes, Isaiah still speaks to us. Our fears, our despair, our weariness in the world can be transformed. Look for the new opportunities. Don't overlook what God can do.

O Lord, thank you for walking with me. I trust you always are doing a new thing in me—even as I celebrate this, a new day, which is your gift. Create a new spirit in me this day. Amen.

TUESDAY, APRIL 2 ~ *Read Isaiah 43:19b-21*

In May of 2016 I received my *compestella* (certificate) for having walked the Camino de Santiago in Spain. This pilgrimage was the longest journey I had made on foot. It involved overcoming not only physical barriers (rain, mud, rocks, heat) but also the mental and spiritual barricades and pitfalls that we often encounter in life.

One of my most powerful experiences on the Camino involved water. My friend and I had been walking much of the day in a rising heat, over parched ground and uneven path, when we at last crossed a small footbridge spanning a large stream. Nearby, a fountain of purified water invited us to fill our empty water bottles and to sit for a time in the shade as we replenished our bodies and spirits.

I thought of God's promise that day as I drank deeply of this water. "I will make a way in the wilderness," Isaiah writes, "and rivers in the desert."

Not only the physical limitations of life need to be replenished by God's abundance. We have spiritual deficiencies within us. We experience moments that seem depleted of love, faith, or joy. Sometimes, our energies are depleted. Other experiences reduce our levels of trust, hope, or finances. In short, we need the refreshing abundance of God.

When we walk through the dry places, we can remember that God's refreshment is not far off. God will make a way.

Many experiences zap our energies, wreak havoc on our emotions, stress our relationships, and fill us with fear. The wilderness is not necessarily a place but any experience in life that causes us to lose sight of God—the source of our strength and hope. But the prophet reminds us—God will make a way for us to push through. This is grace. And it is enough.

Help me, God, to trust you in this day of uncertainty and anxiety. Alleviate my fear and help me to see the hopeful places toward which you call me. Amen.

WEDNESDAY, APRIL 3 ~ *Read Psalm 126:1-3*

For many decades, *Reader's Digest* has featured a humor page entitled, "Laughter Is the Best Medicine." Many readers turn to this page first as a source of inspiration, comfort, and healing.

Can laughter have this kind of effect upon us?

Many believe so. In fact, the psalmist recounts how God restores the ancient city of Zion. In that memory there is laughter and joy that transforms a people and lifts the lives of others. The same holds true today.

We can find healing and hope in laughter, in the positive attitudes that shape our relationships and circumstances, and even in pleasant memories. In times of deep sorrow, we can discover the amazing comfort that comes from remembering the good, lifting up the positive, holding on to those memories of special times. Often we gather at the table with family or with good friends to raise ourselves above our difficulties with the uplifting atmosphere of laughter.

When we consider what God has done for us—how God has offered hope through grief or been present through troubled times—we often discover joy. Wonderful memories of God's provision shape our faith.

Take a moment. Consider what God has done for you and your family. Count your blessings. Consider the joy of it all. Surely laughter can be a part of the equation. God is good. God is the author of joy.

God, you are the giver of all blessings, and all good gifts come from your hand. Thank you for giving me a joy today that the world cannot take away. In Jesus' name I thank you. Amen.

THURSDAY, APRIL 4 ~ *Read Psalm 126:4-6*

One young man in my congregation is a particularly positive influence. He uses a wheelchair, and his engaging spirit and his smile are infectious. His attitude and demeanor have changed our congregation. And I have known many others who bring joy and affirmation to the lives of others. We all need these positive people. Our lives are made all the more joyous when we can create optimistic outlooks and outcomes in others.

Certainly, the psalmist understands this too. Life isn't all negative. Life is a journey of joy and gratitude—especially when we recall the wonderful gifts of our Creator God.

In the bottom drawer of my filing cabinet I keep a small cardboard box filled with an assortment of cards and handwritten notes. These letters, which I have collected over thirty-five years of ministry, are mostly letters of appreciation I keep because I have discovered that I need these reminders of friendship, helpfulness, and love. I need them when the outcomes of my work don't seem so rosy and I am tempted to believe that life is a crock—filled with nothing but darkness and despair. Reading one of these letters during difficult days reminds me that life may have tears, but it also has joy and hope.

What are some of the ways that you recall God's goodness? Perhaps you have rituals, special times for reflection, or even a corner of your home dedicated to these visual reminders.

We may have difficult days in the planting; but like a farmer reaping a harvest, we also experience many seasons of joy. Take a few moments today to note your own blessings, and then lift your gratitude to God—the source of all good things.

> *Gracious God, how marvelous are your gifts! Give me joy today that will transform my struggles and turn darkness into light. Amen.*

FRIDAY, APRIL 5 ~ *Read Philippians 3:4b-14*

In the summer of 2017, my wife and I were blessed to walk in the footsteps of the apostle Paul as we journeyed through Greece. This special trip was made all the more remarkable by reading Paul's letters as we visited these ancient sites. At times, we found ourselves imagining what it was like to walk these same streets and avenues in antiquity. In many respects, Paul's letters also came alive on the journey.

Paul's experience in Philippi was not easy. When Paul wrote to this church, he was in prison. He could not speak in the synagogues or marketplaces. His freedom was limited.

Yet this letter is Paul's most uplifting and positive. Paul doesn't shy away from acknowledging his chains, but he gives thanks for his blessings and circumstances in Christ. He realizes that he can still write, that he is in the prayers of the church. He shares that despite being under duress, God's goodness and the communion of the saints continue unabated. Nothing can remove him from God's care.

Reading Paul's beautiful affirmations in Philippians 3, we do well to note how the faithful help one another. Our common experiences can serve as a source of strength. Like an athlete running a race, we know that we have not yet reached the finish line, nor the prize. We press on through Christ's love.

Might we follow Paul's attitude here? Although we experience grief, pain, brokenness, and hardship, our ultimate outcomes are not defined by these trials. Rather, we can rejoice in what God has given us in Christ as we press on toward the goal of our heavenly call. Christ is our true freedom and hope. Nothing can separate us from God's love in Christ.

God of Love, I am not defeated; I cherish what you have offered me in Christ. Help me to make today a blessing to others. Amen.

SATURDAY, APRIL 6 ~ *Read Philippians 3:4b-14*

People around the world love sports. In fact, we might say that sports have become a religion to some, and the athletes who compete often are revered as gods.

The apostle Paul uses a sports analogy to describe the Christian journey. There is a race to be run—a goal that awaits us. Some of these goals can be run each day, while others—like the ultimate goal of finding our life in Christ—are eternal.

Much of the life of faith consists of perseverance, persistence, consistency, and faithfulness. In fact, if we live in Christ and if Christ lives in us, we find that we are energized by love and generosity, by helpfulness and service. These attributes allow us to run the longer distance, knowing that life is not a sprint but a marathon. Most often, our life's journey is filled with any number of valleys and demanding hills. But we don't get to the finish line without struggle, without sacrifice. God's strength, however, prepares us to go the distance.

These details of the Christian life remind me of my grandparents, who lived at the intersection of many changes in their lifetimes. Transportation, energy, and communication technologies all changed, and yet they were able to embrace these changes and make their journey through faithfulness and helpfulness.

We live in a time of no less adaptation—the world is ever changing, and changing rapidly. But we can approach our life's journey with faithfulness and perseverance.

Today is just another leg of the journey, but it counts. Run your best. Finish strong. And then press on.

Gracious God, thank you for giving me the strength I need to face today's challenges. I press on in your love. Amen.

SUNDAY, APRIL 7 ~ *Read John 12:1-8*

FIFTH SUNDAY IN LENT

Would I have given Jesus anything so costly? Have I ever given to Jesus so sacrificially? These are the questions I ponder when I read about Mary's extravagance. She gives Jesus a gift that she cannot recoup. Her gift is a once-in-a-lifetime sacrifice.

Throughout Lent, it is helpful to consider our gifts to God and God's gifts to us. These gifts are not equal. God has given far more than we can repay. This is the very definition of grace. God has given us the extravagant gift of grace at Christ's expense. Our gifts can be a means of saying to God, "Thank you."

One of my friends has always kept a small paper doll on her shelf to remind her of God's grace. The doll—given by a child years ago—reminds her that we receive gifts of mercy and great extravagance. A child's prize can become our prize too. Any gift given in love has the potential to change our attitude and spirit.

I often marvel at our call to give. God calls us to be good stewards of our blessings. I can give. You can give. Together our gifts can add up to God's work—a blessing that we can share with the world in Jesus' name. These gifts don't have to be expensive. They just have to come from the heart.

As we consider the gifts we give, perhaps new gifts come to mind. There may be people we long to help, situations we hope to impact, suffering we desire to help alleviate with our generosity or intervention or prayer. God desires our partnership and our commitment to sharing these gifts with all God's children.

O God, help me to open my hand and heart today to give all that I can. Help me to give out of gratitude for your grace. Amen.

The Blessed One, Servant and Son

APRIL 8–14, 2019 • MELISSA TIDWELL

SCRIPTURE OVERVIEW: Blessed is the one who comes in the name of the Lord! Psalm 118 is a song of rejoicing, yet it also includes the prophecy that the cornerstone must experience rejection. Isaiah speaks of physical suffering, of being beaten, disgraced, and spat on. We see elements of this in the Gospel reading, where Luke describes the final moments of Jesus' life. Bloodied and beaten, Jesus hangs on the cross and breathes his last. In Philippians, Paul places this drama within the eternal narrative of God's redeeming work. Jesus leaves his rightful place and becomes flesh. He experiences pain and suffering, even the most humiliating form of death, crucifixion. Jesus can empathize with our suffering because he has suffered. Blessed is the one who comes in the name of the Lord!

QUESTIONS AND SUGGESTIONS FOR REFLECTION

- Read Isaiah 50:4-9a. How does the Suffering Servant speak to your life today?
- Read Psalm 118:1-2, 19-29. How do you hear differently the familiar verses of this psalm when you read them together?
- Read Philippians 2:5-11. Do you find it paradoxical to live as a beloved child of God and as a servant? If so, how do you live in this paradox?
- Read Luke 19:28-40. How do you experience the extreme emotional highs and lows of Palm Sunday and Holy Week, even knowing how it will all turn out?

Pastor of the Westminster Presbyterian Church in Xenia, Ohio; former editor of *Alive Now!* magazine; author of *Embodied Light: Advent Reflections on Incarnation*; writer on the topics of metaphor, music, maps, and zombies.

In four different passages in the book of Isaiah, the prophet speaks of the Suffering Servant (42:1-4; 49:1-6; 50:4-9; 52:13–53:12). We understand the Servant as a universal figure standing for all who suffer. The Servant might have been modeled on a historical person like Hezekiah, Josiah, or Cyrus. Christians can see Jesus in this model as one who is unjustly accused, who suffers for righteousness and waits for vindication.

Isaiah's words mean one thing to the original audience and can mean something different to a later age. The message is not bound to one situation but is thick with meaning. The many layers of meaning in scripture help us continually reinterpret the past in light of the present's demands, which a living, dynamic faith requires.

The words of the Suffering Servant reveal the wisdom of one who knows how to hold things in balance—speaking and listening, honor and humility, acting and acceptance. The Servant offers his face to be spit on, accepts the insult and shame, because he knows the One who will vindicate him is near. That kind of humility might seem passive and powerless to some, but passivity does not drive the Servant's actions: confidence does. He knows God will be his vindication.

Most of us will never know the level of indignity and pain suffered by the Servant. But we all experience moments when we must choose how we will respond to pain and injustice around us. We can choose to respond to the angry voices we hear by trading insult for insult, or we can be guided by the Servant's equanimity. The Servant stands without shame or hostility and as a reminder for all who suffer that God has transformed suffering into triumph in Christ.

Lord, help me speak and listen and learn to respond to the challenges I face with the confidence that you are my vindication. Amen.

TUESDAY, APRIL 9 ~ *Read Isaiah 50:4-9a*

Both Jesus and the Servant face scorn and suffering with the help of God. The Servant has had his ear opened in a receptive posture to receive the word, which he will pass on to sustain the weary. The Servant accepts abuse without retaliation because he is sustained by God.

We see Jesus hold a similar servant-like posture. Perhaps the servant song inspires Jesus to teach his followers to maintain their serenity in the face of oppression. Jesus teaches the practice of turning the other cheek (see Matthew 5:38-42) in the same way the servant turned both cheeks to those who insulted him. Jesus instructs his followers to go beyond retributive justice, beyond an eye for an eye, by refusing to take any violent action. If an enemy "demands your shirt," says Jesus, "give your coat as well" (Matt. 5:40, AP). Imagine that scene: Doesn't the act of going beyond what is required make the oppressor look a little foolish?

The posture of Jesus and the Servant was the spiritual basis for Martin Luther King Jr.'s teaching of nonviolent resistance during the US Civil Rights movement. King and the leaders of the movement taught that love is stronger than hate. Their witness of dignity in the face of hatred inspired more people to join the movement despite beatings, imprisonment, and bombings. Their courage sustained the weary.

When Jesus is tested, scorned, and abused, he does not respond in anger. Instead he relies on faith in God. Like the Suffering Servant, Christ has the confidence in his vindication; he knows that he will be redeemed—and his redemption is ours.

Lord Jesus, sustain us when we are weary with the power of your word. Help us not retreat from challenge but remain rooted and grounded in your mercy and truth. May our confidence in your vindication give us the power to live in peace. Amen.

WEDNESDAY, APRIL 10 ~ *Read Psalm 118:1-2, 19-29*

Psalm 118 is like a biblical greatest hits playlist; it contains many lines we sing or pray in worship. Beginning at the first verse, "O give thanks to the LORD, for he is good," this great psalm contains words and images that teach and inspire us.

The image of the stone the builders reject is so relevant to the life of Christ that it is referenced in three places in the New Testament: Matthew 21:42 as Jesus cleanses the Temple, Acts 4:11 as Peter gives bold testimony, and 1 Peter 2:7 where the author calls Christ a "living stone" and calls believers to become temples that reflect the holiness of Christ the cornerstone.

"Blessed is the one who comes in the name of the LORD," an affirmation of hope and longing the crowd repeats on Palm Sunday, is one we often repeat in the celebration of the Lord's Supper.

Parts of Psalm 118 might remind us of our own spiritual journey. You might remember times you have thanked God for the goodness that has brought you through trials, blessed you, or enriched your family life. Or you might feel connected to the cornerstone imagery as you remember times you have felt rejected or misunderstood and have held fast to the realization that Christ—while rejected by some—is truly the cornerstone, the point on which everything in heaven and on earth comes together. You might remember times in worship when you have felt moved to praise the one who comes in the name of the Lord.

Review those moments from your experience alongside this psalm. Ask yourself when or where you might have been the one speaking these words in hope or in faith, in doubt or in comfort.

Christ our cornerstone, blessed are you. May we know you as the rock of our salvation, the cornerstone of our faith, in whom our trust is always secure. Amen.

Paul's letters are not abstract theological treatises but practical communications meant for a particular place with a particular context. We do not know the exact details of all the situations to which Paul writes, but it seems clear that the Philippians are experiencing conflict among strong-minded parties.

Paul urges the Christians in Philippi to put aside their desire to have their own way and instead to develop a Christ-like outlook. Then Paul quotes a hymn, one his audience likely knows. In cosmic imagery, this hymn praises the pre-existent Christ, the eternal second person of the Trinity who exists before the Incarnation. Christ, says the hymn, "did not consider equality with God something to be used to his own advantage" (NIV) but instead remains humble as a servant.

The prologue to John's Gospel alludes to this idea of a pre-existent Christ. Pre-existence is a complex proposition; it is abstract and metaphysical. Why, then, do we read this passage as we prepare for Holy Week's real, concrete portrayal of a human Jesus suffering a human death?

The hymn of Philippians seems to perfectly illustrate the paradox of Incarnation: that Christ, as perfectly divine, could have avoided the humiliation of arrest and execution. But in his choice to be human, Jesus takes on a role that leaves him vulnerable, mortal, and susceptible to harm. Allowing this harm to befall himself is a powerful statement of God's concern for and solidarity with all those who suffer. Paul shows us Christ with two aspects: human and divine, son and servant. Given that example, how do we approach the paradox of humanity? How do we find the mind, the outlook, the sense of purpose Jesus holds?

Incarnate One, human and divine, we praise you as servant and son. Teach us to embrace our own call to be children of God, servants of all. Amen.

FRIDAY, APRIL 12 ~ *Read Philippians 2:5-11*

I remember more than a few Sunday school lessons that contrasted various Greek words for love, like *philios* (fraternal love) and *eros* (romantic love), with *agape*, the love of Christian caring. Most of us can relate to all three types of love these words describe. Yet Paul offers us another Christlike action I would argue is worth emulating as a type of love: *kenosis*, or emptying and taking the form of a servant.

In his letter to the Philippians, Paul uses the text of a hymn to urge his readers to have the same mind, the same outlook, as Christ. This way of living does not seek to further its own aims or to hype its own awesomeness. Instead, the way of Jesus is about giving ourselves away for the sake of love.

The self-emptying Paul describes can be a difficult idea to embrace. Does exalting servanthood lead to a distorted view of human worth? If we give ourselves away, do we negate the divine personhood gifted to us by God? It is a knotty question, but it helps to consider that Jesus does not erase his self-identity. He offers it, extends it as a gift, pours it as a libation. Perhaps in the pouring out we find that like the waters of abundant life, there is yet more love welling up to regenerate the love freely offered.

While most of us will never be faced with the choice to literally give our life as Jesus does on the cross, we have the opportunity to pour out our gifts, our faith, and our commitment in the same kind of humility shown by our Lord. That is a love worth naming, practicing, and making the goal of all we do.

Generous God, continue teaching us to love in more depth and breadth, so that we can have the mind of Christ as our goal. Amen.

SATURDAY, APRIL 13 ~ *Read Luke 19:28-40*

The Gospel of Luke has a long section, chapters 10–19, in which Jesus makes slow progress toward Jerusalem. Along the way he tells stories, heals the sick, and speaks to crowds. Before Jesus' final entry to the city, Luke pauses once more to show us in detail the preparations for this entrance that pair joyful and sober moments, from the joyous acclaim of the crowd to Jesus weeping over the city that refuses to accept him.

Before the joy and weeping, Luke tells of the two disciples sent into the city to fetch the colt Jesus will ride. They know what kind of colt it is—one young enough to have never been ridden. They also know where to find the animal and what to say if they are asked why they are taking it. The scene develops exactly the way Jesus says it will.

That detail may seem incidental, but many theologians wonder how much Jesus knows about the way his mission will unfold. In the Gospels, Jesus speaks of his impending death in a way that suggests he knows exactly what will happen. Yet Jesus' prayer in the garden of Gethsemane, where he asks for his cup to pass from him, makes us wonder whether Jesus feels there is more than one possible ending to the events that loom before him.

This passage invites us to consider how we can experience the story of Jesus' passion, even knowing how it will turn out, while praying for insight through which the power of the gospel might come to us anew and deepen our discipleship.

Gracious God, open our spiritual imagination to find ourselves in these events of Jesus' life during Holy Week. Strengthen us to be steadfast in following you with hearts that can be changed by the power of your living word. Amen.

Palm/Passion Sunday

As Jesus enters the city, the crowd begins to throw their cloaks on the ground to make a carpet as if for a royal procession. They take up the joyful song of the disciples, a version of Psalm 118. The crowd changes "Blessed is the one who comes" to "Blessed is the king who comes." It is a provocative twist for the people to speak of a new king under the noses of the Romans.

Perhaps that provocative proclamation makes the Pharisees nervously suggest that Jesus should calm the crowd. At other times in his ministry, Jesus tries to keep his messianic identity secret. But on this occasion, he allows the joy of the moment to resound with the singing of the crowd. The singing is unstoppable, he tells the Pharisees. If the people stop, the stones will pick up the tune.

The image of singing stones reminds us of other images of the earth responding joyfully to the presence of God. In Isaiah 55:12 the joy of the returning exiles will cause the trees to clap their hands. In Psalm 65, the meadows and the valleys sing together.

Sometimes the joy of Palm Sunday seems muted or compromised by the knowledge that the crowd who lauds Jesus will turn on him. On the other hand, if we fail to give ourselves over to the joy of praise, we fall into the same fearful posture as Pharisees in this text. If we focus on our fear, how many opportunities for joy might we miss? Responding to God's presence with gratitude and worship can fill us with the strength to continue walking the gospel way through Holy Week and throughout our lives.

Blessed is the one who comes in the name of the Lord. Blessed are you Jesus, bringer of joy, bearer of good news. I will praise you with my heart and mind and voice. Amen.

When the Passion Gets Personal

APRIL 15–21, 2019 • JAMES A. HARNISH

SCRIPTURE OVERVIEW: The readings for Holy Week focus our attention on the sacrifice made by the Messiah. The prophecies in Isaiah speak of it. The Psalms tell of confidence in God even in the midst of betrayal and suffering like that experienced by Jesus. The author of Hebrews celebrates Jesus' death as the final and perfect sacrifice. Paul describes crucifixion as the center of our teaching as Christians. We follow these events through the eyes of two Gospel writers, particularly John. Jesus foreshadows his death in multiple ways, but even his closest followers struggle to understand and accept its meaning. Why would the Son of God experience such alienation and suffering? It is all for us, the ultimate work of love. But then he conquers the grave! Praise be to God!

QUESTIONS AND SUGGESTIONS FOR REFLECTION

- Read John 13:21-32. When have you noticed darkness planting seeds of betrayal in your heart? How did you follow Jesus' light?
- Read John 13:1-7, 31b-35. What status symbols do you hold on to that keep you from following Jesus' example of humble service?
- Read Isaiah 53:1-5. On Good Friday, God enters into human suffering. When have you felt God's presence in your suffering?
- Read John 20:1-18. How has Christ found you?

Retired pastor, Florida Conference of the United Methodist Church; author of *A Disciple's Path* and *Easter Earthquake*; husband, father, and grandfather; blogs at www.jimharnish.org.

MONDAY, APRIL 15 ~ *Read John 12:1-11*

I would guess that Mary has not planned to break open her perfume jar that evening. She may be saving it for her wedding night or as financial security for her future. I suspect her decision is one of those spontaneous things we do because we couldn't live with ourselves if we did anything else.

But this is Jesus—the one who raised her brother, Lazarus, from the grave. Since then, opposition to Jesus has been building. She instinctively knows that sooner rather than later, Jesus will end up in a tomb too. This might be her last opportunity to express her gratitude and love.

Without weighing the consequences, she breaks open the jar, empties the perfume onto Jesus' feet, and wipes his feet with her hair.

Judas asks why the perfume isn't sold and the money given to the poor. Mark's version of this story indicates that all the disciples are angry. None of them can understand why Mary squanders her most precious possession in this spendthrift way.

But Jesus understands. He knows that she knows the end is near. In Mark's version, Jesus says, "She has done what she could" (Mark 14:8). He receives her gift as a beautiful act of selfless gratitude for the self-giving love of God that will be revealed at the cross. It is all she can do.

Sometimes the only reasonable way to confront the unreasonable evil, pain, and suffering of our world is to do whatever we can with whatever we have in our hands. The only way to respond to the costly love of God at the cross is to offer our own act of costly love. Sometimes it's all we can do.

Were the whole realm of nature mine, that were an offering far too small; love so amazing, so divine, demands my soul, my life, my all. (UMH, no. 298)

TUESDAY, APRIL 16 ~ *Read John 12:20-36*

Do these Greek pilgrims find what they were looking for? John doesn't answer that question. All we know is that they want to see Jesus and that their coming marked the turning point on the way to the cross.

People like them keep coming: spiritually sensitive people searching for something they can't define; broken people longing to be made whole; skeptical people who have been abused by versions of Christianity that have nothing in common with the way of Jesus; idealistic people drawn to something larger than narrow self-interest. They're like Bono singing, "I still haven't found what I'm looking for."

No one expects Jesus to respond by saying that like a seed that dies in order to bring forth fruit, only those who lose their lives will find them. They don't expect him to say, "Whoever serves me must follow me."

The disturbing truth is that seeing Jesus means seeing him on the cross. Finding Jesus means finding him at the place where he takes upon himself our suffering, sin, and death. Following Jesus means surrendering our self-serving narcissism to God's self-giving love.

C. S. Lewis learned this lesson while riding on the top of an English bus. He sensed he was being invited to surrender, to let go, to lose his life in order to find it. He said that when he let go, he felt like "a man of snow at long last beginning to melt."* He found what he was looking for. Have we?

---

*C. S. Lewis, *Surprised by Joy: The Shape of My Early Life* (San Francisco: HarperOne, 2017), 274.

Long my imprisoned spirit lay, fast bound in sin and nature's night; thine eye diffused a quickening ray; I woke, the dungeon flamed with light; my chains fell off, my heart was free, I rose, went forth, and followed thee. (UMH, no. 363)

WEDNESDAY, APRIL 17 ~ *Read John 13:21-32*

The words, "And it was night," aren't just telling time. John's Gospel opens by celebrating the light that "shines in the darkness, and the darkness did not overcome it" (1:5). Only John's Gospel records Jesus' saying, "I am the light of the world. Whoever follows me will never walk in darkness but will have the light of life" (8:12). Now John ushers us into the darkness that will overshadow us until the women come to the tomb on Sunday morning (20:1).

Jesus and Judas know what the rest of the disciples do not know. "The devil had already put it into the heart of Judas . . . to betray him" (13:2). Jesus knows that the decision has already been made. Judas' betrayal that night begins in his heart sometime earlier.

How did the darkness work its way into Judas' heart? Selfishness? Greed? Pride? Resentment? However it began, Judas allows it to overtake the light he had once seen in Jesus. He could choose to follow Jesus and walk in the light, but he allows the darkness to overcome that light. Having mutated in Judas' heart, it leads to that moment when he leaves the table and goes into the night.

We can easily miss the ways in which we are like Judas. Like him, betrayal begins in our hearts. It takes root in shadowy temptations in the deep, hidden desires we try to deny. Over time, we make our choices. We either allow the light of Christ to overcome the darkness or we allow the darkness to overcome that light. But if we walk with Jesus, we will find the light that darkness can never overtake.

O God, who calls us from darkness to light, help us to acknowledge the subtle temptations that draw us away from Jesus. Strengthen us to walk in his light. Amen.

MAUNDY THURSDAY

In *The Road to Character,* David Brooks notes a common pattern among people whom we know to have great character: "They had to go down to go up. . . . They had to humble themselves . . . if they had any hope of rising up transformed. . . . In the valley of humility . . . they had opened up space for grace to flood in."*

When Jesus takes off his robe, ties a towel around his waist, and starts washing the disciples' grungy feet, he takes the role of the lowest servant in the house. When he puts on his robe, returns to his place, and tells his disciples to do to others as he had done to them, he is commanding them to lay aside their symbols of status and self-importance to serve others with the same humility he has demonstrated.

Paul proclaims this truth when he describes Christ as one who "emptied himself, taking the form of a slave . . . humbled himself and became obedient to the point of death—even death on a cross" (Phil. 2:7-8). He challenges us to "do nothing from selfish ambition or conceit, but in humility to . . . look not to your own interests, but to the interests of others" (Phil 2:3). When he summons us to "let the same mind be in you that was in Christ Jesus" (Phil. 2:5), he calls us to lay aside our status symbols and approach life with the same servant-shaped humility as our Lord.

Every time we gather around the Lord's table, whether we include foot-washing or not, we are invited to experience the grace that floods in when we learn the way of humility.

---

*David Brooks, *The Road to Character* (New York: Random House, 2015), 13.

O Servant Lord, you showed us the way of humble, self-giving love by washing your disciples' feet. Draw us close to you. Set us free from our narrow self-interest so that we may love as you loved, live as you live, and serve as you served. Amen.

FRIDAY, APRIL 19 ~ *Read John 19:16-30; Isaiah 53:1-5*

Good Friday

The Gospel writers don't linger on the gory details of Jesus' flogging and crucifixion. The descriptions are scarce. The sentences are simple. The ghastly wounds on Jesus' body are the same as the wounds on the bodies of millions of innocent people across the centuries and throughout the world. The Gospel writers are more interested in recounting *why* rather than *what* Jesus suffered.

At the cross we see the shocking truth with bloody clarity. God does not magically eradicate human suffering or the scars we carry from it. Instead, we see the naked, bleeding, vulnerable love of God enter fully into the naked, bleeding, vulnerable suffering of humanity. Jesus bears the brutal scars of the world's sin and of our own.

The gospel doesn't provide glib answers or simplistic solutions to our inexorable questions about innocent suffering and human sin. Instead, we experience the God who enters fully into the suffering we inflict on others and the pain that is inflicted upon us in a sin-broken, violence-addicted world.

Beyond our explanation but not beyond our experience, we know that Jesus bears our infirmities, that he is wounded for our transgressions, and that the extravagant love of this wounded God can heal us. Through Jesus' obedience in suffering, he becomes the source of our salvation. Even his resurrection doesn't wipe away those scars. For his disciples, Jesus' scars confirm his identity as the risen Christ (John 20:20).

Upon that cross of Jesus mine eye at times can see the very dying form of One who suffered there for me; and from my stricken heart with tears two wonders I confess: the wonders of redeeming love and my unworthiness. (UMH, no. 297)

SATURDAY, APRIL 20 ~ *Read John 19:38-42*

Holy Saturday

My mother was living in a nursing facility near us in Florida when she died at age 95. Our last conversation was during the residents' Christmas party. She was enjoying the festivities when she said, "I'm ready to go. Take me home." When I started to roll her wheelchair toward her room, she said, "No! Take me home to Pennsylvania." We fulfilled her last request by taking her ashes to the cemetery in the town where she lived most of her life and where many people she loved are buried.

We all make that journey. Like Joseph and Nicodemus, we carry the remains of our loved ones to the grave. But because we know the rest of the story, we do not "grieve as others do who have no hope" (1 Thess. 4:13). I received a sympathy card from two faithful friends who are the same age as my mother. They ended their message with the words, "We know there's more."

Before he went to prison for his resistance to Hitler, Dietrich Bonhoeffer wrote to his students to report the death of three friends. "Now they sleep with all the brothers who have gone before them, awaiting the great Easter Day of Resurrection. We see the cross, and we believe in the resurrection; we see death, and we believe in eternal life; we trace sorrow and separation, but we believe in an eternal joy and community."*

Because of Jesus' resurrection, we face the stony silence of Holy Saturday in hope. We carry our loved ones the way we will one day be carried to the grave—knowing that there's more.

---

*Geffrey B. Kelly, *The Cost of Moral Leadership: The Spirituality of Dietrich Bonhoeffer* (Grand Rapids, MI: William B. Eerdmans Publishing Company, 2003), 220.

O God, grant that as the crucified body of your dear Son was laid in the tomb and rested on this holy Sabbath, so may we await with him the coming of the third day, and rise with him to newness of life. Amen. (*The Book of Common Prayer*, 283)

EASTER

"Why are you weeping?" is the most absurd question Mary has ever heard.

She is there when they nail Jesus to the cross. She sees them lay his body in the tomb. She hears the funereal thud when they roll the stone in place. She comes in darkness, prepared for sorrow, but not for surprise. When she finds the empty tomb, the only reasonable conclusion is that as a final insult, Jesus' opponents have stolen his body. Why wouldn't she be weeping?

We weep with her too when we face the darkness of death, when we realize that the best life that ever lived was put to death by the worst that is within each of us.

Then she hears another question, "Whom are you looking for?"

John's Gospel begins with Jesus asking, "What are you looking for?" (1:38). It's the question that haunts every human heart, particularly when we face the questions of life and death. What are we really looking for? But now it becomes, "Whom are you looking for?" With personal intimacy Jesus says, "Mary," and she realizes who he is. The light overcomes the darkness. The One for whom she is searching finds her. Mary announces to the disciples, "I have seen the Lord!"

In the risen Christ, what we are looking for finds its answer in the One who finds us. The eternal becomes personal. The hungers of the human soul are not found in what we think or what we do, but in whom we find.

Having come in tears, Mary goes away with joy. She becomes the first person to sing, "You ask me how I know he lives? He lives within my heart!" (UMH, no. 310).

Almighty God who raised Jesus to new life, may this be the day we experience the Risen Christ and find in him the answer to the deepest questions of our hearts. Amen.

Uprising/Rising Up

APRIL 22–28, 2019 • SUSAN T. HENRY-CROWE

SCRIPTURE OVERVIEW: After the resurrection of Jesus, the disciples are unable to remain silent. They go to the Temple to proclaim the gospel. Some receive the message, while others do not. This causes turmoil within the community, but the apostles stand firm in their testimony, inspired by the Holy Spirit. Psalm 150 might be on the lips of those early apostles. Everything that has breath should praise the Lord! The author of Revelation recounts a vision that he receives from the risen Jesus Christ, who one day will return as Lord of all nations. In John we learn more about the source of the confidence of the apostles. They have experienced Jesus in the flesh, and this experience gives power to their proclamation of the reality of his resurrection.

QUESTIONS AND SUGGESTIONS FOR REFLECTION

- Read Acts 5:27-32. When has your faith compelled you to rise up, stand up, or kneel down in obedience to God rather than earthly authorities?
- Read Psalm 150. When have you praised God with great noise? When have you praised God with quiet service to creation?
- Read Revelation 1:4-8. How do you see peace arising out of violence in the Bible and in the world around you?
- Read John 20:19-31. How have your experiences of witnessing violence or the results of violence helped you to understand that violence does not have the last word?

General Secretary of the United Methodist Board of Church and Society; Dean of the Chapel and Religious Life, Emerita, Emory University; clergy member, South Carolina Annual Conference of the United Methodist Church.

MONDAY, APRIL 22 ~ *Read Acts 5:27-32*

A*nastasis*, which means "up" or "rising," is the ancient Greek word used by Orthodox Christianity for what the churches of Western Christianity call "resurrection." While the English translation of the word is "resurrection," *anastasis* holds a somewhat different understanding from the modern Western Church. The Western Church (rooted in Augustine) describes resurrection individually: Christ rises triumphantly and magnificently—but utterly alone. The Eastern Orthodox Church celebrates a more universal resurrection. Christ rises triumphantly and magnificently—and takes all of creation with him. Universal resurrection underlines the contrast between Rome's violence and Jesus' nonviolence.

In today's reading, the apostles have been arrested and brought to the high priest for defying the order of the Sanhedrin not to teach in Jesus' name. The apostles are charged with intending "to bring this man's blood upon us." Peter and the others say, "We must obey God rather than any human authority."

Like the apostles, we know unquestioning obedience and loyalty to the powers of the state can lead us to dark places. We remember that blind obedience to Nazism led to the horrible violence of the Holocaust. After the death of Jesus, his followers become a persecuted community, and the apostles resist the obedience imposed by both the religious establishment and the state. We can see such resistance to injustice in our contemporary world. In recent months we have seen athletes "take a knee" as nonviolent resistance to racism as part of the Black Lives Matter Movement. Carefully and prayerfully ponder disobedience as an act of faithfulness.

Glory to you, Lord Christ; your death we show forth, your resurrection we proclaim, your coming we await. Amen. Come Lord Jesus.

TUESDAY, APRIL 23 ~ *Read Acts 5:27-32*

From Western and Eastern Christian traditions, resurrection/*anastasis* carries an individual and a communal quality. In the days after the tragic school shootings in Parkland, Florida, and in dozens of others before, the question arises: How do communities, families, and friends grieve, lament, and heal after death? Grief is a long and painful journey. How do survivors live on after experiences of sickness, disease, hatred, violence, and death? How do communities move from grief to restoration? This scripture reading gives us a glimpse into life in community after death.

Mary, the mother of Jesus, his friends, his followers, share something with the parents, grandparents, and teachers who witness such violence and killing. They carry unbearable pain. The world has long been filled with violence against the innocent—children, people who are poor, those living with mental illness, those who are estranged and isolated—and against Jesus himself. Often the messengers of movements of nonviolence are blamed. Martin Luther King Jr., Harriet Tubman, and the apostles are blamed for the violent acts of others.

Mourning can be done alone; yet within the embrace of community, those who suffer from unspeakable sorrow caused by violence, neglect, and conflict heal and keep an open heart.

In the days following the school shooting in Parkland, young people—like the apostles in today's reading—raise their voices to those with political power and come together to say, "This must stop. We will rise to end gun violence." Motivated by pain, sorrow, and suffering they are rising up. They are turning their grief into a movement for nonviolence.

O Jesus, Light of Life, this is the world for which you died. This is the world for which you rose. This is the world for which you come again and again. We witness to these things. Amen.

WEDNESDAY, APRIL 24 ~ *Read John 20:19-31*

In the first days after loss of a beloved, absence is palpable. Sorrow runs deep. We feel as if there is a hole in the solar plexus. Raw feelings—yearning, unbelief that our loved one is gone—dominate our emotions. As Emily Dickinson says, "The Nerves sit ceremonious, like Tombs—"*

After a terrible death, I felt such a sense of deep loss. I was sad and primordially restless. My profound sense of absence sparked a desire to go looking. I was dazed, frightened, and sick to my stomach; my instinct was to howl and wander aimlessly. In the verses before today's reading, Peter looks for Jesus in the tomb. Our instinct is to go to the tomb, the site of the wreck, the place where the body lay. But we will not find love and life there.

After a while someone suggested I go to the Children's Hospital and rock a baby. That focused my grief. It turned my gaze from death toward life. It did not take away the grief but turned it toward healing. It became a metaphor for me: When there is death, anxiety, and fear, go cradle life.

In the following days, this One who is risen does not enter through doorways but appears in the midst of the community, on the road to Emmaus, in the house, in anxious rooms behind locked doors. Christ appears bridging the divine and the human, emerging from within, and calming anxiety and fear. Though the followers of Jesus often do not recognize what they are seeing, they hear and feel Christ's words of comfort, "Peace be with you. As God has given me to you, I give you to the world" (AP) The world does not give security or peace. This Risen One "does not stop the chaos of the world. Rather [Christ] is present within it, calming and untroubling the heart."**

---

*Emily Dickinson, "After great pain, a formal feeling comes—" *The Complete Poems of Emily Dickinson* (New York: Little, Brown and Company, 1960), 162.
** John Shea, *Spiritual Wisdom of the Gospels for Christian Preachers and Teachers: The Relentless Widow, Year C* (Collegeville, MN: Liturgical Press, 2006), 108.

O God, let not our hearts be troubled, nor afraid. Amen.

THURSDAY, APRIL 25 ~ *Read John 20:24-31*

Emmett Till was 14 years old when he was tortured and murdered in Mississippi on August 28, 1955. He was accused of flirting with a white cashier, Carolyn Bryant. His mother, Mamie Elizabeth Till-Mobley, insisted that her son's funeral be open-casket because "I wanted the world to see what they did to my baby." The families of children who die in violent, terrible acts want the world to know what happened in the hopes that it will never happen again.

In today's reading, Thomas wants to see the evidence that the risen Christ before him is the Jesus who suffered violent death. Jesus says, "'Put your finger here and see my hands. Reach out your hand and put it in my side. Do not doubt but believe.' Thomas answered him, 'My Lord and my God!'" Mrs. Till-Mobley wanted the world to see the wounds and marks of such profound violence on her son. Those who see and touch such wounds are astonished. "My Lord!" can be the exclamation of belief or of unbelief. When we see and believe, we exclaim, "My Lord!" Often our exclamation means more: "I can believe but this is an unbelievable act." When our perception of violence leads to our belief in it and our unbelief of its power, we honor life and death.

The Gospel writer tells us, "These are written so that you may come to believe that Jesus is the Messiah . . . and that through believing you may have life." We tell stories of our witness to violence because we know that death is not the final word. Life and love in Christ will triumph.

Sun of justice, ray of blessings,
form of light, cherished desire. . . .
Let your light dawn, your salvation be swift,
your help come in time, and the hour of your
arrival be at hand*

---

*Saint Grigor Narekatsi, *Speaking with God from the Depths of the Heart,* trans. Thomas J. Samnelian (2002), 467-68.

FRIDAY, APRIL 26 ~ *Read Revelation 1:4-8*

We can find a love story written in the story of our faith in Revelation. The beauty and wonder of the Christian story is that it is set in a complex world of persecution in a community that believes in love and that challenges empire. John, the author of Revelation, tells the Christian story in a world that used violence to kill the One who is Love. John's account begins with a greeting of peace for all eternity from the One who is and who was and who is to come.

Despite its violence, John's revelation is the account of love forever—the love that created paradise, that healed the brokenness of humankind, that promises salvation through the divine love that enters human history. Revelation promises that the world of violence and death does not have the last word and instead offers us a world in which death is no more when heaven and earth become one. This new world is populated by the cloud of witnesses and is the story of love forever.

The new world John's vision offers calls us back to the beginning: the beauty of the night, where the darkness was on the face of the deep, and the joy of the light of day. God saw that it was good. Out of that goodness, our faith and John's vision of the future insist that every child should hear this story of love with a full tummy, clean water, loving arms, no worry of war, and in a bed in which they sleep each night. God tells us all, "I love you and set you free to love."

God of all that you call good, help us to tell your story of love out of our world of violence, and help us to work toward your world where death is no more. Amen.

SATURDAY, APRIL 27 ~ *Read Revelation 1:4-8*

Today's reading offers God's gift of love to all of us. As Christians, we live the story of God's love and of this blessing week after week with thankful hearts through the sacrament of Communion. When I served as Dean of the Chapel and Religious Life, the Christian community celebrated Communion every Sunday. Students, faculty, staff, and friends came from many Christian traditions (or none). Some of the people came from faith communities that observed weekly Communion and others had never or not often observed Communion. Yet it did not take long for students of many denominations and backgrounds to fall in love with this sacrament of life in faith.

Students eagerly signed up to be chapel deacons to bake the bread, pray prayers, set the table, serve the meal, clean the table, and delight in the feast. Each week we told the story of the Christian faith, and it became emblazoned on our hearts. The Great Thanksgiving animates and transmits faith.

This community gathered for many reasons: their Dean loved them, the preaching was quite good, the space was perfect for a wide array of faith expression, and the music was amazing. But the liturgy of Communion, in which we tell the story of Christianity again and again, held it all together.

Blessed are you O Holy One, the beginning and the end.
O God of resurrection and new life:
Pour out your Spirit on us and on these gifts of bread and wine.
Bless this feast, grace our table with your presence.
Raise us up as the body of Christ for the world.
Breathe new life into us. Come Holy Spirit.
With your holy ones of all times and places,
With the earth and all its creatures
We praise you, O God now and forever. **Amen.***

---

*Adapted from Holy Communion Setting IV (Ash Wednesday—Day of Pentecost), *Evangelical Lutheran Worship* (Minneapolis: Augsburg Fortress, 2006), 111.

SUNDAY, APRIL 28 ~ *Read Psalm 150*

Psalm 150 serves as our doxology this week as it affirms myriad ways to praise our Creator. Everything that breathes offers praise to God.

There are extravagant acts of praise: dance, symphonies, orchestras, rock bands, art, hikes, space travel, and oceanography. And there are simple acts of praise. One day, Dash, my then four-year-old grandson, and I visited a bookstore. It is one of our favorite activities. After spending time in the store and making our purchase, we sat on the cement steps outside the store basking in the sun. Dash is a reflective and deep thinker. After a little bit he said, "Do you want to do something good for the earth?" I was curious about what he was thinking. "Of course," I replied. He said, "We could pick up all this trash." And so we did. Picking up trash was our act of praise that day. It was our small way of giving praise for creation by honoring it.

We can help everything that breathes praise God by revering all things that God has made and has done. Through dance, music, picking up trash, cleaning up rivers, saving timberlands, caring for children, protecting cultures, respecting older people, and nurturing the human family, we give praise to God.

Let everything that has breath praise God.

Embodying the Resurrection

APRIL 29–MAY 5, 2019 • JOHN FREDERICK

SCRIPTURE OVERVIEW: Saul is one of the primary obstacles to the early spread of Christianity. The death and resurrection of Jesus does not fit his paradigm for the Messiah, so it cannot be true. It takes a miraculous intervention by Christ himself to change his mind. Psalm 30 reminds us that the light will always chase the darkness. We experience true suffering and true loss, but God can turn our mourning into dancing in God's own timing. In Revelation, John takes us to the throne room of God, where angels and creatures proclaim the glory of the Lamb of God who has defeated death and reigns forever. Returning to the Gospel of John, we read more about Jesus' post-resurrection appearances, which here include a seaside breakfast and a quiz for Peter.

QUESTIONS AND SUGGESTIONS FOR REFLECTION

- Read Acts 9:1-20. Jesus' resurrection calls us to an embodied faith. How do you bear the gospel?
- Read Psalm 30. Recall a specific time when you depended on God.
- Read Revelation 5:11-14. Have you ever worshiped the Lamb with your whole body? What keeps you from falling down to worship God?
- Read John 21:1-19. The author reminds us that Jesus calls us to be shepherds and sheep. Which role do you most often fill? How can you take on a new leadership role or allow others to lead you?

Lecturer in New Testament at Flinders University and Trinity College Queensland; author of *Worship in the Way of the Cross*; pastored and planted churches in Boston and Phoenix as an Anglican priest.

MONDAY, APRIL 29 ~ *Read Acts 9:1-16*

Evangelism occurs through our embodiment of the gospel. God calls Ananias to heal Saul of Tarsus, but Ananias understandably is anxious about taking up this mission. After all, Ananias knows that Saul is in the habit of "breathing threats and murder against the disciples of the Lord."

Nevertheless, God commands Ananias to "go" because God has chosen Saul as a vessel to bear the gospel to the world. Most modern translations render the passage "an instrument whom I have chosen to bring my name." Yet, in the New Testament, the verb *bastaz* is never used to express message-carrying. It usually refers to the bearing of a burden (Jesus bearing our illness [Mark 8:17]; bearing our own cross in order to be Jesus' disciples [Luke 14:27]; bearing one another's burdens [Gal. 6:2]).

Thus, God refers to Saul not as the mere instrumental deliverer of a message but as the incarnational embodiment of the message. Paul's call is not to engage in his mission as a postman but rather to evangelize through embodiment—by becoming the message with his whole being in his thoughts, words, and deeds, bearing the gospel in his body as a vessel—for the sake of the world.

Are we following in Paul's footsteps? Are we bearing in our bodies the message of God's sacrificial, redemptive love? Or are we simply carrying it as a message? Let us pray that we become those who practice evangelism through embodiment.

Father, Son, and Holy Spirit, assist us in becoming missional messengers of the gospel through embodying the sacrificial love of Christ in our thoughts, words, and deeds. Amen.

TUESDAY, APRIL 30 ~ *Read Acts 9:16-20*

Verse 16 of our reading reiterates the idea of embodied evangelism, the suffering to which God is calling Paul for the sake of the gospel. God calls Paul to a cruciform ministry, a ministry formed by the way of the cross, the way of the self-giving, suffering love of Jesus Christ.

Jesus is the root, source, and summit of the ministry of suffering, divine love. (See Acts 3:18; 17:3.) This embodied evangelism is found throughout the New Testament. Peter exhorts believers to endure suffering by emulating the example of the cruciform love of Jesus. (See 1 Peter 2:19-23; 3:14-18; 4:1.) Paul teaches that believers are granted to believe and to suffer for the sake of Christ (see Philippians 1:29; 2 Corinthians 1:6; 1 Thessalonians 2:14; 2 Timothy 1:12), and that through our suffering we are joined together in solidarity and communion as the church. (See 1 Corinthians 12:26.)

Our suffering in service to the gospel is not for a sadistic God who might seem to have a divine propensity toward pain and punishment. Rather, it is a sanctifying suffering that conforms us to the image of the holy God who is, in Triune essence, suffering love. Let us consider the extent to which we are willing to live out the suffering love of Jesus Christ in our own lives. Do we rightly perceive our own suffering as an embodiment of the love of Christ that transforms ourselves and others? Or, do we seek to avoid the sanctification that comes through suffering?

Almighty God, we pray that you conform us to your image by teaching us to learn divine love through living out the suffering love of Christ for the sake of others. Amen.

WEDNESDAY, MAY 1 ~ *Read Psalm 30*

The psalmist exclaims: "You . . . clothed me with gladness" so that "my glory may sing your praise" (ESV). God clothes sinners with gladness to sing praise to God because of God's own glorious grace shining through us.

The psalm's richness resides in its focus on the reality of our absolute dependence upon God for life and salvation. Verse 1 expresses this concept by using the metaphor of drawing up water from a well. Imagine this: We as human beings are so completely incapable of attaining our own salvation that apart from the miracle of God's grace freely given to us, we have as much chance of rescuing and redeeming ourselves as water does of drawing itself up out of a well! This psalm provides a crucial reminder for those of us living in a culture of individualism and self-reliance that without the grace of God, we are without hope in the world and powerless against the pervasive pull of sin and death.

The theme of complete dependence on God continues as the psalmist recalls instances of God's saving action in his life. On the basis of God's gracious initiative and saving power, the psalmist cries out to the Lord, seeking anew God's mercy and help. This psalm teaches that our gladness is a result of God's grace, which leads us to praise God's glory as it is displayed in our lives through God's faithfulness and lovingkindness.

Triune God, renew in us a feeling of complete dependence on you, so that in every endeavor of our life we can rest in the comfort and peace of your gracious gospel and divine provision. Amen.

THURSDAY, MAY 2 ~ *Read Revelation 5:11-14*

Jesus is praised and worshiped because he is the God who is the Lamb. The concept of praise based upon God's sacrificial death as the Lamb constitutes an unexpected radical revelatory revision of the sacrificial theology of the Old Testament. In the cross of Christ we discover that God—the one who previously required sacrifice—has now become the sacrifice.

The point here, however, is not about formulating theories of the atonement; it is about recognizing that Christ as the sacrificial Lamb reveals to us the very being and essence of God—namely, that God is self-sacrificing, death-defeating love. God does not require blood; God spills it on our behalf to redeem us from the power of death. God is not a vindictive deity who demands retribution. Rather, God is the divine Lamb who relinquishes power and thereby kills the myth of redemptive violence and rises victorious over it in the resurrection.

The God who is love transforms the world into the image of love and ushers in a new creation, a new Jerusalem, powered by the energy and vitality of divine, cruciform love. As we meditate on the sacrifice of God today, let us praise the power of Christ's revolutionary love, and let us become agents of reconciliation in a world of brokenness and violence.

Triune God, may your sacrifice give us rest in you so that we might become reconcilers for your kingdom of peace, salvation, and life. Amen.

FRIDAY, MAY 3 ~ *Read Revelation 5:13-14*

Christ's sacrificial death culminates with a focus on worship in today's passage. In response to the Lamb's sacrifice, the elders fall down and worship. This act helps us understand the true character of Christian worship. The Greek word for worship, here *proskuneo,* already indicates reverent prostration. With the addition of the verb *pipto* (to fall down), the two-verb structure links this verse to a common Old Testament phrase that utilizes the same combination of verbs in describing acts of prostrated worship to God (see 2 Chronicles 7:3; Job 1:20) and powerful human beings (see 2 Samuel 1:2). Revelation makes clear, however, that worship is reserved for God alone. (See especially 19:10.)

Too often in the church we focus on the style rather than the disposition of worship. We engage in "worship wars," where we argue about the degree to which our liturgies are meant to be flexible or rigid. In many churches the meaning of worship narrows to the point that it becomes a mere synonym for "musical praise."

Yet our current ecclesial simplifications and distractions about worship miss the disposition of worship that precedes and directs all subsequent acts of worship. The reverent worship of the worthy Lamb is meant to be the humble, submissive, spiritual, and physical posture of human beings who have come into the presence of the holy God crucified and raised for the salvation of the world. We can express our humility through prostration, bowing, and falling down. When is the last time that you fell to your knees in the worship of God? Or laid prostrate in reverent prayer to Christ?

Triune God, let our disposition be one of holy humility before you as we bow our souls and our bodies to you in complete submission and awe through spiritually transformative worship. Amen.

SATURDAY, MAY 4 ~ *Read John 21:1-14*

The New Testament intentionally affirms the bodily and physical—as opposed to the merely spiritual—resurrection of Jesus. In John 20:24-31, Thomas touches the risen Lord in order to verify the bodily nature of the resurrected Christ. Today's passage highlights the physicality of Jesus' resurrection by telling a quirky story about Jesus' miraculous production of fish, which subsequently get tossed on the barbie for a seaside breakfast.

Imagine how strange this breakfast must have been! First, Jesus appears and causes 153 large fish to fill the empty nets of his disciples. Next, he shouts out, "Come and have breakfast." Of the many things you might expect the resurrected Christ to do, having an apostolic cookout is likely not one of them. Yet that's what happens! The meal is awkwardly silent with Jesus' disciples not venturing to ask who he is because "they knew it was the Lord."

Elsewhere, in Luke 24:36-43, the post-resurrection Jesus appears to his disciples, wishes them peace, and then proceeds to ask, "Do you have anything here to eat?" Perhaps remembering Jesus' choice of cuisine at the prior barbecue, the disciples hand him a peace of broiled fish which Jesus proceeds to eat. It is evident here too that Jesus is aiming to get his disciples to focus on the mysterious yet physical nature of his resurrected body. As we focus today on the bodily nature of the resurrection, let us ask the Lord to reveal to us the ways in which our spiritual lives are connected to God's renewal of all things, including our bodies.

Help us, O Lord, to recognize the goodness of your creation and the holistic nature of your redemption, in which all that you create is on a trajectory of cosmic physical and spiritual renewal. Amen.

SUNDAY, MAY 5 ~ *Read John 21:15-19*

Reading John 21 from start to finish reveals a theme that one might otherwise gloss over: Before Jesus tells Peter to feed his sheep, Jesus feeds his sheep. In yesterday's reading from the chapter, Jesus performs a miracle in which the disciples catch 153 fish. Jesus then prepares and serves these fish to Peter and the other disciples. Along with the fish, "Jesus came and took the bread and gave it to them" (21:13), which reminds us of Jesus' words during the last supper accounts in the other three Gospels. Only after Jesus feeds and communes with the disciples does he call Peter to feed others.

Jesus asks Peter, "Do you love me?" and commands Peter to feed his lambs, to tend his sheep, and to feed his sheep. Jesus charges Peter with shepherding the flock, but Peter never ceases to be a sheep in need of communion with Christ, the living bread.

This is an important lesson for us as ministers, whether we are ordained or lay. Before we can feed others, we must be fed by Christ; after we become shepherds, we remain sheep in need of shepherding. Christ calls all of his disciples to continually become like little children, living in complete dependence upon him so that we can experience the reality of the kingdom of God. As we reflect upon our walk with Lord, let us pray to be both sheep and shepherd.

O Lord, renew in us a childlike dependence upon you, that we who seek to lead might ourselves be fed by the life-giving grace of the gospel through our shepherd, Jesus Christ. Amen.

Conviction of Things Not Seen

MAY 6–12, 2019 • G. SUJIN PAK

SCRIPTURE OVERVIEW: The imagery of sheep plays a prominent role in three of this week's readings. Psalm 23 uses the relationship between the shepherd and the sheep as its guiding metaphor. The Lord is our shepherd and leads us to safe and fertile places. Even when we pass through a dark valley, the Lord is there protecting us with a shepherd's weapon, a staff. In the Gospel reading, Jesus describes himself as a shepherd who calls his sheep. Because they are his, they hear his voice. In Revelation, Jesus becomes the sheep—or more specifically, the Lamb that was slain on our behalf. Those who endure will praise the Lamb forever. Acts is different in that it focuses on a resurrection story, a manifestation of God's power working through Peter.

QUESTIONS AND SUGGESTIONS FOR REFLECTION

- Read Acts 9:36-43. How can you be a witness and a vessel for God's activity?
- Read Psalm 23. Reflect on the questions the author poses in Tuesday's meditation. Allow God's guidance and correction to be comforting.
- Read Revelation 7:9-17. How does knowing Christ as both Lamb and Shepherd help you work to bring about things not yet seen?
- Read John 10:22-30. How does your faith allow you to hold gently your convictions without needing to grasp tightly to certainties?

Faculty member in history of Christianity and Vice Dean of Academic Affairs at Duke Divinity School; specializes in the history of Christianity in late medieval and early modern Europe with a recent focus on views and uses of prophecy in the early modern era.

MONDAY, MAY 6 ~ *Read Psalm 23:1-4*

Sheep heavily rely upon their vision. The placement of their eyes enables a wide field of sight for them to scan their surroundings quickly for any surprises, particularly predators. Since their sense of security depends on being able to see other sheep, a good shepherd knows to keep sheep within visual contact of one another to ensure their physical and emotional well-being.

Consequently, sheep are reluctant to go into any territory in which they cannot see. They avoid shadows and dark places. Verse four holds more significance than we might first realize: "Even though I walk through the darkest valley"—or "the valley of the shadow of death" (KJV)—"I fear no evil." Here, the sheep must reach for a trust beyond dependence on sight to a trust rooted in what has come before: the ways the shepherd has hitherto led them to provision, protection, and restoration. In this frightening period in which they cannot see the next step, the sheep still follow the shepherd because they have known and experienced the shepherd's love, care, and protection.

Note how the sheep know the shepherd's presence in such times of darkness: "Your rod and your staff—they comfort me." These tools of the shepherd serve both protective and corrective functions. Shepherds use the rod as a club to defend the sheep from predators and use the hook of the staff for gentle redirection, correction, and rescue if a sheep wanders or falls into an area seemingly out of the shepherd's reach.

We all have times in our lives when we cannot see what comes next or feel we are surrounded by darkness. If we rely upon sight alone, despair threatens to engulf us. Jesus, our Good Shepherd, calls us to a conviction of things presently unseen—a conviction that our Shepherd's guiding influence reaches beyond mere sight.

Lord, you are the Good Shepherd. Strengthen a faith in me that reaches beyond my current circumstances. Amen.

TUESDAY, MAY 7 ~ *Read Psalm 23:4-6*

Readers tend to focus on what Psalm 23's Shepherd does for us—with good reason! The Shepherd provides for our needs; guides us into places of peace, safety, and prosperity; and leads us through darkness to abundant life.

Yet, this psalm exhorts us to certain activities. Trusting in the Shepherd's guidance, we may be surprised to realize that the Shepherd sometimes leads us into the dark valley, the valley of the shadow of death. Yet is it so surprising? Jesus Christ precisely and obediently faces the world's darkness and death. He becomes obedient to death—even death on a cross—so that resurrection is possible. Indeed, resurrection by definition follows some form of death. Christ invites us to participate in his death and resurrection symbolized in our baptism. You may ask yourself, *What in my life needs to die so that resurrection can take hold? What blocks me from following Christ and receiving the abundant life Christ promises? Will I surrender these to the Shepherd in the conviction of resurrection not yet seen but assuredly promised?*

In times of asking what needs to die in our lives so that resurrection can prevail, we often experience God through the corrective staff and protective rod. In such experiences of discipline and correction, we frequently fail to see their roots of God's love and protection. Putting to death the idols of our lives is a painful process that requires practices of godly and loving discipline. This psalm calls us not to fear and to recognize God's discipline as a comfort that demonstrates God's resurrecting presence in our lives. Only then can we proclaim and claim a future reality not yet seen—that goodness and mercy shall follow us all the days of our life and that we shall dwell in the house of the Lord.

Lord, I surrender the idols of my life to you. Help me to live into your promise of resurrection. Amen.

WEDNESDAY, MAY 8 ~ *Read Acts 9:36-43*

By the time we arrive at Joppa and the story of faithful Tabitha, the signs and wonders of Peter and the apostles are known widely. When Peter is in Jerusalem, people bring their sick into the streets just so his shadow might fall upon them and bring healing. (See Acts 5:15.) Peter and John lay hands on the believers in Samaria so that they receive the Holy Spirit. (See Acts 8:17.) Just prior to today's passage, Peter heals a paralyzed man in the nearby city of Lydda.

There is good reason to believe that Peter could heal a sick Tabitha. But Tabitha has died. Logic dictates that the situation has reached a point beyond redemption. Yet, the disciples in Joppa have a conviction of things not yet seen. They imagine the possibility of something more. They imagine the impossible. So they send for Peter and ask him to come quickly.

The elements of this text echo aspects of the accounts of Jesus raising the widow of Nain's son from the dead (see Luke 7:12-15) and resurrecting Jairus's daughter (see Mark 5:22-24, 35-42). Both Jesus and Peter "put all the people outside." The command of resurrection varies by a single letter in the original Aramaic—"Tabitha [Talitha] cum." One difference is equally significant: Peter kneels down and prays before resurrecting Tabitha, for Peter knows none of this is about him or within his own power; he serves as a witness and vessel of God's activity.

As Jesus tells his disciples, "If you have the faith of a mustard seed, nothing will be impossible for you" (Matt. 7:20). What seems impossible in your life today? Will you follow the disciples of Joppa in their conviction of things unseen? Will you practice resurrection faith—faith in resurrection of something seemingly unredeemable? Will you pray as Peter prayed?

Jesus, help me to imagine the impossible with the eyes of resurrection faith. Amen.

Earlier in John 10, Jesus depicts himself as the good shepherd who willingly lays down his life for the sheep. He warns that one must enter the sheepfold by the gate, whereas thieves try to find another way. Indeed, explains Jesus, he is the gate: "Whoever enters by me will be saved" (John 10:9).

According to the Johannine text, many of the Jews dislike these claims. They are divided concerning how to understand the discrepancy between these strange words that run counter to Jewish expectations of the Messiah and Jesus' actions of healing that display divine power. So, the Jews address Jesus saying, "If you are the Messiah, tell us plainly!"

How many times have we also cried to God, "Tell me clearly what to do, what to believe"? Too often we desire certainty. But certainty is not faith; indeed, it runs counter to faith. The author of Hebrews defines faith as the "assurance of things hoped for, the conviction of things not seen" (11:1). If something is certain, what need does faith fulfill? Things not yet in evidence require faith.

Yet a vast difference exists between certainty and conviction. Certainty grips firm control to secure a claim on truth, often to wield it for a particular agenda. It seizes power rather than relinquishing power to the Almighty. Conviction, however, grasps softly with the knowledge that the journey of faith is always under construction. Faith recognizes that all human knowledge is finite. At any moment God might reveal to us a deeper truth, a truth that could overturn parts of what we thought we knew. Likewise, some might claim certainty about who are the true sheep and who are not, but such certainty is not ours to claim; rather, we live by faith.

God, help me recognize where I have demanded certainty. Enable me to embrace the more difficult, more beautiful path of faith. Amen.

FRIDAY, MAY 10 ~ *Read John 10:27-30*

Jesus says, "My sheep hear my voice. I know them, and they follow me." At first this sounds like a logical, easy progression of events. We hear God's voice, and we follow. Except, in actual experience, it can be difficult to know when we've heard the voice of God. Frequently, it is unclear whether the advice from a trusted friend, colleague, or pastor is really a word from God or just another random piece of counsel. Through all the clamor of myriad messages with which the modern world increasingly surrounds us, we struggle to distinguish the voice of the Shepherd. Even as we try to discern the voice of God, we struggle to know.

Just as the sheep recognize their shepherd's voice through repeated experience and practice, so also we become more adept at recognizing the voice of God. We would be wise, then, to cultivate practices of silent meditation and carve out spaces of quiet to enable godly listening. Yet, here is the good news: The Shepherd knows us. As we foster attentive ears ready to hear God in any given moment or situation and take that first step of faith in conviction of things not yet seen, the source of our assurance is not so much our knowledge of God but the Shepherd's perfect knowledge of us. God knows our every need, weakness, and fear. God knows our every gift and our heart. The Good Shepherd always seeks our well-being, and no one can snatch that away. Rather than relying upon our own questionable ability to know, we can hear and follow in the absolute assurance that God knows us and anticipates our every need.

Lord, quiet the world's perpetual noise, saying, "Peace, be still!" Help me learn to be still enough to hear your voice. Teach me to rest in the assurance that you know me and have anticipated my every need. Amen.

SATURDAY, MAY 11 ~ *Read Revelation 7:9-12*

Sometimes when I look at the world, I begin to despair. There seems not enough space for the thousands of refugees worldwide fleeing war, genocide, brutality, and injustice. Even if we realize there is enough space, the generosity of nations with stability and peace increasingly frays under the inrushing of numbers difficult to manage or adequately support—sadly, at times, yielding to other forms of racism. The United States in particular is faced with the question of how it will define its "greatness" in the present historical moment. Will it become increasingly insular, protecting its borders at any cost? Will it disregard its immigrant roots and narrate an American identity that forgets its founding cry for "liberty and justice for all" and the invitation to "give me your tired, your poor, your huddled masses"?

As Christians, this is exactly the moment in which we must hold intently to an eschatological reality yet unseen. We catch a glimpse in Revelation 7 of God's ultimate vision for God's people: "a great multitude that no one could count, from every nation, from all tribes and peoples and languages, standing before the throne and before the Lamb." Every person equally beloved and given refuge at the seat of the throne. Together they live into a new doxological reality. Every path, every nation, every race, every language, every person joins in a singular gaze upon the Lamb and a singular hymn of praise. John's Revelation offers us a vision of diversity honored and preserved—an exquisite portrait of unity precisely in embodied diversity. This vision of all creatures living into the fullness of God's inestimable goodness is the hope—the *telos*—of all life itself to which we are called today to embrace with a conviction of things yet unseen.

Lord, help me today to find concrete ways to embody your promised eschatological reality so that I may be a more loving and just presence in the world. Amen.

SUNDAY, MAY 12 ~ *Read Revelation 7:13-17*

Several scripture readings this week depict Jesus as our Shepherd, describing his care for the sheep. When coupling Revelation 7 with Psalm 23 and John 10, a striking reversal leaps from the page. The Shepherd is now the Lamb! "Salvation belongs to our God who is seated on the throne, and to the Lamb!" (7:10). Those coming out of the great ordeal have "washed their robes and made them white in the blood of the Lamb."

Jesus, though God, becomes human. Jesus, though the Shepherd deserving of all power and authority, becomes one of the sheep—lo! He becomes the sacrificial lamb. Jesus proclaims that the good shepherd lays down his life for the sheep (John 10:11); yet, he undertakes more. He takes up our life and all our sins and the burdens of this broken world so that we have access to true and everlasting life—so that we can participate in the Triune life of God. Jesus willingly and lovingly bears the suffering, violence, and injustice of this world in order to embody, enact, and manifest new and renewed creation, in which there is no hunger or thirst; and something that was meant to bring life (like the sun) will no longer cause pain and death.

There is one last reversal. The Lamb is now the Shepherd—for "the Lamb at the center of the throne will be their shepherd and guide them to springs of the water of life." The One who knows our every fear, injustice, sorrow, and wound now sits on the throne so that love, righteousness, peace, and justice may prevail and every tear be wiped from our eyes. In this conviction of something yet unseen, we find hope that makes us alive again and gives us strength for today and for tomorrow.

God, help me to recognize the reversals needed in my life. May I experience and embody your intended love, righteousness, and peace. Amen.

Working Our Way Through Change

MAY 13–19, 2019 • R. MICHAEL SANDERS

SCRIPTURE OVERVIEW: Change can be difficult. It is easy to get comfortable with what is familiar. In Acts, some in Jerusalem criticize Peter for having fellowship with the Gentiles. Peter explains that his actions are not his own idea but are inspired by a vision from God. This change leads to the spread of the gospel. Revelation speaks of a new heaven and a new earth. God cares for the earth that God created, but at the end of time everything will be changed and made better. Jesus tells his disciples in John a new commandment, namely that they should love one another. This is how others will know that they are truly Jesus' disciples. Psalm 148 is not about change but is pure praise for the works of the Lord.

QUESTIONS AND SUGGESTIONS FOR REFLECTION

- Read Acts 11:1-18. God calls Peter to initiate change. How do you respond to changes in your church's culture? How do you discern what changes are from God?
- Read Psalm 148. The next time you sing, focus on praising God and sharing God's love through your words and melody.
- Read Revelation 21:1-6. How do you live a full life in the waiting for the new heaven and new earth?
- Read John 13:31-35. In the wake of betrayal, Jesus calls his followers to sacrificial love. When have you needed to heed the call to this type of love?

Writer; Pastor of Topinabee Community Church and First Congregational Church of Wolverine (Evangelical Association), Topinabee, Michigan.

MONDAY, MAY 13 ~ *Read Acts 11:1-18*

When God seeks change, God calls persons in ways they can understand. Along with the other disciples, God charges Peter with the daunting task of changing a religious culture.

In the past, those seeking to follow God completely went through a long process that led to being a proselyte. Then they were circumcised, lived by a dietary code, and strictly observed Sabbath. In this passage we notice a shift: God's only criterion is "the repentance that leads to life."

Peter goes to Jerusalem to explain what has happened, and he meets keepers of the old culture. Their first concern is not about the new faith of the Gentiles but about Peter's eating with them. Often critics of change will protest new ways with minutia of the old ways. Peter knows their true quibble so he tells his own story step by step. He doesn't begin with "I'm Peter the Rock, listen to me. I know better than you." So that they will know he has had a holy experience, he starts by telling them he went up on the roof to commune with God.

In his vision, a blanket comes down with all kinds of animals, some of which are considered unclean. When he is told to take and eat, he responds with the proper reply of the old culture. But God says, "What God has made clean, you must not call profane." God says this three times so that Peter will understand.

Visitors arrive while Peter is still puzzled. These Gentiles want to know about Christ. He goes to Caesarea with other believers and there they bear witness of the presence of the Holy Spirit as the Gentiles repent.

And so the church now knows that God welcomes all persons—regardless of position, past religion, or ethnicity. No one is unclean.

God, help me to see all who call your name as your beloved children, no matter their past. Amen.

TUESDAY, MAY 14 ~ *Read John 13:31-35*

Despite what romantics say, love is not blind. Attraction may obscure others' flaws, but genuine mature love recognizes all shortcomings and understands and accepts others as they are.

Jesus calls his followers to love, but Jesus speaks neither in a vacuum nor as a professor teaching doctrine. Consider the context: Jesus has just dismissed Judas. Not only does he instruct Judas to leave; he requests that Judas betray him quickly. Only after Judas is gone does Jesus turn back to the others and call them to live a deeper love. As he teaches this love, his attention does not drift back to the one who just left: the one who followed him, ate with the five thousand, and saw Lazarus come forth; the one who has just set into motion the greatest act of love the world has ever known.

What is this love so profound that Jesus calls it a new commandment? This love is more than warm feelings. It weathers the times when love cannot be felt, when only faith can overcome disappointment and hurt. It triumphs over hurt and loss and is given freely when there may be no immediate return.

Later in this teaching, when Jesus says, "No one has greater love than this, to lay down one's life for one's friends" (15:13), he offers not theory or fantastic notion but a hint at what is coming in a matter of hours.

This love forgives from the cross; it is not worn around the neck as an emblem of faith, but comes bearing blood as proof.

Jesus calls us all to this kind of love. It grows within us through the divine power of the Holy Spirit as we walk with God.

Lord, help me to know that I can do all things through you. Amen.

WEDNESDAY, MAY 15 ~ *Read John 13:31-35*

How is it that Jesus has been glorified already? He has dismissed Judas to set in motion his crucifixion. There is no turning back.

Jesus neither pleads with Judas to reconsider nor calls the others to grab hold of the traitor and shut down the whole process. Jesus follows what he knows to be the will of God.

Jesus carries out God's will through obedience, even obedience to the cross. The salvation God promises is imminent, and thus God is glorified.

How do we seek God's glory? God's glory comes not from mighty achievements that bring us accolades but from submitting to God's will for our lives rather than personal glorification.

How often have people sought glory for God's kingdom in the wrong places? How many great buildings and ministries' cornerstones should have read, "For the Glory of God by the Pride of Men and Women"? We find God's glory by the singular simple act of giving all to follow the will of God.

Many years ago, wandering through a bookstore, I picked up a book by Dietrich Bonhoeffer entitled *The Cost of Discipleship*. I stood there carelessly thumbing through the pages, past many wonderful words written by this great martyr of the faith. But then eleven simple words jumped out as if they had been printed in bold type, and they changed the direction of my life: "When Christ calls a man, he bids him come and die."*

In that moment all the sermons my pastors had preached on following Christ and all the lessons my Sunday school teacher had led, suddenly made sense. My life path changed, and I turned to follow the greatest of all plans.

---

*Dietrich Bonhoeffer, *The Cost of Discipleship* (New York: Touchstone, 1995), 89.

Lord, help me to take up my cross and follow you. Amen.

THURSDAY, MAY 16 ~ *Read Psalm 148*

I find it intriguing that one entire book of the Bible, Psalms, is a book of songs. Words to be sung, not merely read. All cultures have their own music; it is almost impossible to find a people without song.

One of the cross-cultural powers of the psalms is the flexibility of Hebrew poetry. They do not depend on special rhythms or rhyme. They are based on repetition and rhyming of thought and ideas. Repetition brings home meaning and allows for easier translation than do strict rhyming schemes.

Many of the psalms are hymns of praise. We continue to sing their words in traditional hymns and in more contemporary songs. Such singing is an act of obedience. The Bible is full of God's call to sing. (See Colossians 3:16; Ephesians 5:18-20.) While song styles vary from worship service to worship service, all our songs help us to praise the Almighty.

Since singing words of our faith brings us together as we worship, we can make room for many different styles and each of our favorites. I am learning to leave room for a song that blesses others but does not speak to me as I hope others do likewise.

Singing is also a profession of faith. "About midnight Paul and Silas were praying and singing hymns to God, and the prisoners were listening to them" (Acts 16:25). After hearing their hymns of faith and their concern for him, the jailer reaches out to know their faith.

Our songs of faith have the power to build our faith and speak to those who do not yet know the grace and love of God.

Dear God, by your power help our music build our faith and speak truth to your world. Amen.

FRIDAY, MAY 17 ~ *Read Psalm 148*

We praise people to affirm them, but God doesn't need our affirmation to be God.

We praise others to encourage them to continue on a certain path, but God works in God's way.

We praise people to keep them from being discouraged and quitting too soon, but God doesn't have this human failing.

So why do we praise God? We praise as an act of obedience. Simply doing what is right or what we have been asked can be powerful.

We praise God because we are thankful. Our failure to be thankful can promote self-centeredness. Praising God cures our pride. It turns our focus away from ourselves toward God.

We praise God as a testimony of our faith to those around us. Our praise shares God's wonder with others.

Our praise turns us to the Center of Reality. Our praise speaks of an infinite, loving, righteous, and holy God. We understand, in that moment of praise, who God is and who we are. As the priest tells the young protagonist in the movie *Rudy*, "I've come up with only two hard incontrovertible facts; there is a God, and I'm not him."

We praise to encounter the living God. In the act of praise, we encounter God. As we worship, we enter into direct communion with God, just as we do in the sacraments of Communion and baptism.

We praise in obedience, in gratitude, as a testimony, and as a reality check. And for the most precious of all moments, to be in the very presence of God.

Praise be to God, Father of us all!

SATURDAY, MAY 18 ~ *Read Revelation 21:1-6*

Revelation 21 begins with the powerful statement that we need a new world; the old world is unable to embrace what God has for us next.

Sometimes we can repair broken things. But there can come a time when something broken is too far gone and we must begin again.

Years ago, my daily walk took me past an empty and untended house. I would stop to look at the old house that leaned precariously to the west with an unsure foundation, busted windows, and dilapidated roof.

The former owners had died, leaving the house to feuding relatives who could never agree on selling or repairing the structure. Year after year it deteriorated. By the time I moved to the area, it was beyond renovation and seemed to be begging for something new to arise. Years later, I returned to the westward leaning home to find that the rotting house was gone—replaced by a beautiful new building brimming with the love and laughter of a family.

John's Revelation offers us an image of a time when God might look upon our humble planet and say that it is time for something new and perfect.

Our world may reach that point, a point of no return. Used up and worn out. The good news is that the One who set all of this in motion has the power to bring a new world where "there will be no more death or mourning or crying or pain" (NIV).

Creator of all things new, teach me to celebrate the good in my world while I look forward to your new world where there is no pain or loss. Amen.

SUNDAY, MAY 19 ~ *Read Revelation 21:1-6*

He will wipe every tear from their eyes. Death will be no more." When I was young, these words held little meaning. I was busy building a life and a ministry and these good things consumed my thoughts and prayers.

Over time, family and friends suffered injuries and passed away. Tears come more frequently now as time takes its measure of my loved ones.

Today when I read these words, I find great comfort in God's promise and I smile. Still, I live between the promise and the fulfillment. Am I to long for that painless world but scorn today? How do I honor the promise and the present grief?

Part of the answer came to me as I pastored a small church made up mostly of farmers. During the cold of winter when nothing grew and the fields lay dormant, they prepared for the certain return of spring. They repaired old equipment while checking the interest rates for loans in case the old needed to make way for the new. They waited not with folded hands or lazy minds but in active preparation for the new season of growth.

Jeremiah 29:4-7 offers an answer as well: God has promised to rescue the children of Israel from Babylonian captivity. While they wait, they send word to Jeremiah and ask what they are supposed to do until God's promised return. He tells them to build houses, have children, and pray for the place in which they live. The prophet tells them that waiting is not only a time for renewal and preparation; it is life itself.

What is our biblical response to waiting until death shall be no more? We are to love our families, work our jobs, pray for our communities, and wait on the certainty of spring, when God makes everything new.

God, thank you for today and for the promise of tomorrow. Amen.

At Home with God

MAY 20–26, 2019 • CAROL W. BUMBALOUGH

SCRIPTURE OVERVIEW: The kingdom of God is constantly advancing by the power of the Holy Spirit. In Acts, Paul is driven forward in his missionary activity by the Spirit. He moves westward to Macedonia, where a woman named Lydia becomes the first known convert in Europe. This becomes a base for subsequent mission. In Revelation, the Spirit shows John the new Jerusalem, in which the Lamb will provide light for all nations. Jesus' disciples wrestle with the idea that he would leave them. He teaches them that he will not leave them alone; he will send the Holy Spirit to empower them. The psalmist does not mention the Spirit but declares that all nations, not just the Israelites, will sing for joy because of God's saving power.

QUESTIONS AND SUGGESTIONS FOR REFLECTION

- Read Acts 16:9-15. Recall a specific time when you have followed God. How did you discern God's voice? What did you do to follow through on God's call?
- Read Psalm 67. How do you share God's blessings with the world?
- Read Revelation 21:10, 22–22:5. What would it mean for there to be no separation between nations? no separation between you and God?
- Read John 14:23-29. When have you experienced the Holy Spirit as your Advocate?

Adult Discipleship Program Director, Brentwood United Methodist Church just outside Nashville, Tennessee.

MONDAY, MAY 20 ~ *Read Acts 16:9-10*

In today's passage, Paul and his companions are on their second missionary journey, departing from Antioch and heading west. They have chosen to take the land route this time to visit cities where they have preached and won converts to Christ.

Have you ever wondered how Paul decides where to go? With the whole world waiting to hear the good news, how does Paul know where to start?

Our reading today gives us a hint: The Holy Spirit comes to Paul in a dream and shows him a man from Macedonia standing and pleading with Paul to "come and help us!" Verse 10 says, "Immediately after he saw the vision, we prepared to leave for the province of Macedonia, concluding that God had called us to proclaim the good news to them" (CEB).

This passage makes clear that God can guide us in our decision-making if we open ourselves to God's influence. God's tools are various: Sometimes God presents the "open door"—the opportunity that comes our way. Sometimes God shows us the "closed door"—when circumstances change and we no longer can pursue a course of action. Sometimes God guides us through the word of a wise friend or a complete stranger. And God even comes to us in dreams as we sleep.

All these ways of divine direction rely on a common thread: Our willingness to seek and perceive God's guidance and to be obedient to God's leadership when it comes.

Paul and his companions "immediately" respond to God's direction. What guidance from God do you need to respond to "immediately"? Be open, aware, and obedient.

Loving God, help me to open my heart and mind to your guidance and to respond in obedience to your direction. Amen.

TUESDAY, MAY 21 ~ *Read Acts 16:11-15*

Once Paul and his companions get the green light from the Holy Spirit to enter Macedonia, they proceed to the city of Philippi. Paul's usual strategy in a new city begins with proclaiming the good news in a Jewish synagogue. The fact that he goes outside the city gates to the river on the sabbath strongly suggests that Philippi does not have a synagogue within the city.

When Paul and his companions arrive at the meeting place, they come upon a group of women gathered for prayer. They sit down on the river bank and share the good news.

One of the women, Lydia, is singled out. She is described as being a Gentile who worships God and who is also a dealer of purple cloth. This business woman listens eagerly to Paul, and "the Lord enabled her to embrace Paul's message" (CEB).

Lydia's positive response to the gospel seems dependent upon God's action. Various translations emphasize God's proactive stance: "The Lord opened her heart to listen eagerly;" "The Lord enabled Lydia to embrace Paul's message" (CEB); "As she listened to us, the Lord opened her heart, and she accepted what Paul was saying" (NLT); "The Lord opened her heart to respond to Paul's message" (NIV).

It seems that accepting the good news is a two-part process. God opens the door, but we must choose to walk through it. Notice what happens next—once Lydia's heart has been opened, she acts. She is baptized and then opens her home to Paul and his companions.

Lord, open our hearts to your good news and enable us to embrace your guidance and provision. Once we have opened our hearts, help us to be generous with those around us. Amen.

WEDNESDAY, MAY 22 ~ *Read Psalm 67*

When our children were babies, my husband and I would often go into the nursery while they slept just to gaze at their little bundled-up forms. They weren't doing anything unusual—just breathing rhythmically and occasionally making little muffled sounds or yawning. But to our eyes, they were the most fascinating creatures in the world. Our faces literally shone with joy when we gazed at them.

Today's psalm begins with the prayer that God will "make his face to shine upon us." Like a child dependent upon her parent for every good thing in life, the psalmist looks to God for the abundance of God's blessing.

The psalmist also asks that God's ways may be known in the earth and God's salvation may be known among *all* nations. The call to praise God is not limited here to the nation of Israel because God's guidance and blessing extend to all nations on earth.

When we share our blessings, we help make God's "saving power" known in all the earth so that everyone may be blessed. The psalmist invites us to envision a beautiful circle of blessing, praise, more blessing, and more praise.

In our world today, when so much divides us and nations look upon each other with distrust, the psalmist's image can encourage us: One day all the nations will "be glad and sing for joy" and will recognize that God judges with equity. In our own churches and communities, we can demonstrate the same generosity and openness to all that God demonstrates to us.

God of all blessings, thank you for demonstrating your love to us through your abundant provision. Help us to use our blessings to make known your "saving power" to all those with whom we come in contact. Amen.

THURSDAY, MAY 23 ~ *Read Revelation 21:10, 22–22:5*

In biblical times, cities are surrounded by walls that serve to protect citizens from a multitude of threats: marauding armies, bands of outlaws, and wild animals. The gates are left open during the day to facilitate trade and commerce but are shut tight at night to keep out danger. In our passage today, we read about a heavenly city, the new Jerusalem, where God resides and the gates "will never be shut by day—and there will be no night there." God-worshiping people from all the nations will fill the city and nothing evil will enter it. In a world full of terrorism, wars, cruelty, and greed, we long for this holy city without night and without evil.

Those who enter this city—to which God invites all—will find no divisions. Nothing is accursed; a river bears life-giving water to persons and to trees that bring fruit and healing; no darkness separates the light. And there is no separation between God and the people: God and the Lamb dwell not in a temple but amongst the nations within the city.

We long to share God's abundance and light with people from all the nations and join together in praising God and sharing God's abundant blessings. We long to find our home in God's presence. Faith in this heavenly vision keeps us focused on how we should live each day. Instead of walling ourselves off from potential dangers or from those persons who are different from us, John's vision of God's new heaven and new Jerusalem invites all of the good from all nations into God's light. Peace comes not from lack of difference but from lack of separation. As we seek to live together despite our differences, God will dwell among us.

God, our dwelling place, keep the vision of your heavenly city burning brightly in our hearts so that we may be motivated to seek your peace with God-loving people from all nations. Amen.

FRIDAY, MAY 24 ~ *Read Revelation 22:1-5*

Today's passage recalls another important Bible story—Adam and Eve's rebellion in the Garden of Eden. A quick look at Genesis 3 yields the scene where God forbids Adam and Eve from partaking of the Tree of Life. Genesis 3:22-23 says, "Then the LORD God said, 'See, the man has become like one of us, knowing good and evil; and now, he might reach out his hand and take also from the tree of life, and eat, and live forever'—therefore the LORD God sent him forth from the garden of Eden, to till the ground from which he was taken." God exiles Adam and Eve from the Garden because of their direct and willful disobedience of God's commandment. God banishes them from their perfect home and removes them from the intimate relationship they had shared. No longer will they converse with God in the cool of the evening as they did before they rebelled. A barrier erected by sin separates human creatures from their Creator.

In today's passage in Revelation, we see the consequences of humanity's original rebellion being reversed. Redeemed humanity now has free access to the Tree of Life and its lush and abundant harvest. Not only does the tree provide nourishment in the form of fruit which ripens each month, it also offers healing properties from its leaves. No longer separated from God by their sin, the residents of the new Jerusalem see God face-to-face. In the new city of God, the new Jerusalem, God restores the intimacy humanity knew in the Garden of Eden.

Lord, we long for your new Jerusalem, where you restore our face-to-face intimacy with you. We long to feast on the ripe fruit plucked from the Tree of Life. We long to drink from the crystal clear river that flows from your throne. Bring us to your new city and restore what we lost when we rebelled. Amen.

SATURDAY, MAY 25 ~ *Read John 14:23-24*

Home. What do you think of when you read that word? Does it bring memories of dinners around a table covered with steaming platters of food? Does it conjure up scenes of laughter and tears with people you love?

Home has been an underlying theme in our readings this week. In Acts 16, Paul and his companions share the good news with Lydia and she invites them to her home—a way of living out her new faith. In Psalm 67, the psalmist longs for face-to-face intimacy with God and cries out in verse 1, "May God be merciful and bless us. May his face smile with favor on us" (NLT). Revelation 21 and 22 describe the new Jerusalem where redeemed humanity and God make their home together and the citizens see God face-to-face.

Home is a word fraught with many emotional connotations. Beyond a shelter from the elements, the concept of home speaks of intimacy—of knowing and being known. It speaks of relationships. It speaks of comfort and love. And Jesus says in today's passage that if we love him and obey his commandments, he and his Father will make *their* home with us.

Obeying Jesus' commandments boils down to loving God and loving our neighbor. As we make time in our daily life for God and neighbor, as we serve others and share our resources generously, we will find ourselves surrounded by God's love as well. We will find ourselves at home with God.

Heavenly Father, we long for home—to be with you in intimacy and comfort. We want to know the joy born of obedience and trust. Send your Holy Spirit to guide us in keeping your commandments so that you and your Son will make your home in our hearts. Amen.

SUNDAY, MAY 26 ~ *Read John 14:25-29*

Several years ago my husband and I went to Rome on vacation. We wanted to see the major tourist sites, and we wanted to make the most of our time there. We knew that Rome is a crowded city, so we hired a tour guide to show us around. It was a great decision. She took us to places at the Colosseum where tourists didn't have access. She interpreted the historical and cultural significance of the sites and told us things we would not have known to ask. She made our day in Rome more meaningful than if we had tried to do it on our own.

In today's passage, Jesus tells his disciples that he is going away, but that his Father will send them a guide—the Holy Spirit—to help them after he has gone. The Greek word *paraclete* literally translates as "one who comes alongside." English versions variously translate it as Advocate, Counselor, Comforter, or Encourager. Whatever word we use, the meaning remains: The Holy Spirit is one who guides, assists, and helps.

Just as we read in our first reading of the week, wherein the Holy Spirit guides Paul and his companions to Macedonia to share the good news, this Advocate—this Counselor—is available to guide us today. The Holy Spirit is a personal, indwelling guide to help us love God, stay close to God, remember Jesus' teachings, and remain in God's peace.

How do you need the assistance of the Advocate most right now? Do you need guidance? Do you need comforting? Do you need the power and ability to complete an overwhelming task? The Advocate comes alongside you to strengthen, encourage, and empower you.

Jesus, thank you for sending us the Advocate, the Holy Spirit, the one who helps us. Amen.

Discerning the Spirits

MAY 27–JUNE 2, 2019 • JACO LOUW

SCRIPTURE OVERVIEW: How did you first hear about the gospel? Was it from your family or a friend? Or was it from a completely unexpected source? This week's readings remind us that God uses many different techniques of revelation. Paul and Silas are in prison in Philippi, and the guard of the prison has no idea that he is about to encounter the power of God and come to faith. The psalmist says that creation itself reveals God's glory and power. In Revelation, Jesus speaks directly about his future return and reign, as attested by his messenger and by the Spirit. Jesus prays in John for his followers, because through their unity the gospel will be proclaimed to others. Although Jesus ascends to heaven, the revelation of his plan and purpose does not end.

QUESTIONS AND SUGGESTIONS FOR REFLECTION

- Read Acts 16:16-34. Recall a difficult time in your life. Were you able to continue to praise God through this time?
- Read Psalm 97. Write your own word picture of what it means to be a child of God, who is in control.
- Read Revelation 22:12-14, 16-17, 20-21. How has Jesus' invitation to partake of the water of life changed you?
- Read John 17:20-26. What signs of division do you see in your community? How can you work toward the oneness to which God calls us?

Methodist minister in sunny Durban, South Africa; passionate about ecumenism, spirituality, assisting those with addiction problems, and walking on the beach.

MONDAY, MAY 27 ~ *Read Acts 16:16-24*

Today's reading consists of many layers of past experiences and future expectations laced with the role that business concerns and cultural norms play in the eventual imprisonment of Paul and Silas.

A woman with a divining spirit follows Paul and Silas for many days as they make their way in the city. This woman shouts out exactly who Paul and Silas are: "These people are servants of the Most High God! They are proclaiming a way of salvation to you!" (CEB). It is as if she senses something of the kingdom of God and has become a proclaimer of faith despite the still-raging darkness deep within her soul; she cannot help but tell all and sundry that salvation is at hand.

We do not know how genuine the woman with the divining spirit is. Does she make her proclamation about God and the apostles because she sincerely believes or because she sees a Spirit bigger than the one within her? We know that Paul discerns the "wrong" spirit and commands it to leave the life and the body of the woman afflicted. We see some of God's grace-already-at-work in the life of this woman.

Today's reading speaks of the reality of Jesus and of what happens when fortunes are reversed. While we can only imagine what happens to the enslaved woman after Paul sends out the spirit, we know that her owners can no longer profit off her suffering. For that, Paul and Silas are thrown in jail. But it is only the beginning of the reversals their ministry will bring to this city.

Lord, help us to discern the voices around us from your true voice whispering deep within us. We ask in the name and Spirit of Jesus. Amen.

TUESDAY, MAY 28 ~ *Read Acts 16:25-34*

In today's reading, we find incredible descriptions of the difference in worldview that exist between Jews and Gentiles, between those enslaved to the ways of the world and those set free by faith in God.

Paul and Silas are imprisoned. They should be sulking at best or enraged at worst for their unfair treatment and imprisonment. Instead, we find them singing hymns of praise—at midnight! The result of their joy is mind-blowing; it causes an earthquake, and the prison doors swing open.

I wonder whether the earthquake and opened doors come about because of Paul and Silas's prayer and singing or whether these things come about because of their faith that God works according to God's holy and perfect will. In the scene that follows the earthquake, we find a description of how an entire household comes to faith in Jesus. We see, therefore, that the previous events (the enslaved woman's spirit, Paul and Silas's worship, and the earthquake) serve as catalysts for the jailer and his entire household to be baptized after they come to believe in God.

Recently, in Zimbabwe, President Robert Mugabe stepped down after nearly forty years in power. Many lauded his resignation and now hope for a more fair and humane government that "will sort out things." In a similar fashion, nations around the world often look for a reprieve from oppressive regimes. Let us remember, however, that God will only open our prison doors in order to serve God's kingdom purposes.

Holy God, we come into your presence to ask you to listen to the cries of the oppressed—those who are ill-treated, those who are being treated unfairly. We pray this in the name and Spirit of Jesus. Amen.

WEDNESDAY, MAY 29 ~ *Read Psalm 97*

In a world fraught with intrigue and composed of opposing parties often fighting for dominance, today's psalm comes as a refresher course in what God has in mind for us. The psalmist starts off by declaring, "The LORD rules!" (CEB) and then goes on to describe exactly what this rule looks like.

We often think that the Jewish people of the Hebrew scriptures believe that only they are God's chosen people. The islands mentioned in the Common English Bible version of the text refer to other non-Jewish nations while the clouds and thick darkness surrounding God are reminiscent of the events surrounding the giving of the Law to Moses at Mount Sinai. The implication is clear: God is as much the God of other nations as the God of Israel.

The words *righteousness* and *righteous* occur four times in this psalm and reveal one of God's attributes. The psalmist considers righteousness so powerful and so life-changing that the psalmist likens it to a fire melting mountains and a violent thunderstorm. The message once again is clear: God is king and God is in control. Nothing stands before God's power.

When I was about seven or eight years old, our family went up Table Mountain in Cape Town by cable car. I wasn't scared, and I remember some of the magnificent views the city and environs offered. Psalm 97 is like that; it offers us a word picture of what it means to be a child of God.

The closing lines emphasize the discerning marks of God's redemptive promises in the life of those who belong to God, saying: "Light is planted like seed for the righteous person; joy too for those whose heart is right" (CEB).

Lord, we thank you for mountaintop experiences in our lives as we continue to follow you. Amen.

THURSDAY, MAY 30 ~ *Read Ephesians 1:15-23*

ASCENSION DAY

In our reading on Monday, we read how Paul's discernment leads to a confrontation between the Spirit of Jesus and a false spirit. Yet we can also understand this moment as one of the fresh beginnings of the early church, the becoming-one of Jew and Gentile through God's grace-that-went-before.

For the last few years in South Africa, we have struggled with the debilitating symptoms of many deep-seated attitudes and hurts left unresolved from the past. In today's reading the writer speaks of having heard of the Ephesians' faith and love toward all God's people and then says the following: "I pray that the God of our Lord Jesus Christ, the Father of glory, will give you a spirit of wisdom and revelation that makes God known to you" (CEB).

As in the life of Paul and the enslaved woman, and as was the case in the early Christ-following community in Ephesus, and as is the case in present-day South Africa, the writer's call is clear: We are called to unity in and through the Holy Spirit, but we can only authentically be so and do so if we have a discerning and loving spirit. The question begs to be answered: "How can we be more discerning followers of Christ?"

As we remember the ascension of Jesus today, we remember that it serves as a reminder that he has been where we still need to go. As we know and follow the ascended Jesus, we shall receive a spirit of wisdom and revelation. Discernment, therefore, finds its root in a solid relationship with Jesus when we allow his presence and influence to fill all of our life.

Holy Jesus, we invite your life-giving Spirit to fill and empower our whole being. We pray that your Spirit shall connect with our spirit. Amen.

FRIDAY, MAY 31 ~ *Read John 17:20-26*

I still remember very well one of the first racially integrated church services I and some members of our predominantly white church attended. South Africa was emerging slowly from years of forced racial segregation, and people from all levels of society were talking together, sharing together, and worshiping together. As we made our way toward an Easter Sunday evening service, my heart was throbbing in my throat, and I was looking forward to the service with bated breath. Things turned out well that evening, and I cherish those memories. Things for our country, however, have not always been that great; poverty continues to increase, and inequality is on the rise.

One thing has kept me going over the years: I look for signs of God's kingdom. I always attempt to discern signs of the unity among God's people, regardless of denominational affiliation.

In our reading today, we hear some of Jesus' special prayer to his Father. Jesus asks that everyone who believes in him be one. He then continues to say that his people have been called to unity so that the world may believe that his Father has sent him.

I always have held firmly to the opinion that says: "Where there is division, Christ is not." For me, one of the kingdom-signs is our ability to work, love, and co-exist side-by-side as God's children.

Attending a racially diverse church has led me to laboring among people from different denominations, faiths, and backgrounds. The welcome I received that Easter evening humbled me and showed me that God's *basileia* (kingdom) is and can be a reality, even when it seems as if negativity might gain the upper hand. So, let's stand together and know that we worship one Lord, who is God and Father of all.

Holy Father, Son, and Spirit: We confess that you are three in one and one in three. Help us to follow you through our words, thoughts, and actions. Help us to become instruments of unity among your people. Amen.

SATURDAY, JUNE 1 ~ *Read Revelation 22:12-14, 16-17, 20-21*

I once spoke to a person who told me that she refuses to read Revelation. When I asked her why, she told me that all the violent imagery and scenes of death and destruction scare her so much that she cannot motivate herself to read it.

Just as Genesis tells the story of creation, so Revelation tells a story of re-creation. We can talk about Revelation as a kind of measuring stick that clearly points out the good, the bad, and the ugly within us and around us. This magnificent piece of literary art, however, is far more significant and life-giving than a mere instrument for blaming and shaming. We can read Revelation as a love letter that gives us a final and important clue in discerning what true salvation looks like. Verse 14 of today's reading speaks about people washing their robes. This scene alludes to the process of getting rid of all things that stand between us and a healthy relationship with the risen and living Jesus.

We find the most powerful message of today's reading in verse 17, where the author invites anyone who wishes to take the water of life as a gift. None of the characters in this scene (Jesus, the Spirit, or the bride) orders or coerces us; we are invited to partake of the life Jesus has in mind for us and walk with him. That is true *metanoia* or repentance. Once we drink from the water of life, we truly are blessed by the One who offers it—Jesus the Christ.

God, thank you for sending us your Son so that we can see what it means to be fully human. Jesus, thank you for the water of life that flows from you in which we can wash our old selves and from which we can drink life abundant. Amen.

SUNDAY, JUNE 2 ~ *Read John 17:20-26*

Over the years, I have learned that I will never forget books or plays that continuously repeat the same thing over and over. Even Hollywood has learned the lesson of repetition. Think of lines like "I'll be back" from the Terminator movies or "In a galaxy far, far away" in the Star Wars movies or "Wax on, wax off" in 1984's *The Karate Kid*. We remember these movies in part because of these repeated lines.

In today's reading, Jesus keeps saying the same thing but using different words with each repetition. It is as if he holds a cut diamond in front of him and lets each facet manifest the different nuances of God's will.

Jesus prays for those who believe in him because of the testimony of those who have had a firsthand experience with him. He then asks that these two groups be one and undivided, as he and his Father are one and undivided.

Not long after Jesus prays these words, the ever-widening rift between Christian Jew and Christian Gentile becomes problematic. Despite the work of Paul and Barnabas, this rift is only partially solved by the first council in Jerusalem. (See Acts 15.)

Since the advent of democracy in South Africa, the widening gulf between rich and poor is of concern to many. However, there always has been the realization that all are one in and through Christ. May we all pray Jesus' prayer as we seek unity with him and among ourselves, thereby giving glory to God.

Dear God of all whom you create, help us to seek unity among your children. In the name of Jesus Christ, the One who prays for us. Amen.

Awaiting the Spirit

JUNE 3–9, 2019 • MICHAEL E. WILLIAMS

SCRIPTURE OVERVIEW: In preparing for Pentecost, we focus again on the work of the Holy Spirit. Acts 2 recounts the famous story in which the disciples are miraculously able to speak in other languages in order to preach to the crowds in Jerusalem. The psalmist states that God creates and renews creation through the Spirit. According to Paul, if we are led by God's Spirit, the Spirit confirms that we are children of God. In the Gospel of John, Jesus promises to send the Helper, the Holy Spirit, who will teach us how to love him and to keep his commandments. In some branches of Christianity, fear of excess causes hesitation about the Holy Spirit; however, we must never forget that the Spirit is central to God's redeeming work.

QUESTIONS AND SUGGESTIONS FOR REFLECTION

- Read Acts 2:1-21. The miracle of Pentecost is not only in the multitude of languages but also in the act of listening. How can you experience worship in many languages or offer deep listening this Pentecost?
- Read Psalm 104:24-34, 35b. How do you witness God's experience woven through all of creation?
- Read Romans 8:14-17. The author reminds us that *spirit* also means *breath*. When have you felt led by the breath of God?
- Read John 14:8-17, 25-27. How has fear kept you from trusting God?

Retired pastor, Tennessee Conference of the United Methodist Church; Writer/Storyteller-in-Residence at Martin Methodist College; author of *Spoken into Being*. Michael Williams died during the production of this volume.

MONDAY, JUNE 3 ~ *Read Psalm 104:24-34, 35b*

I love to go hiking in the Nashville area's many parks. Our city offers the blessing of many public parks both within the city limits and nearby. I experience a sense of peace and belonging as I walk along a trail and look at the sunlight slipping around the trees' limbs and dappling the leaf-blanketed ground as far as I can see. I feel at home and at peace.

I think I feel such a sense of peace in the woods because I grew up in a rural area and spent many days walking through the woods exploring the area near our home. As I explored, I would let my imagination run free, seeing in my mind's eye the original inhabitants and early settlers in the land where I lived. I became familiar with the trees and flowers that surrounded me. Occasionally I would happen upon an abandoned car or house. Preachers in the churches where I grew up did not talk much about God's presence in creation. Rather, the Creator of all that is taught me about the many and varied ways that the creation speaks. I know that each leaf, each tree, and each stone reflects the greatness of God. I know that the imagination that allows me to enter in to that environment is a gift from God as well.

The sense of being centered and at peace and at home that I feel as I wander the woods today—well, we know where that comes from too. Psalm 104 reminds us that God not only made everything, but the presence of the Creator is woven through all creation. All we are and all we have are gifts from God and speak of God. Today when I hike I know whom to thank for everything that surrounds me.

God of all creation, help me listen for your good news in all the places and things of earth. Amen.

TUESDAY, JUNE 4 ~ *Read John 14:8-17*

The older I grow the more I resemble both my mother and my father. When I look in the mirror I see many of my father's features in my own face. He once said to me that the Williams family had strong characteristics. He was correct about that. Once, after I told stories at a church near where I grew up, an older man came up to me and said, "You're Tid Williams's grandson, aren't you?" My grandfather died before I was born. I never met him. Still, this man recognized my grandfather in me.

My personality is more like my mother's. I love people, and I love to talk. While my father was very reserved, almost a recluse, my mother was gregarious. She told me many times that the Cherrys (her family) "talked to hear their heads rattle." Even many of my mannerisms are like hers.

Both my mother and my father are "in" me. When you look at me you see them because I embody so many of their characteristics. Looking at the human traits we inherit from our parents may help us understand what Jesus says to his followers. When Jesus says the Father is in him and he is in the Father, he is suggesting that when we look at Jesus we see God.

God comes to us as one of us in Jesus. If we want a snapshot of who the God of Jesus is, all we have to do is look at the person, life, and teachings of Jesus. Jesus embodies the God of love. Perhaps this is the reason that writers in the early church claimed that Jesus was both fully human and fully divine.

God, whom we see in Jesus, help us to embody your love. Amen.

WEDNESDAY, JUNE 5 ~ *Read Romans 8:14-17*

When I was a boy I was afraid of the dark. We lived in a trailer, behind which we had built a small cinder block house with a washing machine, tools, and storage. Occasionally, my mother asked me to go out to "the little house" to get something for her after dark. I always hesitated.

As I walked the thirty yards between the trailer and the house, I would imagine fearsome creatures and people hiding along the way and hands (or claws) coming out of the darkness to grab me. So, I would always ask my mom to watch me as I walked through the darkness. Just the fact that she was willing to look out the tiny kitchen window above the sink in the trailer brought me courage. I knew that if I turned to look behind me, I would see her face illuminated by the kitchen light, smiling, waving, urging me on. She never turned away from that window. Knowing that my mother was watching over me gave me the courage to walk to the little house and retrieve whatever she had asked me to bring her.

The courage it took to do what my mother asked came from knowing that she was present with me and watching over me, just like God does for all of us. God does not want us to be enslaved to a spirit of fear, a spirit that keeps us from doing what we are asked to do by God. Like my mother, God is watching over us to comfort us and give us courage as we make the journey through the darkness, through our fear, to do what God asks us to do.

Ever-present God, help me know that you are watching over me so that I will not be enslaved by my fear. Amen.

THURSDAY, JUNE 6 ~ *Read Romans 8:14-17*

In both Greek and Hebrew one word means spirit, wind, and breath. When Paul writes that God's Spirit witnesses with our spirit that we are children of God, he describes a kind of conspiracy—a breathing together—between God and us. To conspire simply means to breathe together.

As a theater student I learned a number of improvisational games that we played as a group. To play one of those games, called "parts of a whole" or "machine," each person makes a particular sound or action. In short, we created a machine with our bodies, with each part having its particular sound or motion like no other part but moving in rhythm with all the other parts. We could speed the machine up or slow it down at the very same rate. Sometimes the person instructing the game would ask us to slow the machine until it stopped. Then he or she would tell us to begin again all together "on the breath." This meant that all of the parts of this machine (the players) had to listen carefully to the breathing of all the others. Once our breathing synchronized, we could begin to move once again all at the same time. When that happened it was magic.

I wonder what it would be like to pay such close attention to God that our breath synchronized with God's breath, our desires and hopes synchronized with God's desires and hopes for us and for the world. At that point we could enter into a truly divine conspiracy, our breath witnessing with God's breath that we, and all people, are God's beloved children.

God, who breathed into us the breath of life, help me synchronize my breath, wishes, hopes, and desires with yours. Amen.

FRIDAY, JUNE 7 ~ *Read John 14:25-27*

Jesus tells his followers not to be afraid as he prepares them for a time when he will no longer physically be present with them. Not because there isn't plenty for them to be afraid of. After all, look what happens to Jesus. He will be arrested, tried, whipped, and crucified. The powers of that time could do a lot to make people suffer. Jesus knows this. Instead, it seems that Jesus is concerned with the kind of people into which fear could turn his followers.

When we are afraid we become suspicious of others, sometimes even paranoid. When we are afraid we look for other people to blame for our fear, and too often we hate, revile, and demonize those whom we blame. Jesus doesn't want his followers to fall into that trap. He knows that the only antidote for fear is love.

In this passage, Jesus ups the ante, as he often does with his followers. Not only does he tell those whom he loves not to be afraid. He instructs them not to let their hearts be troubled by the circumstances that might otherwise prod them into that fearful place. Jesus replaces fear and a troubled heart with a sense of trust in the God of love and in himself as he has revealed that loving God to them. Jesus knows that fear stems from deep distrust and that the troubled heart leads us to do things we would never do otherwise.

Trusting in God allows us to begin to trust in others, which is a step toward loving others as Jesus loves us. Jesus offers us an escape from slavery to freedom—freedom from fear and a troubled heart and from the kind of destructive behavior fear cultivates.

Trustworthy God, help us to leave our fear and troubled hearts behind as we learn to trust in you. Amen.

SATURDAY, JUNE 8 ~ *Read Acts 2:1-4*

Pentecost did not begin as a Christian holiday. The followers of Jesus gather together to await the visitation of the Spirit that Jesus promised, but hundreds and perhaps thousands of other Jewish people from across the world have come to Jerusalem to celebrate the Jewish holiday *Shavuot,* or the Feast of Weeks, which was called *Pentecost* in Greek. The Greek name is based on the word for fifty because this holiday comes fifty days after Passover.

Too often when Christians read Acts 2 we focus on the fact that the disciples speak in languages that are not native to them and that they have never studied. As remarkable as that experience must be, it is incomplete, however, unless there is someone to hear and to understand the words of the languages they speak. Perhaps the greater miracle of Pentecost is that people from many countries who speak many languages hear the good news of God's love for them in a language each can understand. Perhaps listening and comprehending belongs at the heart of our celebration of Pentecost.

In our day and time we don't listen to each other very carefully. Often we listen in a distracted fashion or only partially as we prepare our response. Perhaps the best way we can celebrate Pentecost as Christians is to open our ears, to focus our minds, and to listen deeply to those around us. We might hear some comments that disturb us as well as some words that encourage us. We might hear some things that make us sad as well as some that give us joy. But if the heart of Pentecost lies in listening, may listening become the spiritual practice at the heart of who we are as the followers of Jesus, just as it did on that Shavuot long ago.

Speaking God, help me to listen for your voice in the voices of others. Amen.

PENTECOST

While I was serving as pastor at Blakemore United Methodist Church in Nashville, Tennessee, the congregation welcomed into their space a congregation of Rwandan refugees who had come to the United States to escape genocide. Ordinarily the Rwandan congregation's services were conducted on Sunday afternoon, so they used the sanctuary in the afternoons after the Blakemore UMC congregation held our services in the mornings.

Hutus and Tutsis attended the Rwandan services. If they had been in Rwanda, these two groups might have been stirred up to kill one another. That was exactly what had been happening in their homeland because of hatred that was tearing them apart. Instead, they gathered in a sanctuary to thank God for the love that binds them (and all of us) together. It was a remarkable experience to attend a service conducted in a number of different languages, including French, English, and several Rwandan languages.

One day the Rwandan pastor, Boniface Senturo, called me to plan a revival for the Saturday evening before Pentecost Sunday. On that Saturday night my Rwandan colleague called to tell me that the evangelist's plane had been delayed. He asked if they could change the time to Sunday morning, when the Blakemore congregation met. They were willing to have it in the fellowship hall, so the two services were scheduled for the same time.

At Blakemore, the fellowship hall is immediately beneath the sanctuary. We conducted our usual Pentecost service upstairs, and each time we paused for silence we heard the sounds of singing from the revival just below us. That multitude of languages wafting up through the floor bringing peace to people who otherwise might be harming each other meant that on that Sunday we had a true experience of Pentecost.

God of all people, help me listen for your good news in those who are different from me. Amen.

God Delights in You!

JUNE 10–16, 2019 • STEVE HARPER

SCRIPTURE OVERVIEW: In our society we often privilege intellect and expertise. However, in Proverbs we read that God values wisdom. Wisdom has been present since the beginning, and some early theologians understand this Wisdom to be none other than the Son of God. Part of wisdom is understanding our place in the universe. The psalmist marvels at the vast display of God's power in the heavens yet also recognizes that humans are a manifestation of God's glory. The New Testament readings invoke the Trinity as we approach Trinity Sunday. Paul says that we have peace with God through Christ, and we are given the Holy Spirit. In John, Jesus Christ has received everything from the Father, and the Spirit will guide his followers into all truth.

QUESTIONS AND SUGGESTIONS FOR REFLECTION

- Read Proverbs 8:1-4, 22-31. When have you heard God calling out to you?
- Read Psalm 8. The author reminds us that our shortcomings are not because we are *only* human, but because we fall short of our humanity. How do you strive to be *more* human—a little lower than God?
- Read Romans 5:1-5. How do you allow God's peace to calm you when you feel your life swirling around you?
- Read John 16:12-15. To which person of the Trinity do you feel "closest"? How can you develop your relationship with the other two persons?

Retired Elder in the Florida Annual Conference of The United Methodist Church; retired Professor of Spiritual Formation and Wesley Studies.

MONDAY, JUNE 10 ~ *Read Proverbs 8:1-4, 22-31*

Sadly, we have done a good job using religion in general and Christianity in particular to give people the idea that God is mad at them. Over the years, I have met person after person (including professing Christians) who feel that God is fed up with them—on the verge of saying, "I've had it with you!" and walking away. If they stick with religion at all, they practice it as a never-ending, performance-oriented attempt to show God they are spiritual and worthy of love. Truth be told, I have felt that way myself sometimes.

The problem is that this is not what the biblical story says. Rather than saying God is mad at us, the Bible says God is madly in love with us. It says that God delights in us. Every reading this week provides us with some aspect of God's delight.

Today's passage from Proverbs tells us that God has delighted in us from the beginning. Wisdom says, "I was having fun, smiling before [the Lord] all the time, frolicking with his inhabited earth and delighting in the human race" (CEB). We all exist in the context of smiling and frolicking. God's delight in us is fun and eternal.

In theological language, we call this "original righteousness." It is the story recorded in Genesis 1–2, before original sin in Genesis 3 altered the picture. Original righteousness is the starting point for God's understanding of us. Along with everything else God made, we are good. We are made in the image of God. From the beginning until now, we put a smile on God's face and set God's feet to dancing!

Meditation: Imagine walking into the holy Presence and seeing God smile at you. How does that make you feel?

TUESDAY, JUNE 11 ~ *Read Proverbs 8:1*

For every negative word spoken to us, it takes many more positive words to compensate for the pain. Words that hurt do great damage and last a long time despite any accompanying healing words.

Maybe that's why our reading from Proverbs begins with the words, "Doesn't Wisdom cry out and Understanding shout?" (CEB). Over against the negative signals we receive and carry around with us, God turns up the volume so we can hear the truth. God shouts to get our attention.

We have all raised our voices to make a point or get across an important message. Others know we really mean it when we speak louder. When it comes to life-and-death crises and emergencies, we call out even louder. Pay attention! Watch out! Get this! Listen up!

We read yesterday that God has delighted in us from the beginning—smiling, playing, and dancing as we came into existence. Today, we discover that God's delight is no small thing. It is something to be exclaimed. The writer of Proverbs uses words to paint a picture of God crying out to us, Whatever you do, don't fail to hear that I delight in you! Don't allow anyone or anything to make you think otherwise!

Since we have never met, I have no idea how often others speak negatively to or about you. All of us have received negative messages about us at one time or another. Some of us have heard we're "no good" for so long and in so many ways that we now tell ourselves the lie. Today, God comes shouting, Don't you believe it! I delight in you!

***Meditation:** Cling to God's positive words and dump the negative ones others have said to you.*

WEDNESDAY, JUNE 12 ~ *Read Psalm 8*

In verse 4, the psalmist ponders why God would even pay attention to us. Out of genuine appreciation for God's attention, the psalmist poses a staggering answer: We are only "a little lower than God." This answer reminds us that God's delight in us is real, not imaginary.

This revelation has the potential to destroy us or to give us life. Recognizing our closeness to God becomes destructive when it makes us prideful, when it inflates our ego with arrogance, and when it lets us envision ourselves a caricature of humanity. Paul describes this as thinking too highly of ourselves (see Romans 12:3), and we now recognize such self-aggrandizing as a deadly sin.

Yet there is no virtue in thinking too lowly of ourselves. God delights in us so much that we are crowned with glory and honor and have been given this earth. The psalmist's discovery strikes the proper balance—we are not God, but we are made in the image of God. Locating ourselves here saves us from pride on the one hand and despair on the other. "A little lower than God" is precisely what it means to be human.

Sometimes a person will say, "Don't blame me—I'm only human!" But that's wrong. Our problem is not that we are human, it is that we are not human enough. Living beneath our nature, falling short of our potential to be a little lower than God, leads us to say such things. Our first task is not to become Christian but rather to become human—to claim our sacred worth and let God delight in us.

Meditation: Dare to believe you are of inestimable worth to God. Then pray for the grace to acknowledge your sacred humanity and to become who you already are.

THURSDAY, JUNE 13 ~ *Read Romans 5:1-2*

When I was a child, one of my favorite toys was a small snow globe. When I shook it, the snowflakes swirled around so much that they nearly hid from view the skier in the middle of the globe. Only when I stopped shaking the globe and held it still so the flakes settled to the bottom could I see the skier clearly.

Today, Paul sheds light on our response in knowing we are God's delight. He says we have peace through God's faithfulness given to us through our Lord Jesus Christ. Jesus comes to us and stops the swirling that keeps our lives clouded and confused. Our response is peace. We no longer have to be agitated by the lies others have told us or by those we tell ourselves.

This peace not only makes us calm, important as that is, but grants us "access to this grace in which we stand." We can see the skier! We see ourselves as we truly are.

When I think of the word *access*, I think of an open road, a formerly blocked highway now open for traffic. God's peace opens the way for us to move past the lies and into the truth, the truth that God delights in us. God's peace abides in our hearts. It rises above our understanding (see Philippians 4:7) and surpasses whatever agitation we feel.

The traditional American spiritual says it well: "He's got the whole world in his hands." The shaking has stopped, and we can see ourselves as we really are. The noise has subsided, and we can feel God's peace.

Meditation: Sit quietly and whisper to yourself, "Peace with God through our Lord Jesus Christ." Feel God's grace.

FRIDAY, JUNE 14 ~ *Read Romans 5:3-5*

When we experience the peace that comes in knowing God delights in us, we have a place to stand for facing all life's adversities. We can find strength in knowing God's love for us. Paul describes our strength in an interesting sequence, a kind of upward spiral: suffering, endurance, character, and hope. With the peace and strength of God's love, our problems become pathways rather than pitfalls.

When Holocaust survivor Victor Frankl was a prisoner of war, he observed his own suffering and the suffering of those around him. In his book published in English as *Man's Search for Meaning*, he recorded that those who fared best in the midst of suffering were those who did not lose hope—an observation very close to what Paul says in today's reading.

The most mature people of faith I know have grown in ways that include "going against the odds." They do not wear their suffering on their sleeve, but they carry it in their heart. Because they know God delights in them, they continue to have hope in the midst of problems and pains.

Paul says this hope is not theoretical; it is concrete in real-life situations. It is not superficial or fleeting; it is deep and abiding because "God's love has been poured into our hearts through the Holy Spirit."

Meditation: How have you experienced the strength of hope through periods of suffering?

SATURDAY, JUNE 15 ~ *Read John 16:12-15*

We ended yesterday's reading thinking about the Holy Spirit, and we pick right back up with the Spirit today. The Gospel lesson for this week falls within the larger context of Jesus' teaching about the Holy Spirit, which begins in John 14:16. The Holy Spirit's presence offers the ultimate proof that God delights in us. Jesus calls forth the revelation of truth, and the Spirit guides us into the truth.

Robert Boyd Munger's booklet *My Heart, Christ's Home* describes this process. Comparing our heart to a many-roomed house, we might see Jesus enter and move about room-by-room, renovating our lives—including the closet at the top of the stairs where we have locked away our secrets. This total life transformation, according to Munger's Jesus, is because "I value your fellowship."* Munger has Jesus articulate what we've been learning all week: God delights in us.

Jesus describes the unfolding process of how we will come to know God's love for us: The Spirit will proclaim to us what Jesus has said and done. The Spirit "takes" whatever part of Jesus' words and deeds we need to know and declares it to us. We are never overwhelmed with everything at once; the Spirit moves us step-by-step into the experience of amazing grace.

---

*Robert Boyd Munger, *My Heart, Christ's Home* (Downers Grove, IL: InterVarsity Press, 1986), 28.

Meditation: What particular aspects of God's grace have you been given by the Spirit at just the time you needed them?

Trinity Sunday

Today is Trinity Sunday. The Holy Trinity is Christianity's most distinctive offering to religion about the nature and activity of God. We struggle to explain the doctrine fully, but God reveals it to us clearly. Today's reading serves as one example of its revelation: In just two verses, the Son references the work of the Spirit and the dominion of the Father.

Trinity Sunday helps us wrap up our exploration of God's delight, for in the various daily readings we have read how each person of the Trinity reveals God's delight in us. The readings in Psalms and Proverbs refer us to God. In Romans, Paul opens the lens wider to include "our Lord Jesus Christ." And the Gospel lesson describes the actions and relationships of all three persons of the Trinity.

This means the whole Godhead delights in us. Father, Son, and Holy Spirit together. God's delight does not vary from one member of the Trinity to the next. Through and through we are God's delight.

The Trinity's symbiosis is important. Some Christians feel "closer" to one person of the Trinity than another. But we end our meditations this week knowing we do not have to pick and choose. God's delight is found comprehensively in the Trinity. God's steadfast love surrounds us and sustains us.

Meditation: Approach each person of the Trinity in your heart. What do you want to say to the Father about God's delight in you? To the Son? To the Spirit? Perhaps you might end up singing the hymn "Holy, Holy, Holy" or at least this much, "God in three persons, blessed Trinity" (UMH, no. 64).

Between Fear and Faith

JUNE 17–23, 2019 • CHELSEY D. HILLYER

SCRIPTURE OVERVIEW: The fact that we trust in God does not guarantee that life will be easy. Believers suffer discouragement as well. Elijah is a powerful prophet of God who faces profound discouragement. He looks around and sees faithlessness and desolation, as does the psalmist wrestling with his own sense of despair. In both cases the person's spirit is revived—by divine visitation to Elijah and by the psalmist's self-talk about the truth of God's faithfulness. The New Testament readings take us in a different direction. Paul speaks of the freedom we have when we are in Christ, heirs to all of God's promises. The Gospel writer tells of another kind of freedom, the freedom experienced by a man delivered from demon possession.

QUESTIONS AND SUGGESTIONS FOR REFLECTION

- Read 1 Kings 19:1-15a. Recall a time you ran to a silent place. How did God send you back into the world?
- Read Psalm 42. The author asks us to imagine the words of this psalm coming from the mouth of Elijah and the Gerasene man. Consider how these words might be yours as well.
- Read Galatians 3:23-29. How does your faith in Christ help you to embrace the freedom that comes from lack of division rather than to flee in fear?
- Read Luke 8:26-39. What true story do you have to tell to the world of what Jesus has done for you?

Elder, Missouri Annual Conference of the United Methodist Church; passionate Midwesterner who loves to garden, paint, and have dance parties with her spouse and daughter; writes at www.chelseyhillyer.com.

MONDAY, JUNE 17 ~ *Read 1 Kings 19:1-9a*

It's disappointing, isn't it? The way that Elijah flees from Jezebel. The way he seems to believe his life may really be in her hands and not God's.

Hasn't he seen the Lord heal the sick? Doesn't he shame the Israelites who run after lesser gods? Hasn't he won a barbecue contest against all the prophets of Baal using only wet wood? I want for Elijah to be better than this. Better than running from a simple threat. Better than spending a night under a scraggly bush and begging for his own death.

I want to hear a story of triumph over Jezebel. I want to hear of how Elijah stands up to Jezebel and how the Lord set things right. I thirst for this story. I hunger for this story. But no messenger of the Lord sets down what I long for, telling me to wake, to eat, to drink.

Fear makes Elijah run. Elijah is human. And I'm disappointed. I want Elijah to be better than me. Because if Elijah cannot stay and face Jezebel, how can I face cruelty and injustice in the world? How can I oppose the forces and rulers who hold people captive from their own lives?

I peer out from beneath my own broom bush to read this passage, and I long for a different story. I want a hero, not a simple prophet. I want certainty, not a crisis of faith.

But this is the story we have. Elijah fears. Elijah flees. I want to resist it, to flee myself, but something pushes me to look again. Is there nourishment here? More than what I want, is this story what I truly need?

Lord, help me to long for what you offer, not just what I desire. Amen.

TUESDAY, JUNE 18 ~ *Read Psalm 42:1-5*

If you listen closely, you can almost hear Elijah whispering these words. Can you imagine him sprawling under a bush or wandering on his forty-day and -night journey to Horeb going over and over recent events in his mind? *My whole being thirsts for the living God. When will I come to see God's face?* An angel provides food and water, but Elijah remains convicted by the question that hangs in his heart, Where is your God now?

A lament psalm isn't simply a sad prayer. It's a call for help. But whom does the psalmist call upon? Who, exactly, is expected to bring help?

The psalm moves ever inward, from remembrances of joy in the presence of God to the painful questions of the present. *Why,* I ask myself, *are you so depressed?* It is as if by drawing a straight line from joy to sorrow, the distance between them could be bridged: Loneliness could bloom into connection, and isolation could melt into reunion. Hope in God! The psalm demands of itself, as if by shaking itself hard enough hope will pop out of the desolation in which it is lost. And yet, there is awareness that what is really needed is God. Not just memories of God but the living God.

How often are we stuck in our own laments of self? I imagine Elijah on his journey through the wilderness trying to self-diagnose and heal his lack of faith, when only an experience of God will set his heart right again.

When we lose our nerve or lose our faith, it is easy to become stuck within ourselves, trying to jump-start our faith internally. But is this really what God asks of us?

God, I long for you. Lead me in freedom to experience you today. Amen.

WEDNESDAY, JUNE 19 ~ *Read 1 Kings 19:9b-15a*

At least Elijah wasn't just running away. At least he wound up in the place we all do eventually when we've lost our own sense of faith or direction—in the presence of God, having to answer the question, "Why are you here?"

The question echoes throughout the cave and through Elijah's heart, as if there is someplace else the Lord might have expected him to be. Does God expect Elijah to be able to admit that fear set him on this journey?

Elijah tries out the stiff words of the speech he's composed for this moment. The language is flimsy and awkward: "I have been very zealous for the LORD, the God of hosts." He must know how flimsy it sounds. And yet he tries it again, this time into God's very face. This time, he speaks it into the silence that allows for no illusions.

Why is Elijah here? Because God saved him. That's why. Because when Elijah flees without food or drink, messengers of the Lord keep him alive, giving him food, water, and direction, even when he has no will to seek it on his own.

If Elijah is asking for protection, his request is not clear. For instead of further respite, the Lord sends him back to the world of human politics, back to the work of a prophet.

In the silent place we come to after fleeing what we fear, God will not hesitate to send us back into the world. God's need for our action is greater than our human need to feel safe. But sometimes we need the noise of our doubts and voices of our enemies to be silenced in order to figure that out.

Lord, help me to find the silence that will send me back into the world. Amen.

Jesus meets him as soon as Jesus gets out of the boat. By now, Jesus must be accustomed to welcome parades made up of people in need of healing. But this man approaches him with suspicion, not supplication, with the expectation of torture, not of teaching.

His fear is not unfounded. The man has been separated from his community and himself. Far from free, he has been chained and set apart when his demon has raged within him; at least until he escapes to the wilderness to wander amongst the tombs. He expects nothing different from Jesus. Fear and isolation will do that to a person.

But instead of the man begging for his life, the demon begs Jesus not to send it back. Liberator that he is, Jesus frees the demon to its fate, to drown in the bodies of pigs.

Do not be surprised when those whose communities have harmed them in the name of helping are suspicious of the motives of Jesus' followers. Do not be surprised when someone you meet asks not for healing but instead for you to help them to destroy what keeps them from wholeness.

Where is the lake of Galilee in your community? What boundary might you need to cross to come into contact with those who live in isolation? Chances are, you know. What unspoken force keeps you away? Would you be able to overcome the suspicion that you are there to do harm? Would you be able to do good?

These are not flippant questions. They are the ones that Jesus' actions hold up to his disciples as a mirror. Do we have any genuine help to offer those who suffer in our community without harming them with what *we* think they need? And will we offer help?

Jesus, guide me to the places where you would go. May I be a force of healing and not of bondage. Amen.

FRIDAY, JUNE 21 ~ *Read Psalm 42:6-11*

If you listen closely, you can almost hear the Gerasene man whispering these words. How often has he come to the shoreline and thought about throwing his body into the waters of the deep that beckon him with the promise of an end to his torture and isolation? How often does he wonder why God has forgotten him?

The psalm continues to turn inward, to rehearse a script to share with God upon meeting: *Why do I have to walk around sad, oppressed by enemies?* What keeps us from actually taking this prayer to God? What keeps us turning it around within ourselves instead? We come back again, to the refrain of hope, as if this is the only way to approach God.

I know so many people who move through life this way. Sometimes I am one of them. To bring to light what is heavy and hard, what is depressed and sad can seem like an impossible task. The risk of ridicule, the potential for shame, the possibility of relationships cut off because of an inability to relate can keep many in silence about feeling lost and disconnected. It's easier to hide behind hope than it is to own our despair.

But what healing is possible when someone hears us! The psalmist takes the time to write down these words as a way to say, "Me too. If you've felt this way, know that you're not alone."

We know that God does not expect us to dwell in our own negative emotions. Yet easily we forget. The caring and radical acts of listening, of presence, of non-judgment can be like coming face-to-face with God. Connecting with others connects us to God. How might you be called to connect today?

God, help me to connect with someone today. Remind me that I am never alone. Amen.

SATURDAY, JUNE 22 ~ *Read Luke 8:37-39*

We know from Elijah's story earlier this week that our own fear can send us running. But here in Luke, we hear how fear can also chase off what would free us from fear. The Gerasenes, having witnessed a miracle, promptly ask Jesus to leave.

And in the midst of it all, the man who has been restored is lost again. He has not belonged in his community for many years. And he begs to find community amongst the disciples.

Perhaps the man feels fear himself, since his own restoration is the impetus for the community's fear. *Will they focus their fear on him in Jesus' absence? Could he find safety with Jesus?* But Jesus does not take in the man, does not pull him aboard the boat with a pat on the back and an embrace. Instead, Jesus sends him back into the community that exiled him.

This moment echoes Elijah's story: The Lord sends Elijah to continue his work as a prophet. Elijah is equipped only with his experience of God. Jesus sends the Gerasene back to his community, equipped only with his story of what Jesus has done for him.

How vulnerable he must have felt, watching Jesus' boat disappear into the horizon. How exposed—even more than when he walked the tombs naked and suffering. But he turns anyway and goes throughout the city proclaiming the good news for him and for all.

The power of a true story sets us free from our own inward-facing fears and from our fear of others. A true story of mercy and healing cuts through cynicism and fear in ways that a heroic tale cannot—by connecting humanity to our true identities in God rather than portraying us as gods.

Jesus, don't allow me to hide in fear. Send me back to the world to tell my true story. Amen.

SUNDAY, JUNE 23 ~ *Read Galatians 3:23-29*

Paul roots us firmly in our God-given identities: We are God's children, no exceptions; heirs to God's promises throughout the generations as those who have been given the gift of faith.

With the old lines of division removed, what will we do with such freedom? Will we claim the inheritance of a tradition that promises life? Or will we scramble in fear, clambering for safety in rules and laws?

Faith comes with the gift of hope. It flickers at the edge of these questions and invites us to claim it. Hope, not forced, but offered. Hope as an invitation, not a demand. Paul writes, "But now that faith has come, we are no longer subject to a disciplinarian." This freedom offers comfort in some ways. But it also requires us to manage our own fears, to find the tenuous balance between fear and hope that all people of faith seek.

We know that we will not do this perfectly. Sometimes fear will send us running. But faith comes bubbling up; whether in silence or in remembering, in restoration or in retelling, hope remains. We need only master the fear that keeps us from gripping this gift of faith with everything we have and from allowing all markers of status to fall away as we trust that our identity in Christ is enough. We will be fed, we will be given water, we will be given direction, we will be restored, we will be sent back to tell our stories. This is the way of faith as it always has been and always will be.

God of Abraham, Elijah, Jesus, and the Gerasene man, thank you for the gift of faith. Help me to cling to it more fully from today onward. Amen.

Investing in Others

JUNE 24–30, 2019 • JOHN A. FISCHER

SCRIPTURE OVERVIEW: This week's readings open with the dramatic scene of Elijah's departure. As the prophet is taken into heaven by fiery chariots, his cloak falls to his successor, Elisha—symbolic of the continuation of God's prophetic work. The psalmist praises the Lord for being the source of all good. The Lord gives guidance, protection, security, and joy. Paul reminds us that freedom in Christ comes with responsibility. We cannot live to satisfy our fleshly desires. If we live in the power of the Spirit, then our manner of life should stand out and bear godly fruit. In the Gospel reading, Jesus challenges his followers with the cost of discipleship. His statements here may seem extreme, but he is pointing out that we can be tempted to find excuses for not proclaiming the kingdom of God.

QUESTIONS AND SUGGESTIONS FOR REFLECTION

- Read 2 Kings 2:1-2, 6-14. When has fire—real or metaphorical—changed your life? How have you seen God working in this change?
- Read Psalm 16. Recall a time when you needed God's protection. How did you keep God in front of you?
- Read Galatians 5:1, 13-25. Along with our freedom, we are given a responsibility. How do you use your freedom to serve others?
- Read Luke 9:51-62. When have you heard Jesus' call to follow? What have you had to leave behind to follow the one who has "set his face to go to Jerusalem"?

Retired Financial Planner; Pastor Emeritus, United Christian Church (Disciples of Christ), Aberdeen, Washington.

MONDAY, JUNE 24 ~ *Read 2 Kings 2:1-2, 6-14*

Change is in the air. As Elijah's long ministry draws to a close, he offers us some good guidance.

Knowing his time is short, what does he do? Puzzlingly, he tells his heir apparent, Elisha, to stay put in Gilgal for the Lord has called Elijah to go to Bethel. Elisha wants no part of such a separation. Forget it—"As the LORD lives, and as you yourself live, I will not leave you."

So Elisha goes with Elijah across the Jordan. Elijah says to Elisha, "Tell me what I may do for you, before I am taken from you." Elijah cares what happens to the Lord's prophetic ministry that he will soon leave behind. He wants to make sure that the good work will continue, even abound.

What does Elisha ask for? That double portion. He is not asking for a spirit greater than Elijah's, but for a double portion of Elijah's spirit—like what a firstborn son would inherit from his father. And as Elijah is taken up to heaven in a whirlwind chariot, his cloak descends on Elisha, anointing him for the Lord's service. God's work will thrive!

Chances are that today will not be our last. So, what can Elijah show us? During times of transition and change, think about others' needs, the effect of change on their lives, and the loose ends tossed into their laps. Elijah is sensitive to Elisha's feelings; he allows him to go with him to Bethel. For us, we can imagine being in someone else's shoes and can let them share whatever is on their hearts and minds.

As life changes, let's think about others and their needs, praying for God's double portion on their work. Invest in others for the sake of God's kingdom.

Lord, thank you for caring for us through all of life's changes. In Jesus' name. Amen.

TUESDAY, JUNE 25 ~ *Read 2 Kings 2:1-2, 6-14*

Elijah and Elisha are out walking one day, talking with each other. But it is hardly a normal day. Fire breaks out. Fire from the Lord—a chariot and horses from heaven. It separates the two of them and Elijah ascends to heaven in a whirlwind.

Throughout the Hebrew scriptures, fire comes from God. Moses communicates with God through the burning bush. (See Exodus 3.) Fire by night gives light and warmth to Israel as God's people wander in the desert those forty long years. (See Exodus 13:21.) Now more fire comes to bring Elijah home to heaven.

So, what can we make of this story for us today? Possibly everything is going along quite nicely at the moment. But you may wonder when a "fire" will break out and disrupt your life. Or perhaps stress and worry already have turned up the heat. Are you experiencing unwanted separation from who or what means the most to you? If so, fire has broken out in your life.

It may be time to step back and ask, "Whats next, Lord?" For Elijah, all heaven breaks loose! Elisha is anointed with great power to continue the Lord's prophetic work.

For you and me the question remains: What's next? Will God's fire consume us? No, probably not. God promises a fire to help us—to light our way and warm our heart. We may find the temperature of God's fire disagreeable or even unbearable when we're unsure what is going on. But we can step back and wait for God's answer. A cloak may yet descend upon us with new purpose for the days ahead.

Thank you, Lord, for your fire that offers reassuring warmth and light. In Jesus' name. Amen.

WEDNESDAY, JUNE 26 ~ *Read Psalm 16*

Such a reassuring psalm, isn't it? When King David cries out for safekeeping, he knows where his security lies: "Protect me, O God, for in you I take refuge." David knows he is safe in God, who will protect him from whatever threatens.

In most English versions of the Bible, this psalm bears a heading. Does your Bible say, "A Miktam of David"? What does *miktam* mean? No one knows for sure. It could be a musical term or a way to introduce a particular kind of psalm.

One possible definition of *miktam* is "to cover." Perhaps David feels vulnerable to his enemies and sings this as an affirmation of trust and safety to God. David knows whose hand he can safely hold.

When we offer support to others, we often say, "I've got you covered." We hope we can follow through with our promise. Sometimes we do; other times we miserably fail. We may wonder, *Will the Lord fail me?* David knows the answer: Never! I remember seeing a sign above the chancel in a church that read, "Jesus Never Fails." King David would have yelled out a booming "Amen!" for sure.

While we will fail many times, we can count on the Lord never to let us down. David reminds us God is right next to us. God shelters us and holds us up when we become unsteady.

Does this mean that life will always be rosy? That nothing bad will ever happen? Hardly. This world can deal some tough blows, but remember that God covers us: "For you do not give me up to Sheol, or let your faithful one see the Pit." David reminds us that God has promised us an eternal safety.

Lord, thank you for standing with us as our secure covering. In Jesus' name. Amen.

THURSDAY, JUNE 27 ~ *Read Psalm 16:8-11*

I've unearthed a nugget of gold in the mine of Psalm 16. It is twenty-four carat and priceless. Interested? Of course you are! Join me in reading verse 8: "I keep the Lord always before me; because he is at my right hand, I shall not be moved." King David has cried out to the Lord for protection. The king faces numerous obstacles, some of his own making. He knows he cannot clean up the messes he encounters.

David turns to the Lord for help. And so do we. We know where our help can be found, don't we? David says, "I keep the Lord *always* before me." Always. I think that means all the time, don't you? You say that's terribly difficult. It certainly is for all of us. But it is a matter of our will, our commitment to invest our lives in the One upon whom we can always depend. It's a matter of willpower, a decision to discipline our lives with our focus on God.

Keep your eyes on the Lord. Like when driving we say, "Keep your eyes on the road." We have a large windshield to look through, but only small side and rearview mirrors. Yes, we glance back and to the side once in a while. But the large windshield in front gets most of our attention. Today, look forward. Keep your eyes on the Lord as you follow David's advice to keep the Lord always before you.

Lord of refuge and counsel, thank you for your constant presence. Help me to keep you before me and to keep my eyes on you. Amen.

FRIDAY, JUNE 28 ~ *Read Galatians 5:1, 13-15*

It's Friday. The weekend beckons. We have free time to enjoy and to worship. Paul writes to the Galatians, "For freedom Christ has set us free." Freedom not only for the weekend, but for time and eternity. Now that's what I call freedom. Free from the shackles of the law. Free from the consequences of our sin. Free from slavery to ungodliness.

But Paul has more to say about our newfound freedom. He warns his readers against using their liberty as an excuse for self-indulgence to pursue a dissolute and decadent lifestyle, for which Jesus has not set them free.

Then for what purpose? It's really quite simple, yet hard to perform. Paul writes, "Through love become slaves to one another." Freedom to become slaves? I knew there was a catch. It seemed too good to be true. But it's not. Jesus grants us life as we give ourselves to others. It's simple, yet we see so little evidence among us. How often do we think about someone else rather than ourselves? Before we open our mouths, do we consider others' feelings? Does our lifestyle brag about our possessions? This is not the type of freedom for which we've been set free.

In Jesus, we're free to invest in others. When I was a financial planner, my primary purpose was not to make the most money for myself. Others assured me that the more I could help others achieve their financial dreams, the fewer nightmares I would have about money.

The same premise holds true for followers of Jesus: The more we help others, the more free we will feel. Invest in the spiritual and worldly lives of others. Jesus set us free to love one another; this is freedom as it was meant to be.

Lord, we want to live our lives for you and for others. Thank you for this kind of freedom in Jesus. Amen.

SATURDAY, JUNE 29 ~ *Read Galatians 5:1, 16-25*

In Galatians 5, Paul contrasts the "works of the flesh" with the "fruit of the Spirit." Between the two is a chasm as great and wide as the divide of the Grand Canyon in the southwestern United States. "Works of the flesh" refers not to life in our human bodies, which are good and created in the image of God, but rather to the sludge that flows from our sinful nature, which works its way through to harm us and others. What may feel good winds up destroying. Self-centeredness runs amok. Ungodly living lets loose.

Opposed to works of the flesh is the fruit of the Spirit—good works we do and fruit we bear. Fruit grows from healthy plants and trees in good soil replenished with nutritious ingredients. We don't create good fruit. It comes as a byproduct of blooming, thriving, and maturing health. It comes when a plant is nurtured and well-fertilized, protected from predators and the harshness of the elements. Good fruit comes from the abundance of God's grace through the Holy Spirit.

Bearing the "fruit of the Spirit" results from our exercising godly disciplines like what you're doing right now: spending time in devotion to the Lord. It comes from giving ourselves to God, caring for others, attending church, eagerly serving with our brothers and sisters in Christ, and digging deeper into our wallets when we have the opportunity to help someone else.

We can prepare and nourish the soil of our souls with times of prayer throughout the day. We can protect new growth by confessing our sins to the One who loves to forgive. We can dig in the soil of our lives and work the compost of failure that produces compassion and understanding in our hearts. When we invest in our spiritual health and in others' lives, we will bear good fruit, the fruit of the Holy Spirit.

Lord God, we pray for good fruit in our lives as we live for you and others. In Jesus' name. Amen.

SUNDAY, JUNE 30 ~ *Read Luke 9:51-62*

As with the prophet Elijah, the time rapidly approaches for Jesus' return to heaven. He focuses on Jerusalem, where he knows he will pay the ultimate price to love his own, you and me. Throughout this passage, Luke calls us to follow Jesus. The word follow appears three times in these twelve verses: "I will follow you," "Follow me," "I will follow you." Because of all Jesus has done for us, wishy-washy discipleship is no longer an option.

Jesus sends his disciples ahead to prepare the way and to proclaim the kingdom of God even in hostile territory. When they encounter rejection, some disciples ask Jesus if he wants them to cast divine judgment on these scoffers. How easy to let anger get in the way of investing in what's good for others! But Jesus says "no" and tells them to move on to more receptive places.

Jesus encounters three men on this journey. The first asks to be part of the Lord's team, to go wherever Jesus goes. Rabbis in Jesus' time are notable figures of great respect and status. Comfortable benefits often come to their followers. Jesus wants this man to know that there may be no comforts for his followers except to walk in the steps of God's Son. That may be all, and it should be enough.

The next two men have family responsibilities to attend to, worthy and honorable tasks at home, before they can follow Jesus. Jesus' harsh retorts serve not to abrogate familial duties, but to emphasize the supremacy of following him first and fully, before everything else. We can invest well in others only after we have invested our all in Christ.

Lord, may we be faithful followers of your Son, who gave his all for us without excuse. Amen.

Listening for Instructions

JULY 1–7, 2019 • ELIZABETH HAGAN

SCRIPTURE OVERVIEW: The readings from the Hebrew scriptures describe what can happen when our own strength fails us. Naaman is a great military commander from Syria, but he has no power to heal himself. The psalmist, traditionally David, has become too comfortable in his prosperity. Both men must humble themselves before they can experience healing and restoration from God. How often do we let our pride stand in the way of our healing? Paul admonishes his readers to carry themselves with humility and to build up one another. What they do will always come back to them; what we sow, we reap. The story in Luke warns against being proud even of the gifts that God gives us. Our greatest joy is not that we can do things for God but that God already has accepted us.

QUESTIONS AND SUGGESTIONS FOR REFLECTION

- Read 2 Kings 5:1-14. When have God's instructions been more involved than you expected? How did you respond?
- Read Psalm 30. How can you continue to praise God during the dark, lonely, and hopeless times?
- Read Galatians 6:1-16. When has your faith community struggled with members' lack of humility? How did you resolve the situation so that you could welcome and nurture new Christians?
- Read Luke 10:1-11, 16-20. When have you misconstrued God's accomplishments as your own successes? How did you refocus your life or ministry on serving God?

Senior Minister, Palisades Community Church, Washington, DC; author of *Birthed: Finding Grace Through Infertility*.

MONDAY, JULY 1 ~ *Read 2 Kings 5:1-8*

Naaman finds himself in a set of helpless circumstances. This commander in the army of the King of Aram aches with a terrible disease, leprosy, for which there was no cure. Though known commonly as a skin disease, leprosy stems from the nervous system. Patients of leprosy often experience very painful disfigurations of their hands, feet, and even nose. We can imagine that Naaman wakes up every morning and goes to bed each night with a lot of pain.

Yet, thanks to a courageous servant in his household, Naaman gets a second chance at life. A servant girl suggests that he travel to her home country of Israel and ask for the prophet. She knows Naaman can find healing if he asks.

We, like Naaman, may find ourselves in a time of trouble today. Our circumstance may look and feel bleak. We may be seeking a cure to a physical, emotional, or spiritual disease that troubles us but for which we have no answer. Naaman's story reminds us that a journey of faith must be rooted in persistence. Who knows what answers another email might bring? Or phone call? Or conversation? Sometimes God answers our prayers for help as we put feet to the answers we're seeking.

God, it's easy to grow tired as we wait for your answers. Help us today to keep asking, keep seeking, and keep listening for your gifts of help. We don't want to miss them when they arrive. Amen.

TUESDAY, JULY 2 ~ *Read 2 Kings 5:9-18*

Naaman's head must fill with expectations as he approaches the prophet Elisha's house. Finally, he can be cured, he hopes. We imagine that Naaman has dreamt of this day for so long. So long that he knows what his cheers of "I'm healed! I'm healed!" will sound like all the way back to Aram. He might remember what his wife's touch will feel like again. He may think of what the gazes of strangers will be without his outcast status. He knows. And he cannot wait for it!

But then healing does not come as Naaman has imagined. Naaman has envisioned that Elisha would come out to him, pray to God, and heal him on the spot. Instead Elisha tells Naaman to go to the Jordan River and wash himself seven times. This requires Naaman to do just one more thing. In hearing such news, Naaman is angry and disappointed. He fires back to Elisha questioning his judgment. Why did he have to come to Israel's river? Aren't there acceptable rivers back at home? Naaman feels overwhelmed by the dissonance between what he wants and reality. So, Naaman almost misses his chance for healing. If not for a servant's encouragement to heed Elisha's instructions, Naaman would have missed his cure from leprosy.

How often do we, like Naaman, miss out on an experience of God because we're upset life is not unfolding as we imagined it? We balk at the instructions offered to us through wise counsel. If it's not our idea first, we don't want to try it. Yet, the story of Naaman encourages us to consider how God's guidance for our lives appears differently than we would have expected. Our job is to listen and to obey when the instructions come.

God, clear our minds of ideas or plans that are not the ones you have for us. Give us courage this day to be willing to receive whatever it is you want to give us. Amen.

WEDNESDAY, JULY 3 ~ *Read Luke 10:1-11, 16*

If you have spent time around new Christians, you have seen how eager so many are to share their faith. Christ's love has flooded their stories. They cannot wait to tell everyone who will listen the good news of what Jesus has done for them. We can imagine that the first disciples of Jesus shared this posture. Following Jesus changed everything about their lives, and they were ready to share the story.

Yet, as our Gospel reading for today begins, Jesus has some words of caution. It is as if you can feel Jesus pulling back the eager disciples from heading out the door, saying, "I'm so glad you're excited, but listen to me first." Jesus' instructions include wanting the missionary teams to go out in pairs. He wants them to know that not everyone will meet their excitement with approval. He wants them to be open to how God will use them to heal the sick. Jesus also gives practical instructions about how to live on the road. They are to eat whatever is put in front of them, only to enter houses where they are welcomed in peace, and not to stay long in a town if they are not welcome.

Like the first disciples, we too are called to listen to Christ's instructions as we share the good news. Our journeys may not look like the one Luke describes, but we can learn much from this first missionary venture. Not everyone will welcome us with open arms. Not every house will be full of peace. Not everyone will cheer us on. But God is with us. God will guide us to where our ministry can thrive. Today, let us not be hasty in new ventures, but instead seek the Lord's leading first.

Lord, you teach us to share the good news of what you're doing in our lives. Help us today to proceed with wisdom. Amen.

THURSDAY, JULY 4 ~ *Read Luke 10:17-20*

Jesus teaches the value of servanthood and humility in the kingdom of God. Our mission is not to make a name for ourselves or to seek personal recognition for our achievements. Rather our mission is to follow God's leading so that the activities of our lives have eternal significance.

After the disciples' first big missionary adventure ends, they seek out Jesus to share their enthusiasm. They have given willingly of their time to share the good news with any who would listen. They have followed Jesus' instructions. As a result, they have brought hope, healing, and restoration to many. They have seen those possessed by demons cured. Coming home, they are riding a high and seem to want Jesus to offer a pat on the back. Much to their surprise, Jesus does not praise them. Jesus reminds them of the great things he has done. For Jesus knows the disciples are in danger of confusing the power of the gospel with their own personal power. He reminds them again that their gifts for ministry come from God, the Almighty One, who deserves all the praise and honor.

Like the first disciples, we can confuse our ministry successes with our own strength. Quicker than we might realize, we draw attention to ourselves. We seek closeness with those in positions of influence so that our accomplishments shine brighter; all the while we forget the One who gave us the gifts to be of service in the first place. As an alternative, Jesus invites us to stick close to our relationship with God and to listen only for God's voice. For as we draw closer to God, Jesus says, we remain grounded in the eternal.

Jesus, thank you for your invitation today to invest our lives in that which lasts forever. Keep us this day from the distractions of pride so that we can hear you clearly. Amen.

FRIDAY, JULY 5 ~ *Read Galatians 6:1-10*

Paul cares deeply about how the members of the church relate to one another. He has seen the church at Galatia at its best and at its worst. He sees how their conflicts and quarrels keep them from creating a beloved community. So, Paul writes to convey two basic truths.

First, the members belong to one another. The members are responsible to one another. Therefore, they should check their pride at the door. Thriving faith communities are governed not by ego, Paul writes, but rooted in humility. This kind of humility can be counterintuitive. It goes against that within us that wants to shout, "Me, me! Love me now!" But the exhortation to bearing with and for one another remains the same.

Second, Paul writes that all members contribute unique gifts to make the community thrive. Sometimes this means receiving instruction humbly from an unlikely person. Sometimes it means continuing to work hard even when one's contributions are not appreciated. And often it means planting seeds of faith even if the harvest does not come for years. Regardless of how our gifts are received, we're asked to offer them.

Like in the early church, nothing kills our community life faster than members' feelings of self-importance. Showing up at church believing that we're better than someone else not only kills any spirit of Christian unity but also keeps others from feeling welcome. Today, we hear again the call to bear one another's burdens, walk with one another, and uplift one another. As we respond to that call, our church becomes a stronger witness for the way of Christ while becoming a community of faith where newcomers feel welcome and find ways to grow in their faith.

God, committing our whole hearts to community life is tough work. But it's the work you've called us to do. Bring to mind today one person we need not only to pray for but to go out of our way to show kindness to this week. Amen.

SATURDAY, JULY 6 ~ *Read Galatians 6:11-16*

Rule-following can offer us the gift of satisfaction. We convey this message to children from a young age: Learn the rules; act accordingly. Often, following the rules equals happiness and ignoring the rules equals unfavorable consequences. Then as adults, few of us like to learn that the rules in which we've always believed have changed. It can feel overwhelming when a leader suggests a change after we've done the same thing the same way for such a long period of time. Rules provide us security and presumed assurance of a reward.

Paul's ministry among the early church constantly engages in a conversation about the rules. Paul fights an uphill battle in trying to give the church at Galatia new instruction. In Paul's first visit to Galatia, he teaches that circumcision is not necessary for converts to the Christian faith. The teachings of Jesus make everything new. The law of the Torah does not need to be followed in the same way. After this first visit, the church embraces the change. But then, much to Paul's dismay, some new teachers come to town saying Paul's interpretation is wrong and circumcision is required. Confusion sets in. The church at Galatia wants to follow the rules. So, how are we to interpret Jesus' teaching?

In today's reading, Paul writes about grace to the church at Galatia. Do not stress over knowing the rules and following them, he says. If you want to be circumcised, that's fine. If you aren't circumcised, that's great too. Following Christ is most important. Following Christ means embracing a journey of not knowing what lies ahead but believing in the freedom Christ gives. As Christian people, we are bound only to Christ.

Jesus, giver of all good gifts, help us to lay aside our love of rules and to embrace your gifts of grace. Amen.

SUNDAY, JULY 7 ~ *Read Psalm 30*

The psalmist we meet in this passage has known a life of trouble. Although we don't know the specifics, we can imagine that tears have fallen, the air has felt thick with sadness, and days have come and gone where life didn't feel worth living. Where is the spring of new life—of hope and comfort?

But, in dramatic fashion, we read that the season has changed. Something new has transpired. Hope is born anew. The psalmist can't help but shout for joy to any who will listen. Everyone must know the good news. God is to be praised. No more sackcloth is needed. Cue the "Hallelujah" chorus being sung in the background.

We might wonder how such a spiritual movement transpires. It is no small thing to have your mourning turned into dancing or to go from crying a bed of tears to leaping forth in the morning ready to take on the new day. It is no small thing to thank God from our internal wells of the deepest gratitude. The psalmist finds joy in waiting on the Lord. For the psalmist, waiting means telling the Lord exactly how he feels and relying on God's ability to be in control of his life. Waiting on the Lord means seeking instructions for how to move forward according to God's plans.

While we may want to try to fix our own circumstances in times of personal crisis, Psalm 30 invites us to wait on the Lord, to wait for answers to our prayers in God's time. We can wait with the belief that something beautiful comes in the silent times, the lonely times, and the hopeless times. Most of all, God is worthy of our praise as we wait.

God, though I may not always see your plans at work in my life, help me to trust you, to listen for you, and to praise you as I wait. Amen.

Getting Unskewed

JULY 8–14, 2019 • DOYLE BURBANK-WILLIAMS

SCRIPTURE OVERVIEW: Amos is a farmer called by God to deliver a message to Jeroboam, the king of Israel (the Northern Kingdom in the divided monarchy). Because the king has not listened to the warnings from God, judgment will come. The psalmist also warns of judgment, in this case for those who oppress the weak and needy and fail to protect them from the wicked. Such heartless people will surely be brought low by God. The opening to the letter to the Colossians is a prayer of thanksgiving for their faith in Christ and the spiritual fruit they are producing in the world. The parable in the Gospel reading challenges our human tendency to ignore need. Jesus teaches that mercy should overcome any reason we might find to harden our hearts.

QUESTIONS AND SUGGESTIONS FOR REFLECTION

- Read Amos 7:7-17. Look for God's plumb line in the world. In what ways is the ground you stand on askew?
- Read Psalm 82. If you sit on the council of the Most High, how does this change your perspective on the world?
- Read Colossians 1:1-14. Prayers of mere words are just the beginning of prayer. To what prayerful actions do your prayerful words call you?
- Read Luke 10:25-37. The author writes, "Even those trying to be faithful walk askew." Consider how you live out Jesus' call to love your neighbor.

Artist in ministry; Pastor, New Visions Community United Methodist Church in Lincoln, Nebraska.

MONDAY, JULY 8 ~ *Read Amos 7:7-9*

Tucked in among the tourist traps of the South Dakota Black Hills is a self-entitled "Mystery House." The mystery of the Mystery House is that water seems to run uphill, and objects dangle strangely out of plumb. But the mystery involved is not in the house; it is in our brains. The house is built off-kilter, but once inside a visitor has no external frame of reference. Because our brains are used to seeing floors as level and walls as parallel, our grey matter goes to work inside the Mystery House to reread the tilted floor as even and the walls as square. Unconsciously, we read the room as normal and are mystified when the water runs uphill.

That is precisely the type of situation Amos is addressing in Israel. The people have become accustomed to living in a skewed house. The primary concern of a biblical prophet is to call the people back into covenant with God. In Amos's eyes, the people have strayed from their promises. The heart of the covenant with God is deep compassion for the poor, the widow and orphan, the migrant and foreigner. But Israel has abandoned those passions and priorities. Like the Mystery House, the oblique angles are exposed when a covenant plumb line is dropped.

Which leads me to wonder what my out-of-kilter heart and brain have compensated for in our skewed world today. We inherit priorities like success and progress and power, and we rarely stop to get our covenant bearings. When a messenger of God drops a plumb line, all too often we wonder why it hangs at such an odd angle. But maybe the ground we stand on is askew.

Reorient the level of my heart, O God, not on the ground of society's values but on the plumb line of the passion of your heart. Amen.

TUESDAY, JULY 9 ~ *Read Psalm 82*

The Saint Benedict Center in Schuyler, Nebraska, is a beautiful spiritual retreat center. It has soaring ceilings and long, expansive hallways. The breathtaking perspective its ceilings and hallways offer communicates an essential message: You are small, especially in comparison to the awesome beauty of God.

Psalm 82 begins with that familiar perspective. Our God is the High God above all other gods, sitting in council over the state of the world. God is high above us, out of our league. God castigates lesser gods for their lack of compassion for the lowly, the poor, the destitute, and the powerless. The High God asks the lesser gods, Why have you abandoned the fortunes of these most vulnerable of God's children? (Remember yesterday's covenant thing?)

Yet here again things seem askew. The world likes to reinforce the diminishing message that keeps us powerless, too tiny to make a difference. The poor remain poor, the defenseless remain at the mercy of their abusers, and there is nothing we can do about it. While much of religion makes us feel small, the psalmist sees things differently. "I hereby declare, 'You are gods, children of the Most High—all of you!'" (CEB).

We are not small in God's eyes. Psalm 8 tells us that we are just a little lower than God. Divine perspective empowers the lowly and challenges the powers that be. It never reinforces them. God empowers us to take on the causes of those who are closest to God's heart. We sit in council with the Most High God, considering the situation of the world. How's that for a different perspective?

Change our perspective, Most High God. Teach us to see the hope you place in our hands, and then use those hands to change the world. Amen.

WEDNESDAY, JULY 10 ~ *Read Colossians 1:1-14*

Nightly news about the economy, politics, and world affairs is often bad news. We hear of attacks, abuses, pollutions, starvations, and contaminations. Most nights we wonder why we don't ever hear any good news.

Yet Paul writes to the folk in Colossae because they have heard good news. Paul does not give any details about the good news, but he calls it "the true message" and acknowledges the people as sisters and brothers in Christ because of that good news. Jesus' vision of the kingdom seems to be parallel to the priorities of God's covenant from its earliest days: compassion for the poor, the vulnerable, the outcast. Something in the life, death, and resurrection of Jesus is good news for the people at Colossae. It changes their lives.

That good news changes the way we see ourselves, each other, and the world. We are no longer on the bottom rung of life; we are among those gathered together by Christ's love—love that values us beyond measure. Paul notices that the good news changes the way the Colossians live. They now "bear fruit in every good work and as [they] grow in the knowledge of God." The good news unskews the lines in our lives that no longer are parallel to the lines of unconditional justice and love that God embodied in Jesus.

All the bad news we digest is just evidence of lines skewed by fear and greed and hate. The gospel (which means good news) reorients those lines back to the meridians of love and grace that God intends.

What good news will change my life in the ways that you invite, O Christ? Take my life and draw it back into the parallel lines of your love and grace. Amen.

THURSDAY, JULY 11 ~ *Read Amos 7:10-17*

Yesterday we pondered the good news that changed the people at Colossae. Today we go back to Amos. Amos's words are difficult, and they feel like anything but good news. This passage from Amos fits the stereotype of a gloom and doom prophet and offers a prime example of why people avoid reading Hebrew scriptures. If these words accurately reflect God's nature and temperament, no wonder people reject God.

As Christians we proclaim good news. Not easy news or happy news but, in one way or another, good news. It is incumbent upon us to wrestle good news out of even the darkest texts. Amos tests that proposition.

The royal court doesn't like what Amos has to say, and they ask him to shut up and leave. Amos only turns up the heat. Amos says God promises awful, terrible things for them all. Clearly Amos doesn't intend this to be good news for them. They have forsaken their covenant with God, and the wages of sin is . . . well, you know. (See Romans 6:23.) We pray that this doesn't apply to us, while we harbor a deep suspicion that it does.

If Amos prophesies bad news for those in charge of Israel, for whom would it be good news? It is a weighty prophecy for those who want the world to continue operating as usual. But for those neglected by an unfulfilled covenant, those who desperately need and long for the world to change, it comes as good news indeed. If we do not find ourselves in that position, can we open our hearts enough to empathize? Can we proclaim good news for someone other than ourselves? When the world skews toward injustice, will we see the line that shows it all off plumb?

In a world skewed toward injustice and hate, righteous God, help me embody the good news of Christ for those who need it most. Amen.

FRIDAY, JULY 12 ~ *Read Colossians 1:9-12*

Most houses are not plumb. Some were never built that way; others have settled or shifted. It is almost impossible to bring an out-of-plumb house back into true. We think of the world that way too: We just have to learn to live with it, askew as it is.

The good news of Jesus Christ, though, is that reality will change. Jesus taught and embodied the nearness of God's kingdom, a new reality becoming present in this world. And Jesus called disciples to join in that work.

What tools might we bring to the task of bringing the world back into the plumb of God's justice and love? It's not easy work to do, and the tools will have to be up to the job. Paul points us in the right direction. He says that since hearing about the blossoming spirit of the Colossians, he hasn't stopped praying for them.

It sounds trite to say that our primary tool at bringing our world back into plumb is prayer. But maybe our concept of prayer is skewed. We tend to think of prayer as words we think or say aloud. But words are the merest form of prayer. Our tears when we see a child refugee's body are prayer. Muscles aching from cleaning a flood-ravaged home are prayer. Late night hours spent with someone struggling with depression are prayer. Good words might indeed true an out-of-plumb wall by just a bit, but prayer brings so much more than words to the task. Paul prays that the Colossians might live lives pleasing to God, living prayers as it were. Those prayers not only reshape us; they expose the walls and floors that are askew, walls and floors that need us to pray them back into true.

Open our eyes to the off angles of life, O Christ, that our prayers of words might start the work of prayer that brings us back into plumb. Amen.

SATURDAY, JULY 13 ~ *Read Luke 10:25-28*

If tradition holds true and Jesus was a carpenter, it is interesting that he never pulls a plumb line out of his toolbox for a parable or two. Nonetheless, much of his teaching shows the places where we have drifted off level. That is the case in this passage, certainly.

A legal expert comes to test Jesus. "What must I do to inherit eternal life?" Even 2000 years ago, people spent a lot of energy on the question of saving our own tailbones. Jesus turns the test back on the quizmaster and asks how he sees it. The expert responds with what we call the Great Commandment: to love God with everything we have and to love our neighbor as we love ourselves.

Jesus' standard of love hangs as a plumb line here, showing the slant of the expert's stance. The question begins by asking about his own inheritance: "What must I do?" Remember that for Jesus, the heart of the kingdom of God are the disenfranchised, the vulnerable, the exiled, and the excluded ones. The concern for the "I" is off track in Jesus' understanding. Jesus lets the ancient wisdom of the Torah speak the corrective, though. The first step is to love God, then love another. It does not say love yourself first and foremost. Putting the focus of love on someone else is the key to the best inheritance. Selfless love holds steady the plumb line of the kingdom.

Focusing on our own situation skews our faith life. The plumb line of Jesus' love levels us and directs us to the needs and pains of others. Giving up life for others leads to eternal life. Loving generously is Jesus' true standard.

O Carpenter Christ, free me from a life lived askew, spent too much on myself. Put me on the level surface of your love and grace so that I may see new ways of loving completely. Amen.

SUNDAY, JULY 14 ~ *Read Luke 10:29-37*

True story (pun intended): As a boy grew, he developed a noticeably odd way of walking. He leaned to one side. Doctors put him through a battery of tests but found no cause—no scoliosis, no muscular abnormality, everything normal. Then his father walked into the doctor's office, leaning obviously to one side. "Why do you walk like that?" the physician asked the father. "I lost a couple of toes in a mower accident years ago." His son walked off-kilter because his dad walked that way.

Much of what we do in our faith and church journeys happens likewise. We lean because we have been taught to lean. The priest and the Levite have been trained to lean away from the beaten victim. This is not a moral failing. They both have duties to perform that ritual uncleanness would prevent. They are doing their best to maintain the covenant as they have been taught. So they walk by on the other side, leaning away.

The Samaritan walks differently, though. He walks straight to the bloody, beaten victim and tends his wounds. With no thought of obligations to come or propriety to be followed, he gets his hands bloody and uses his financial resources to bring the victim back to health. When Jesus tells this parable, he mentions nothing of piety or devotion. We do not know whether the Samaritan possesses deep faith or none at all. But the Samaritan shows deep compassion, a compassion that overrides common sense. Jesus tells this story because deep compassion is the plumb line of the kingdom he proclaims. Even those trying to be faithful walk askew. But the one walking upright in compassion is the measure that Jesus gives us to emulate. "Go," Jesus says, "and unskew likewise."

Help me examine all my actions by the standard of your compassionate love, O Christ, that my leaning gait may never carry me past on the other side. Amen.

Feeding the Christ Within

JULY 15–21, 2019 • SHARON SEYFARTH GARNER

SCRIPTURE OVERVIEW: This reading from Amos provides more indication of the reasons for God's coming judgment. Too many in Israel have been oppressing the poor. They cannot wait for religious festivals to end so that they can make more money through corrupt trade, including what we now call human trafficking. If we understand the psalmist to be David, the warning he issues in this passage concern Saul. Because Saul has turned to evil, God will not allow him to remain in power. While God is love, God also sometimes brings judgment. The author of Colossians extols the elevated status of Christ, who has reconciled us to himself through his death. In Luke, Mary prioritizes spending time with Jesus, while Martha focuses on working for Jesus. It is Mary who receives Jesus' praise.

QUESTIONS AND SUGGESTIONS FOR REFLECTION

- Read Amos 8:1-12. Who in your community has been left behind in the famine from hearing the words of the Lord? How can you care for them?
- Read Psalm 52. How do you remain rooted in God's steadfast love when you cry out against injustice?
- Read Colossians 1:15-28. What do you need to let fall away to reveal the mystery of Christ in you?
- Read Luke 10:38-42. How do you focus on Christ even as you attend to the necessary tasks of daily life?

Contemplative colorer; UMC Pastor and Founder of Belly of the Whale Spiritual Direction and Retreat Ministries; author of *Praying with Mandalas: A Colorful, Contemplative Practice* and *Mandalas, Candles, and Prayer: A Simply Centered Advent*; wood-fired pizza aficionado.

MONDAY, JULY 15 ~ *Read Amos 8:1-12*

Every week during the summer, I pick up a delicious basket full of summer fruits and vegetables from UpCycle Farm—tomatoes, zucchini, watermelon, strawberries, and more. My family eats, stores, or shares the food right away because if we neglect our food in the basket, it will rot quickly in the summer heat.

Amos, a herdsman by trade, understands the implications of his vision of a basket of summer fruit. The people of Israel have neglected the word of God for too long, and they have become "rotten"—songs in the Temple have become wailings, people die in the streets, the poor are cheated in the market place, and merchants rush through the sabbath so they can get back to the business of "buying the poor for silver and the needy for a pair of sandals." As a result of these deceitful practices, God says "I will send a famine on the land; not a famine of bread, or a thirst for water, but of hearing the words of the LORD."

That famine of hearing the words of the Lord continues today: People are dying in our streets, we trample on the needy, and we justify almost any behavior that will turn a profit. We glorify violence and sex and then seem shocked when our communities are beset with violent crime and sexual harassment.

We would do well to remember the basket of summer fruit. Rather than neglecting God's word and pursuing the "rotten" practices of deceitful self-promotion, we need to be about the work of loving one another. May we feed on the word and bear the fruits of God's love and grace in our daily lives.

Lord, nourish us by your word so that we may offer food and nourishment to a world in need. Amen.

TUESDAY, JULY 16 ~ *Read Psalm 52*

A headline about Psalm 52 might have read something like this: "Saul orders slaughter of priest and family, over eighty-five dead." In 1 Samuel 21 and 22, we learn that David, fearing for his life, visits the house of the priest Ahimelech of Nob, who provides him with bread for sustenance and the sword of Goliath for protection. When Saul learns of this apparent betrayal, he orders Doeg, the Edomite, to kill Ahimelech and his entire family (eighty-five men plus women, children, infants, and animals). It is a gruesome and tragic story.

Psalm 52 is David's response to this horrific news. He cries out, "All day long you are plotting destruction. Your tongue is like a sharp razor, you worker of treachery. You love evil more than good." David is enraged. He cries out against the injustice that led to the deaths of so many innocents.

Yet David does not get lost in his anger. After raising his voice against the evil he has seen, he returns to the goodness of God. Like a green olive tree, David will bear fruit, trusting in the steadfast love of God. Even amidst all the destruction he has witnessed, David still says, "I will proclaim your name, for it is good."

Amidst the tragic headlines that inundate our twenty-four-hour news cycles, we see plenty of injustice to cry out against—and cry out we should! Yet, we must not get lost in our anger. Our faith calls us to raise our voices *and* to remember that God is good. We are the green olive tree, planted in the house of God, where we will be rooted in the steadfast love of God forever.

God, guide my tongue so that I can speak out against injustice while remaining rooted in your steadfast love. Make me like a green olive tree, bearing fruit and proclaiming your name, for it is good. Amen.

WEDNESDAY, JULY 17 ~ *Read Psalm 52*

Music beautifully and mysteriously blends sound and silence. Even the lovely bird songs of the early morning naturally mirror this gift of both chirping and quiet. The balance between notes and rests creates the unique beauty of each melody. Without the silence, the notes would be an endless cacophony. Through the collaboration of silence and sound, the beauty of the music emerges.

Many scholars suggest that the term *Selah,* found in Psalm 52 and many others, is a musical or liturgical note indicating the need for a rest or moment of silence in the psalmist's melody. *Selah* reminds the listener or reader to take a moment of silence to absorb one section of the psalm before continuing on to the next section. Moments of Selah help us to listen deeply and to let what we have heard sink in, otherwise the endless stream of words can become like a noisy gong or a clanging cymbal.

In our daily lives, we could use more moments of Selah—time for silence—so that we can understand more deeply what we have heard or experienced before moving on. Silence is a counter-cultural concept in our world full of perpetual motion and constant contact. May we embrace the gift of Selah so that we can set aside the cacophony of the world for just a moment and listen for the still small voice of God in the midst of our everyday lives. *Selah!*

God of silence and sound, God of singing birds, chattering squirrels, and breezes in the leaves, slow me down so that I may receive the blessing of Selah amidst the never-ending noise that surrounds me. Fill me with your love so that the words I speak may be grounded in an awareness of your silent stillness at the center of my being. Amen.

THURSDAY, JULY 18 ~ *Read Colossians 1:15-28*

It is said that Michelangelo could look at a plain block of marble and see what was invisible to everyone else: the image that dwelled beneath the surface, waiting to be made visible by the hands of an expert artist. He reportedly said, "I saw the angel in the marble and I carved until I set him free."

This image can help us better understand Paul's message to the Colossians when he says, "[Christ] is the image of the invisible God" and "Christ [is] in you, the hope of glory." The image of God that had been invisible to the world is made visible in Christ. That alone is a powerful statement, but Paul takes it one glorious step further. Not only is God's image made visible in Christ, but Christ continues to be made visible through us. In other words, we are each like a block of marble with Christ inside of us, and through our living, we carve until we set it free.

In my ministry of spiritual direction, I companion others on their journey of faith as they seek to walk more closely with God in their daily living. Many of my directees struggle mightily with the idea that Christ is in us. They feel like they have messed up too many times for God's image to exist within them. Yet Paul states without question the mystery of faith that "Christ is in you, the hope of glory." Whether we feel worthy or not, Christ is in each and every one of us. Christ is in you. Christ is in me. Look closely!

God, open my eyes to see the hope of glory that is Christ in me and in each person that I meet. Amen.

FRIDAY, JULY 19 ~ *Read Luke 10:38-42*

We live in a society that celebrates our inner Marthas; we are affirmed for being productive, busy, and active. Our inner Marys, on the other hand, receive minimal, if any, encouragement. Taking time to sit quietly at the feet of Jesus is often seen as lazy, unproductive, and a waste of valuable time.

We all too easily identify with the overworked, irritated Martha. "Seems like I am always the one doing all the work," we readily complain. And when Martha approaches Jesus to speak her mind, we cheer her on and say, "You go, girl!" We have been in her shoes and long to be acknowledged for our hours of unrecognized hard work.

However, as is often the case, Jesus turns our expectations upside down and inside out. Rather than encouraging Mary to get up and help, he encourages Martha to slow down and rest. Jesus says, "Martha, Martha, you are racing around like a chicken with its head cut off, distracted from what really matters. No need to worry so much about your 'to do' list. Mary has found the better way by slowing down and being present with me" (AP). Note that Jesus does not chastise Martha or tell her that her work is unimportant. He points out that she approaches her tasks with a spirit full of worry rather than full of an awareness of Jesus' presence.

When we make time to sit at the feet of Jesus, even for just a moment, our souls are refreshed. We can then tend to our tasks full of assurance and trust rather than full of worry and distraction.

Gracious God, help me to release my inner Martha and embrace my inner Mary. Open my eyes so that I will know how to make time and space to sit at the feet of Jesus and to be filled with your calm and peace. Amen.

SATURDAY, JULY 20 ~ *Read Luke 10:41-42*

As I strive to release my inner Martha and embrace my inner Mary, one huge distraction stands in the way—my cell phone. For years I have been encouraging my kids to let go of their dependence on technology. Yet somehow I have managed to ignore my own advice and have become addicted to that little screen; I glance at the phone on and off all day long without even realizing it.

When my cell phone died recently and I nearly fell apart, it became strikingly clear that I needed to step out of the world of virtual reality and back into the tangible world of three-dimensional reality. How could I recognize Jesus with my nose constantly buried in my cell phone? In order to set aside my Martha-like worries and distractions so that I could embrace my Mary-like attention to Christ, I needed to turn off my cell phone.

So, I have begun a new spiritual practice called cell phone sabbath—time to intentionally turn off my devices and be present with those around me. Perhaps you or those you know could also benefit from a cell phone sabbath. On our journey into a deeper experience of faith, may we set aside our worries and distractions. May we unplug from technology and plug into God by sitting at the feet of Jesus.

God, help me to embrace a regular practice of cell phone sabbath so that I can be more fully present in the real world rather than getting lost in the cyber world. Help me to turn my attention to you so that I will be able to recognize your gracious presence in all that I do, in all whom I meet, and in all that I perceive. Amen.

SUNDAY, JULY 21 ~ *Read Luke 10:38-42*

Saint Francis de Sales reportedly once said, "Every one of us needs half an hour of prayer each day except when we are busy—then we need an hour." At first this phrase seems counter-intuitive, but upon closer reflection it holds profound wisdom. If we are hungry, we do not say, "I am too busy to eat today." We make time to eat. If we are thirsty, we do not say, "I am too busy to drink water today." We make time to drink. If we are feeling short of breath, we do not say, "I don't need so much air in my lungs today!" We make time to sit down and catch our breath.

So, if we are feeling busy, overwhelmed, and spiritually depleted, why then would we make less time for spiritual nourishment rather than more? Prayer is food for our spirits, thirst-quenching water for our souls, and the fresh air we need for our spiritual survival. Prayer grounds our lives in the word of God, in our relationship with God, and in our awareness of the presence of Christ in each person we meet.

How will you make time to pray—to sit at the feet of Jesus, to feast on the fruit of God's word, to be the hope of glory, and to trust in God's steadfast love? I encourage you to explore refreshing new prayer possibilities—contemplative coloring, prayer beads, yoga, centering prayer, or cell phone sabbath. Whatever your prayer practice may be, embrace it fully and allow it to feed the presence of Christ in you so that you can be the presence of Christ in the world.

Lord, open my eyes to refreshing new ways to pray so that I may feed the Christ within me. In so doing, may I gain the sacred strength and divine wisdom to raise my voice for peace and justice in a deeply wounded world. Amen.

Restored

JULY 22–28, 2019 • BO PROSSER

SCRIPTURE OVERVIEW: Hosea can be a difficult book. This prophet is called to live with an unfaithful wife as an image of how Israel is unfaithful to God. Yet even in this initial statement of judgment, God includes a promise of restoration. Psalm 85 appeals to God's steadfast love. God has become angry with the people for their unfaithfulness, and the people appeal for God's mercy, which they are confident they will receive. The Colossians reading warns against replacing or even supplementing the simple truth of the gospel with human wisdom, religious rules, or anything else. We have fellowship with Christ through our faith. Jesus teaches us to ask God for what we need and for what we want just as we would ask a human parent.

QUESTIONS AND SUGGESTIONS FOR REFLECTION

- Read Hosea 1:2-10. How is God reminding you of your covenant relationship?
- Read Psalm 85. When have you needed to pray for restoration in your life? in your relationships with family and friends? in your relationship with God?
- Read Colossians 2:6-19. Paul teaches us the value of community. How has your community restored you as you seek to be like Christ?
- Read Luke 11:1-13. How has praying regularly changed you? If you do not pray regularly, start a practice now. Look for the ways it changes you.

Catalytic coach and consultant, Cooperative Baptist Fellowship; speaker, retreat leader, and author.

MONDAY, JULY 22 ~ *Read Hosea 1:2-10*

My given name ends with "Jr." I was named for my dad, by my dad. He hoped and prayed that I would grow to be a good man. My dad knew me, named me, and nurtured me. He also called me "Bo." It's a nickname; my dad was a nickname kind of guy. My nickname came from a clown doll I carried as a baby. With that nickname came the responsibility to bring laughter into the world. And I believe we need more laughter in our world.

In today's reading, the Lord speaks to Hosea and gives a name to each of Hosea's children. Their names serve as specific prophetic warnings to the house of Israel, each with a special and specific meaning. God knows these children, names them, and nurtures them in the midst of a desperate situation. Each name carries meaning in any attempt to restore Israel to the covenant with God. These children, their names, mean something significant to God and to Hosea and Gomer.

What does your name mean? What is its significance? Perhaps you are named after someone significant in your family's story. Perhaps you are named after a specific place or a significant event. Perhaps your name reflects your parents' hope for your future—the type of person you may become or the life you may live. Hosea's children are named as warnings from God about the future Hosea's people can expect if they do not return to their covenant with God.

Despite the harsh warnings of Hosea and Gomer's children's names, God renews the covenant: "It shall be said to them, 'Children of the living God.'" This week we will read about God's continued faithfulness in restoring our covenant relationship.

God, I know you by so many names. Jehovah, Yahweh, Elohim, El Shaddai, Abba. May each name remind me of your covenant with me. Amen.

TUESDAY, JULY 23 ~ *Read Psalm 85:1-7*

Restore us, O God! The more things change, the more the refrain stays the same. The psalmist yearns for a return to past glories. The psalmist remembers (perhaps accurately, perhaps not) a time when God overlooked, pardoned, and forgave the iniquities of the people.

The words of this psalm could certainly be sung in today's world. Many of us yearn for a return to our own glory days or wish desperately for a return to greatness in our nation, our churches, our economy, or our individual lives. We pray earnestly to God for restoration, for revival, for a return to our former glory when God seemingly overlooked, pardoned, and forgave our iniquities. We know that our mind often plays tricks on our memory. We, along with the psalmist, may hold more fantasy than reality in our memories of past glory.

God doesn't dwell in the past. God is here. Now. Are we aware of God's presence? Will it really take a revival of the past for us to rejoice in God? Will it really take a restoration to past glory, individually or corporately, for us to rejoice in God? Surely not!

God is here, now. That thought alone is worthy of rejoicing. When we busy ourselves wishing for the "good ol' days," we miss the glory of right now. When we try to manipulate God's working, we miss the miracles happening around us. We can rejoice in God's ever-present glory regardless of whatever else might be happening.

God, forgive me when I try to manipulate you. Forgive me when I forsake your present glory for memories of the past. Help me, O God, to rejoice in you. Amen.

WEDNESDAY, JULY 24 ~ *Read Psalm 85:8-13*

The haunting line woven through the first half of this psalm sets the tone for the second half. Verse 5 asks, "Will you be angry with us forever?" Can you feel the depth of despair in this line? The question lingers in the mind of the psalmist and the pain translates across the pages of time. Many of us have wondered this same question when in the midst of pain and suffering.

Yet even as this refrain lingers, the psalmist turns to hope: "[God] will speak peace . . . surely his salvation is at hand." We begin to hear a song of hope rising up from the refrain of fear and despair. We set aside our fears of the future and begin to hope for a brighter present. We dare to sing this hope.

In the midst of pain, fear, and despair, the psalmist dares to sing of peace, restoration, love, and goodness. What about us? Are we so mired in the pits of despair and pain that we can neither hope nor hear a note of hope? A song of hope dares to emerge. Do we sing along? Can we hope for a new transformation?

God is here! God's presence does not relieve us from fear and pain, but God's presence does relieve us from having to face these alone. God is with us; God has always been with us. God restores us. Righteousness breaks forth before us. Let us hope boldly! And let us sing!

God, forgive me when I let fear and despair drown out my song of hope. My hope is in you from everlasting to everlasting. Help me to sing. Amen.

THURSDAY, JULY 25 ~ *Read Colossians 2:6-15*

Paul writes to the Colossians to redirect them from false teachings being introduced into the church. Paul gets to the point clearly, "Live your lives in [Christ] . . . just as you were taught." Paul gives practical examples about what teachings to ignore.

As we interact with the world around us, many of us get sidetracked. We need spiritual community and spiritual mentors (like Paul to the Colossians) to redirect us and bring us back on course. Being a Christian is quite simple: Live in Christ. But being a Christian is quite challenging: Live in Christ. Some in the Colossian church have been distracted from their beliefs and their actions. So, Paul intervenes.

Christian community and spiritual mentors are God's gifts. A sense of belonging grounds us and gives us focus. When we are sidetracked from our beliefs, the community (or the mentor) brings us back to the center. Paul is not harsh. He lovingly calls back the church to the basics of the faith and the rootedness of their community.

Most of us have been nourished in the love of a faith community. We have been nurtured in the truth of Christ. And we have been set free to continue to grow as disciples. Our belonging to a community roots us to a strong foundation. Our beliefs put in place a system of being and doing the work of God. Our becoming more like Christ moves us along this faith pathway, growing ever closer to God and one another. And, when we fall short, the community lovingly dusts us off, embraces us, and sends us out again restored.

Thank you, God, for the community of faith that has nurtured me in your love, for the spiritual mentors who have helped me understand your truth, and for your continued guidance as I become the disciple that you have called me to be. Amen.

FRIDAY, JULY 26 ~ *Read Colossians 2:16-19*

What does a "normal" Christian look like? Paul warns the Colossians that some people will condemn them. He warns that some will even try to "disqualify" their faith.

Those same warnings hold for us today. Never before has our world been so divided. Never before has the need for Christ's love been more apparent. Never before have so many tried to confuse and distort the truth of Christ!

Recently I asked my small group, "What does a 'normal' Christian look like, sound like, act like?" One dear saint in the group meekly responded, "About like everybody else!" Despite her intended sarcasm, I think she is on to something.

Jesus does not seek to lord himself over those who follow him. He seeks to be part of the community around him, to be a little yeast in the dough. Jesus challenges us to live to higher standards but to be humble, to be last, to be least. We will have trouble being a disciple if we choose authority over humility. We will have trouble being incorporated into our communities if we choose arrogance over understanding.

Paul warns us that as we become part of the community around us, as we serve, as we are transformed by Christ, there will be those who don't want us to be "normal." They will want us to all look alike, think alike, act alike, and be in lock step with their understanding of normal. That's uniformity, and Jesus came to offer us freedom from that!

Thankfully, Jesus calls us individually, by name, in the uniqueness of who we are. Working together, we form a beautiful patchwork of "normal" Christians. Fearfully and wonderfully made, we are Christ's workmanship.

God, forgive me when I want everything to be easy and want everyone to conform to my idea of normal. Help me to live humbly and to embrace the uniqueness that each person brings into this wonderful community of believers in Christ. Amen.

SATURDAY, JULY 27 ~ *Read Luke 11:1-4*

We generally don't consider the Lord's Prayer a particularly exciting passage. Many of us have prayed this prayer since childhood. We think we already know how to pray. But in this passage we hear the disciples asking Jesus to teach them how to pray. We would think they would already know how.

In church we often assume others already know how to pray. This passage confronts us and our culture at a time when people are seeking prayer rituals, reading self-help books, and desiring genuinely deeper spirituality. Perhaps we should examine all of these "spiritual" things in light of the prayer Jesus teaches his disciples. Surely, Jesus' life was prayer-filled. We read about his praying in a variety of situations: at baptism, before choosing the Twelve, while on the Cross. Jesus models prayer for those who follow him. We know his disciples pray and fast. Yet, they want a deeper understanding of *how* to pray. And so begins the lesson.

Half of this prayer discusses what God wants from us. Jesus teaches us that prayer is grounded in humility and dependence upon God to keep us spiritually strong. Acknowledging these helps us approach prayer and leads us to the genuine spirituality we seek.

Still, knowing *how* to pray is never as important as the act of praying. And, while there are many ways to pray, trust your own heart. Let your needs spill honestly from your heart. Praise God sincerely for blessings and goodness. Thank God for the deep love we know through Christ. And wait patiently.

As you pray today, be concerned with your "how," but be more concerned with your "what." You can even just sit still and spend time focused on God. Let your soul have fellowship with the heart of God and be nourished by God's presence.

Lord, when I don't know how to pray, open my heart to feel your love in the quiet stillness. Amen.

SUNDAY, JULY 28 ~ *Read Luke 11:5-13*

Prayer changes things. We respond as the disciples, "Lord, teach us to pray," but we continue to doubt whether God hears or cares about our prayers. After giving the disciples a model for prayer, Jesus then gives an illustration to emphasize his teaching and to reassure us that God not only hears but cares and responds.

Prayer is not a superstitious recitation or a blank check to fulfill our wishes. Prayer does not guarantee financial prosperity. Prayer is a discipline. Prayer is asking, seeking, knocking, and waiting. And God, the perfect parent, hears and responds.

Prayer is spending time with God. We can talk with God about relationships within our community, about the needs of others, and about ourselves. Sometimes, life overwhelms us and we have no words at all.

Jesus encourages us to pray often and to persevere in our prayers. God is not only high and holy but also close and intimate. God cares more for us than we can comprehend. Jesus reminds us that as much as we love our families and friends, God loves us even more.

Prayer changes things. Prayer changes me as I discipline myself to spend time with God. Prayer changes my outlook on the world as I pray deeply for healing in our world. Prayer changes how I relate to those around me as I pray for them and for our relationships. Prayer changes how I see others and how I see myself.

Loving God, help me to keep a discipline of prayer for the sake of change in myself, in others, and in the world. Remind me that praying is spending time with you. Amen.

Be the Gospel

JULY 29—AUGUST 4, 2019 • DEVONNA R. ALLISON

SCRIPTURE OVERVIEW: Hosea relates a further message from God. Israel has repeatedly ignored God's teachings, even though God continues to reach out with love and kindness. Although a just response would be wrath, God will respond instead with mercy to restore the people. The psalmist echoes this teaching about God's enduring love. Although some have gone through periods of distress, when they call out to God, the Lord responds with steadfast love. We then explore guidance for the life of a Christian. In Colossians we read that we should focus on heavenly realities, not the physical world. Rather than pursuing our own pleasure, we should put on a new self and behave more like God desires. The parable that Jesus tells reinforces this point. We should focus on storing up heavenly treasures, not earthly ones.

QUESTIONS AND SUGGESTIONS FOR REFLECTION

- Read Hosea 11:1-11. How have you suffered the consequences of turning away from God? How has God welcomed you back?
- Read Psalm 107:1-9, 43. What stories of God's goodness does your family tell to the next generations?
- Read Colossians 3:1-11. How has Christ renewed you? How do you see Christ in others?
- Read Luke 12:13-21. How has greed shown up in your life—as racism, wealth-mongering, or myths of scarcity? How do you combat greed in all its forms to live out of a mentality of abundance?

Author, speaker, and freelance writer from southern Michigan; member at Locust Grove Mennonite Church in Burr Oak, Michigan.

MONDAY, JULY 29 ~ *Read Luke 12:13-21*

The West African country of Senegal has a tradition called "storying" where storytellers relate important tales of national or personal history through words, actions, and singing. Senegalese Christian women meet together discreetly to learn how to tell and perform Bible stories in this traditional manner. While one woman reads the stories, the others listen carefully and memorize so that they in turn can relay the stories to an audience.

Only forty percent of the Senegalese population can read, so storying is a way for Christian women to share their faith with their friends and neighbors. Sharing the Christian faith is not illegal in Senegal, but persecution for proselytizing is very real and carries great risk. These women have decided, despite the dangers, to "be" the gospel for their loved ones. They use their traditional form of sharing knowledge to share their love for Christ with others.

This week in the stories of Hosea 11 we'll read of the warnings of turning apostate and God's promise of restoration. In Psalm 107 the psalmist encourages us to remember the many ways the Lord has led and delivered us. In Colossians 3, Paul reminds us to live as those made alive in Christ. And in chapter 12 of his Gospel, Luke tells us the story of when Jesus uses a story to teach us that we are foolish to prize this life and its treasures over heavenly concerns.

There's an old saying, "We may be the only gospel some people ever read." When we live out our faith or tell its stories to others, we heed the call to "be the gospel."

Dear Lord, be with us this week as we study your word with the aim of enlightening, encouraging, and strengthening ourselves, not only for our own good but for the good of others. Lead us into a life of being the gospel for others through action and story. Amen.

TUESDAY, JULY 30 ~ *Read Hosea 11:1-7*

Hosea preaches to Israel and Ephraim in the Northern Kingdom during the same time frame as Isaiah prophesies in Jerusalem in the Southern Kingdom. Hosea and Isaiah's preaching leads us to believe that this time before the destruction of Jerusalem is a time of great apostasy.

In today's reading, Hosea lays out a tragic litany of the people's betrayals and the Lord's warnings of dire punishment for their misconduct. Their sin and their fickle relationship with their Creator, despite God's great love for them, will result in the severe consequences of judgment.

Israel's history can serve as a cautionary tale for us as we read it these many years later. Just as Israel's neighbors influence their behavior, our society's norms can and do challenge us daily. Our daily news provides plentiful evidence that we live in a fallen world amongst fallen people.

However, rather than allowing life's negativity to overwhelm us, we can make it our priority to remain grounded in faithfulness. We can cultivate habits that encourage us in our faith and reconnect us with our Lord. Bible reading and memorization, prayer, Christian service, and regular worship with other believers fortify us and help to keep us faithful. We can choose to honor and please God with a life of holiness and devotion apart from the sins of this world.

Dear Lord, help us to align ourselves with you by practicing holiness and distancing ourselves from conduct that would steal our loyalty from you. Make us sensitive to the sin in our own lives and mindful of anything that would separate us from you and your protecting hand. Amen.

WEDNESDAY, JULY 31 ~ *Read Hosea 11:8-11*

"May the memory of them be a blessing," is a common honorific for the deceased among Jewish people. It's based on Proverbs 10:7, "The memory of the righteous is a blessing."

In the Bible, forgetting or being forgotten accompanies punishment. Israel is said to have "forgotten the Holy One" when they turn aside to idols, and Job grieves that he is "forgotten by his companions" in his time of great suffering. To be lost is terrible, but to be forgotten is infinitely worse. It implies one is no longer being sought after.

In today's reading, we look at a continuation of Hosea's warning to the people of Israel that judgment is coming. But as with any loving parent, God promises that discipline will be tempered with mercy. In verse 8 Hosea reminds the people of God's great love and compassion and says that God cannot treat Israel as God treated Admah and Zeboiim.

Deuteronomy 29:23 records that God wiped out Admah and Zeboiim along with Sodom and Gomorrah. But, unlike Sodom and Gomorrah, the Bible tells nothing else about these two cities. They are essentially forgotten. So what is the legacy and lesson of Admah and Zeboiim? Through their mention in Hosea, they help us to understand that though God may punish God's children for a time, God will not forget or utterly abandon the people as God did those two cities.

With this assurance of being remembered by God, the people will respond to God's correction, repent, and return to the Lord. Hosea assures us that though we may suffer the consequences of turning away from God, the Lord will return us home.

Thank you, Lord, for remembering us even when we sin against you. Thank you for welcoming our repentance with open arms. Amen.

THURSDAY, AUGUST 1 ~ *Read Psalm 107:1-9*

I feel fortunate to come from a family of storytellers, men and women who keep our family's history alive by recounting to younger generations the tales of days gone by. Each old story inevitably holds a valuable lesson for today. We learn a lesson in honesty from the story of a Minnesota farm boy who confesses his wrongdoing expecting punishment but receiving mercy. We learn a lesson of trust from the blind workhorse who will outpull any other horse as long as his master's hand is at the reins. We learn courage from the small dog who faces down an angry bull and thereby saves my grandfather's life. We hear stories of war and of times of celebration and of surviving the Great Depression. Our family stories make us laugh, make us cry, and make us think.

In today's reading, the psalmist reminds readers to be grateful for the many different times and ways the Lord God has led them. The psalmist reminds us of the desert places from which we've been delivered and the lean times when God has been faithful to provide. These memories are meant to invoke in us gratitude for all the Lord has done for us.

The psalmist instructs us not only to recall the ways the Lord has led us but also to tell others what the Lord has done for us. Our Bible, full of stories with continuously relevant life lessons, serves as our example. We read and tell these stories to remember the Lord's goodness and love for us.

Take a moment to ponder all the times the Lord has answered your prayers, delivered you from distress, and met your needs. How can you share your stories? With whom?

FRIDAY, AUGUST 2 ~ *Read Colossians 3:1-11*

Pete had been a scary man. He trusted no one, and people avoided his gruff nature and angry face. No one knew Pete's story; his deep anger stemmed from years of abuse he had suffered as a child. One day, Pete's younger brother reached out to Pete with the message of the gospel, and, miracle of miracles, God changed Pete. The man who had felt nothing but hatred was overwhelmed by the love of God through salvation. People cannot help but notice the undeniable change in Pete. He smiles. He greets people. He has stopped hanging out in the rough places with the rough crowd and is now a faithful attendee of church and Bible study. His language has changed, his appearance has changed, and his purpose in life has changed. He enthusiastically shares with others his story and the miracle of transformation God wrought in his life. Pete is a new creature in Christ, and his life reflects his choice.

In today's passage from the letter to the Colossians, Paul entreats the followers of Christ in Colossea to embrace their new nature in Christ and to guard their lives from sin. This advice is for us too. What do our daily practices say about our priorities? Are there attitudes and actions that creep into our lives that are out of place in the life of a follower of Christ? Let's look at Paul's warnings to the Colossians and examine our own life practices: "Put to death . . . whatever belongs to your earthly nature. . . . Rid yourselves of all such things. . . . Do not lie to each other, since you have taken off your old self with its practices" (NIV).

Assess your life story in the light of the gospel today. What do your actions tell others about your life in Christ? You do not need to have experienced as dramatic a change as Pete did to have a story to tell.

SATURDAY, AUGUST 3 ~ *Read Luke 12:13-21*

In 2010, while reporting on the work of mission workers around the world for the Mennonite Mission Network, I came to know Isabella. Isabella recently had moved to Paris to attend a university. She was lonely for her home in the Caribbean when she discovered a welcoming congregation of believers in the Parisian neighborhood of Chatenay-Malabry. The demographics of this traditionally white, Christian, middle-aged, French community had changed dramatically in the past decade. Large immigrant populations had arrived from many other countries. With these many arrivals has come now-famous conflicts between native French and France's 6.8 million immigrants.

Isabella's new congregation, however, decided to make a difference in its neighborhood, opened its doors to immigrants, and began ministering to them. The congregation grew in membership as they helped new immigrants find jobs, homes, and assistance with the staggering array of government paperwork.

One of the first ways members of the church connected with the new members of their community was through sharing prayer needs. Prayers for housing and jobs or for sick or absent family members were simple concerns all church members could relate to. Reaching out in compassion and understanding was making these strangers into brothers and sisters in Christ.

Racism is, at its heart, greed—a fear that "we" will lose out if we accept "them." In Luke 12:13-21 Jesus warns against greed. A rich man, with a crop so large his existing barns could not contain it, was focused on how to store even more. Think of all the people he could have helped with his wealth! But that was not his focus; his greed made him think only of himself. What good did all his wealth do him when the time of his death arrived?

We live in a world that is increasingly divided into "us" and "them." When we give of ourselves to others, we embody the gospel and invite a blessing to both "us" and "them."

SUNDAY, AUGUST 4 ~ *Read Psalm 107:43*

Our ten-month-old grandson is our joy and delight. During one of his visits to our house, I was busy in the kitchen when I noticed he had gotten uncommonly quiet in the living room. I looked into the room just in time to see him about to put an electrical cord into his mouth. Instinctively I shouted, "No!" which startled him so much he not only dropped the cord but burst into tears. I scooped him up and comforted him to reassure him that I loved him.

How like a loving parent is our God. The Bible is filled with warnings, as we read in Hosea 11; accounts of guidance and protection as found in Psalm 107:1-9; and instructions in righteousness, as in Colossians 3:1-11 and Luke 12:13-21. Yet these texts assure us that even God's harshest warnings come from a heart of God's parental love.

In 2 Corinthians 3:2-3, Paul writes to the Corinthian believers, "You yourselves are our letter, written on our hearts, known and read by everyone. You show that you are a letter from Christ" (NIV). Paul tells the Corinthians that they are the living gospel to all those they come across. And so are we today.

In order to "be the gospel" to those around us, we must first love them. Loving others can be difficult, but I rely on the old saying: "Our walk talks, and our talk talks; but our walk talks louder than our talk talks." In other words, actions speak louder than words. When our actions show God's love, we are being the gospel.

Dear Lord, help us to be the gospel both within ourselves and to others every day. Help us to live authentic Christian lives; lead and direct our hearts, minds, and mouths. In Jesus' name. Amen.

Doing Good, Seeking Justice

AUGUST 5–11, 2019 • LARRY J. PEACOCK

SCRIPTURE OVERVIEW: The prophet Isaiah brings a harsh message to the Southern Kingdom of Israel. Although they are performing sacrifices and observing feasts, they have lost their heart for God. God wants no more meaningless sacrifices but instead wants the people to repent. The psalmist proclaims a similar message from God. The people's sacrifices have become pointless because they have forgotten God. The primary offerings that God desires are thanksgiving and ethical living. The author of Hebrews sounds a note of harmony, emphasizing that Abraham's faith in action—not his performance of religious duties—brings him favor with God. Jesus teaches that we cannot rest on our laurels of having faith. Instead we should remain vigilant and continue to perform acts of charity, including caring for the poor, as a response to our faith.

QUESTIONS AND SUGGESTIONS FOR REFLECTION

- Read Isaiah 1:1, 10-20. Consider the author's difficult questions: Is there blood on your hands? Does your worship lead you to acts of mercy and justice?
- Read Psalm 50:1-8, 22-23. How do you offer thanksgiving as sacrifice and go in the right way?
- Read Hebrews 11:1-3, 8-16. How do you demonstrate faith as a verb, not just a noun?
- Read Luke 12:32-40. God promises us a bountiful kingdom, but we cannot take our worldly possessions there. How do you work toward living as if you are already in God's bountiful kingdom? How do you help to create it?

Director, Franciscan Spiritual Center, Portland, Oregon; retired United Methodist minister; retreat leader and author of *The Living Nativity: Preparing for Christmas with Saint Francis*.

MONDAY, AUGUST 5 ~ *Read Isaiah 1:1, 10-15*

The longest prophetic book in the Hebrew scriptures begins with complaints about the rebellious people of Judah in the Southern Kingdom with its capital of Jerusalem. The readings this week address their worship practices and their evil ways that oppress the most vulnerable in society.

The book of Isaiah begins not with the customary call to prophesy (Isaiah's call is told in chapter 6), but rather by his calling the people to listen to what God has against them. Isaiah tells the people that proper offerings and rituals in the Temple mean nothing if not accompanied by proper treatment of people outside the Temple. As reported by other prophets, notably Amos in chapter 5, God has had enough of fatted animals, festivals, and incense if the poor remain oppressed and the orphan children forgotten.

How many churches have battled over worship: what kind of music to play, where to place the announcements, and how long the preacher should preach and on what? How much time goes into planning worship with great pressure to be "entertaining" and attract a younger crowd, while so little time goes into planning to change systems that make adoption difficult, that underpay working widows, or that encourage luxury condos over affordable housing? Isaiah is direct. God will not listen to our prayers—a stunning indictment of how we so glibly say, "God, hear our prayer." Verse 15 leaves us with a difficult question to begin the week: Is there blood on our hands? Isaiah calls us to deep reflection, Does our worship lead us to acts of mercy and justice?

God of Justice and Compassion, open my ears to hear the cries of the poor, soften my heart so I can feel the pain of the wounded and hungry, make ready my hands to build a new beloved community where the smallest and most vulnerable are cared for and all are valued and respected and fed and housed. Amen.

TUESDAY, AUGUST 6 ~ *Read Isaiah 1:16-20*

In frustration, we may ask, "What do you want me to do?" We long for clarity and direction, even though we may not like the answers we receive and think we know better in making our own choices. God, through the prophet, provides clear direction: "Cease to do evil." Isaiah revisits the actions of the people and the leaders of the nation throughout the first ten chapters and offers a summary of their evil in chapter 10: He accuses the leaders of writing crooked laws, robbing the poor, and oppressing widows and orphans. (See Isaiah 10:1-2.)

It is not enough just to stop doing evil; we must also "learn to do good; seek justice, rescue the oppressed." Isaiah looks at the people most in need, the folks at the bottom of the social scale. The prophet uses strong words, active verbs: "rescue, defend, plead." Isaiah urges us to lift up those who have no means to come back into the community. The widows and orphans have no family structure to sustain them, no champion for their cause. Isaiah instructs us to be willing and obedient learners, to be diligent and persistent in doing good.

Bishop Reuben Job distilled John Wesley's General Rules into three simple rules that echo the prophet. Do no harm. Do good. Stay in love with God. The Bible weds its persistent and prophetic focus on justice with personal practices of prayer, worship, and spiritual formation. Isaiah weaves those insights together in the first chapter with clarity and urgency. The words find New Testament expression in the words and life of Jesus, who announces he has come "to bring good news to the poor . . . release to the captives . . . to let the oppressed go free" (Luke 4:18).

Holy God, help me to slow down for prayer, to stand up for the homeless and oppressed, and to breathe deeply of your love. Make me a willing and obedient servant of your compassion for all. Amen.

WEDNESDAY, AUGUST 7 ~ *Read Psalm 50:1-8, 22-23*

On the heels of Isaiah comes a psalm of judgment. While we may prefer psalms of comfort, like Psalm 23, or psalms of praise and thanksgiving, like Psalm 8, psalms of lament and psalms of judgment give us language for our troubles. Sometimes we complain to God in colorful and angry laments and sometimes God complains about us, taking us to court for our misdeeds. Sometimes God takes our side to praise our deeds of compassion, but in Psalm 50, God testifies against us.

The lectionary's selection of verses does not lay out the case against us, but Isaiah and other prophets list the errors of the leaders of God's chosen ones, the sins of the people who forget they were once foreigners, and the iniquities of those who mistreat the widows and orphans. And in verses 18-20, a portion of the psalm omitted from the lectionary reading, the psalmist adds some new specific sins: befriending thieves, keeping company with adulterers, speaking evil, and slandering one's kin.

God is both attorney testifying against us and judge deciding our case. In verse 22, God proclaims a harsh sentence. Some people experience God as this kind of judge as their pastors preach condemnation, though often for a list of personal sins rather than the societal sins of injustice named by the prophets and found in these judgment psalms. Yet, even within this psalm of judgment, we hear that God prefers prayer, thanksgiving, and going the right way. Our reading from Isaiah this week offers us an explanation of going the right way: "do good, seek justice, rescue the oppressed, defend the orphan, plead for the widow" (1:17). In the early church, Christians were often known as people of the Way, and even today we strive to be followers of the compassionate and loving Jesus, staying true to his Way.

What would be God's court case against your faith community? How is God inviting you to live with more gratitude and more prayer?

THURSDAY, AUGUST 8 ~ *Read Hebrews 11:1-3*

The writer of the letter to the Hebrews, whom scholars believe is not Paul, is a theologian and a storyteller. The eleventh chapter begins by setting out the direction and the definition of *faith*. Faith is an orientation to the future. For the writer, faith is not a set of beliefs, though we often use *faith* as a noun when we refer to "the Jewish faith or the Christian faith." But *faith* is better understood as a verb, a foundational base of trust in God as we move into an unknown future. Faith is stepping out, leaning forward, and trusting that God goes before us.

Faith does not depend on proof or visible results. Faith draws our heart toward a new relationship, hopes for a bright future, and invites us to sail toward a new horizon or march to a new country. For the author, even creation, which God called into being and which can be seen, testifies to the unseen hand of God.

We walk by faith and hope, believing the work we do, the kindness we share, and the care we offer make a difference.

I recently visited the Martin Luther King Jr. Memorial in Washington, D.C. The statue by sculptor Lei Yixin renders Dr. King's bust protruding from a large granite rock as if he were carved out of a large mountain. Many see and have claimed the monument as a stone of hope hued out of a mountain of despair. As a person of faith, Dr. King walked toward an uncertain future, let go of the status quo, and marched forward as a "drum major" for justice.

Holy and loving Creator, teach us to grab your hand as we step forward on curving trails, stony paths, or barren deserts. Give us confidence in your love, guidance, and care as we risk bold ventures, conviction to speak up when we see injustice, and strength to live each day as instruments of your peace and compassion. Amen.

FRIDAY, AUGUST 9 ~ *Read Hebrews 11:8-16*

The writer as storyteller spends the rest of the eleventh chapter of Hebrews naming people of faith who put their trust in God in myriad circumstances. This week's lectionary reading speaks of Abraham and Sarah who follow God to a new place and trust in God's power of procreation even though they are old—"too old." Such trust leads to many descendants, uncountable like stars or sand, from the highest heavens to the lowly earth.

Sarah and Abraham are called to move, to experience life as foreigners in a strange, new land. Later, the psalmist and many of the prophets remind the Hebrew people that their experience as strangers should teach them to be kind to the foreigners in their midst. But often they forget and treat foreigners as enemies. The writer of Hebrews links the earthbound experience of being foreigners to the seeking of a better country beyond death, a heavenly home that welcomes them. God prepares a city for them, a large city, it seems, since the descendants number as many as grains of sand in the desert.

A speaker I recently heard says he prefers to use the term "people move," instead of the often more charged words "refugees" or "immigrants." Going back to Abraham and Sarah and throughout history, people move for many and varied reasons. Sarah and Abraham let go of their established life, their familiar surroundings, and set out to follow God's call. It is not easy to move, to pack up and go without a new address waiting. The tent symbolizes their transient status.

For the writer, willingness to follow God's call demonstrates faith. Listening and obeying, trusting and moving forward; these skills and practices continue to prove useful today as we discern God's call for our life.

Loving God, soften my heart, unstop my ears, and shrink my fears so that I may hear and respond to your call. Amen.

SATURDAY, AUGUST 10 ~ *Read Luke 12:32-34*

Do not be afraid." The angel's words to Zechariah and then to Mary in Luke 1 appear again on Jesus' lips in today's reading. These words and variations of them appear frequently throughout scripture to remind us to let go of anxiety, worry, and fear and to trust in God's care and provision. God is pleased to love us and to give us the kingdom. Jesus reminds the anxious disciples not to worry about what to wear, eat, or drink. These sweet words offer affirmation to the disciples—the little flock Jesus addresses—and by extension to us. Do not be afraid. God wants to give us the kingdom.

The kingdom God promises does not include wealth or possessions; it does not promise bank accounts, big houses, or the mountain chalet or lake cabin. In fact, with knowledge of God's kingdom, we can sell our possessions and give to the poor. Jesus invites us to look where our attachments lie. What do we cling to? What are we holding on to? What gets in the way of responding to God's call to live lightly and joyously in the kingdom?

I heard a story about the death of a stingy rich man in a small community. People were curious about his money. One person asked the funeral director, "How much did he leave?" The director replied, "All of it." We cannot take anything with us. Maybe that can shake us loose from the constant striving, acquiring, and worrying about the future.

God wants to give us the kingdom, the assurance of being loved, forgiven, accepted as we are and thus empowered to live in peace and harmony with all creation and all people. Set your heart on living in God's grace and be at peace with all.

Repeat throughout the day, "Do not be afraid."

SUNDAY, AUGUST 11 ~ *Read Luke 12:35-40*

Live in readiness. Be dressed for action. Keep your batteries charged. Jesus does not equate waiting with doing nothing.

Life is lived in the present, and Jesus has just instructed the disciples not to be anxious or afraid but to trust in the ongoing graciousness of God who feeds the birds and clothes the flowers (12:22-27). Yet, life is also about preparing for the future, waiting for the return of Christ.

Some, maybe most, in the early church expect Jesus to return within their lifetime. Such immediacy calls forth a certain kind of readiness: not holding on to possessions, not getting married, and, for others, foregoing work and relationships to live in the desert.

Now, centuries later, the ever-relevant call to readiness means something a bit different for most of us. We feel called to live each day alert, alive, and grateful. Many of us recite Psalm 118:24, "This is the day that the LORD has made; let us rejoice and be glad in it." God's creation fills us with holy anticipation and surprising wonder, so we must be awake and ready to celebrate.

The ongoing call to preparedness is not a disaster drill but faithful work to create a more just and peaceful world. Preparedness is centering ourselves in the grace and forgiveness of our loving God, looking for places where the light of Christ is present, and joining in the celebration and construction of the new reign of God. We can work for the kingdom to come on earth as in heaven as we live with joyful expectation and genuine acts of kindness and compassion.

Coming God, teach us to live with eyes open to see you working for good in your world and in our lives. Teach us to keep our hands open to receive your gifts and ready to work for justice and peace. Dress us in kindness, clothe us in compassion, and keep us awake to your presence always. Amen.

No Greater Love

AUGUST 12–18, 2019 • JESSICA LAGRONE

SCRIPTURE OVERVIEW: Isaiah compares the people of Israel to a vineyard that God has planted. However, the grapes that grow there have become wild. There is no justice, no right living in the vineyard so God is considering letting it be destroyed. The psalmist bemoans the state of God's people using the same metaphor. The vineyard has been overrun, burned, and cut down. The psalmist appeals to God to restore the vineyard. The author of Hebrews presents many more examples of people of faith in past times. All these exemplars now surround us and cheer us on in our life of faith. In Luke's Gospel, Jesus cautions that following the gospel requires full commitment. For some, this will mean tension in relationships, even within families. Following Jesus is not a commitment of convenience.

QUESTIONS AND SUGGESTIONS FOR REFLECTION

- Read Isaiah 5:1-7. Recall a time when you lovingly prepared a place. What would prompt you to destroy it?
- Read Psalm 80:1-2, 8-19. How has God restored you when you have been at your most vulnerable?
- Read Hebrews 11:29–12:2. Who makes up your personal Faith Hall of Fame? How does each person cheer you on in your spiritual journey?
- Read Luke 12:49-56. What does it mean for your life of faith for Jesus to have come to bring division?

Dean of the Chapel, Asbury Theological Seminary in Wilmore, Kentucky.

MONDAY, AUGUST 12 ~ *Read Isaiah 5:1-2*

Love often takes the shape of preparation. A young man showers and shaves and washes his car as he thinks of a date with his beloved later that day. A mother-to-be prepares a nursery for the arrival of her first child.

The beloved in this story from Isaiah is a gardener. His preparation is as meticulous as his love is boundless, even before a single seed drops into the dirt. He searches for a hillside with the best soil and clears all the stones that would hinder the vines of his dreams. After gently dropping grape seeds into the ground he prepares in faith by building a wall, a watchtower, and a winepress. A wall will protect: He desires to see the vines kept safe and secure. A watchtower will guard: He expects that the vines (though yet to be seen) will be of great worth. A winepress anticipates an abundant harvest worthy of making fine wine. He looks forward to the only way the vines can return his love: by producing good grapes, a crop of faithfulness in return for an introduction of love and care.

We discover that this meticulous gardener is the Lord God. God expresses love by preparing. God gives to each of us a gift that we call prevenient grace, a grace that comes to us before we ever respond to God. Perhaps you can see ways in which God has gone before you to lay a path of grace before you ever walked it. You may be able to peek into God's plans for you and to see elements of walls, watchtowers, and winepresses that anticipated you would be of great worth before you ever took your first breath.

Lord, whether the crop of our response has been sweet or bitter, we can see that you have loved us well by sowing mercy and grace for us to find. Amen.

TUESDAY, AUGUST 13 ~ *Read Isaiah 5:1-7*

Today we learn the outcome of the gardener's investment of care. When he harvests the grapes, they are not the sweet, wholesome fruit for which he prepared. They are wild grapes, bad grapes.

Just as the gardener's caring preparation in planting the vineyard requires deep emotional investment, his response is just as passionate. He responds to his deep hurt by reversing his original work: He tears down the hedge and wall and allows the wild animals to trample the fields and the ground to return to thorny wild pasture. When finally he commands the clouds to withhold rain, we remember this is no ordinary gardener. This is the Lord Almighty, commander of clouds and climate. This passage seems to confirm all our worst fears of a vindictive, angry God. We worry: *What will God do to us if we are not faithful?*

I offer one note to help us put this parable in perspective: It is written in a way that shows a God capable of deep love and deep pain. It assures us that at the heart of the universe is not a set of rules being checked off but a relational God who cares deeply enough to be affected by our actions. This is at once both reassuring and terrifying. Then the last sentence of the passage gives the final clue of what stirs the gardener enough to prompt such a severe response: injustice and bloodshed, cries of distress unanswered.

God responds passionately here because God is passionate about justice. God sows Israel kindness, and Israel responds by sowing bloodshed and injustice. God cannot ignore or continue to nurture this kind of fruit. Change must come. As Christians, though, we remember that when the fruit of injustice runs its course, God wears the thorns that bring justice. The wine of salvation comes not from our grapes but from God's giving of God's self for our iniquities.

Lord, help us to bear the good fruit of justice. Amen.

WEDNESDAY, AUGUST 14 ~ *Read Psalm 80:1-2, 8-19*

Today's setting feels like déjà vu all over again to those of us who spent the last two days in Isaiah 5. We're back on the farm. Once again Israel is the vine that God has planted, and the psalmist locates a tender shoot under the watchful eye of a gifted gardener.

This time, though, we're given a different kind of history. The vinegrower transplants this tender shoot out of Egypt and brings it to this prepared and beautiful place. Is there any more vulnerable life force than a plant taken out of its soil? We are totally dependent on God, the watchful protector who makes a place better for us than the arid lands we formerly inhabited.

The psalm is a communal lament, a crying out of a people who have known peace and prosperity in the past but now suffer and struggle to make sense of the brokenness in which they find themselves. So many communities and families could make this pattern their own heart's cry: God has done something wonderful for us (the transplant of a tiny shoot) and we have prospered (growing to cover the mountains). Only now we have been devastated, destroyed. Once strong, we are weak again and plead for the mercy of God's tender care and restoration. How many times have we gone through this same cycle of growth, loss, and a return to utter dependence on God in our own lives?

The psalmist closes with a beautiful picture of our one true need in moments of deepest despair: "Restore us, LORD God Almighty; make your face shine on us, that we may be saved" (NIV). Our greatest need is not soil or shade or rain but for God's face to shine on us. This holy photosynthesis alone will restore us to light and life.

Lord, shine on those in pain and grief. Restore us to light and life. Amen.

THURSDAY, AUGUST 15 ~ *Read Hebrews 11:29-40*

Too many of us have grabbed hold of the notion that people of faith are perfect, unwavering examples to be lifted up because of their endless strengths. Actually, reading the Bible is a dangerous activity if you want to hold that kind of view. The characters you'll find there are, well, characters. Not only do they have checkered pasts; their presents aren't too spotless either. Instead of fearless pillars of faith, we often find reluctant followers whose successes come only by sticking close to a faithful God.

We often refer to Hebrews 11 as the Faith Hall of Fame. The names and stories lifted up in brief review here are meant to inspire us and drive us to desire and pursue a closer walk with God. But these stories encourage us not because their stars are in some way superhuman. Surely the Israelites' knees knock in fear as they pass through the Red Sea; surely some whisper disbelief as they march around the walls of Jericho for the sixth time with no result. This list includes martyrs and prophets who help turn generations back to God. But then there's Gideon, who never quite gets over his self doubt, and Barak, who cannot believe God will use a woman to accomplish God's will. David's story is marred by adultery and murder, Rahab's by prostitution, and Jephthah makes the worst oath in the Bible with the worst results.

These are our Hebrews 11 heroes. In all their human frailty, how do they shut the mouths of lions and quench the fury of the flames? These ordinary human beings rely on an extraordinary God. These stories make the hall of fame not because their actors are famous but because their actors lift up our faithful God. That's a kind of hero I can aspire to follow.

God, make your name famous through our imperfect stories of faith in you. Amen.

FRIDAY, AUGUST 16 ~ *Read Hebrews 12:1-2*

What does it mean to run a race surrounded by witnesses? In the first Olympics of modern times in 1896, the crowd not only cheered but literally surrounded one runner. The games had returned to their place of origin in Greece to inaugurate a new era. One of the largest crowds had gathered in the Olympic stadium, the location of the finish line, to witness the end of the marathon.

As word began to spread that the front-runner and likely gold-medalist was one of their own, a Greek athlete, many of the onlookers poured out of the stadium and ran backward along the route to greet the leader of the race. When the crowds got to him, they began running alongside him, almost crowding the course too much for the runner to pass. Finally passing through the crowds leading up to the stadium, the winner entered to the sound of deafening cheers and then, remarkably, both the Crown Prince and Prince of Greece jumped down from the royal box and ran across the finish line with him. Then they carried him with them in triumph up to the royal box.

Can you picture the kind of excitement that comes when a hopeful crowd knows that one of their own runs toward their home turf? That's the scene playing for us here to close out the Faith Hall of Fame in Hebrews. The long list of ordinary heroes made remarkable in the Lord is here not just for entertainment value. Instead, these remarkable saints surround us on our journey and cheer for us. The author of Hebrews encourages us to rid ourselves of the things that weigh us down and to keep Jesus firmly in our sight. Jesus has run before us and will carry us over the finish line.

Lord, give me a cheering section, and make me a cheering section for someone else. Amen.

SATURDAY, AUGUST 17 ~ *Read Luke 12:49-53*

In 2014 I had the chance to spend a week with a group of leaders from the underground church in Iran. The Americans were assigned to be their teachers at a weeklong training, but we found quickly that these amazing Christians were far more equipped to teach us than we were to teach them.

I loved hearing their stories about how they learned of Jesus and decided to follow him. In a country that punishes by death conversion and baptism to the Christian faith, those who had shared Christianity with each of them had risked their lives in order to do so. In some cases, God had revealed Godself to them in dreams and visions that sounded as though they came straight out of the biblical story.

Because every one of these Iranian Christians was a first-generation convert to Christianity, each had to make a hard decision about what and when to tell their family of their decision. In one case, after an adult son told his father that he was now a follower of Isa Masih (Jesus Christ), the father called all the family together and announced that the son and his wife and children were no longer part of their family and that no one would speak to them again. Without hesitation, the son pulled his key chain out of his pocket and removed the key to his parents' home (where he and his family lived) and the key to his father's shop (where he and his wife worked) and placed them on the table, saying, "No home or job or even family is as valuable to me as Jesus the Messiah."

In this passage in Luke, Jesus does not praise family quarrels, but he does say that there should be no force on earth stronger than our loyalty to him. Is there anything that stands between you and a life fully devoted to following Jesus?

Isa Masih, give us undivided hearts where you are first in all things. Amen.

SUNDAY, AUGUST 18 ~ *Read Luke 12:49-56*

Jesus' declaration that he has come not to bring peace but to bring division is unsettling. Images of a peaceable kingdom where lions lie down with lambs float further away as we see Jesus' ministry causing more conflict than it resolves.

Since history is always written afterward, the authors of the Gospels have the benefit of knowing what is coming in Jesus' story. They know that the baptism he has to undergo is a violent and excruciating death. We too read the Bible with the end in mind. We know that the Resurrection will bring a happy ending to the Crucifixion and that the last pages of scripture herald God's final victory. The trouble with knowing the end of the story, for us and for Jesus, is that we live in the middle. In today's passage, Jesus tries to alert the crowd of the storms that lie ahead.

Predicting storms is tricky business. Jesus admonishes the crowd for being good meteorologists of the signs they see in the weather conditions while being clueless of the signs of the times. The crowds gather not to hear from a man who will die in shame on a cross but in the hope for a glimpse of a miracle worker, a chance at victory with a military Messiah come to conquer their oppressors and set things right. They cannot interpret the signs that the coming storm will dash all their hopes before God will fulfill them in the most unlikely way.

We too have hopes. We look anxiously for signs that the best of our hopes will come to pass. But to follow Jesus means to cling to him as our only hope, even if it means clinging to him through storms on the way to eternal calm.

Lord, be our peace in the storms of our lives. Amen.

Refuge Is Sabbath

AUGUST 19–25, 2019 • LAWRENCE RANKIN

SCRIPTURE OVERVIEW: The readings in Jeremiah and Psalm 71 are repeated in a pair from earlier in the year (January 28—February 3). They describe the authors' confidence that God has had plans for their lives since even before they were born. God similarly knows each one of us and has a calling on our lives. The reading in Hebrews gives us confidence in the permanence of the kingdom of God, to which we have access through the sacrifice of Jesus Christ. We are not to take this lightly; we should worship God with due respect. In a synagogue on the sabbath, Jesus teaches a lesson about mercy. When he encounters a woman in need, he places her need above religious regulations. If religious traditions trump mercy, then our priorities are out of alignment.

QUESTIONS AND SUGGESTIONS FOR REFLECTION

- Read Jeremiah 1:4-10. How do the children in your life live out God's call on their lives?
- Read Psalm 71:1-6. How do you continually praise God as your refuge?
- Read Hebrews 12:18-29. How do you discern what is required of you in praising God in the new covenant?
- Read Luke 13:10-17. How do you observe the sabbath now? What sabbath practice might you start that puts God's reign into action?

Retired ordained member of the Florida Conference United Methodist Church; former Conference Secretary for Global Ministries; board member of Club Success; member of a covenant between the Cuban and Florida conferences; husband, father, and grandfather.

MONDAY, AUGUST 19 ~ *Read Jeremiah 1:4-10*

Baby brother came home from the hospital with his proud parents to meet his sister. The four-year-old asked her mom and dad if she could be with her brother alone. Anxiously, they allowed her. She went into the baby's room, closed the door, and moved toward the crib. Her parents, their ears pressed to the door, heard her whisper, "Quick, tell me who made you. Tell me where you came from. I'm beginning to forget!"

When God calls young Jeremiah, God makes sure that Jeremiah will not forget who he is and to whom he belongs. "Before I formed you . . . I knew you . . . I consecrated you; I appointed you a prophet to the nations." Jeremiah struggles to believe God and his ability to fulfill God's call. "Ah, Lord God! Truly I do not know how to speak, for I am only a boy."

When the bishop laid his hands on my head and intoned the words of ordination, "Take thou authority as an elder to preach the Word of God," I was unsure I could fulfill God's call on my life either.

But God calls each of us to our vocation. Whether we work as a minister, a business professional, or in the trades, God calls each of us and gives each of us a mission. As Christians, Jesus Christ calls us as he did the disciples. And Christ's call to all Christians, no matter our vocation, invites us to co-create the kingdom of God, today and into eternity. "Go therefore and make disciples of all nations" (Matt. 28:19).

God of prevenient grace, when you call, help us to listen. Amen.

TUESDAY, AUGUST 20 ~ *Read Psalm 71:1-3*

My friend Sergio was born with a severe hearing impairment and a defective heart. When he was a six years old, his parents brought him to Florida from Mexico. They entered the United States as undocumented immigrants. After many years, his family continues to live in fear of deportation. Sergio is temporarily protected by the Deferred Action for Childhood Arrivals (DACA), but the government can revoke his status at any time. Nevertheless, for now, DACA is his refuge from losing everything.

The psalmist trusts God's protection. "In you, O LORD, I take refuge. . . . In your righteousness deliver me and rescue me. . . . Be to me a rock of refuge, a strong fortress, to save me."

Refuge, *chasah*, has many interpretations in the Hebrew scriptures. A refuge is a shelter, a dwelling, a tent, a sanctuary. In a refuge, one gains strength. Sergio discovered this strength from his refuge while growing up, playing, working in the fields, and going to school. I mentored him until he graduated from high school. He earned a scholarship to study to be an auto mechanic. He hopes to be able to support his parents so they won't have to work picking fruit and vegetables. He finds his strength to overcome the obstacles put before him by trusting in God's refuge.

The psalmist calls on God to be a refuge with faith that God will rescue him. Like the psalmist, we can trust that the Lord who has supported us since taking us from our mother's womb will be our rock and our fortress.

"O LORD, my strength, and my fortress, and my refuge in the day of affliction," (Jer. 16:19, KJV) may you extend your tent around me so that I may boldly proclaim your salvation. Amen.

WEDNESDAY, AUGUST 21 ~ *Read Psalm 71:4-6*

Jesus' enemies often threaten to arrest and kill him. He admonishes his disciples, "Whoever does not take up the cross and follow me is not worthy of me. Those who find their life will lose it, and those who lose their life for my sake will find it" (Matt. 10:38-39).

German pastor, theologian, conspirator, and martyr Dietrich Bonhoeffer challenged the churches to reject the Third Reich. Most didn't. Bonhoeffer was found out, imprisoned, and executed a couple of weeks prior to the end of the war. Bonhoeffer may have prayed from his favorite songbook, "Rescue me, O my God, from the hand of the wicked, from the grasp of the unjust and cruel. For you, O LORD, are my hope, my trust."

I met Maria Cristina Gomez during a visit to El Salvador in the mid 1980s. I served as a mission interpreter with Alfalit Latinoamericano, a Christian literacy and grass-roots community development ministry. Maria was a teacher at a Baptist school in her war-torn country. She directed Alfalit's women's program and was a leader of a teacher's union. One day heavily armed men burst into her classroom and dragged her away while her students watched in horror. The next day, her body was found on a trash heap.

Are we willing to witness to Christ even to the ultimate sacrifice? When we bear witness to Christ to others, we too are martyrs because witnessing is martyrdom, no matter the cost.

Whenever Maria's community remembers her and other martyrs, the people shout in solidarity, "Maria! Presente!" because Maria indeed is present with the resurrected Christ.

Jesus, what am I willing to die for in order that I may live in you? Help me to witness to you. Amen.

THURSDAY, AUGUST 22 ~ *Read Hebrews 12:18-24*

The writer of Hebrews encourages the first-century followers of Jesus to persevere in their faith in the long-awaited Messiah. The writer reminds them what it was like to live under the law of the old covenant. God was perceived as unapproachable and vengeful, something to be feared. And woe be unto those who disobey the law. Even Moses trembles with fear.

The writer reminds them that Jesus brings a new covenant that fulfills the old covenant. Jesus' life and love highlight another aspect of God as the God who loves, forgives, and offers salvation for all humanity through extravagant grace. Fear and judgment no longer serve as the motivators for people to obey God. The law of love has been around since creation, even in the midst of humanity. Therefore, the writer assures the followers of Jesus that they are loved by God and are called to love others even as they love themselves.

The writer declares, "You have come to Mount Zion . . . the heavenly Jerusalem . . . and to Jesus, the mediator of a new covenant, and to the sprinkled blood that speaks a better word than the blood of Abel." We no longer need to offer endless sacrifices to appease God. Jesus has forgiven all sin, once and for all, through his blood on the cross.

As followers of Jesus, we live in the covenant of Zion. Our Christian faith invites us beyond the covenant of Sinai fraught with fear to follow Jesus "marching upward to Zion . . . to fairer worlds on high" (UMH, no. 733).

God of salvation, you love us so much that you invite us to march upward to Zion. Guide us on our journey. Amen.

FRIDAY, AUGUST 23 ~ *Read Hebrews 12:25-29*

The writer of Hebrews reminds his contemporaries about their Israelite ancestors: "Indeed, by faith our ancestors received approval. By faith we understand that the worlds were prepared by the word of God, so that what is seen was made from things that are not visible" (11:2-3). "Therefore, since we are surrounded by so great a cloud of witnesses, let us also lay aside . . . sin . . . and let us run . . . the race that is set before us, looking to Jesus the pioneer and perfecter of our faith" (12:1-2).

Today's reading from the latter part of chapter 12 references Jesus' reading of Isaiah 61 at his home synagogue in Nazareth. He is surrounded by men who remember him as a boy. And he proclaims, "Today this scripture is fulfilled in your hearing" (Luke 4:22). Through his death and resurrection, Jesus is revealed as the Messiah, who says, "Do not think that I have come to abolish the law; I have come not to abolish but to fulfill" (Matt. 5:17, AP).

The writer warns, "At that time his voice shook the earth" and recounts God's words, "Yet once more I will shake not only the earth but also the heaven." Those things that are shaken from the old shall be removed. Those that are not shaken are the new creation Christ establishes. "Therefore, since we are receiving a kingdom that cannot be shaken, let us give thanks, by which we offer to God an acceptable worship with reverence and awe."

With Christ's fulfillment of the Law and the Prophets, God shakes off the requirements once fulfilled by the people in covenant with God. Through Christ, we have direct access to God as our refuge.

O God, may we know the difference between those things that are shaken from those that are not. May our daily lives be acts of acceptable worship to you. Amen.

SATURDAY, AUGUST 24 ~ *Read Luke 13:10-13*

Many years ago I met a woman whose real name I did not know; I knew her by her nickname, Cat. Cat shuffled into the dorm where I worked the night shift. She greeted me and mumbled about a poem she had written that she wanted to read to me. Cat was born with cerebral palsy and with a brilliant mind. Her parents institutionalized and abandoned her as a child, assuming that she belonged in a facility for persons with intellectual disabilities because of her cerebral palsy. Years later, the staff realized her intellect and restored her independence. She became a ward of the state because she had nowhere to go.

When Cat, now in middle age, approached me that night, I first heard only gibberish. But as I listened more closely, I heard her beautiful, poetic words. She had a voice. I realized that I was in the presence of a wonderful soul trapped in a body devalued by others and our society. With determination and a deep faith in Jesus Christ, she was "set free" as her soul "stood up straight." I too was transformed by having known this wonderful woman, who uttered words of inspiration to all who would listen.

The woman in today's reading is among the most famous of the many unnamed women in the Bible. Jesus sets her free from her pain by seeing her. And though it is the sabbath, he does not let that barrier stop him from healing her. What self-imposed barriers do you carry that ail you? When Jesus calls you over, have you given him permission to lift these from you? Remember that you are set free to praise God by the one who offers you God's overwhelming grace.

God, remove the barriers within me to see past others' differences and to value them for your love and grace within them. Amen.

SUNDAY, AUGUST 25 ~ *Read Luke 13:14-17*

The woman has suffered from bodily and social pain for eighteen years. She has been victimized and abused as a sinner by the religious leaders. She has been exiled, rejected, despised, and denied her full humanity.

When Jesus sees her, he lifts her up to the highest status in Jewish society. He declares her a "daughter of Abraham" and names the source of her suffering as not her own sins but the binding of Satan. When Jesus is rebuked for healing on the sabbath, he shames the religious leaders for their lack of compassion—that they would value rules over human life and suffering. He calls them hypocrites. He teaches them and all of us that keeping sabbath is about more than refraining from physical labor. Jesus teaches that sabbath is the practice of shalom—love in action. God's reign comes into our midst on the sabbath to divinely and outrageously interrupt our lives.

Walter Brueggemann writes in his book *Sabbath as Resistance: Saying No to the Culture of Now* that sabbath requires being neighbor to all without distinction. Sabbath means joining with God to co-create in God's reign. Jesus' healing of the unnamed woman reminds us of God's great reversal, that the "least of these" (Matt. 25:40) become the first to receive God's grace. When others see Jesus putting God's reign into action, "the entire crowd, rejoic[es] at all the wonderful things that he [is] doing."

How might you live sabbath beyond just obeying it?

Lord of sabbath, may I rest in you for the rest of my days, when sabbath is fulfilled in me. Amen.

God of Enough

AUGUST 26—SEPTEMBER 1, 2019 • CARA MEREDITH

SCRIPTURE OVERVIEW: Jeremiah (the "weeping prophet") is not very popular in his time. In this passage he relates a message from God that the people have forsaken God (living water) and put their trust in things that can never satisfy (leaky cisterns). The psalmist expresses similar frustration from God. Israel will not listen to God's voice or receive God's provision, so God allows them to experience the unfortunate consequences of their choices. The author of Hebrews provides practical advice for living the Christian life: showing hospitality, caring for those in prison, honoring marriage, and avoiding materialism. This ethical living is an offering to God. Jesus reinforces this in his parable of the banquet. We should be generous to those who need it most, not just to those who can provide us some benefit in return.

QUESTIONS AND SUGGESTIONS FOR REFLECTION

- Read Jeremiah 2:4-13. When have you missed the fountain of living water springing up before you?
- Read Psalm 81:1, 10-16. How is God seeking to provide for you? Are you willing to accept God's satisfying provision?
- Read Hebrews 13:1-8, 15-16. How do you or your faith community share hospitality? Do you distinguish between friends and strangers?
- Read Luke 14:1, 7-14. Whom do you invite to your home and to your church? Do you invite those who cannot repay you or only those who can?

Writer and speaker from the San Francisco Bay area; author of *The Color of Life*; follow her on Twitter @caramac54.

The print that hangs in a corner of our dining room reads: "When you have more than you need, build a bigger table, not a higher fence." My family tries to live by this wisdom, and it provides me a much-needed daily reminder of God's provision, God's nature to care for and feed God's people.

In Luke 14, Jesus attends a meal at the home of a Pharisee. After observing how the guests choose their seats, Jesus tells a parable about a meal. Jesus recommends guests take the lowest seat because they do not know their level of distinction compared to the other guests. Then, when the guest of honor comes, the host will invite the guest in the lowest seat to move up higher rather than having to ask the guest to give up the seat. Jesus recommends this practice as an act of humility that will lead to honor.

Perhaps like the Pharisees who listened to Jesus' story, we need the reminder to choose humility. We can practice such humility by recognizing that God gives us enough. The Great Feeder provides us with every ounce of sustenance, both metaphorically and physically. Out of this overabundance of grace, we can build a bigger table, invite more people to it, and give away our seat of honor to take the seat of a servant. After all, we are no better than the person to our right or left. In building bigger tables instead of higher fences, we acknowledge that God alone is enough. And maybe, when that happens, we will begin to recognize anew that we have enough to share abundantly and that all are worthy in the eyes of God.

God, sometimes praying for humility is the hardest prayer of all. Show me what it means to believe that you are enough, so I might act generously out of your provision for me. Amen.

Christmas carols remain the song of choice in my family all year. Earlier this morning, my five-year-old sat on the floor of the living room, singing his own version of "Repeat, repeat the sounding joy!" Sometimes the "re" syllable in "repeat" came out like "pe," and I heard "pepeat the sounding joy." And it wasn't "sounding" joy; it was "sound of" joy. Despite his adaptations, the Christmas message of repeating the good news remained the same.

In Psalm 81, the psalmist sings of the one who feeds and provides. God chimes in and commands the Israelites to open wide their mouths with a promise to fill them. Although prophets have repeated over and over again God's truth, the Israelites do not obey God. The story becomes cyclical: God makes a declaration of love, but the Israelites do not listen. God makes a declaration of love, and the Israelites listen. Repeat, repeat. As outsiders looking in, we easily see the repetition within the psalm, which drives home the call for us to trust and obey in the One who is enough.

But are we all that different from the Israelites? Don't we fail to hear and believe God's message repeated time and time again? Perhaps we should start singing a Christmas song of our own so we can hear the truth that God's love is enough for us.

O Lord, I need to hear the repeated sounds of joy and truth again! Clean out my ears so I can hear you and believe in the depths of your love. Amen.

WEDNESDAY, AUGUST 28 ~ *Read Hebrews 13:1-8*

Last week, a handful of friends gathered at my family's house for dinner. Take-out pizzas, compostable paper plates, and red plastic cups filled our table. Three hours later, most of the adults remained deep in conversation while the children ran circles around us.

The unknown author of Hebrews takes it a step further, encouraging the community of God not only to show love to one another but also to love the strangers in their midst. In showing hospitality to strangers, we might very well entertain the likes of angels! Ancient readers of scripture would have understood the full meaning of *hospitality*. The Greek word, *philoxenia,* comes from two words: *philos,* which means friend, and *xenos,* which means stranger. True hospitality is showing friendship not only to those we already know and love but to strangers far from home who show up on the doorstep in the middle of the night.

Christ, the most famous sojourner of all, travels from village to village as an immigrant. While fully dependent on the goodwill of others, he proclaims the good news, heals the sick, and performs miracles. I wonder if the men and women who show hospitality know they are entertaining the greatest guest of all!

When I dig into the roots of biblical hospitality, I cannot look at my dining room table the same again. It's easy to entertain friends unawares, but might the gift be even greater and holier to the strangers in my midst?

God, give me the courage to show hospitality to the sojourner, the immigrant, the refugee, and the stranger. Amen.

When I was an English teacher, I loved teaching about contrast in literature and helping my students to understand what happens when we consider together a pair of two strikingly dissimilar objects, things, or persons. The created juxtaposition often serves a greater literary purpose, and we find such an example in full at the end of today's reading from Jeremiah.

Speaking through the voice of the prophet, God claims the moniker, "the fountain of living water." God is a naturally flowing spring whose sustenance is always enough. A cistern, on the other hand, is made by humans. When God's people choose to ignore the living water springing up before them, they miss the point of God as water. Their best efforts result in broken cisterns, worthless things. The contrast between a naturally flowing spring and shattered vessels that cannot profit their makers is blatant from our twenty-first-century perspective: as one theologian said, it's like "digging a canal alongside a navigable river."* The people of Jeremiah's time could not recognize the gift of God directly in front of them.

Today, Christ springs up all around us. The gifts of God beckon us to take notice, to breathe in the aroma of pine trees on a walk around the lake, to chew slowly the tomatoes and lettuce from the backyard garden. Whether in nature, in people, in scripture, or in silence, God offers life abundant. Too often we overlook this fountain of living water as we seek to make our own way. May we heed Jeremiah's call and not miss God's bountiful, evident gift of enough.

---

*Alexander Maclaren, *Expositions of Holy Scripture: Isaiah and Jeremiah* (New York: A. C. Armstrong and Son, 1906), 250.

God, give me the eyes to see, the ears to ear, the mouth to taste, the fingers to feel, and the nose to smell the gift of you already all around me. Amen.

FRIDAY, AUGUST 30 ~ *Read Luke 14:12-14*

Recently, my sons and I encountered a man experiencing homelessness asking for assistance. I rolled down my window to give him a package of Pop-Tarts. A conversation about building houses and providing food for those who don't have enough ensued. "Mama, the workers will build a house for them!" my three-year-old said with enthusiasm. I nodded my head along with him as I wished for just an ounce of his faith.

At the end of the parable in Luke 14, Jesus calls us to share our abundance with those who could never repay us. As Christians, we are to extend hospitality to "the poor, the crippled, the lame, and the blind"—for such is the kingdom of God. Though I find it easy to roll down my window and hand someone a breakfast item, I find it far more difficult to stretch my hospitality a step further toward the heart of Jesus' words. Jesus comes not only for those who look put together and have financial security. Jesus comes not only for those of us who attend church every Sunday, who tithe regularly, who repent of our sins, who vote the way we feel is right, and who know all the right people. This passage reminds us of the subversive nature of God, who reverses our expectations and understandings and who promises that those who host the marginalized out of their abundance will be "repaid at the resurrection of the righteous."

As much as I want to live by this upside-down, counter-cultural social system, I don't always know how to make it happen. I think it requires a step beyond a package of Pop-Tarts. My next step might be asking someone's name and issuing an invitation to my house for dinner.

God, I believe your kingdom extends far beyond the borders I usually place around me. Help me to extend my borders to include all whom you send my way. Amen.

SATURDAY, AUGUST 31 ~ *Read Hebrews 13:15-16*

Years ago, I kept a gratitude journal. Without much space to jot down more than a thought or two, its narrow pages became a genuine and authentic way for me to reflect on all I had to be thankful for at the end of the day: *God, thank you for Mike, who jump-started my car this morning. Thank you for a lovely conversation with Holly. Thank you for getting me through the day.*

I wonder if this is part of what it means to "continually offer up a sacrifice of praise to God." By the final chapter in Hebrews, readers should know who God is and what God has done on our behalf. All the heroes of the faith in chapter 11, all the instruction on correct living, and all of the other truths and teachings packed into the book of Hebrews point to one thing: Jesus Christ. Is there any proper response but praise? How could we not give thanks to God? The unknown author of Hebrews uses the metaphor "fruit of lips" to paint a picture for the reader. Although *fruit* most often describes produce, fruit can also mean the results of our actions. We should praise God for Jesus' personhood and God's good gifts throughout the day. After all, what other choice do we have but praise?

Today's passage makes me want to get back into the practice of praise and thanksgiving. Perhaps I'll begin another gratitude journal, or I may hang a sticky note with the words, "Give thanks!" over my kitchen sink. Either way, I want the fruit of my lips to exude gratitude.

O God, my God, there is so much to thank you for, to whisper and shout and speak praise to your name. May this be a ritual in my life and of my lips. Amen.

SUNDAY, SEPTEMBER 1 ~ *Read Psalm 81:15-16*

A year or two ago, I cut sugar from my diet in an effort to decrease arthritis inflammation. Eager to experiment and find a sugar substitute, I delighted in finding I could consume honey to my heart's content! This sweet, edible substance is not only used by humans across the globe; it is a taste as old as time. The Bible mentions honey in a literal and figurative example over sixty times.

I find it helpful to look into the greater meaning behind "the finest of the wheat" and "honey from the rock." Of the latter, the land of Canaan abounds with honey, where bees make their home in the clefts and holes of rocks. A delicacy then just as it is now, honey is one of the only sweeteners available to the Israelites; but even more so, its sweetness serves a metaphorical purpose, as a sign of abundance and prosperity.

Now when I open the honey jar for my morning coffee or substitute it in a batch of cookies, I see honey in a new way. I see the promises of God—not only the promises that should have been but the promises that very well will be—as I trust and hope in the enough of the Holy One.

Dear God, as I trust in your abundance, feed me with the sweetest of substances, with hidden honey from the rocks. I will forever relish the sweetness of your love. Amen.

The Grandeur and Grace of God

SEPTEMBER 2–8, 2019 • J. PHILIP WOGAMAN

SCRIPTURE OVERVIEW: Jeremiah brings another warning of impending judgment. If the people will not turn to the Lord, God will break the nation and reshape it, just as a potter breaks down and reshapes clay on a wheel. The psalmist praises God for God's intimate knowledge of each one of us. Even from the moment of conception, God knows us and has a plan for our lives. Philemon is often overlooked, but it packs a punch. A text that some used in the past to justify slavery teaches a very different message. Paul warns Philemon not to enslave Onesimus again but to receive him back as a brother. Secular power structures have no place in God's kingdom. In Luke, Jesus uses striking examples to teach us that the life of faith cannot be lived well with half-hearted commitment.

QUESTIONS AND SUGGESTIONS FOR REFLECTION

- Read Jeremiah 18:1-11. As clay, how can you better respond to the Potter's guiding hand?
- Read Psalm 139:1-6, 13-18. God knows you better than you know yourself, yet God has given you the ability to make your own decisions. How do you respond to God?
- Read Philemon 1-21. How do you honor the full humanity of those who serve you through their work?
- Read Luke 14:25-33. What does it mean for you to take up the cross in your life?

Professor Emeritus of Christian Ethics, Wesley Theological Seminary, Washington, D.C.; author of *What Matters*.

MONDAY, SEPTEMBER 2 ~ *Read Luke 14:25-26, 33*

Today's reading is one of the most troubling passages in the whole Bible. Is Jesus calling upon us to abandon our families? Those who are nearest and dearest to us? The ones who have loved and nurtured us? Those who depend most absolutely upon us? Are we even to hate them? And "even life itself"? Not to mention our possessions? What?

Here Jesus has engaged in a bit of hyperbole to make a point that is no exaggeration. None of our earthly loyalties is as important as our commitment to God. God is everything to us. Anything else is relative. We remember that Jesus himself displays attachment to his own family: his mother, his brother. The fact that he refers to God as "Father" suggests that his relationship to his earthly father is intimate and caring. But these and all other earthly attachments cannot be as central as our devotion to God.

Twentieth-century theologian H. Richard Niebuhr wrote about the importance of our "center of value," the basis on which we evaluate everything else. He spoke of how most people value their group (family, community, nation, etc.) as more important than anything else. But we cannot allow these loyalties to take the place of God. Verse 33 speaks directly to one of our most tempting idolatries: our possessions. Our culture can lead us to be pretty materialistic. We all need material things, but they are not our central life purpose. As Jesus reminds us, giving up our material attachments is a prerequisite to being his disciple.

Dear God, help us gain new perspective on what really matters. Liberate us from false attachment to lesser things. Amen.

TUESDAY, SEPTEMBER 3 ~ *Read Psalm 139:1-6*

We pause over the deep implication of this psalm: God is present all the time and everywhere. The psalmist expresses that implication in personal terms: God knows everything about us. On the larger scale of the whole universe, there isn't any place where God is not present. To the psalmist that means especially that God is deeply, personally present to each of us. That isn't so easy for us to understand, much less to accept. Can the God of this vast universe know each of us and care for each of us?

The psalmist writes a long time before modern cosmology began to discover the incredible immensity of the universe. Reputable scientists agree that there are at least a trillion galaxies in the universe, each (like our own Milky Way) holding millions of stars and who-knows-how-many planets. The psalmist couldn't know these numbers, but even in the ancient world, the immensity of creation is wonderfully evident. The psalmist's faith in God's intimate presence to each and every human being is deeply rooted in the psalmist's wonder at the vastness of creation.

When we affirm our faith in God's presence with each of us, we are all the more aware of the sheer grandeur of God. How can the God of all that is be so present to each of us? Theologian Paul Tillich reminds us that God is not just one "thing" among others. God, he writes, is the "ground of all being." God is involved in everything. The intimate presence of God means all the more in light of the grandeur of God. We are invited to see the loving presence of God and to respond to God's ubiquitous and intimate presence.

Thank you, God, for the incredible gift of this universe in which we have our home, and for your intimate loving presence with each of us. Amen.

WEDNESDAY, SEPTEMBER 4 ~ *Read Psalm 139:13-18*

The psalmist continues to express, in the most intimate terms, how totally God knows us and has formed us. These words do not compel us to conclude that God literally made every aspect of our bodies and minds or that God intended, from the beginning of all creation, that we would be exactly who and what we are. That would suggest a kind of determinism that excludes the actions of our parents and their parents (*ad infinitum*). But it reminds us that the potentiality of all creation stems from God. God has, from the beginning, enabled the emergence of people like us with the capacity to respond to God and to join creatively in God's purposes.

The psalmist lingers over the wonder of human life. Whether or not God specifically intended each of us to be created as we are, one thing is sure: We had no part in our creation. We had no say in the crucial decision in our life: our conception and birth. For each of us it is a given. Suddenly, here we are. What we do about that may depend upon us in large measure, but our life and the life of all our ancestors comes from God.

That said, how we respond to the incredible gift of life depends on us—at least in large measure. God knows each of us intimately. But God has also gifted us with the freedom to respond to the gift of life given by our Creator.

O God, how can we begin to take hold of the immense gift of life and to respond to your invitation to be a part of your creative purposes? Guide us as we seek to follow you. Amen.

THURSDAY, SEPTEMBER 5 ~ *Read Jeremiah 18:1-6*

In this striking analogy, Jeremiah pictures God as the potter, fashioning vessels out of clay. This would be a very familiar image to Jeremiah's readers. The clay in this imagery represents people. God shapes the clay, but some of it doesn't work as planned. At first reading, this narrative seems to say that God, the potter, will do with the clay whatever God wants to do. But Jeremiah isn't really saying that we are inert lumps of clay. Clay can resist the potter, and we can spoil God's creative purposes. We are invited, not forced, to be active participants with God, the potter.

What are those purposes God has for us? Jeremiah doesn't spell it out, and we cannot presume to know it all. But, in the deeper reaches of our faith, we can discern that God's purposes are grounded in love. When we are fully responsive to God, we recognize and relate to the workings of that divine love wherever we are. Most immediately that means performing acts of love for those who are closest to us, seeing their potential, and enabling them to be good persons. It also means reaching out to people in need whom we may never know personally. And it means discerning the hand of God in the world of nature, treating its beauties and resources as gifts to be treasured rather than exploited. God may not plan the details of our lives, but within each of us God has planted extraordinary possibilities to be realized as we respond to the evidences of love all around us.

Have thine own way, Lord! Have thine own way! Thou art the potter; I am the clay. Mold me and make me after thy will, while I am waiting, yielded and still. Amen. (UMH, no. 382)

FRIDAY, SEPTEMBER 6 ~ *Read Jeremiah 18:6-11*

Jeremiah sees God at work in our lives and invites us to respond. God's presence draws us into deep communion with God and the loving purposes that infuse all of creation. We may be tempted to read this assertion in individualistic terms—God the potter seeking to make something beautiful out of me, the clay. Okay, that's there; but Isaiah offers us something more. God gets involved intimately with the kingdoms of this world, seeking to fashion goodness out of the collective life of humankind. God will do good for nations and kingdoms that renounce evil and seek good. But God will destroy nations and kingdoms that turn away from God. In other words, God does not ignore the political life of humankind. Jeremiah does not live in a democracy, so he does not provide this as an essay on responsible citizenship. Jeremiah reminds us that the way nations exercise political power cannot be removed from their spiritual life. The good or evil done by our state implicates us all.

And thus God through Jeremiah invites us to seek loving justice through our actions in the public sphere. We can do our part to seek the better in a public order that is neither perfectly good nor fully evil. Our faith calls us to care for the marginalized and victimized, to seek peace and reconciliation in the wake of violence, to recognize and relate to the hand of God even when others are given to cynicism, and to seek civility in public life.

O God, we trust that you are the God of all the ages and that your purposes will ultimately prevail everywhere. Grant us your light in the presence of so much evil and confusion, and make us humble about our own righteousness. Amen.

SATURDAY, SEPTEMBER 7 ~ *Read Philemon 1-21*

In this familiar story, Paul sends Onesimus, who is probably an enslaved man who has run away, back to his master, Philemon. Paul appeals to Philemon not to enslave Onesimus but to accept Onesimus as "a beloved brother." Most societies no longer permit the ownership of one person by another, so we ask, Does this story still have spiritual significance? Yes, in this sense: Whenever we treat other people only as instruments for our service, we have denied their humanity. When we reject the humanity of others, we are questioning humanity itself—and that includes ourselves. Martin Luther King Jr. asserted that the first victims of racism are racists themselves because they reduce their own humanity to superficial skin color.

We make use of other people all the time: those who work to provide our goods and services, custodians, shopkeepers, bus drivers—everyone who contributes to our economic and social well-being. We ourselves act in service of others in a variety of ways. As we serve one another, Paul's words to Philemon call us to recognize and to appreciate the full humanity of others, no matter their location on the economic or social scale. We can cultivate such awareness through words of thanks to those who serve our needs and through prayers on their behalf for their well-being.

We wonder whether Philemon takes to heart the message and receives Onesimus in the spirit of Paul's appeal. We can't know. But we know that the letter is preserved and perhaps treasured by whoever receives it. We can continue to treasure its message by loving all those who serve as siblings in Christ.

Gracious God, thank you for the gift of humanity that we share with others. Make us more sensitive to the fact that we are all siblings in your intended family of humankind. Amen.

SUNDAY, SEPTEMBER 8 ~ *Read Luke 14:27-33*

Today we return to Luke 14, where Jesus counsels his followers to give up their idolatries if they would be his disciples. Now we note the hardest part of this call: "Whoever does not carry the cross and follow me cannot be my disciple." What does it mean to carry the cross? We usually begin our interpretation in physical terms: We must be prepared to endure suffering with a courageous spirit if necessary. To Jesus the cross meant much more than physical suffering.

Why does Jesus himself take up his cross? Not to be a hero or to demonstrate great courage, but for the sake of love. He could avoid the cross by retreating quietly to Galilee and abandoning his ministry. But he would have to turn away from those who have experienced him as the Incarnation of God's love. Taking up the cross, with its painful death, is a supreme gift of love for those to whom he has ministered and to all of humanity. Jesus' teachings are important, but the cross represents an expression of love beyond words.

So how do we take up the cross? In rare circumstances it can mean physical martyrdom. More often it means lovingly accepting those our society's prejudices and stigmas reject no matter the social consequences. Even when society then casts us aside, taking up our cross means we do not reject those who have rejected us. Instead we repeat Jesus' words from the cross: "Father, forgive them; for they do not know what they are doing" (Luke 23:34). We invest our whole self in God's loving purposes, knowing that in the long run, God's grace will prevail and that in the short run, taking up our cross is the key to abundant life.

O God, your grandeur surpasses our understanding and your grace fills us. Even in our weakness, we seek to follow Jesus, the one who gave his all out of love. Amen.

Returning to God

SEPTEMBER 9–15, 2019 • HIRHO PARK

SCRIPTURE OVERVIEW: Jeremiah's warning of coming judgment continues. The children of Israel have become foolish, have ignored God, and have become good mainly at doing evil. God is going to respond to this situation. The psalmist describes the state of all who are foolish: they deny God and follow their own corrupt desires, including the oppression of the poor. The author of First Timothy, traditionally Paul, says that this was also his former way of life. He has been foolish and ignorant, a persecutor of the followers of Christ. In fact, he had been the worst of all sinners; yet Christ has shown him mercy, not judgment. Jesus tells two parables to reveal God's heart. Rather than neglecting the ignorant, the foolish, and the lost, God searches to find each one of us.

QUESTIONS AND SUGGESTIONS FOR REFLECTION

- Read Jeremiah 4:11-12, 22-28. How do your actions show others that you know God?
- Read Psalm 14. When have you, like the psalmist, felt that no one knows God? How did you have faith that God would restore God's people?
- Read 1 Timothy 1:12-17. Recall a time when you felt unworthy of Christ Jesus' full acceptance. How has that experience made you more grateful for Christ's mercy?
- Read Luke 15:1-10. In a world full of death and violence, how do you rejoice when God finds one lost person?

Executive Director of Clergy Lifelong Learning and UMC Cyber Campus at The General Board of Higher Education and Ministry of The United Methodist Church; oversees the continuing education, online education, and spiritual formation for clergy; provides support for United Methodist clergywomen and racial and ethnic clergy in the areas of theological education, enlistment, and research.

MONDAY, SEPTEMBER 9 ~ *Read Jeremiah 4:11-12, 22-28*

This week's reading starts with a feeling of the Creator's agitation and the image of creation being dismantled. The disappointment with human beings and our unfaithfulness reaches the point of an utterance of nothingness, "no light," on God's part. It almost sounds like a deconstruction of what God did in the beginning. Is God regretting the act of Creation?

It seems like all hope is lost in Israel. However, Jeremiah reminds us that "[God] will not make a full end." God still calls Israel "my poor people." God cannot stop being a loving parent. In spite of our abominations, God declares that we are God's own. God never gives up on us even when we want to give up on ourselves; God waits and hopes for us.

We learn two lessons from Jeremiah's prophecy. First, God is the God of compassion. The heart of God is always open regardless of our circumstance. A mother of a missing child left her front door unlocked for nineteen years just in case her daughter returned. The fear of a stranger entering the house could not overcome the love she had for her child. Likewise, God waits for us to return just as the father of the prodigal son waited. (See Luke 15:11-32.)

Second, God intends not only individual salvation but also creation's salvation. Sinfulness impacts the entire creation. The earth "was waste," "the birds of the air had fled," and "the fruitful land was a desert" all because of "foolish" people who did not have any understanding of doing good.

The love of God stands alone. Return to God, return to home, and respond to God's love.

Help me, O God, to be a steward of your creation. Help me start by being in tune with your Spirit. Amen.

TUESDAY, SEPTEMBER 10 ~ *Read Psalm 14*

How many times do we forget to "call upon the Lord"? Seeking after God is not an easy task for contemporary Christians, especially when there are so many distractions. What would it mean for us to seek after God?

Every human being is born to participate in life in the communities that surround us. We are social—relational—beings and spiritual beings. As relational beings, we build relationships with people around us every day. We often think of building a relationship as a social activity, but we can connect spiritually with one another regardless of religious affiliations.

The question becomes, "How do we build relationships when we are so different?" What concrete practices can we live out to connect with others as spiritual beings? Seeking God on this earth means having a spiritual practice of building relationships beyond differences.

People who create a supportive and harmonious atmosphere among others harvest the act of seeking God. After all, God reveals Godself through people. In our ever more diverse global context, language, class, gender, culture, race, and education could prevent us from deepening our relationships with others and could create friction among Christians.

However, we can connect with others by building positive energy intentionally and practicing simple principles as spiritual beings, such as being intentional in acknowledging differences, breaking out of a habit of stereotyping, allowing others to open the door to a new insight of life, and being responsive to changes. From this perspective, building a relationship itself is a spiritual practice of seeking God. It is because "otherness" is a point of the other side of God's creation. In a multifaceted, pluralistic, and fast-paced global context, building relationships is essential to creating a livable community that seeks after God.

Living God, help us see the beauty of your creation in the "otherness" of people so that we may seek you. Amen.

WEDNESDAY, SEPTEMBER 11 ~ *Read 1 Timothy 1:12-17*

What has Jesus called you to do? How has the overflowing grace and love of God enfolded you and empowered you, especially in times when you have made poor choices out of ignorance or pride or spiritual weakness? You aren't alone in these situations: In yesterday's scripture—Psalm 14—the psalmist speaks of our weaknesses, even going so far as to say, "There is no one who does good, not even one" (v. 3, NIV). When was the last time you shared with someone what Jesus has done in your life? Are you thankful for being a disciple of Jesus Christ?

Today's reading begins with the author of First Timothy's simple confession of thanks to Jesus who has fully accepted him: "I am grateful to Christ Jesus our Lord." I am grateful to Jesus Christ for my calling. A calling from God is a burning desire that gives urgency to do something about what Jesus has imprinted on our heart. I have been the first Korean-American woman to serve in many of the roles I have filled in the United Methodist Church. I am opening a door for future generations of Korean-American women. Imprinted on my heart is the desire to advocate for those who are marginalized—women and persons who are among racial and ethnic minorities—so that they experience "full acceptance" of God. As a response to my call, I am extra diligent in my work and ministry. God's mercy and grace strengthen and empower me when I face tokenism, discrimination, and prejudice.

I thank God for my "holy burden." At times it seems too much to carry, and at times I fret over it. But then, I stop and acknowledge that this burden is accompanied by God's sufficient grace upon me. What a privilege of knowing this God who brings us together in the midst of diversity!

I am grateful, O God, for what you have done through Jesus Christ in my life. Now help me testify about your grace and love to others. Amen.

THURSDAY, SEPTEMBER 12 ~ *Read Luke 15:1-10*

One day I lost my earrings. My daughter had bought them for me with her first salary, so you can imagine how precious they are to me. I thought I had left them in a beauty salon. I called the salon, but the earrings were not there. I looked for them everywhere. I finally found them on the floor of my car. Somehow, I had dropped them while putting them in my purse for safekeeping. Can you imagine how elated I was to find them?

I am sure that Jesus feels a thousand times more excited when one lost member of his family comes home. I imagine this as Jesus putting together a puzzle. Jesus needs that one more piece of the puzzle, and that could be you or me.

Can you believe that your presence could bring so much joy in heaven? You don't have to do anything; you can just be yourself and turn to God.

Jesus says, "There is joy in the presence of the angels of God over one sinner who repents." What is repentance? The word *metanoia* means turning around or "a transformative change of heart," according to Webster's dictionary. Repentance does not have to be an event like Saul experienced on the road to Damascus. (See Acts 9.) We can turn around anytime.

Once we realize that we are on a wrong road, it's easy to turn around as soon as possible: simple repentance. Our turning around will bring tremendous joy to God, just as the sheep that was lost brings joy in the parable.

Do you need to turn around at this juncture of your life? Remember, God wants you home.

Wise God, thank you for letting me join in your joy when I turn around toward you. Amen.

FRIDAY, SEPTEMBER 13 ~ *Read 1 Timothy 1:12-17*

How do we experience God's mercy? Paul testifies that he received mercy even though he was the foremost of all sinners. The word *mercy* presupposes an acknowledgment of unworthiness on the part of the receiver.

I am a good organizer and have a lot of energy. I can do many things well. I believed that I could control my life by planning well and working hard to accomplish goals. Then, one day I found myself doing good work but grumbling all the way through. I was contributing much, but there was no joy in my heart. My heart was heavy, and my body was aching. I was moving only by my impeccable plans, not by the Holy Spirit. Once I realized the situation, I acted upon what Jesus calls us to do: "Come to me, all you that are weary and are carrying heavy burdens" (Matt. 11:28). I laid down before Christ my personal ambition and concerns for the future. Frankly, I was embarrassed about going to God; I was ashamed of my arrogance, yet I confessed, "Here I am, Lord. I am letting things go. I am in your hands." Suddenly, I felt like I could breathe again. It was like I was slowly opening my clenched fists. My heart was light, I exhaled with relief, and even my sore muscles were relieved. It was refreshing to have an unburdened heart. I received God's mercy on that day. I questioned myself, *Why did it take so long going to God?*

Receiving mercy is about experiencing grace, compassion, and full acceptance of God—therefore, peace.

Merciful God, your invitation to "come to me" lingers. Help me to experience your mercy in my life today. Amen.

SATURDAY, SEPTEMBER 14 ~ *Read Luke 15:1-10*

The theme of this week is "Returning to God." With such a theme, we can't help but think of death. Even though death is so close to us with reports of terrorism, school shootings, gang violence, suicide, and murders, it is a subject we don't really like to discuss, maybe because we cannot fully understand it.

John Locke, a seventeenth-century English philosopher, argued that experience determines human knowledge. From this perspective, John Locke's emphasis on empiricism (relying on experience) makes sense to me; we do not understand death since we have not experienced it yet and the dead cannot tell us what it is like to die.

As Christians, it is as important to understand death as it is to understand life. Death and life are two sides of one coin. Going to church on Sundays presents us a prototype of a circle of life. We go "home" every seven days and find peace and spiritual breathing space. Then a pastor summons us to "go out to the world" again.

We travel this journey called life in the world then finally arrive at our eternal home. Can you imagine the joy and celebration we are able to share with God when we arrive at our eternal home? God is elated that we are home at last! What a joyful day that will be! That is the day of ultimate acceptance of being who we are. That is the day that fireworks will go off in heaven because we are home; those who were lost are found. "Where, O death, is your victory?" (1 Cor. 15:55).

Eternal God, help me live my life to the fullest until I make it home. Amen.

SUNDAY, SEPTEMBER 15 ~ *Read Jeremiah 4:22-28*

Recently, I visited Bethune-Cookman University in Daytona Beach, Florida. It is one of the United Methodist Church's historically black universities. There, in the middle of campus, I found this epigraph written on the tombstone of the school's founder, Dr. Mary McLeod Bethune: "She has given her best, that others may live a more abundant life." With $1.50 in 1904, Dr. Bethune started a school for girls; after 115 years, Bethune-Cookman now is a coeducational university with more than 3,700 students.

I thought of an anguished God who once proclaimed in Jeremiah 4:22: "My people are foolish, they do not know me." On this campus it was with joy that I saw this isn't the case; people know God. Faculty and students were interacting with one another with words like God, prayer, faith, and hope.

Do we know God? Or are we among the foolish ones of whom Jeremiah writes—the ones who are skilled in doing evil but know neither good nor God? What does it look like to live as though we know God?

Knowing God will push us to care enough to act, as Dr. Bethune did in establishing the school. Knowing God is when we cannot put a lamp under the bushel basket; we cannot help but let light shine. (See Matthew 5:15-16.)

We may not see God's presence all the time, but the unmovable God is there in the form of the Holy Spirit. The promise of God is there for us to trust; nothing in all creation will be able to separate us from the love of God. (See Romans 8:38-39.) Remembering that "we live and move and have our being" (Acts 17:28) in God grants us confidence to act on what we believe through our faith in Jesus Christ: love, peace, freedom, equity, prosperity, and justice.

O God of eternal presence, help me to know you better so that others may see my good works and give you glory. Amen.

Search after Freedom

SEPTEMBER 16–22, 2019 • CHARLES PERRY

SCRIPTURE OVERVIEW: The "weeping prophet" grieves for the plight of his people. They have provoked God's judgment by following foreign gods, and now there is no comfort to be found. The psalmist cries out to God from a similar situation of despair. Foreign nations have overrun the land, destroyed Jerusalem, and killed many of its people. The psalmist cries out to God for compassion and restoration. The author of First Timothy gives his readers two commands. They should pray for and honor their leaders, and they should be faithful to the one true God, with whom they have a relationship through Christ Jesus. Jesus in Luke tells a strange parable about a dishonest manager who is commended for his shrewd business sense, but Jesus turns his story to a teaching about good stewardship.

QUESTIONS AND SUGGESTIONS FOR REFLECTION

- Read Jeremiah 8:18–9:1. When have you called out to God in your distress?
- Read Psalm 79:1-9. As you search after a solution to life's problems, how do you demonstrate God's call to love and to justice?
- Read 1 Timothy 2:1-7. How do you pray for your local, state or province, and national leaders with whom you agree? with whom you disagree?
- Read Luke 16:1-13. How do you negotiate the complexities of Jesus' call to be a good steward of your resources as you seek to serve God rather than money?

Retired minister of the Methodist Church of Southern Africa; husband, father, and grandfather; preacher; worship leader and provider of pastoral care in Methodist Retirement Village.

MONDAY, SEPTEMBER 16 ~ *Read Jeremiah 8:18–9:1*

There is a continual search after freedom of one kind or another throughout the world. In South Africa, the long search after political freedom eventually came in 1994. On April 27, 1994, a new era dawned as every eligible adult gained the freedom to vote.

In his prophecy Jeremiah tells of the cries of the people of Judah as they seek after freedom from exile in Babylon. They long to be back in Jerusalem where they know they can find the Lord. Jeremiah mourns with a broken heart the plight of his people because freedom has not come. God becomes angry because the people have begun to worship foreign gods. Jeremiah is dismayed because time has passed and still God has not saved the people. No amount of medicine can restore the relationship of the people of Judah to God.

Just as Jeremiah longs for healing, salvation, and freedom from oppression for the people of Judah, so people around the world look for healing and salvation in their current situation. But when we seek healing and salvation, we sometimes look in the wrong direction like the people of Judah who turn to cultic gods. Then, like Jeremiah, we cry out in our distress and wonder where God has gone.

We will go in the right direction when we look toward God. Our relationship with God offers us a healing medicine that will set us free—free to be God's people in the world.

Together with the prophet Jeremiah I cry out, O God. Hear my cry to be healed and set free. Help me to look to you as my source of life and hope. Amen.

TUESDAY, SEPTEMBER 17 ~ *Read Psalm 79:1-4*

A church building in the center of a South African city had to be pulled down because its structure had become unsafe. It was a sad day, as countless preachers had proclaimed the good news of Jesus from its pulpit, and thousands of people over the years had worshiped there.

Thousands of years earlier, and for very different reasons, an invading army destroyed the Jerusalem Temple. The destruction of Jerusalem and its Temple saddens the psalmist, but the death and devastation the Babylonians leave in their wake deeply troubles the psalmist. This destruction challenges the faith of the people of Jerusalem. Yet in the midst of all that happens to the people of Judah, the psalmist turns to God. In the eyes of the psalmist and the people, the Temple is God's domain and the people who have died are God's people. The taunts and jeers of Jerusalem's neighbors humiliate the psalmist even further.

The destruction of God's creation by war and the desire of a few for power over the earth likewise challenge our faith today. We, like Jeremiah, may wonder whether any medicine can bring healing and wholeness to our broken world. In this world of warfare, terrorism, and persecution we can follow the psalmist's example and turn to God.

The world's suffering and brokenness challenges our faith. We search after a solution to our problems. Yet even as we search, we know that the solution to the world's problems and our own difficulties lies in our relationship with God.

God of love, we come to you in the midst of the brokenness in the world and the brokenness in our own life. We seek your guidance and love. Hear us and build up our faith. Amen.

WEDNESDAY, SEPTEMBER 18 ~ *Read Psalm 79:5-9*

I write today's meditation on a South African public holiday known as "Women's Day." As I write, people march in one of our major cities against the abuse of women and children. The cry goes up from people of faith, "How long, Lord?" How long before women and children are treated with love and respect? How long before those who abuse others are brought to justice?

The psalmist cries out to God wanting to know when God's anger will be turned against the nations that have destroyed Jerusalem, indeed all of Judah. The psalmist then pleads with God not to hold the wrongdoings of past generations against the people who have suffered so much at the hands of the Babylonians. The psalmist calls upon God to rescue the people of Judah and to blot out any memory of their sinfulness.

We believe in a God of justice, but we also believe in a God of love. This psalm calls us to a spirit of justice and love. There are times when we may feel as the psalmist that God should be roused to anger and bring an end to the oppression of people and the abuse of women and children. At such times our faith calls us to remember that God has shown us another way in Jesus, the way of love and right living. Following the way of Jesus, we can demonstrate to the world what it means to love and to act justly.

We turn to you, God of love, and call upon you to bring an end to oppression and abuse. Help us, as your people, to act with love and in a spirit of justice toward anyone we meet. We pray in Jesus' name. Amen.

THURSDAY, SEPTEMBER 19 ~ *Read 1 Timothy 2:1-7*

The church my wife and I attend has a large candle on the Communion table that the pastor lights at every worship service before announcing a particular subject for prayer. The focus for prayer each Sunday varies; topics include the government, the poor, the abused, road users, and many more.

The letters to Timothy are likely written at a time when the Roman Empire expects all its people to pay homage to the Emperor. First Timothy calls the early followers of Jesus to pray for those in authority. Today's passage urges prayers of intercession for government officials so that Jesus' followers may practice their religion in peace. Ultimately such prayers are for all people so that all will find salvation and the truth in Jesus.

We sometimes find it difficult to put into practice the words written to the early church. If we live in a country where we disagree with the actions and policies of the government, we may feel that our prayers are not being heard as the authorities continue to disregard God's truth revealed in Jesus.

No matter how we may feel about those who govern, God calls us to pray for them. In praying for those who are in authority in our country, we can pray that they will seek after and do what is right and true. Give some thought to those in authority in your country, state, or province. What in particular do you think you need to pray about so that you and other people may live in peace and in the way of Jesus?

God, help me as I pray for those who govern my city, state or province, and country. May my prayers display your love for all people, and may those who govern come to know your love. Amen.

FRIDAY, SEPTEMBER 20 ~ *Read 1 Timothy 2:4-7*

A testimony given by the leader of a Lay Witness Mission team held the congregation spellbound. As he finished speaking, people were invited to come forward and commit their lives to Jesus. Many of the congregation came to the altar rail to receive the offer of salvation in Jesus or to renew their commitment to follow our Lord.

The first letter to Timothy calls us to hope and pray that all people will come to know the truth in Jesus—the salvation from sin Jesus offers. The writer of this letter reminds its readers that there is one God, and the way to God is through Jesus Christ. Jesus gives his life on the cross so that all people may find freedom from their sin and freedom to worship the one true God revealed in Jesus.

As followers of Jesus we know that we find life and the truth about salvation in Jesus. Together with the early followers of Jesus, we are called to offer to the world the message of freedom from sin and freedom to worship God. This is not an easy task; some people resist and others remain apathetic. Yet we continue to pray faithfully for all people and to proclaim our witness with others as we share the love of God in Jesus Christ.

God of salvation and life, thank you for setting us free from our sin and giving us the freedom to worship you. Help us, in the name of Jesus, to worship you and to witness to the freedom that comes from you alone. We pray in the name of Jesus, the one true mediator between you and us. Amen.

SATURDAY, SEPTEMBER 21 ~ *Read Luke 16:1-8*

Unemployment is a problem in many countries. I have known persons who have been retrenched, and I have seen its difficult effects. Many persons face crises about their worth and about their future when they experience unemployment.

The steward in the parable Jesus tells faces the crisis of unemployment. He feels he is not strong enough to do manual work, and he does not want to beg. After being dismissed, he sets about meeting with his master's debtors and lessening their debt. By doing so, he ensures that the debtors (who do not yet know he has been dismissed) will think highly of his master and may appreciate the steward's reduction of their debt enough to welcome him into their homes.

This parable teaches the followers of Jesus to learn from the ways of the world. The steward uses his resources to ensure that he will be taken care of once he loses his employment. Jesus uses this parable to tell his followers to use the resources available to them as they follow him.

Jesus calls us, too, to be resourceful as we seek to follow him. Crises of a personal nature come our way, as do crises in national life. Whatever we face, we can put our minds to following Jesus. We can be as resourceful as the entrepreneur who works hard toward building a successful business or as an athlete who trains for hours to win a race.

Being resourceful in following Jesus will mean growing in grace and in the knowledge and love of God. Spiritual growth comes in many forms. Give some thought to your own spiritual growth. What do you need to do to grow in knowledge and love of God and neighbor?

God of love, help me to love as you have loved me in Jesus, my Lord. Amen.

SUNDAY, SEPTEMBER 22 ~ *Read Luke 16:9-13*

Money plays a large role in the lives of most people in the Western world. The contrast looms between the affluent person who needs to decide how to spend or invest money and the poor person who wonders how to earn enough money to live. Then there are those who have enough to live on but who are neither affluent nor poor.

In commenting on the parable of the unjust steward, Jesus reminds his followers not to allow the wealth of this world to corrupt them. He goes further as he calls upon his disciples to act honestly, both in terms of worldly wealth and spiritual wealth. Jesus ends this part of his teaching with a clear message: We must choose between God and money.

Money can easily rule our lives whether we are rich, poor, or in between. We become so concerned about what we have or don't have that we neglect our spiritual welfare. When it comes to spending our time thinking about either money or our spiritual welfare, we can think of what God would want us to do.

Speaking on the subject of a "simple lifestyle," a colleague once said that we often learn more by looking at the person who has less than the person who has more. Then we will not want more but be grateful for what we have been given. We are stewards of what God has given us. When we remember this, we turn toward God and find ourselves to be giving, loving people.

Loving and giving God, in our search for freedom from the love of material things help us to be good stewards of what you have given us. We are grateful for what we have received at your hand. Empower us through your Spirit to be giving and loving servants in the name of Jesus, our Lord. Amen.

Inexplicable Hope

SEPTEMBER 23–29, 2019 • KATHLEEN STEPHENS

SCRIPTURE OVERVIEW: While Jeremiah is in prison, God tells him to buy a field. This transaction shows that in the future life will return to normal. It is an "enactment prophecy," where a prophecy is given through actions instead of just words. The psalmist rejoices in the protection that God provides to the faithful. God is a fortress, a covering, and a shield. Paul admonishes his readers not to fall into materialism. The love of money, not money itself, is the root of all kinds of evil, and those obsessed with it build their hopes on shifting sands. Jesus tells a parable about a rich man who has fallen into that very trap. Only after death, when it is too late, does he realize his mistake.

QUESTIONS AND SUGGESTIONS FOR REFLECTION

- Read Jeremiah 32:1-3a, 6-15. How do you live as if God's promises were already true?
- Read Psalm 91:1-6, 14-16. How do you turn toward God with hope in times of darkness?
- Read 1 Timothy 6:6-19. Whether you have few or many possessions, how do they get in the way of your following Jesus?
- Read Luke 16:19-31. God knows each of us by name. Do you know the names of the persons in your community who have obvious or internal unmet needs?

Member of Christ Episcopal Church, Temple, TX; former editor, *Weavings* and Upper Room Books; freelance editor and writer who is happiest when traveling to far-flung destinations.

MONDAY, SEPTEMBER 23 ~ *Read Jeremiah 32:1-3a, 6-15*

There are times when God asks us to do something that may seem ridiculous to others and even to us. Leave a comfortable, secure job for work that feeds the soul but leaves us worried whether we can pay our bills. Forgive an abuser who hasn't acknowledged the abuse. Buy a piece of land when we know that it soon will be taken over by our enemies.

That last example is found in our scripture reading today. Jeremiah has warned the people of Israel that the Babylonians are coming to take their land and to send them into exile. He has pleaded with them to repent of their sins so that they escape God's judgment. Instead of heeding Jeremiah's warning, the people have ignored him and the king has locked him up for treason.

Then comes God's baffling instruction to Jeremiah—buy a relative's piece of land. Jeremiah knows that the field in question will soon belong to the Babylonians. Exile is coming. Realistically, it is not a good time to invest in real estate. But right in the midst of this seemingly hopeless circumstance, God offers Jeremiah a chance to demonstrate inexplicable hope. Jeremiah's purchase of the field is a concrete sign to the people of Israel that though the future looks bleak, God will have the final word. And that word is *restoration*—the people will be restored to their land.

We may be asked to demonstrate our hope in God's promises. A faithful response is particularly difficult when circumstances seem dire and we are exhausted physically and emotionally. But because of our relationship with a faithful God, we can find the courage to trust God enough to do what on the surface may seem incredulous. When we are willing to take that step, we find strength in our faith and in that of others.

Help me, God, to listen and to be willing to do whatever you ask of me today, no matter how inexplicable it may seem. Amen.

TUESDAY, SEPTEMBER 24 ~ *Read Jeremiah 32:1-3a, 6-15*

As we already have seen, Jeremiah lives in the midst of a darkness where he is the only one who has any light. Jeremiah's light comes in the form of an unbelievable message that the future belongs to God and to God's people. God has promised that one of these days all will be made right, and the land will be restored to Israel.

But first, Jeremiah has to act on that message of light. By buying the land that will soon be seized by the enemy, Jeremiah demonstrates his inexplicable hope in Israel's future. For this message to ring true, Jeremiah has to risk some things. He risks his investment of money but also his reputation and his faith in God's promises. He has to put some skin in the game. And so Jeremiah buys the land and has the deed put into an earthenware jar so that it will last a long time—long enough for God's restoration of the people to their land.

We too are called to put some skin in the game when it comes to believing and acting on God's promises. This kind of risk demonstrates that our faith is genuine. Rather than simply repeating God's promises, our faith calls us to act upon them as if they were already true. We demonstrate this kind of inexplicable hope to the world today by buying our own piece of land—by building up God's kingdom and working for justice, righteousness, and peace. Each day brings abundant opportunities for us to risk our time, our money, and perhaps our reputation to prepare the ground for the future and present coming of God's kingdom on earth.

What is it, Lord, that you want us to risk today? No matter the cost, no matter the risk, may we have the courage and faith to invest in your kingdom. Amen.

WEDNESDAY, SEPTEMBER 25 ~ *Read 1 Timothy 6:6-19*

Today's reading presents us with a stark choice: Will we depend on our wealth for security, or will we instead take hold of eternal life? It may seem an easy choice. But in a world that constantly bombards us with erroneous messages that we find happiness in material things, we can lose our way. When we've lost sight of God's promises to us, we can be tempted to find hope in a job promotion, a bigger house, expensive clothes, or stock market gains. We can be tempted to think having all these things buys us security in an insecure world.

Today's passage reminds us that our security isn't in this world. Because, unfortunately, we can't take any of our stuff with us when we leave. The security of the prosperous is only temporary. When we focus on fleeting things of this world, we lose sight of what really matters in the long run—pursuing godliness, faith, love, and gentleness.

So how do we live a godly life? Is it wrong to be comfortable financially? Our attitude toward our belongings matters more than how much we own. If our possessions get in the way of our trusting God and hinder our following Jesus, they are a problem. Scripture makes clear the right response to our abundance: "Do good, be rich in good works, generous, and ready to share." As we live this open-handed kind of life and pursue godly virtues along with it, we discover that we have found the life that is eternal life.

God, when everyone seems focused on money and the temporary pleasure it brings, help us fix an inexplicable hope on the things that are eternal. Amen.

THURSDAY, SEPTEMBER 26 ~ *Read Luke 16:19-31*

In his parables, Jesus often challenges our usual way of doing things. He punches holes in our preconceived notions and reveals our misguided methodologies. In today's reading, Jesus upends another common trope—that rich people are more important than poor people. We notice that something is up as soon as Jesus begins the parable. "There was a rich man . . ." he says; but as he continues, this rich man is never named. Rich people are always called by their names. If you possess money and power, everyone knows your name. Dropping the name of a wealthy person opens doors to places previously off-limits to most of us.

No doubt the unnamed rich man of the parable does not know the name of the beggar who sits at the gate of his house either. But in the parable the beggar has a name—Lazarus. It is the only time Jesus ever uses a name in a parable. To the rich man, the beggar is nameless, just a person to be ignored, invisible. But to God he has a name. He is not known as "a beggar." He is Lazarus.

As with Lazarus, God calls each one of us by name. In Isaiah we find this statement: "Do not fear, for I have redeemed you; I have called you by name, you are mine" (Isa. 43:1). God knows us personally and cares about us as unique individuals. Think about it: The Creator and Sustainer of the universe knows us!

In our world, rich people's names are known and beggars are often treated as nameless. But in the parable, as in God's realm, the beggar is called by name. Each one of us matters to God.

God of the named and nameless, we are astounded—and grateful—that you, the Creator and Sustainer of the universe, care enough for each of us to call us by name. Amen.

FRIDAY, SEPTEMBER 27 ~ *Read Luke 16:19-31*

If we look beneath the surface of the parable about the rich man and Lazarus, we will see that Jesus has more to say to us than how to use our wealth. Jesus also speaks to us here about perception and recognition in two ways. One is what we perceive and recognize with our physical senses. The other involves perceiving with our imagination, creativity, inspiration, and empathy.

Just like the rich man who passed by Lazarus every day and never really saw him, we can miss perceiving with empathy. We often ignore the reality of people in desperate need. Sometimes their needs are obvious—food, shelter, clothing—and sometimes they are deeper and less obvious—the need for acceptance, meaning, understanding, love.

We may ignore people with needs, avoid looking into their eyes and listening to their stories, in hopes of escaping the pain we recognize there. We desperately need the kind of perception that opens us to understanding and helps us to recognize that we are not so different from our siblings—these children of God.

Jesus reminds us that our eternal life is connected to how we serve and treat our neighbors who wait outside our gates now. Whether their inexplicable hope is realized depends on how we respond to them. There is a relationship between this life and the next, Jesus says. The choices we make, meeting needs or turning away, will have consequences.

Our own problems may seem more than enough for us to deal with right now. But Lazarus sits there at the gate, in front of us every day. We can recognize our neighbors and respond as imaginatively and graciously as God has responded to us.

God of Abraham, when we are tempted to turn away from the deep needs of our neighbors, give us courage to do what we can because we know that they—and we—are your beloved children. Amen.

SATURDAY, SEPTEMBER 28 ~ *Read Psalm 91:1-6*

Our home place is a sacred memory for many of us. Nothing warms us like a vision of family gathered together to work, to play, to eat and sleep, and to share the ups and downs of everyday life. If our memory of home isn't so cheery, we still are drawn to the concept of home as a place where we are accepted and valued as we are. Home conjures an image of safety and security and belonging.

Today's scripture reading refers to God as our "refuge" and "fortress." God is what we long for when we long for home. The psalmist tells us that in God we find freedom from fear and anxiety. We find someone who cares deeply for us and for what matters to us. When we have cultivated a deep relationship with our Creator, we find that we are able to trust, to rest, and to hope that all will be well for us.

We will all experience trouble and sorrow in this life, but we do not go through these things alone. We believe we have a loving Guide who will be with us all along our way.

It has been said that to take a general truth and make it our own by personal faith is the highest wisdom. Here is a truth we can make our own: God is our fortress, our refuge. And so we can experience inexplicable hope, no matter what troubles we face. We find our hope here: God is our home.

Whether our home in which we live reflects a Hallmark movie or brims with tension and conflict, we have the promise of a safe, warm, and welcoming home in God.

When we draw close to you, God, we can truly know what it is to be welcomed home. Amen.

SUNDAY, SEPTEMBER 29 ~ *Read Psalm 91:14-16*

In the past week's meditations we have looked at reasons for inexplicable hope in God's promises. We've seen the examples of Jeremiah and Lazarus. We've been challenged to participate in bringing and being hope to people in need. We've been reminded that our security is not in material possessions but in eternal things. And we've been encouraged to remember that the home we all hope for is found in God.

Today's reading gives us more reasons for hope. Listen to these incredible promises made to all who have made their home in God. To believers, God says, I "will rescue . . . protect . . . answer . . . deliver . . . and honor" you. And if that isn't enough, God also adds, "With long life I will satisfy [you]."

But while we have basked in the wonders of hope this week, it is also important to say what hope is not. It is not the belief that everything is or will be fine. Everywhere we look we see suffering and despair. Whether on a global, local, or personal scale, we often feel as if we're hurtling toward some imminent catastrophe. The things we see as fundamental to our identity may be gone or quickly fading away. We may feel we are being enveloped in darkness.

What do we do in days like these? How do we find courage to hope? How do we respond to the darkness? In the shadow of despair, we are to turn toward the darkness of this world with God's light of love. As we work to bring hope for those in despair we will find our own darkness turning to light. When we dare to give our lives for others of God's people, we find we are moving closer to God, in whom our hope has always been grounded.

Lord God, especially in dark times, may we turn again to each other and to you as we recognize the singular gifts of our lives that call us toward hope. Amen.

Faith, Strength, and Servanthood

SEPTEMBER 30—OCTOBER 6, 2019 • TOM CAMP

SCRIPTURE OVERVIEW: Lamentations opens with a description of the plight of the people of Judah, the Southern Kingdom. The people have been taken into exile as part of God's judgment for their idolatry. The psalmist struggles to sing the songs of the Lord. In fact, those who overthrew Jerusalem have forced them to sing for their amusement, so the joy is gone. The psalmist prays that one day God will repay the invaders. In Second Timothy Paul praises God for Timothy's faith and for the legacy of faith that comes through his family. He charges him to preach boldly and without hesitation the gospel of Christ. In the Gospel reading, Jesus challenges the disciples to show greater faith and to understand that we are all servants in God's kingdom.

QUESTIONS AND SUGGESTIONS FOR REFLECTION

- Read Lamentations 1:1-6. How do you allow your imperfections and failings to transform you?
- Read Psalm 137. How do you remember your spiritual traditions and sacred places without clinging to them in the rapid changes of our world? How do you look for God's work in change?
- Read 2 Timothy 1:1-14. What spiritual practices help you to "guard the good treasure entrusted to you"?
- Read Luke 17:5-10. How might a posture of cyclical servanthood to and with all creation transform or increase your faith?

Retired Elder, North Georgia Conference, the United Methodist Church; Marriage and Family Therapist; Yoga Therapist; Enneagram Teacher and Spiritual Guide.

MONDAY, SEPTEMBER 30 ~ *Read Lamentations 1:1-6*

We often face difficult and painful—and sometimes even devastating—experiences. We encounter defeat, failure, loss, and death. Such experiences may seem to be punishment, and we can begin to feel vengeful toward someone or something we blame for causing these experiences. Even in scripture, people regress to vengeance in the face of defeat and failure.

Human life is finite. It has limits. These limits include not only the reality of death but also the reality of occasional failure and defeat. Each of us is finite, and no matter how enduring they seem, our culture, society, institutions, and government are finite. They will change, fail, and be defeated in ways we do not expect. Accepting our finitude opens us to a more gracious way of experiencing failure and defeat.

How does our faith enable us to deal with the realities of failure, defeat, and death? What was once a wonderful life is now desolate. At one time I experienced myself as capable, liked, and competent, but now I feel a failure and rejected. Maybe something has changed in my church, community, or nation that has led me to these feelings of failure and defeat.

In faith we can see these experiences as teaching moments that shock us back into realization of our imperfection as human beings in an immense cosmos. They are wake-up experiences! Our failings can remind us that we are God's creatures.

Our imperfections are not evidence of total failure, defeat, or final death. Rather, they are doorways through which we enter spiritual transformation. Human imperfection invites us to let go of our ego and to live in faith in God's ultimate love.

Imagine letting go of your balance and falling backward into God's strong and loving hands. Ask God for faith to do so, and express gratitude to God for promising to hold you in love.

TUESDAY, OCTOBER 1 ~ *Read Psalm 137:5-9*

We moved from our hometown when I was entering middle school. We left a community in which I felt known, valued, and loved. The center of our life was the little brick church with colored windows and five tiny Sunday school rooms. We'd had many picnics in the grassy area out back. I loved that place.

I returned to my childhood hometown in my adult years and found that my church had been removed and there was now a convenience store in its place, complete with a large trash dumpster where we had once picnicked. I was sad and deeply disappointed. As I looked at the pavement where there had been grass and the gas pumps where there had been a church, I sensed the presence of those who meant so much to me. I remembered the spirit that had permeated that congregation. As I relaxed and concentrated, this presence became more real. Even without the tangible symbols, the memories of what had been there were still alive. I felt my Sunday school teacher's warm embrace, heard the joyful music, and sensed the love of those who affirmed and nurtured me in childhood.

Today's scripture calls us to remember Jerusalem, that tangible manifestation of God's community. Having something manifest—a person, building, or symbol—helps us remember, but it is not necessary. The felt presence of those who love and nurture us is a manifestation of God's Holy Spirit, and that presence is always with us. Our sacred memories of loved ones and loved places represent the kingdom of God within us. We can never be apart from it—unless we forget.

Prayer focuses our attention on the presence of God. It is a practice of remembering. Remember Jerusalem, the manifestation of God's presence. Remember every day, every moment, in every relationship.

In the midst of change, may I remember all the ways God is present in my life. May this remembering give me strength and hope.

WEDNESDAY, OCTOBER 2 ~ *Read Psalm 137:1-4*

The Earth rotates at 1,000 miles per hour at the equator. Our world seems to change even faster than that, and such rapid change affects us. Technology and mass media, relatively easy long-distance travel, advances in health, and the easing of barriers to global relationships have brought changes for which we do not always feel prepared.

We encounter various races and faith traditions, diverse ethnic and gender expressions, and fluctuating information about nutrition, health, and relationships. Some jobs disappear and others emerge with different qualifications required. No place is a complete refuge from all this change. Wow! What a strange land!

How do we sing the Lord's song in our strange land? Psalm 137 expresses blame and anger toward those accused of causing the changes, but, as the prophets proclaim, we have our part in these changes and how we relate to them.

Attachment to the way things once were causes us to suffer. If we focus only on the way we lived and worshiped in the past and feel that changes have destroyed these old ways, we cannot move with courage and adventure into the future. Throughout the scriptural record of God's activity amongst us, God is out ahead of us, leading us out of Ur, out of Egypt, out of Israel, out of the Roman Empire, and dispersing us into the world.

When we see the hand of God in the changes in our world, we can celebrate the continuing creativity of God. Jesus proclaims that the movement of God's Spirit is toward a grand feast of abundant life and community for all people. So we sing praises to God's creating Spirit for this creation, even when it is not yet fully revealed.

Creator of continual change, help us to perceive your hand in our evolving world, and give us courage to open ourselves to your will. Amen.

THURSDAY, OCTOBER 3 ~ *Read 2 Timothy 1:1-7*

While hiking in the forest, I was startled by the cracking sound of a large tree as it began crashing toward the ground. I started to run out of its way, but stopped as it was caught mid-fall by another tree with strong limbs. The strength of that tree, standing upright in the strong wind and holding the tree that crashed, amazed me. Strength is a beautiful thing.

Our worldly concept of strength focuses on overpowering or being stronger than our competitors. We imagine strength as large muscles, political victory, or armed might. This is not the strength the Spirit of God gives us.

God is love, we often say, and God gives us strength through the power of love. Love's power comes from deep respect and compassion for each and every person. Love's power stems from our profound awareness of God's presence in and around us at all times. It is our ability to know where and how to express compassion—putting others first and listening with true interest and respect. Such strength involves vulnerability and does not overpower. In the eyes of the world, then, such love is timid, weak.

Yet, like that tree in the wilderness, our power has tremendously strong roots and trunk, for it is open to the loving energy of God flowing through us. Such strength does not defeat but joins, does not overpower but unites, does not hate but loves. It is the strength of the One who created all things. That is real power!

Loving and powerful God, you have given us divine strength. May we trust it, live in it, and share it with all. Amen.

FRIDAY, OCTOBER 4 ~ *Read 2 Timothy 1:8-14*

I was walking several miles every day until I caught a cold and felt miserable. After a week of the cold and a few more days of recovery, I started walking again. My legs hurt and my breath was rapid; I'd lost the strength I needed for a long walk. A few weeks of gradually increasing my distance, however, put me back to where I was before the cold. Resilience!

Those who study our nervous system have found that nerve cells all over our bodies work just like muscles: Use them and they get stronger; do not use them and they deteriorate. And our nerve cells and pathways are resilient just like our muscles.

Awareness and trust in God's unconditional grace and love require mental and emotional focus as well as constant practice. The world constantly pulls our attention away from faith in God. We worry about our safety; we care about being liked and accepted; we are concerned for our physical and financial health. However, these human concerns pull our attention away from faith in God's love.

Practicing awareness and trust in God's love is what spiritual disciplines are about. Just as our muscles require physical exercise, our faith requires daily practice of concentrated awareness of God's abiding love. With the discipline our faith requires, we can even send God's love to people and places all over the world. Awareness of God's presence and prayers of lovingkindness exercise the nerve pathways in our minds that can move our attention from all our worries and concerns to God's presence.

This part of the letter to Timothy is about the "treasure entrusted to you," the gift of full awareness of and faith in God's love for us just as we are. We guard and nurture this treasure with daily practice of remembering and sharing it.

Dear God, thank you for your amazing love. May we intentionally remember your love every day and share it with everyone we encounter. Amen.

SATURDAY, OCTOBER 5 ~ *Read Luke 17:5-6*

When my friend and I finished a several-day hike on the Appalachian Trail, we were many miles from the nearest town. My father was to pick us up in the parking lot between 4 and 5:00 that afternoon. We finished at 5:00, but my father was not there. It was a dreary, rainy, cold day; it was getting dark and we were without shelter. After we had waited a while with no one else around, my friend got anxious: "He's forgotten. We're gonna be stuck here overnight!"

I knew my father would not forget. It seemed like a long time, but it was actually only a few minutes until he finally arrived. He'd had a flat tire a few miles before reaching us.

I had felt some relief but also confirmation. My father did not forget us. I felt that trust in my bones.

Faith is simple trust, as small as a mustard seed, and yet so very powerful. It enables us to relax, release worry, and know deep in our bones that God will not forget us, that we are loved unconditionally just as we are, and that God will be with us through whatever challenges and joys we experience.

If we listen carefully to the many thoughts running through our minds, we will realize how much regret and worry we have about so many things. If we are still and slowly recall the fears lodged in our minds—both past and present—we will see the many places where worry, regret and false hope consume us.

Yet faith offers a profound reliance on the mysterious presence of God with us. Faith sets us free. It releases us to live in trust and frees our energy to do more work, enjoy life more abundantly, and love more fully.

I trust you, O God. Help me release worry and regret as I grow in my faith. Amen.

SUNDAY, OCTOBER 6 ~ *Read Luke 17:7-10*

My visit to a parishioner gave her the opportunity to show me her garden. It was luscious, vibrant, and full of scrumptious fruit and vegetables. She told me she sees herself as a servant of the plants. "It's like a revolving cycle," she said. "I serve them with nurture and care, and they give me sustenance so I can then serve them again."

Servanthood is an attitude we choose, not something cast upon us. An attitude of service involves our taking responsibility in our world and our immense gratitude for all other aspects of life that serve the general welfare—trees providing oxygen, insects pollinating, water moisturizing, people manufacturing goods, truck drivers delivering, health workers administering wellness, and so on. We all serve one another and the cycle of life.

Our servanthood never ends. Even our rest serves our bodies and minds; our study serves our understanding; our recreation serves our living abundantly.

The attitude of servanthood is contrary to the attitude of taking all one can get or being frustrated that one never can get enough. Such is the attitude fostered in our consumer society. In this negative attitude, other people become objects to take care of our desires.

The kingdom of God, as described and modeled by Jesus, promotes a communion of servants honoring and serving one another, grateful for the gift each brings.

Profound faith trusts in the unseen forces and processes that make up the great cycle of love in our world, which we sometimes express as, "What goes around comes around." Service, love, and respect come back around to us so we can send them out again.

God, I surrender to being a loving servant. Empower me with your love. Amen.

Sustained in Exile

OCTOBER 7–13, 2019 • ELAINE EBERHART

SCRIPTURE OVERVIEW: Through Jeremiah, God sends a message to the people in exile: They are to seek good for the city of Babylon, their new home. God will bless the city and in doing so will bless God's people. The psalmist encourages the people to praise God with songs recounting past challenges through which God's powerful deeds have brought them. This can be encouragement for those currently experiencing difficulties. In Second Timothy, Paul encourages his protégé to endure suffering if necessary. In fact, Timothy should expect to experience resistance. Although the apostle is in chains, the word of God is powerful and can never be chained. The story in Luke reminds us of a basic truth: We should remember to show gratitude to God for answered prayers.

QUESTIONS AND SUGGESTIONS FOR REFLECTION

- Read Jeremiah 29:1, 4-7. When have you experienced physical or metaphorical exile? How has God helped you to thrive in your Babylon?
- Read Psalm 66:1-12. Recall a time of division in your family or community of faith. How did God bring you individually and collectively to a spacious place?
- Read 2 Timothy 2:8-15. How do you remember Christ in your actions toward others?
- Read Luke 17:11-19. What boundaries keep you from full wellness that can be found in Jesus Christ?

Member of New Vision Congregational Church, United Church of Christ in Yulee, Florida; associate at Green Bough House of Prayer in Scott, Georgia.

MONDAY, OCTOBER 7 ~ *Read Jeremiah 29:1, 4-7*

Jeremiah writes to the leaders of a community in exile in Babylon. Though he is left behind, many others—religious and political leaders, artisans, and metal workers—are made to dwell in the land of their enemy. Family members are separated, some remain in Judah while others are deported to Babylon. Government, community life, and religious ritual, all of which brought meaning to life in Judah, are no more.

As contrasted with his rival, Hananiah, whose death is reported at the end of chapter 28, Jeremiah does not advise the Judeans to resist their captors nor does he prophesy of God's imminent rescue. Dig in, he tells the exiles, because you will be there for a while. Put down deep roots. Mark engagements and marriages and new babies. Do not allow Babylon to diminish your growth. Living as God's people in exile means thriving in captivity, Jeremiah says, bearing the new reality as a yoke that weighs heavily around your neck but does not break you. Even more surprisingly, Jeremiah asks the exiles to pray for Babylon and to work for its welfare, noting the inextricable relationship between the good of the city and the health of those living there.

Though most of us have not been driven from our homes by force, we have lived in some type of exile, estranged from our families or deported from good health into a foreign land of illness and pain. Such times bring many burdens: money worries, the loss of relationships, and the difficulty of finding meaning in the new reality. God is with us, however, right in the midst of our anxiety and loneliness. God's Spirit transmitted through holy mystery and the ministry of our neighbors makes our Babylons places of a new kind of vitality, one in which we can flourish while still feeling our pain.

Consider when you have lived in a time or place of exile, and thank God for blessing your time there.

TUESDAY, OCTOBER 8 ~ *Read Jeremiah 29:1, 4-7*

Few of us have been exiled to a foreign country, but we are surrounded by people who have. I previously lived in Minnesota, home to the largest Somali refugee population in the country. Somalis were forced from their homes by fighting between rival government factions, drought, and poverty. From camps in Kenya, the refugees were admitted to the United States and sent to Minnesota because of the wealth of settlement support there. Christian social service organizations welcomed the Somali refugees just as they had assisted Vietnamese and Hmong refugees in the past. They offered English language training, housing assistance, and friendship as the refugees adjusted to a climate that so differed from the monsoons and desert heat of Somalia.

Not everyone welcomed the refugees; no community is without racial prejudice and religious intolerance, and economic progress among Somali-Americans was slow and hard-won. In spite of continuing challenges, however, refugees found a place to begin life again. Children and their parents thrived, and new businesses prospered. Refugees pursued citizenship, and a Somali-American was elected to the state legislature. Bringing their culture and stories, their entrepreneurial spirit, and their dedication to their families, the refugees enriched the communities in which they lived across Minnesota.

Jeremiah speaks of God's desire for exiles to flourish even in the most confusing and alien of circumstances. We, who have been sustained during times of exile and have been surprised by gifts of support when we were overwhelmed by pain or loneliness, are called to nurture others torn from their refuges of safety. God bids us to offer abundant hospitality even when that assistance is costly for us, even when it is unpopular or misunderstood. Our brothers and sisters ministered to us with God's comfort when we lived in exile. Can we do less?

As you were with me, O God, when I dwelled in a lonely place, send me to those who need my presence. Amen.

WEDNESDAY, OCTOBER 9 ~ *Read Psalm 66:1-12*

United Methodist annual conferences often open with a hymn that asks whether the gathered have survived another year. Voices echo throughout auditoriums as clergy and laity affirm that the God who has called them in shared ministry has brought them together safely again. That hymn restates the words of Psalm 66: "Bless our God, O peoples, let the sound of [God's] praise be heard, who has kept us among the living, and has not let our feet slip."

Those words, so appropriate for an annual conference gathering, also state our reality as God's people when we gather for weekly worship. Someone, no doubt, has received an unwelcome medical diagnosis. A woman has been trying for months without success to find a job. A teenager has been arrested, and he fears how it will impact his future. A couple, realizing that they can no longer live independently, are grieving as they consider where they should go. Even if these times of exile are not named during the service or around the coffee urn, almost everyone in the congregation bears some burden into the door of the church and carries it out again after the benediction.

Psalm 66 affirms, however, that God wills abundant life for God's people. God is moving in the world bringing love and justice, particularly to those who are on the margins of life. We are called into partnership with God as bearers of love. As much as we want to relieve the burdens of our neighbors, sometimes our efforts simply cannot do so. Sometimes we can only offer a quiet presence and willingness to listen. At those times, perhaps it is enough to tell the stories of exile and restoration again, to remind each other that God sustains us through grace, and to give thanks.

O God, teach me to listen and to be present as a bearer of your life-giving love. Amen.

THURSDAY, OCTOBER 10 ~ *Read Psalm 66:1-12*

How do God's people maintain faith and hope when confronted with divisions in their denominations and in congregations? Well-meaning Christians, purporting to defend the faith and the Giver of faith, draw lines in the sand that make reconciliation difficult or impossible. They support these lines with theology and scripture, with budgets and membership data, and with emotion, fear, and reason. Regardless of the issue, the church can become polarized with each group feeling despair about the future. As most of us have experienced, God's people can become equally agitated by issues as disparate as the inclusion of all people in the body of Christ or the proposed architecture of a church addition.

Are these not the trials that most confound us? When we read in Psalm 66 of God testing us as silver is tried, is there any struggle more difficult, more capable of driving us from the church we love, than one that pits us against our brothers and sisters in the faith?

Again, the psalmist affirms that God moves among the exiled. Even when we find no apparent way to mend a division or to come to a shared understanding of God's mission for us, God brings us to a spacious place. God makes a way through the water and brings us safely through fire. God removes the burden and saves us from the net. More importantly, perhaps, God sustains us while we are trapped in division, while we dwell in a land of hurt feelings and dashed hopes and barriers that seem altogether immovable. And God calls us to affirm together through joyful expressions of praise that restoration is happening even though we may not yet see it.

O God, who has kept us among the living, show us signs of your restoring movement through the church, and guide us as we seek to partner with you in your mission of love and justice. Amen.

FRIDAY, OCTOBER 11 ~ *Read 2 Timothy 2:8-15*

What does it mean to "remember Jesus Christ" in this letter to Timothy? For the writer of the epistle, it means that though he may be held captive, the word of love cannot be bound any more than Jesus was bound by death. For Timothy, the writer affirms that remembering Jesus means that whether the writer's words are welcomed by his hearers or result in his exile in a prison cell, Timothy will be sustained by the Spirit.

For us, remembering Jesus Christ may mean overcoming our fear or apathy when someone on the street asks for our help. It may mean speaking in a city council meeting with a shaky voice when the only playground in a depressed area is in desperate need of repair to make it safe. It may mean praying for strength when we are at the bedside of a friend as she dies. Remembering the Jesus whose humanity brought him face-to-face with all we experience can help us to know that where we are, God is.

What about the verse that suggests that if we disown Christ, we will be disowned? We find little comfort in that verse, for we know that we will fail. Nor do we find reassurance in the next verse, which states that God will be faithful, since it is unclear whether that verse is meant to trump the prior one. Scripture tells us, however, that like Jesus' death on the cross, our mistakes and their consequences are not the final word in God's continuing story of restoration. God will be faithful when we are not; God cannot be chained.

When we gather at the table, when we feel the burdens of exile but forge on with love, or when we retreat in fear in spite of our resolve, remembering Jesus Christ means reminding our hearts and minds that God is with us.

Reflect on a time when remembering Jesus strengthened you to care for your neighbor.

SATURDAY, OCTOBER 12 ~ *Read Luke 17:11-19*

Last fall I traveled with a group of colleagues from the Mayo Clinic to Rome and Assisi in Italy. Since an order of Franciscan sisters along with the Mayo brothers co-founded our institution, our guide asked us to connect the stories of Francis and Clare of Assisi with the values that guide our work. Walking where Francis and Clare walked made real their faithful responses to God's call to love and serve their neighbors. As we trekked through churches important to Francis and Clare, daily sharing the bread and cup in worship, we listened for what renewed calls to service might mean for our lives and work.

Francis was a wealthy young man, and he explored all that eleventh-century life had to offer for someone of his station. Like most people of his time, he was repulsed by lepers and wrote of his nausea when he was near them. In spite of his revulsion, he was moved one day to dismount from his horse, approach a leper, and embrace him. Whether he reflected on the experience in the moment is unclear, but he wrote that after the encounter those he had most feared and avoided became the embodiment of Christ for him. He renounced his family's wealth to share the lot of brothers and sisters living at society's borders, those who were exiled from the practice of their faith and the love of their families.

As Jesus crosses the boundaries of purity laws that prohibit contact with lepers to offer healing and restoration to community, Francis crossed the boundaries of his fears to meet Christ in those who were living as exiles in their own homeland. Many months after our pilgrimage to Italy, I pause at the boundaries standing between me and increased faithfulness and pray for the willingness to cross.

O One who offered new life to ten lepers and who strengthened Francis for love and service, give me courage to reach out in love to those I fear. Amen.

SUNDAY, OCTOBER 13 ~ *Read Luke 17:11-19*

Jesus restores ten lepers to life and community. From their forced separation because of their disease, he gives them access again to their families. Only one, a Samaritan, a foreigner to whom Jesus is forbidden to speak, returns to thank him. The Samaritan falls at Jesus' feet and offers gratitude to God. Why is he the only one to offer thanks? asks Jesus. Ten are offered new life, but only one gives witness to that transforming moment.

What about the nine? They are cleansed and can embrace their families again. They can enter worship and no longer hear their neighbors whisper that their disease is the direct result of a sin they have committed. With a little effort, the nine might even forget that they had been sick. But are they made well? The text suggests that something is missing for them.

When the Samaritan acknowledges the source of his transformation, he finds wholeness, a condition that includes and transcends physical health. Like the nine, he can return from the exile his illness had mandated; but unlike them, he pauses to consider his healing and what it means to him. Knowing that he can do nothing else, he returns to Jesus to give thanks.

Some of us will never know physical or emotional healing from diseases that afflict us. Like exiles who spend their entire lives in Babylon, we may live with an illness or a broken relationship. We may feel deep grief at the death of one we loved. The pain may subside, but it will never completely leave us in this life. Still we are promised the presence of One who dwells with us during our exile. If we seek even the smallest signs of God's sustaining presence and give thanks for them, we will find renewed life and healing even in our brokenness.

O One who wills my wholeness, I acknowledge your presence bringing healing and restoration. Amen.

Trajectory of Mercy and Justice

OCTOBER 14–20, 2019 • JASON BYASSEE

SCRIPTURE OVERVIEW: At last Jeremiah is able to bring a message of restoration and hope. God promises a new covenant with the people, and they will internalize the law in their hearts so that they will keep it. The psalmist rejoices in such a reality. He meditates on God's law all day and has been granted profound understanding. This allows him to walk faithfully in God's paths. The reading from Second Timothy confirms the ongoing power of God's law in scripture, which is given by God for our good. Timothy is charged always to be ready to preach it faithfully. Luke hits on a different theme: the importance of persistent prayer. In the parable a heartless judge finally yields to a persistent widow, so we should be similarly tenacious with our prayers to God.

QUESTIONS AND SUGGESTIONS FOR REFLECTION

- Read Jeremiah 31:27-34. How have you broken your covenant with God? How has God responded?
- Read Psalm 119:97-104. The Jewish laws of the Hebrew scriptures are part of our Christian heritage. How can you delight in the law?
- Read 2 Timothy 3:14–4:5. How can you learn or teach from scriptures you do not normally read?
- Read Luke 18:1-8. Through the familiar call to pray always, the author reminds us that we are called to pray for what God wants. What is at stake when you pray for justice and mercy?

Professor of preaching at the Vancouver School of Theology in British Columbia, Canada.

MONDAY, OCTOBER 14 ~ *Read Jeremiah 31:27-34*

My teenager recently lost a tooth. He's long past the age where he believes a tooth fairy will appear with money in exchange for his dental offerings, but he still put the tooth in a plastic bag and left it for us to find.

Teeth appear at key moments in the Bible. In some volatile instances Jesus promises that in judgment there will be "gnashing of teeth" (Luke 13:28). Even those with minimal biblical knowledge know the Torah's insistence on "a tooth for a tooth" (Exod. 21:24). Most think it a command for biblical vengeance. "An eye for an eye makes the whole world blind," a bumper sticker retorts. But the instruction in Exodus actually limits violence. If someone knocks out my tooth, I am not allowed to take indiscriminate vengeance. Justice must be equal to or lesser than the original offence. In today's text, the prophet Jeremiah agrees—God punishes offenders (those who eat the sour grapes), not their children.

Here again, teeth appear at a key moment as Jeremiah prophesies that God will bring a new covenant to the people of Israel. In this time of planting and building, children will not be held responsible (have their teeth set on edge) for their parents' iniquities. First, Jeremiah says that each person will be held accountable for their own iniquities, but then the point of God's new covenant is made clear: God will forgive God's people, and everyone will know God.

As a child, my son believed talk of his lost teeth was a sign of coming financial gain. As Christians, we don't believe in fairies, but we believe talk of teeth is a sign that something good is coming. And indeed God promises a new covenant where no one's teeth are set on edge as God does what God always does—forgives evil and delights in mercy.

God, thank you for your new covenants built on love and mercy. Amen.

TUESDAY, OCTOBER 15 ~ *Read 2 Timothy 3:14–4:5*

The Bible rarely asserts its authority self-referentially. When it does, we should pay attention. Second Timothy promises that "all scripture is inspired by God." The scripture Timothy refers to—the only scripture the New Testament knows—are the Hebrew scriptures, what we call the Old Testament. It is a gift from God, and it instructs us in the salvation that faith in Jesus brings.

God has given us variegated scriptures. The voice of God's written word comes not as that of a monotone speaker but rather resembles a raucous family argument over good food, stretched out over centuries. The Bible is not a single book, but a library of many (sixty-six for most Protestants; more for other Christian denominations) with different authors and settings. Some parts disagree with other parts. This suggests that God wants us to discern truth through many and varied voices.

Our text from Jeremiah continues Torah's tradition of limiting retribution. Exodus promises that God's mercy extends to a thousand generations. (See Exodus 34:6-7.) That's a heap of mercy. It continues with what seems like a curse—iniquity on children to the third and fourth generations. That's a lot less punishment than mercy, but the prophets are not satisfied. As we read yesterday, Jeremiah 31:29-30 disagrees with Exodus: God punishes no one for their parents' sins. See the trajectory of mercy started in Exodus and continued in Jeremiah?

Scripture is not a word in granite or marble. It is a word on soft, fleshy hearts. (See Jeremiah 31:33.) Discerning its truth—drinking its marrow—requires argument, debate, discernment, and delight. That's how God makes us, mere humans, more like God.

God of all scripture, help me to love your word and to honor it enough to debate its meaning with others as we seek to love you together. Amen.

WEDNESDAY, OCTOBER 16 ~ *Read Jeremiah 31:31-34*

As a member of Generation X, I often warn my baby boom generation colleagues against using sentimental language around "family" to describe the church. The baby boomers were the first to divorce more often than they stayed married. Mine is the first generation where we can ask a total stranger when their parents divorced. Many in my generation know family as the place that harms you, where promises are broken.

Yet harm in the family is not new, as God's prophet makes clear: The new covenant "will not be like the covenant . . . they broke, though I was their husband." Humanity seems to look to break our covenants as soon as the ink is dry. Christians often speak as though this were true only of Israel's covenants, but we are dead wrong. We break covenants whenever we sin, that is, whenever we prove our humanity. (See Romans 3:20, 23.)

Astoundingly, God keeps covenants even when we do not. There are no non-sinners around with whom to make a covenant that will not be broken. So God risks covenants with such as us. God feels the hurt like a spurned spouse. Yet God stays married to us.

During Jesus' ministry, some Sadducees ask him a question many modern readers consider strange: If a woman is married seven times, whose wife will she be in heaven? (See Luke 20:27-40.) The longer we ponder Jeremiah 31, the less strange the initial question seems. God will heal broken promises. What does that mean for dissolved marriage vows? Who knows? Even Jesus punts on the question. But make no mistake: God keeps promises. One day, God will heal our feeble ability to keep promises. God will forgive us, and God will forget we sinned in the first place.

God, thank you for keeping your promises. Despite our failures, help us to keep our promises to you and to others. Amen.

THURSDAY, OCTOBER 17 ~ *Read Psalm 119:97-104*

Psalm 119 is the longest chapter in the Bible. Its 176 verses say one thing over and over: the law is great. It is an acrostic poem, in which each letter of the Hebrew alphabet gets eight lines. The law is beautiful from aleph to tov, from alpha to omega, from A to Z.

Christians do not always speak so exuberantly about the law. Paul considers the law as one of the enemies Christ defeats. (See Galatians 2:16.) How strange then to see our Jewish neighbors, our elder siblings in faith, describe the law as a delight. On the festival of Simchat Torah, the end of the annual reading of the Torah in the synagogue, Jews dance with the scroll. The large Torah scroll is passed around from worshiper to worshiper, each of whom reels with it like a bride on her wedding day.

The Jews are reading Psalm 119, which we also call scripture, better than we do. The law is "sweeter than honey," the psalmist insists. This psalm cries out in ecstasy about the loveliness of the law. The Torah makes the ones praying wiser than their enemies, wiser even than their teachers, their elders. Jews often wear a prayer shawl in worship. It is a symbol of being covered in the law, enveloped by God's mercy. Remember Psalm 119 when you read Paul—he is wearing one of those shawls. He argues that Gentiles have access to divine mercy in Christ without having to live by Torah. His anger is reserved for those who think Gentile converts must become Jews. Jews—go on observing the Torah. Gentiles—no need. All—mercy is here in full, as Jeremiah promises.

Such a proclamation of mercy will set you to writing long poems, to dancing with scrolls, and to delighting in the law, in one another, and in God.

Lord, delight us with your law, sweeter than honey, which sets our feet to dancing. Amen.

FRIDAY, OCTOBER 18 ~ *Read Luke 18:1-8*

The Bible can be funny. Take the judge in today's parable. He "neither feared God nor had respect for people." That is not surprising for a politician. The judge's self-reflection surprises us: "Though I have no fear of God and no respect for anyone. . . ." Sure, he's corrupt, but he's also remarkably self-aware. Preachers who read that in church with a straight face should cause their congregations to laugh aloud.

Here's what's even funnier: Jesus compares God to this judge in a parable about prayer as he admonishes us to pray always. The judge grants the widow justice so she won't wear him out. The notes in the New Revised Standard Version preserve another rendering: "so that she may not finally come and slap me in the face." The judge doesn't want a black eye from the helpless widow. Do you know any politicians worried about being punched out by old ladies? Neither do Jesus or his hearers.

Yet the corrupt, cowardly judge gives the widow what she wants.

This is the sort of story we would forbid in church if it were not already in the Bible. Outrageous! Comparing God to this gutless, spineless, lawless officeholder. The widow with the frightening fists is the patron saint of anyone ever mistreated by any bureaucracy. And this judge is the anti-image of God. Yesterday's psalm tells us that God delights in the law. God will judge all people not just fairly, but mercifully. God has no fear of being beaten up; in fact, in the person of Jesus, God has been beaten. God loves the powerless and becomes one of them to raise up the lowly and bring down the haughty—judges included.

And that's the greatest joke we know.

God, grant justice to all who now lack it and against all who execute it for self-gain. Make right the world you love and over which you lament. Amen.

How do you pray? What do you pray for? In what way? If I'm honest, my prayers are mostly a presentation to God of the list of things I want God to do for me. I treat God as a sort of cosmic butler: do this; don't let that happen. It doesn't work very well. God is remarkably stubborn about having God's way. It's a childish way to pray. It treats God like a talisman, a crystal ball, a tarot card. It's using God to try to alter the course of coming events. I'm a pastor and teach the Bible for a living, yet I still pray this way. Many people go on rejecting for the rest of their lives this childish version of the faith.

Is there a better way?

Jesus' parable suggests one here. He hopes his disciples would learn our "need to pray always and not to lose heart." Always. Not just "bail me out" prayers and "thank you" prayers when things go well, but always. And what for? The widow exists on the edges of society; she represents those for whom God has commanded Israel to care—along with the orphan and the stranger. (See Exodus 22:21-22.) She seeks justice against her opponent. And Jesus tells us the moral of the story—will not God grant justice when we cry day and night? Will God delay in helping?

A prayer for justice. Offered always. Without tiring. Until the Son of Man comes. Jesus calls us to pray not for God to do what we want, but to pray for us—and for those praying with us—to do what God wants.

Lord, thy will be done. Make us into people who pray for justice without ceasing and who long for it more than we long for food and drink. Amen.

SUNDAY, OCTOBER 20 ~ *Read Luke 18:1-8*

This parable is about persisting in prayer, yet its primary content reveals a longing for justice. The story calls us less to persistence as to a longing for justice, which is the heart of all prayer.

And the world could use a little justice right about now, don't you think?

There is always a longing for justice among those whom society oppresses. The widow, the orphan, and the stranger demand more than charity. Justice seeks to level the playing field. Mary sings of this leveling in her magnificat—justice is a matter of God's scattering the proud and filling the bellies of the hungry. (See Luke 1:46-56.) Perhaps the judge is reluctant because justice means a demotion for him. He too would need the assistance due the widow, the orphan, and the stranger.

Justice for the poor preoccupies Luke. His Sermon on the Plain includes not just blessings for the lowly but also curses for the rich. (See Luke 6:20-26.) Jesus takes the side of the oppressed—and according to Luke alone of the Gospel writers—against the oppressor. That is, most of us.

Our world longs for justice now. Protesters take to the streets to ask for it. Many of us relatively comfortable types wish the clamor would die down. But if we stop and listen, we'll notice the clamor is not just a nuisance. It is the very voice of God. The gospel is good news for the poor or it is not good news at all.

Every prayer is actually a prayer for justice, even if those praying remain unaware. So pray carefully in Jesus' name. You could find yourself, like this judge, dethroned; like this widow, ennobled; like all creation, made new.

God, bring your justice. And because we could not stand it otherwise, bring your mercy too. Amen.

God with Us

OCTOBER 21–27, 2019 • TARIQ CUMMINGS

SCRIPTURE OVERVIEW: The theme in the readings from the Hebrew scriptures is abundance. Joel speaks of the time of plenty in the land of Israel. This abundance is not only physical, for it includes a generous outpouring of the Spirit of God. The psalmist sings of abundant rains that allows the land to flourish. The hills, meadows, and valleys all sing praise to God. Second Timothy 4 contains the scriptural passage that brings us closest to the death of Paul. The apostle has been abandoned by many, but the Lord stands by him as he faces his likely imminent death. In the Gospel, Jesus warns us about the dangers of pride. The Pharisee in the parable thinks his personal goodness brings favor with God, but God desires a humble heart.

QUESTIONS AND SUGGESTIONS FOR REFLECTION

- Read Joel 2:23-32. How has rain been a sign of God's impending provision in your life?
- Read Psalm 65. How has God's forgiveness freed you to participate in creation's joy?
- Read 2 Timothy 4:6-8, 16-18. When has God strengthened you in the face of evil?
- Read Luke 18:9-14. What aspect of your life do you need to approach with renewed humility?

Senior Pastor of Ousley United Methodist Church, Stonecrest, Georgia; graduate of Philander Smith College (BA) and Gammon Theological Seminary (MDiv, DMin); 2017 Emerging Leader Award, Gammon Theological Seminary; member of Alpha Phil Alpha Fraternity Incorporated; husband, father, pastor, and friend.

MONDAY, OCTOBER 21 ~ *Read 2 Timothy 4:6-8*

One of my most memorable experiences as a youth was running on my junior high track and field team. I never believed that I would love running. I had never considered myself to be fast or to have the strength and endurance to run a race. However, my time on the team taught me so much more than how to run a race. It showed me the importance of setting a goal.

After I had made several attempts to try to beat my peers with my speed and agility but had failed, I decided to quit the team. As I approached Coach Williams to tell him of my decision, he stopped me and asked, "Cummings, what's your reason for running?" That question changed my life. Though I soon became a decent runner, I became an even better person because I was pushed to find a reason to run.

In his letter to Timothy, the apostle Paul presents his own eulogy in the form of a defense. Aware that his time on earth is drawing to its end, Paul writes of his earthly and spiritual journey—the good fight, the finished race, and his remaining faith. Paul is able to finish his life journey because he is focused during his most trying moments—because only the righteous Judge can provide the crown of righteousness.

What is your reason for running? What prize are you after? From whom do you wish to receive your reward?

Holy God, giver of life, health, and strength, thank you for the ability to run the race you have given me. Help me to focus on my ultimate goal, which is to please you. Amen.

TUESDAY, OCTOBER 22 ~ *Read 2 Timothy 4:16-18*

There is nothing like sitting and listening to the seasoned (senior) persons in my community. They seem to have stories for every situation. They have stories that will make you laugh as well as make you cry. Stories of struggles and stories of triumph. Stories that will make you think and stories that will leave you wondering, *Did I catch their point?* We share our heritage and our faith through stories.

In this letter to Timothy, the apostle Paul instructs Timothy. While Paul shares words of direction, he begins to tell a story of faith and trust in the Lord. Paul tells of how earlier most of his friends had deserted him before the judge, though it seems clear that Paul had expected his friends to support him through this trying season.

I can only imagine how this brief snippet of the story of Paul relates to Timothy, whom Paul entrusts to continue his mantle and ministry. With little to no help, I'm sure that Timothy feels overwhelmed and underqualified. But no doubt Paul's words to Timothy give him great encouragement: Paul writes, "But the Lord stood by me and gave me strength." What a blessed assurance! What a story of faith to know that even when the odds are against us, the Lord will show up and give us strength.

Today, allow the story of Paul to encourage you. Whether in an interview, a doctor's visit, a phone call, or a meeting: If you feel alone, know that the Lord is with you.

Holy God, I thank you for the stories from those who have walked with you. Thank you for their witness to your unfailing love and grace. In times of my despair, help me to know that you are near to me too. Amen.

WEDNESDAY, OCTOBER 23 ~ *Read Luke 18:9-14*

I acknowledged the grace of God awakening me to a call to ministry at an early age. My pastor at the time served an essential role in my discerning process. He would always ask me, "Son, are you humble?" I would affirm, "Yes, sir." He would end with, "Stay humble." This same verbal exchange happened more often than I liked. It would get on my nerves. Out of respect, I would go along, but I could not understand why he continued to ask me the same question.

In the Gospel of Luke, we find Jesus telling a parable to someone wrestling with the issue of pride. Jesus tells of two men entering the Temple to pray. One, a self-righteous Pharisee, prays, "Lord, I thank you that I'm not like other people, for I don't do wrong and I give according to the law" (AP). The other person, a despised tax collector, prays, "God, have mercy on me, a sinner." Jesus says that the tax collector goes home justified before God, not the Pharisee. Pride keeps the Pharisee from being justified before God.

My childhood pastor knew something about success that my teenage mind could not comprehend: success and elevation begin with humility. Looking back on my childhood, I recognize times that I felt pride slipping into my heart and mind. However, the words of my pastor stood at the door of my heart to challenge my pride: "Are you humble?" His words helped save my ministry from being overtaken with prideful pursuits.

What words or thoughts keep watch over the door of your heart, mind, and soul? The words and ideas that keep watch over the gates of our life can determine whether we begin each day in the spirit of pride or the spirit of humility.

O God, I desire to be justified in you. Free me from any prideful thoughts or actions, so that I may live in joyful obedience. Amen.

THURSDAY, OCTOBER 24 ~ *Read Joel 2:23-27*

One night as my son was preparing to go to bed, I heard him listening to the children's nursery rhyme "Rain, rain go away." This song brought back many memories. As a youngster, I was always disappointed when the forecast predicted rain. I viewed rain as a liquid matter that destroyed—or at least altered—the many plans I had made. The rain had ruined many school recesses, family cookouts, parades, sports games, and the list could go on. Now the "rain" that destroys my plans has taken on a new form. As an adult, I've experienced troubles, setbacks, persecution, and trials. Just like rain, they all seem to hit me when I least expect them.

Today's passage reminds us that rain is so much more than an unexpected deterrent. God sends rain as a reminder of God's amazing grace.

The prophet Joel shares a word of hope with a group of people who have experienced an infestation of locusts. The insects flood their lives like the metaphorical rain that destroys our plans. But God sends physical rain with a promise of restoration: The wilderness will soon flow with green pastures, and the trees will overflow with fruit.

Joel calls the people to rejoice in the Lord, who sends us rain to demonstrate God's faithfulness. The last thing the people of Israel want to experience is the dread of cloudy and rainy days. I'm sure they want to experience some beautiful days in the sun. But God uses rain to usher in hope and new life. The care and rain we receive enrich our soil and soul.

Today, be encouraged, whether you are faced with spiritual, physical, or mental rainy days. Know that it is God's way of reminding you that a blessing is on the horizon.

Holy God, thank you for being the God who nourishes our soul and soil. Help us to embrace the rain as a reminder of your commitment to us. Amen.

FRIDAY, OCTOBER 25 ~ *Read Psalm 65:5-13*

Each day, cell phone company commercials interrupt our television and radio programs to explain why their services are better than those of other carriers. There are many cell phone providers, and most carriers have created maps showing their coverage area. Their maps seek to display not only coverage but also the strength of the cellular data service in comparison to other carriers.

God's coverage of grace extends across the land and sea. We all experience times when God's coverage seems spotty, when we feel disconnected from God. But the psalmist reminds us that God offers hope that reaches to "the ends of the earth" and "the farthest seas." Throughout today's reading, the psalmist sings of the great reach and abundance of God's provision. As in yesterday's reading from Joel, water brings new and abundant life to God's people. The psalmist writes of God's sovereignty over creation and God's using this power to make the earth fruitful and productive. God's displays of provision are so great that they inspire awe in the most remote places.

Today's reading reminds us that we can always seek God. When we feel distant from God, we can humble ourselves and go to God in prayer. No matter how far we feel from God, God's coverage of grace reaches to us. God answers and delivers us, and we can expect God to perform remarkable deeds. When God reaches us in our weakest and most remote places, we can sing for joy together with all of creation.

Gracious God, I am thankful that your reach is far and wide. Your deeds are so awesome there are too many to count. Thank you for answering my prayers. May your grace continue to cover those who feel near to you as well as those who feel distant. In Christ's name. Amen.

SATURDAY, OCTOBER 26 ~ *Read Psalm 65:1-4*

I love the celebration of Holy Communion. It is one of my favorite moments in the life of the church. This holy meal, shared with the world, represents God's redemptive love and grace, given freely to the world. This means of grace testifies to Christ's love and presence with us. What a wonderful table to be invited to.

The invitation to the table in the Communion liturgy of the United Methodist Church warms my heart every time I hear it. The invitation includes the opportunity to confess our sins. We seldom willingly take part in confession. Many of us have to be proven wrong by several witnesses before we even entertain the thought of confessing. Though confession has a lot to do with setting aside our ego and pride, it has more to do with the grace that awaits us.

Our human condition has a way of overwhelming us. Pain, world calamities, death, violence, and sins committed knowingly and unknowingly seem to weigh us down. Many times when I become overwhelmed, I find myself asking God, "Will I ever get it right?" At this point, I usually remember the words of the pardon in the Communion liturgy: "Christ died while we were yet sinners; that proves God's love toward us. In the name of Jesus Christ, you are forgiven" (UMH, 12). God's forgiveness is not a hall pass to continue in our sinful way. It is a reminder to invite the grace of God into our lives. I am a witness that the grace of God has the power to change anybody. Though there are times when we will feel overwhelmed by our sins, God's forgiveness will free us for joyful obedience.

O God, forgive us, we pray. Free us for joyful obedience through Jesus Christ, our Lord. Amen.

SUNDAY, OCTOBER 27 ~ *Read Joel 2:25-32*

One of the most significant gifts we can receive is the mantle and spirit of those whom we admire. For me, it would be my grandmother. My grandmother was a strong and courageous woman. She was committed to her family, the church, and God. She taught me her faith by singing songs of praise and reading her Bible as I sat on her lap. Her faith was so real I could feel it through her smile and her actions. To be told that her spirit lives in me reminds me that she is still with me.

In the book of Joel, we see a God who restores us from a place of ruin. To hear the promise that God will give them back what the insects have devoured gives the people of Israel a sense of hope and redemption. What more could God do? What more could God offer? It seems that God has given them everything they need to restart their lives.

When they seem content with what God has given them, God takes love a step further. God pours out God's Spirit. What greater way for God to show love and grace to a people who were poor in resources and spirit? I have gathered over the years that the gift of God's Spirit is the greatest gift anyone could ever receive. We can carry the gift of the Spirit as a reminder of the lessons and promises of God and that we are not alone.

Today, before you thank God for any of your physical possessions, thank God for giving us God's Spirit. For the Spirit reminds us that God has gifted us with much more than we can know.

Holy God, we are grateful for all that you have done and given to us. Most of all we are grateful for your Spirit, which warms us and reminds us that you are forever with us. Amen.

Persistent Praise

OCTOBER 28–NOVEMBER 3, 2019 • YOLANDA M. NORTON

SCRIPTURE OVERVIEW: This week includes All Saints Day, when we remember those who have come before and handed down the faith to us, especially through trials. Habakkuk reminds us that our predecessors sometimes suffered discouragement, but the righteous have always lived by faith. The psalmist also has experienced hard times, but he knows that God's commandments are true and lead to life. The Thessalonians have experienced persecution as well; yet through their strength their faith and love continue to grow to the glory of Christ. May the same be said of us and our church communities! The famous story of Zacchaeus illustrates that the crowd of faithful witnesses that we celebrate on All Saints Day includes those who have been lost—outsiders—for Jesus comes to seek and save the lost.

QUESTIONS AND SUGGESTIONS FOR REFLECTION

- Read Habakkuk 1:1-4; 2:1-4. How can you wait actively for God's response to your prayers and complaints? How will you enact God's response when it comes?
- Read Psalm 119:137-144. How do you persist in following God's commandments in the face of injustice and corruption?
- Read 2 Thessalonians 1:1-4, 11-12. The work of the church has never been easy. How does your faith community work to exude God's love in a time when many reject or feel rejected by church institutions?
- Read Luke 19:1-10. When have you run to Jesus? How can you share your experience so others pursue Jesus as well?

Assistant Professor of Hebrew Bible, San Francisco Theological Seminary; ordained clergy in the Christian Church (Disciples of Christ); womanist scholar whose work lives at the intersection of biblical studies, ethics, and homiletics.

MONDAY, OCTOBER 28 ~ *Read Habakkuk 1:1-4; 2:1-4*

Not every message is made for every season. Often our understandings of God and how God functions limit God's speech to platitudes and orthodoxy. While some patterns of behavior persist in every age, the unexpected happens. Our lives shift in seasons, and the world changes in astonishing and sometimes grievous ways. We all respond differently to these large swings. Some people depend on old modes of being and others find it necessary for a fresh response to the situation.

Habakkuk's story reflects the need for a fresh word in new and difficult times. The prophet is discontent with the political and economic institutions of Jerusalem; he is vexed by the persistence of corruption in God's sacred space. So he is ensconced in an existential question: If God is just, where is God in an unjust world?

For many people this question leads to doubt and disengagement with God. However, Habakkuk realizes his obligation to engage with God even when that dialogue is fraught. Today's readings present two complaints the prophet lobs at God and two responses. The prophet demands from God an answer to the question of how long the suffering will persist. God's initial answer is insufficient and so Habakkuk persists. He first persists in his petition but then the prophet declares: "I will stand at my watchpost . . . [and] keep watch to see what [God] will say to me." Habakkuk is persistent in his desire to be faithful to God's response.

Too often we lob complaints at God without understanding our responsibility to stand at our watchpost and see how God will respond. Habakkuk calls us to be steadfast in our determination to make the world better and to seek justice by continuing to actively wait for God's message. God's response is pointed. Don't be passive. God tells the prophet to "write the vision; make it plain." God's deliverance of God's people requires each of us to listen for God's voice and then actively participate in redemptive moments.

God, help us to be active as we wait for and carry out your message. Amen.

TUESDAY, OCTOBER 29 ~ *Read 2 Thessalonians 1:1-4, 11-12*

Second Thessalonians 1 is prayer. There are three parts to the prayer—an introduction (vv. 1-2), thanksgiving (vv. 3-10), and intercession (vv. 11-12). Verses three and four introduce thanksgiving for each person in the community and acknowledge God's hand in increasing their love for one another. In other words, the author gives God thanks for the humanity that he sees in each person and then acknowledges the power and potential of love. The Pauline writer is not consumed in this moment with the flaws and imperfections of the church; he is not caught up in the institution of the church. He simply is in awe of the way that God has brought people together and allowed love to abound.

In this "age of the nones" when so many people have walked away from the church and when the church has walked away from so many people, we forget that the church is people and love. Church is not about power; it is not about doctrine. The church is the calling and coming together of brothers and sisters to exude love upon one another, not as a sign of who we are but instead as a reflection of who God is.

When God calls us into these spaces, it is not about our reputation. The intercession in verses 11 and 12 reminds us of that sober reality. All the good things that we can do as the church—the gathering of believers—is an effort to be worthy of the call that God has laid before us. Today's reading reminds us that the work is not easy, and that even when we resolve to do the work we are often distracted from glorification of God. This work is so difficult that the author knows that he must intercede on the church's behalf.

God, we give thanks that you have called us together in community. May we always acknowledge in our hearts that you are the center of our calling and our work. Remind us every day to see you in your people so that we may love them with our whole hearts. Amen.

WEDNESDAY, OCTOBER 30 ~ *Read Luke 19:1-10*

Tax collectors during Jesus' time are generally known for their corrupt practices and their relationship with the Roman empire. This is not the kind of person that one might naturally put in close proximity with Jesus. Yet, here is Zacchaeus, a tax collector, intent on seeing Jesus. Zacchaeus finds the notion of Jesus' presence in Jericho so pressing that he will not allow the crowd to get in his way. He wants to see Jesus for himself; he wants to bear witness to Jesus' presence. The problem is that Zacchaeus is short, and despite his wealth, he can not buy access to Jesus.

Zacchaeus reminds me that hearing about Jesus secondhand often is not good enough. Accounts of Jesus' work, mission, and presence are magnificent, but they cannot replace a close encounter with him. I would love it if Jesus would just come to me all the time. Sometimes Jesus does come to us; he meets us in our pain, our woundedness, our strength, and our joy. However, as disciples, we also have a responsibility to doggedly pursue Jesus' presence. We are called to bear witness to Jesus as he moves. Nothing about our status, bank accounts, intelligence, or allegiances will grant us access to Jesus; only our pursuit.

It seems peculiar that the author tells us that Zacchaeus is short, except that Zacchaeus "ran ahead and climbed a sycamore tree." Sycamore trees are huge. I have to imagine that it would not have been easy for Zacchaeus to climb. I suppose that he ran ahead to give himself sufficient time to get to a place where he could see Jesus passing.

And somehow Jesus sees him! He sees him, invites himself into Zacchaeus's home, and Zacchaeus is happy to welcome him. We often make excuses for why we can't rush to Jesus, but this text reminds us that we have everything we need to make our way to Jesus. And Jesus sees us. Jesus invites himself into our presence. All we have to do is welcome him.

God, help us to run to Jesus knowing he will recognize us and welcome us. Amen.

THURSDAY, OCTOBER 31 ~ *Read Psalm 119:137-144*

Psalm 119 is the longest psalm and reads as a litany of prayers and reflections. Today's passage has righteousness as its central theme. The psalmist acknowledges not his own righteousness but that of God and then acknowledges God's presence as reflected in the law.

In a world where so much injustice is ratified by corrupt business and legal practices, it is hard for me to think about law and righteousness as concentric concepts. I know that sometimes people hide behind the law into order to perpetrate injustice. However, the psalmist reminds us that God's law and teaching and instruction is about faithfulness not destruction.

The psalmist is distraught because of those who have forgotten God's word. Shouldn't we all be disturbed by this? God's word is not confined to the Bible, and it is not a word that should be used for our convenience. God's word is righteousness and love. That is the persistent message of God that is "everlasting." We cannot get bogged down in reducing God's word to a series of laws that exclude people with whom we are not comfortable. We are not called to be litigious; we are called to be loving.

God's law becomes a tool that the psalmist can use to alleviate some of the anxiety caused by oppression and taunting. He proclaims that the commandments are his delight. The most popular of God's commandments are found in Exodus 20 and they are a set of laws that call together a community of people to honor God, rest, practice fidelity, honor family, and love justice. Living into that commandment should give us all peace and rest and fortify us for the journey ahead.

Gracious God, may we lean on your word not as a text of exclusion but one that calls us to live righteously and compassionately. Enliven us to hear your words and delight in you even as we mourn an often-broken world. Amen.

All Saints Day

All Saints Day is a liturgical moment when the church pauses to honor the lives and legacies of all those who have passed away. This occasion is not just about the icons of faith or about those individuals whom history has widely regarded; this is a day to celebrate memories of those known by many and those known by only a few.

In the Gospel of Luke's Sermon on the Plain, Jesus lays before the disciples an imperative for life in the Beatitudes. This series of blessings and woes gives insight into the legacy that God desires for all who follow after God. We often use this text as an excuse to absolve ourselves from the responsibility to care for those who are poor, marginalized, and disenfranchised. We use the scripture as a tool to suggest that because suffering on earth is redeemed in heaven, we are not responsible for alleviating miseries of our brothers and sisters.

Yet, on the contrary, Jesus' message is first to a group of his disciples who have left behind their material goods for the sake of his mission. Jesus' sermon calls all of us who are committed to him to prioritize his mission to serve others and be present with all people. God is not opposed to our joy; God is not against our fulfillment. However, God desires that we not become so consumed with our own needs and desires that we are incapable of meeting the needs of others.

This legacy is not reserved for the icons of our faith like Martin Luther King Jr., Mother Theresa, Fannie Lou Hamer, Dorothy Day, and Dietrich Bonhoeffer. We are all called to live out their legacy of deep care for the kingdom of God with a willingness to be bold in our pursuit of equality and justice.

God, give me the wisdom to honor all who have lived to honor you with love, grace, and compassion. Give me the courage to go with boldness to care for your people and your world. Amen.

SATURDAY, NOVEMBER 2 ~ *Read Psalm 149*

Today's reading is a psalm of praise. It is unclear if the psalmist's context is the Exodus or the exile. However, it is clear that the psalmist believes in the sovereignty of God in difficult situations. The psalmist is intent on giving God praise. In verse six, Israel is implored, "Let the high praises of God be in their throats and two-edged swords in their hands." This is sometimes a less palatable vision of praise in our time. The second part of this imperative seems aggressive if not violent. However, its essence is an aspect of praise that we often ignore.

The psalmist outlines a two-part strategy to praise. The first part is our commonly understood meaning of praise: Praise is the vocal articulation of God's goodness. We not only must take note of God's action, but we must give it language. We are called to bear public witness to the ways in which God provides, protects, and sustains.

The second part of praise is one that I often forget. We are called to defend and protect God's mission. This work does not require death and dismemberment. On the contrary, this battle requires that we be willing to work hard to protect those who fall prey to the overreach of empire. If we are to be faithful, our praise is to work for justice and equality. Our praise is to care for others. Our praise is to tear down systems of power that hold people captive. That is the highest praise we have.

Dear God, may your praise always be in our mouths, our hands, and our feet. Remind us that praise is not to heap empty flattery upon you but instead to walk in a way that reflects who you are. Amen.

SUNDAY, NOVEMBER 3 ~ *Read Daniel 7:1-3, 15-18*

Today's passage centers on dreams. In Daniel 1–6, Daniel's job is to interpret the dreams of others. Yet in a pivotal shift in the text, Daniel is now the dreamer. He dreams something that he himself cannot understand. In verse 16 of today's reading, we learn that Daniel must now approach an attendant to "ask him the truth" about the nature of his dream. Daniel's dream is not pleasant and neither is the interpretation; it points the rise of a new empire under Antiochus Epiphanes, who will hinder the religious practices of Israel.

The funny thing about dreams is that they have not rhyme or reason, and they cannot be contained. Some of us are natural dreamers, whether in our waking hours or our sleep. Oftentimes our dreams make no sense and require time and sometimes community to make sense of them. And, like Daniel's, there are moments when our dreams are terrifying. However, God has the capacity to use our dreams to prepare us for the future.

Daniel has to be persistent in his desire to find the meaning of his dream, and he has to be humble enough to ask for help despite his earlier role as interpreter of dreams. We must be willing to engage our best and worst dreams in hopes that they will give us some insight on life. We should never be so arrogant to assume that we will always have the same relationship with our dreams. God calls us to humble ourselves so that we can have an intimate relationship with the vision that God lays before us.

God, may we always pay attention to our dreams, nurture them, and listen to them so that we become better stewards for the days ahead. Help us never to grow weary in the possibilities of our dreams. Amen.

Coming Alive in Christ

NOVEMBER 4–10, 2019 • MICHELLE SHRADER

SCRIPTURE OVERVIEW: Following the return from exile to Babylon, the people of God have much work to do to restore the city of Jerusalem. Haggai is one of the prophets sent by God to encourage them. God promises future material blessings for the people and a time of peace. The psalmist praises God and declares that future generations will pass on the stories of God's wonderful works. In Second Thessalonians, Paul addresses a group that is disturbed because they think they have missed the return of Christ. He assures them that they have not missed the time and admonishes them to persevere in their faith. In Luke, Jesus is asked about marriage in the resurrection, but he focuses on God as the God of the living.

QUESTIONS AND SUGGESTIONS FOR REFLECTION

- Read Haggai 1:15b–2:9. When have you had to rely on God's promises for the future? How did your faith in God's provision keep you focused on the long-term goal?
- Read Psalm 145:1-5, 17-21. How do you share God's majesty and justice with the next generations?
- Read 2 Thessalonians 2:1-5, 13-17. How do you live a disciplined life, trusting in the Lord whether or not the end is near?
- Read Luke 20:27-38. How can you be open to the ways God will answer your questions in unexpected ways?

United Methodist minister from Tampa, Florida; serving Cape of Good Hope District of the Methodist Church of Southern Africa, Cape Town, South Africa.

MONDAY, NOVEMBER 4 ~ *Read Haggai 1:15b–2:5*

Godly work often requires vision beyond the present moment. When God commands the Israelites to rebuild the Temple, some lack motivation. They can remember what the Temple looked like before it was destroyed, and they cannot envision clearly the splendor of the new Temple. Through the prophet Haggai, God tells them to stay strong, to take courage, and to remember that their God is with them. The work of rebuilding the Temple, with all the stops and starts, will take them twenty years; but in the end they will complete it.

In the country of South Africa, during the days of apartheid, many dedicated their lives to ending the evils of the segregating regime. Before Nelson Mandela became the first black president and the first democratically elected president, he spent twenty-seven years in prison. Eighteen of those years he spent on Robben Island. While on the Island, he and many of the other political prisoners continued to teach one another to keep their minds active. They knew it would take dedication to remain strong for the work before them.

As Christians, we commit our life to following the ways of Jesus. We commit to advocating for the poor and the oppressed and to living for a day when divisions among God's children no longer exist. The more faithfully we carry out this work, the more likely we are to face resistance. We can heed Haggai's message to the Israelites: God calls us to be strong, to take courage, and to remember that God is with us.

Loving God, empower us for the living of these days. Grow within us the strength and courage to continue to work toward a life on earth as it is in heaven. Amen.

TUESDAY, NOVEMBER 5 ~ *Read Haggai 2:6-9*

The Israelites fret about the state of the Temple, but Haggai assures them they do not need to live in worry. The Temple will be built and the resources for it will come. Haggai confirms that God indeed has some shaking up to do. Yet God's shaking of the heavens and the earth and the sea and the land and the nations will bring splendor to the house of God, which will outshine the legacy of the glory in Solomon's Temple. Haggai's words call the people to carry on with the work and to trust in the promise of God's provision along the way. The Temple will be rebuilt through their efforts; they can trust in this.

In September of 2017, Hurricane Maria hit the shores of Puerto Rico with devastating impact. The rebuilding efforts no doubt continue to this day. In rebuilding Puerto Rico, the people are rebuilding the infrastructure of their communities rather than a temple. Yet, these catastrophic events shake us in ways that remind us of our humanity as we observe the fragility of life and all that we build.

In times of crisis, we sometimes look for individuals who represent Christ's love, a self-sacrificial love to the point of self-risk. As important as this is, we should also look for a body, the body of believers re-membering Christ and sharing with all the world the gifts of Christ's love alive in them. When devastation strikes—and it will—Haggai reminds us that we are a people who join together to rebuild for the glory of God.

Holy God, remind us again and again of the gift in every moment of our life with you. Receive the work of our hands as one of the ways we lift up praise and worship you. Amen.

WEDNESDAY, NOVEMBER 6 ~ *Read 2 Thessalonians 2:1-5, 13-17*

The year 2000 brought with it the end of the 1900s. Many people believed that it would be the end of time as well. The Y2K computer bug was anticipated to wreak havoc in computers that had not been programmed to roll to 2000. It may have seemed like the end was imminent, but the world continued after 1999. Today anxiety arises with the increased occurrence of natural disasters and superstorms. The question emerges again, "Are we near the end?"

Rather than live in worry over whether or not we are near the end, we can spend our energy disciplining ourselves to hold fast in any circumstance. We will experience times of devastation, but we serve a God who is with us in life, in death, and in life beyond death. As for the day of the Lord, Augustine shared, "So what is this day which the Lord has made? Live good lives and you will be this day yourselves."* And what is good? Micah 6:8 says, "He has told you, O mortal, what is good; and what does the LORD require of you but to do justice, and to love kindness, and to walk humbly with your God?"

We submit ourselves to the sanctifying work of the Holy Spirit so that we can become more alive in Christ. To wait for Jesus is to meet Jesus in the eyes, the ears, and the faces of others who cross our path today. Jesus is clear on his concern for the poor and the oppressed. We must remember what he teaches—that the poor will be with us to the end. It is better for us to spend our time waiting for Jesus with them.

---

*Peter J. Gorday, ed., *Ancient Christian Commentary on Scripture: New Testament IX: Colossians, Thessalonians, 1–2 Timothy, Titus, Philemon* (Downers Grove, IL: IVP Academic, 2000), 92.

Spirit of the living God, shape us in our very being, that we may have love enough for all the world. Amen.

THURSDAY, NOVEMBER 7 ~ *Read Psalm 145:1-5*

This psalm speaks of passing on the praise of God from one generation to the next. One of the great gifts of the Christian faith is to know that we belong to a story that began long before us and will continue on long after we are gone. It is like sitting in a sports arena and participating in the "wave." The wave of our faith never ends—praise upon praise from one generation to the next. This is the life of the Christian people, to have faith that sustains our eternal wave of praise.

However, there are moments in life when we may struggle to lift our voice in praise. Doubts creep in, fear seizes us unexpectedly, and darkness becomes an unwelcome friend along our way. These moments too unite our spirit with the generations who struggled before us. The oral traditions of long ago wove the word of God into the memories of the people until it became a ready word upon their lips. With the stories memorized and recited, the people could recall God's word in moments when faith seemed to be just beyond their grasp. Praise is sometimes the loudest, the most authentic, when it rises from a place of great struggle.

When words fail us, we can remember that the secrets of God's love are hidden in the trees, in the mountains, and in the seas. We are not the only ones created for praise. Poet Rabindranath Tagore wrote, "Trees are the earth's endless effort to speak to the listening heavens."* We can participate in this magnificent movement of love raised to God. All of creation and every generation can be caught up in praise upon praise.

---

*Rabindranath Tagore, *Fireflies* (Gilbertsville, NY: Home Made Books, 2013), 59.

Creator God, you breathed us into being and gave us life. We join with all of your creation lifting praises upon praises to your holy name. Amen.

FRIDAY, NOVEMBER 8 ~ *Read Luke 20:27-38*

The Sadducees confront Jesus with a question that can easily transport modern readers back to the days of mathematical dilemmas: "Train A is traveling 70 miles per hour. It leaves the station, heading toward a city 260 miles away. At the same time, Train B, traveling 60 miles per hour, leaves the city heading toward the station. When do the two trains meet?" These questions very quickly divide mathematical enthusiasts from the mathematically averse.

The Sadducees pose to Jesus the question about whose wife the woman married to seven brothers will be at the resurrection to test his theological acumen just as the train question tests mathematical dexterity. Their question raises their doubts about resurrection. Jesus circumvents the answers they expect. His answer shows them that they have focused on the wrong question.

We can become so fixated on what we think we know that we miss out on the beautiful things God has to teach us through others. As the saying goes, "We can't know what we don't know." But we can remember that there are things we don't know. God calls us to be like children gathered at the feet of a great teacher: always open to learning something new from the God who loves us more than we can imagine and from others with whom we share this beautiful planet.

What lesson can we learn from Jesus' moment with the Sadducees? Perhaps we learn that we can find holiness in conversations with others. Those who differ from us can teach us, but we can only learn if we allow the space between ourselves and others to become fertile ground for teaching and learning, where each has a seed of wisdom for the other.

Enlightening God, create a sense of reverence within us for conversation. Help us not to miss your holiness among us. Amen.

SATURDAY, NOVEMBER 9 ~ *Read Psalm 145:17-21*

Today's psalm of praise tells us two specific and related things about God: God is near, and God is just.

God is as close to us as our very next breath. The Hebrew word *ruach* can mean breath, wind, or spirit. If you sit on a bench and watch a tree for a moment or two, you will soon see the breeze catch the tree and shift its leaves. This sort of watching can be peaceful because it reminds us of the ever-present nature of the Holy Spirit in our lives.

As we can trust in God's nearness, we can trust God's actions to be oriented toward truth, justice, and love. We can understand justice as the way things are meant to be. Justice, then, seeks to make things right in our world. We can rest in knowing that God works toward justice and truth. Knowing this can empower us to work for the good in the world too. Orienting our lives toward justice and God's piercing truth creates a way of living in us that arises from the depths of our being, the place where we unite with God in God's own goodness.

We sing praises to God and we honor God with the way in which we live our life. When we rest in the truth that we are a part of God's great creation—when we walk in God's ways—we can release the worries of our own needs and focus on the needs of others. It is a beautiful thing to get to a place of trust that the divine embrace of God's love is great enough to be enough for us all.

God of justice and truth, draw us into this work with you. Use us to aid you in making all things new. Amen.

SUNDAY, NOVEMBER 10 ~ *Read Luke 20:27-38*

To come alive in Christ is to understand the truth of Jesus' resurrection and its power to awaken us to right living. This story unifies all those who seek to discipline their lives in the ways of Jesus. The Sadducees in this text struggle with the concept of a resurrection and test Jesus about it. They may be interested in who will be married to whom when everyone is resurrected, but they really want to know how what Jesus says about life beyond death can be true. Jesus' life, death, and resurrection reveal the power of the truth Jesus preaches. Through Jesus, we witness living truth.

So often, our fears and doubts create anxiety that separates us from faithful living. To be set free into the truth of resurrection means that we have no reason to fear. As Jesus teaches, we are children of God and God's children cannot die anymore. God's power is greater than the power of death. God calls us to choose the ways that lead to life—to choose the ways of Jesus.

Coming alive in Christ means awakening to injustices all around us and not allowing them to evoke within us a sense of fear. The resurrection message gives us the power to face the challenges before us. God is with us in life, in death, and in life beyond death. We have nothing to fear beyond the grave, for we are children of God, who reigns over and above the power of death. Our trust in God's power can ignite within us a holy sense of inspiration for the living of these present days.

Living God, awaken within us the awareness of the power of your love so that we can be caught up in the fullness of life with you. Amen.

A Perfect World

NOVEMBER 11–17, 2019 • DIRK CALDWELL

SCRIPTURE OVERVIEW: This week we read two passages from the prophet Isaiah. In the first, God promises a total restoration, a new heaven and a new earth—a theme repeated in Revelation 21. The new Jerusalem will be filled with joy and prosperity. Isaiah 12 offers thanksgiving to God for the gift of salvation. God's praise will be proclaimed among many nations. In the epistle, Paul chastises a lazy faction among the Thessalonians. This passage has been misapplied as teaching against providing assistance to the poor, but Paul's target is not the poor; it is those who can provide for themselves but fail to do so because they say they are too focused on waiting for Jesus. In Luke, Jesus foretells future turmoil for Jerusalem at the hands of the Romans.

QUESTIONS AND SUGGESTIONS FOR REFLECTION

- Read Isaiah 65:17-25. How can you play a part in Isaiah's vision for God's people? When do you have to accept that only God can usher in this vision? How do you know the difference between these two situations?
- Read Isaiah 12. How can your words be life-changing for others?
- Read 2 Thessalonians 3:6-13. Who has mentored you in the faith? How has their guidance kept you disciplined and helped you grow?
- Read Luke 21:5-19. How do you speak the truth of Jesus to those who say the end is near?

Ordained elder, Extension Ministries, Indiana Conference of the United Methodist Church; active duty chaplain, United States Navy.

MONDAY, NOVEMBER 11 ~ *Read Isaiah 65:17-20*

With all that we see in our world today, we can grow tired and weary of the heaven and earth we experience. The thought of new heavens and a new earth seems enticing. In fact, I wonder whether what we see in our world is an effort for some to try to create a new existence using their own powers. Sometimes human desires come at the expense of persons around them and may require military intervention.

Today is Veterans Day in the United States. While Isaiah prophesies that the former things will not be remembered nor will they come to mind, those living in the United States do remember. We remember those from among our families and neighbors and towns and cities who have felt compelled to do what they could to defend our nation and its allies. We remember them and are thankful.

Many Americans want to believe that what our veterans spent their energy and time doing was in support of Isaiah's vision of joy and delight manifest in the here and now—a place where God's creation would be honored and nurtured; a place where crying, remorse, and regret would be no more; a place where unexpected and untimely death would not inflict its sting.

American veterans, as brave and courageous as they have been, could not usher in the paradise Isaiah tells us will come. That can only be left to the Divine, to the God that reigns over all creation, who understands the kind of joy and delight that will exist in God's heaven and earth. As part of God's created, we have much to anticipate!

Creating God, help us know that what we create can never be as good as what you create. You have created each of us, so help us live into all that you would have us be. Amen.

TUESDAY, NOVEMBER 12 ~ *Read Isaiah 65:21-25*

A roof over our heads and food on our tables—that seems to be a reasonable expectation for most. And still there are those who have not or cannot realize that expectation in their own lives. The winning purse of a recent boxing match was disclosed to be $100 million and the losing purse a mere $30 million. When I think of the extravagance for some compared to the plight of the unhoused or poor in the world, I cannot help but pray for the vision of Isaiah to come quickly.

Isaiah prophesies that when the new heavens and the new earth come about, people will build houses—and live in them. They will plant food and eat what they plant. God's people—all the people that God created—will live long lives and enjoy their work.

Isaiah's vision seems to be the exact opposite of the reality most of the world's population experience. Today, God's people still go without homes and food. God's created people still are unhappy with their unfulfilling work—some to the point of depression. How can we play a part in Isaiah's vision and God's plan for God's people?

It can be as simple as saying something kind to a stranger. Hospitality is important. It could be that you place a few extra dollars into the offering plates at church. You might take a Saturday—or even every Saturday—and dedicate that day to service in your community so that others can have a house in which they can live, or food to eat, or a job in which satisfaction and enjoyment abound.

Those of us lucky enough to have a roof over our heads and food on our tables can give thanks to God! Our faith calls us to share God's blessing with God's people—and to be thankful.

Gracious God, we want to experience your blessings among us. Help your created people be safe, fed, and happy. Amen.

WEDNESDAY, NOVEMBER 13 ~ *Read Isaiah 12*

Our words carry meaning. When we speak our ideas, thoughts, desires, and fears, others hear them and process them for a meaning in their own lives. Sometimes this valuable exercise can be life-changing. Sometimes the process breaks down and can be confusing.

One day my coworker was tasked with transporting a group of worshipers to a church service. He did exactly as he was told. He left the pickup point at the designated time and drove to the church. But the worshipers were running late. He drove an empty vehicle to the worship service! The words he heard me say were: "Leave the pick-up point at 4:45 p.m. and head over to the chapel." Our words mean something.

Isaiah tells us that at some point, we will praise God. "In that day you will say: Give praise to the LORD, proclaim his name; make known among the nations what he has done" (NIV). What words will come from your mouth and your heart as you praise God?

If you have not thought about what you will say, Isaiah has given us some tremendous advice. Even though you and I fall short of righteous living every day, God continues to reach out to us, to love us, and to offer us salvation. We can speak "on that day" from experience that God has turned anger into comfort, that God is our salvation, and that we can trust and not be afraid. We can speak about how God has protected us and lifted up our hearts and filled them with joy. Our words mean something; if we speak the truth of our divine encounters with God and our authentic relationship with Jesus Christ, then what we speak can be life-changing for those around us.

Holy One of Israel, we will praise you today because you have given us strength, salvation, and joy. Amen.

THURSDAY, NOVEMBER 14 ~ *Read 2 Thessalonians 3:6-9*

The US military is an apprentice organization. It hires personnel with the intent for senior personnel to teach them how to do specific jobs. When I was a beginner chaplain, experienced and wise chaplains trained and mentored me. God willing, I will be able to reciprocate when I am a more experienced chaplain.

The church in Thessalonica is Paul's apprentice. This church body is just developing, so they know nothing about how a community of Christ-followers should behave. Their mentor wants to teach them how to live life in accordance with the good news offered by Jesus Christ: Keep away from idle and disruptive believers and those who do not live according to what has been taught. Idleness and disruption can be damaging and divisive if left unchecked.

Have you thought about where you might fit in to these verses? Do you identify with the hard-working brothers and sisters in your church body? Have you ever thought about how you might be among the idle and disruptive? An honest self-examination might reveal something that unnerves us. We might just be the very individuals Paul warns us against.

All of us are still apprentices. We continue to learn, no matter our age, what it really means to live in a community of Christ-followers. Creating a relationship with a mentor can help us to live in the right ways. Mentors set an example by which we can measure our own lives. And in the end, we have Jesus Christ, the greatest teacher, to show us the way.

God, you have called your people to live in community with all its challenges. Open our heart and mind so that we may learn from you how to be faithful. Amen.

FRIDAY, NOVEMBER 15 ~ *Read 2 Thessalonians 3:10-13*

Idleness and disruption can damage a group of people trying to live and work together.

Every ship's crew is grouped together in teams of members who have been trained to do the same tasks. One group can skillfully navigate the ship. One group expertly handles the ropes. Another group takes charge of the technology and computers. And still another group masterfully maintains all the essential engines. It requires all members in each of those groups to do their job.

Inevitably, the youngest, most novice crew members on ships will not want to participate in the work. They tend to try to avoid it. And inevitably, someone finds out that those young, inexperienced crew members did not complete their work.

The older, crustier, saltier, more experienced crew members offer on-the-spot training. Sometimes that extra training makes life more difficult for the novices than if they had done their assigned work as contributing members of the crew in the first place.

Whatever extra training the older sailors can come up with could not be as severe as Paul's suggestion. He tells the congregation that any members of the community unwilling to work should not eat. Those are pretty harsh consequences. But they drive home a point: If we remain idle how can we obtain food?

But it feels as if Paul has more in mind. Is Paul asking the community to think about this truth in a spiritual context? If we remain unwilling to work in our faith, how can we keep it alive? Life as God intends must be connected to our faith. If we want to live a Christlike life, then we have to be intentional, active, and always in pursuit of the good. To live is to pursue Christ.

God, you have instructed us to do good; so help us do good always. Amen.

SATURDAY, NOVEMBER 16 ~ *Read Luke 21:5-8*

This is the beginning of the end for Jesus, and Jesus knows it. Jesus' contemporaries believe that those nearing death have an extra ability to see things more clearly. Nearing death, they think, is akin to being nearer to God. In such close proximity to the Divine, folks can make sense of what is going to happen to the people close to them.

It is imperative for the dying to relay important information regarding the future of their loved ones. Jesus loves his small community of disciples, so he tells them that the Temple will crumble and that other people will come around claiming to be him.

We have two points to consider today. First, simply by reading Jesus' warning, we are included among his close associates—ones whom Jesus loves. Jesus offers us this warning because he loves us and wants us to be informed of future events that might affect us. He sees that our faithfulness will be challenged and everything we have understood so far will turn into chaos. Deceivers will come and try to pull us away from what we as Christ-followers know to be true.

Second, even though many people are swayed by those who predict the end times, as members of Jesus' close associates we can rest knowing that they have no power over us or our hearts. When we hear deceivers talking about end times, it is easy to get tangled up emotionally and spiritually. But Jesus' instruction is simple: Do not follow them. Predictors of the future are nothing new, and they have often been wrong.

God, in you and you alone will we be free of the deceivers. Thank you for taking the fear out of our hearts. Amen.

SUNDAY, NOVEMBER 17 ~ *Read Luke 21:9-19*

Today's text predicts wars, uprisings, earthquakes, famines, and disease. Jesus says that we will be persecuted and imprisoned, but that we will have "opportunity to testify" to our faith in him.

The author of Luke says that we do not need to be concerned about what we will say, though, because Jesus will fill our hearts and minds and guide our tongues. What Jesus commands from our lips will be enough.

Often, shipmates who have managed to land themselves in trouble must stand before the Commanding Officer, who acts as the judge to determine the consequences for these errant sailors. Typically, the accused have a chance to offer words in defense of their actions. The sailors with a fair amount of courage always have something to say. They open their mouths and all kinds of words issue forth. Commanding Officers can determine easily when they are making up stories and when they are speaking the truth. Sailors' attempts to pull the wool over the eyes of their superiors are rarely well received.

When our time comes to stand in judgment, all we have to do is speak the truth that will be given to us. Jesus will usher forth truth from our mouths and spirits and not a hair on our heads will perish. If we stand firm, we will not need to offer up convincing stories. The testimony we will give of Jesus will be Jesus' words. When Jesus speaks, we can rest assured it will always be truth.

God, help us stand firm so that we may win the life you have waiting for us. Amen.

Longing for the Reign of Christ

NOVEMBER 18–24, 2019 • CANDACE M. LEWIS

SCRIPTURE OVERVIEW: Our readings for the week highlight the Reign of Christ. Jeremiah prophesies about a future King from the line of David who will bring justice, righteousness, and security for the people of God. Luke 1 records the song of Zechariah, the father of John the Baptist. Zechariah praises God for raising up salvation from the house of David as God had promised through the prophets. This child will bring mercy, forgiveness, and light. Luke 23 recounts part of the story of the death of Jesus. Here Jesus, the Light of the world, dies as an act of mercy for our forgiveness. In Colossians, Christ holds first place above everything else. Through his death we are forgiven and brought from the kingdom of darkness into the kingdom of light.

QUESTIONS AND SUGGESTIONS FOR REFLECTION

- Read Jeremiah 23:1-6. How do you trust in God's promises to bring safety and justice as you watch unjust rulers oppress and abandon their followers?
- Read Luke 1:68-79. What will you say when you break your silence?
- Read Colossians 1:11-20. Recall a time when you waited for something in great anticipation. How did your faith help you find patience?
- Read Luke 23:33-43. How do you recognize Christ as King when you experience or witness suffering?

District Superintendent, Florida Conference of the United Methodist Church; enjoys spending time with family and friends, exercising, traveling, and eating at great restaurants.

MONDAY, NOVEMBER 18 ~ *Read Jeremiah 23:1-6*

As we reflect on the reign of Christ through scripture this week, we are reassured that God continues to watch over this world and responds to our cries for leadership that honors God and the people of God. This prayer will be answered in the fullness of time when Christ returns as King. In the meantime, God continues to raise up prophetic voices and leaders who will speak truth and seek justice and righteousness for all God's people.

Longing for the reign of Christ and the return of Christ the King speaks to a desire to see more visible and tangible signs of the peace and power of God in our world today. News headlines bombard us with incidents of gun violence, racial discrimination, nuclear threats, sexual harassment, economic instability, and polarizing political perspectives. We want our current political and spiritual leaders to address these ills and to work toward peace and harmony. Instead we hear of leaders who misuse power and exploit people, which leads to corruption and moral failures.

In today's scripture the prophet Jeremiah speaks out against the kings who have failed to care for God's people as shepherds are to care for their sheep. Their lack of care for God's most vulnerable sheep causes them to scatter, which exposes them to even greater risks. The shepherd's failure to care does not go unnoticed. The prophet warns that God will address the evils of the shepherd and will gather the flocks and bring them back to their folds. God's plan includes raising up good shepherds to lead God's sheep in the way of harmony and peace, not fear and dismay. God's new shepherds will create a place for all to be known and belong.

God, we pray for the day when your scattered flocks are gathered together into one fold where our similarities outweigh our differences, where abundance replaces scarcity and love replaces fear. Amen.

TUESDAY, NOVEMBER 19 ~ *Read Jeremiah 23:1-6*

When ungodly leaders rule, the results can be devastating. We all suffer when our political and spiritual leaders fail to lead, support, strengthen, and govern in a way that protects all of us. In the midst of societal suffering we ask, *Does anyone care? What can we do? I am only one vote, only one voice. Who will hold our leaders, spiritual and political, accountable for the good of all?*

The people of Judah raise similar questions as they cry out to God about the mistreatment they receive from the ungodly kings ruling their nation. In response to their cries, God commissions the prophet Jeremiah to speak. "Woe," says Jeremiah, as he exclaims the pain of the people, the problem, and the pain to be inflicted upon the ungodly as God's response to the cries of God's people.

The prophet declares: God will deal with and visit those who have not cared for and visited God's people. God's message reassures us that God will raise up good shepherds and leaders to guide and care for God's people in response to their present pain. Those who have been scattered due to corruption will be gathered again and will be fruitful and multiply.

Enabled by God, the prophet speaks to the people's present and future suffering. Jeremiah declares that the days are coming when God will raise up a righteous one, who will be called "The LORD is our Righteousness." This coming King will deal wisely and execute justice and righteousness in the land.

The reign of Christ promises us a future filled with possibilities greater than any present paralyzing pain. During this reign, all God's people will live in safety.

Lord, enable us to serve, live, and love in ways that manifest your kingdom in our homes, churches, cities, and communities. We pray for godly leaders who follow and manifest your rule and reign each day. Amen.

WEDNESDAY, NOVEMBER 20 ~ *Read Luke 1:68-79*

It seems appropriate that we share part of the birth story of John the Baptist—Jesus' forerunner—on Christ the King Sunday, which ends the Christian year. Today we get a glimpse of Zechariah and Elizabeth, parents of John the Baptist.

In the lead-up to today's reading, we learn that Zechariah, a priest, has been met by the angel Gabriel, who announces that Elizabeth will bear a son named John. Zechariah does not believe the angel immediately, and so he cannot speak again until the child is born. For nine months, Zechariah has not been able to verbalize his thoughts and feelings.

Many of us can relate to Zechariah. Those of us who are leaders in the church might be mute and not even know it. We might have denied, not believed, or not proclaimed God's promises. There is so much happening in our world today wherein the church largely has remained silent. Have we been silenced for our unbelief or denial? Has the church lost its prophetic voice? Or is the church mute today on purpose?

Eight days after Elizabeth has given birth and the time to name her child has come, Zechariah still cannot speak. He writes that the child should be named John. Only then, after completing the angel's directive, can Zechariah speak. He immediately begins to praise God. After his time of silence, the Holy Spirit fills Zechariah and he speaks the prophecy in today's reading.

If we have been silent because of our unbelief or denial of God's promises, let us reflect on these divine promises with new intentionality. With God-given courage, let us discern a new focus on God and what God wants us to say when we finally break our silence.

God, when given the moment and pivotal opportunity to speak again, may we too be filled with praise and a prophetic message from you that will resonate with your people and proclaim your promises. Amen.

THURSDAY, NOVEMBER 21 ~ *Read Luke 1:68-79*

After nine months of silence, Zechariah has much to say. His prophetic song, known as the *Benedictus,* is a song of praise and thanksgiving. Zechariah proclaims that God has looked favorably upon God's people and has redeemed them by sending a savior. During Zechariah's time, the people are subject to the Romans. They long for a political savior who would deliver them from the Roman Empire's control.

Jesus' mission, heralded by Zechariah and later by his son John, offers us salvation, deliverance, and freedom from captivity to sin. It frees us to love and serve God and others wholeheartedly. This is a part of the good news Zechariah shares in his *Benedictus.*

Zechariah also speaks of the divine purpose of his own son in the fulfillment of God's plan. Imagine Zechariah holding baby John in his arms as a proud parent would at a special ceremonial occasion. He looks at his son and declares, "You, my child, will be called a prophet of the Most High; for you will go on before the Lord to prepare the way for him, to give his people the knowledge of salvation through the forgiveness of their sins" (NIV). John's ministry will usher in light to those who sit in darkness and guide their feet in the way of peace.

John the Baptist will fulfill the call upon his life prophetically spoken by his parent. John will cry out in the wilderness, preaching, proclaiming, and preparing the way for the coming of Christ the King. John will call people to repent of their sins and return to God.

O God, may we hear in John's prophecy a call on our lives to repent and to remember the true meaning of your salvation. Amen.

FRIDAY, NOVEMBER 22 ~ *Read Luke 23:33-43*

We enter the biblical text at the place they call the Skull, where Jesus is being crucified between two criminals. Onlookers sneer and sob. Mockers exclaim, "Save yourself as you saved others." Silent followers weep as they watch their hopes for a political messiah hang on a cross between two thieves. No media, no fanfare, no reporters, no live stream—just eyewitnesses watching the execution of two criminals and a King.

What crime warrants Jesus' crucifixion? In Roman culture, the authorities hang a sign dictating the nature of the crime above the head of the crucified to warn others of actions punishable by death. Jesus' crime, written in three languages, states, "This is the King of the Jews." No one imagines Jesus' crucifixion as the inauguration of the reign of Christ the King and the ushering in of the kingdom of God.

Jesus bears the weight of the world's guilt and shame on the cross. Jesus' death offers an atonement for sins—the innocent dies so the guilty can be set free. Now we can become one with God again. Jesus lives and dies initiating God's kingdom on earth as it is in heaven.

As these horrific experiences unfold, Jesus utters words of forgiveness to those who are crucifying him: "Father forgive them; for they do not know what they are doing" (NIV). Blinded by fear, greed, selfishness, corruption, and living apart from God's divine plan and purpose, they do not know what they are doing when they crucify Jesus. We too are guilty of living apart from God's divine purpose and plan. We too need God's forgiveness, love, mercy, and grace.

Hope is not destroyed at the place of the Skull. Hope and faith are now keys that give us access to a personal, life-changing relationship with God through Jesus Christ.

Thank you, Christ our King, for offering us forgiveness of our sins, peace with God, and access to the kingdom of God. Amen.

SATURDAY, NOVEMBER 23 ~ *Read Luke 23:39-43*

Luke records a conversation among two criminals and a King, who are all being executed by crucifixion. We do not know the lives of the two criminals preceding their being nailed to crosses. We know that Jesus is beaten, bruised, scoffed, and made to carry his cross almost the entire way to the place called the Skull. They are all experiencing excruciating pain as this conversation unfolds. One of the criminals rails, derides, and yells blasphemous accusations at Jesus. Jesus does not respond. In his humanity and human suffering, he cannot bear this man's lament. The other man rebukes the first and defends Jesus. He thinks they are getting what they deserve—they have earned painful death by their actions.

At times in our lives, we all hang on the criminals' crosses next to Jesus. Sometimes, like the first man, we lament and rail and blaspheme against a God we feel has abandoned us to suffering despite possessing the power to save us. Other times, like the second man, we feel sure we deserve our suffering for our sinful actions toward God and others.

As Christians who follow the man in the middle—the one who will be resurrected indeed as King—we recognize that Jesus dies for both men who hang with him. Because Jesus dies, we can rail at God and deserve our suffering. The difference between the two men is in their posture toward Jesus. The first man is excluded from Paradise not because he asks hard questions about human suffering but because he demands proof of Jesus as King in the way he desires it. The second man joins Jesus in Paradise not because he defends him but because he approaches Jesus in a posture of humility that allows him to recognize Jesus as King.

God, may we who are guilty demand nothing yet humbly pray to take part in Jesus' kingdom. May we not ignore our guilt, pain, and shame but ask Jesus to remember us. Amen.

SUNDAY, NOVEMBER 24 ~ *Read Colossians 1:11-20*

Reign of Christ Sunday

In today's text, Paul invites Christ's followers who seek to live faithfully while awaiting Christ's return to give thanks to God. Paul prays that we may be made strong with all the strength that comes from God's glorious power and be prepared to endure everything with patience. We need endurance to get through tough situations and circumstances, and we need patience to deal with challenging people who are part and parcel of these situations.

At times I avoid challenging circumstances and people out of fear that I lack the strength or energy to handle them. But God wants to strengthen me with wisdom and perseverance from God's glorious power bank. I simply need to plug in and stay connected.

Paul calls us to give thanks because Christ enables us to share in his inheritance of the saints in the light. Darkness no longer holds or controls us because of Christ the King. Let us continue to walk in the light as redeemed and forgiven children of God.

In her 1971 song "Anticipation," Carly Simon describes anticipation as that place in our minds that makes us "wait" eagerly as we look forward to a promised encounter. This week we acknowledged through our reading of Hebrew scriptures and New Testament texts our longing for and anticipation of the reign of Christ the King. We long for God's glorious power and strength. We long for light to overcome our darkness. We long for an inheritance that includes redemption and forgiveness.

May we continue to anticipate eagerly the coming of Christ and the fulfillment of God's kingdom. And as we wait, may we live in such a way that we help bring about God's vision for all.

The word of God, for the people of God, thanks be to God.

The Coming of the Kingdom

NOVEMBER 25—DECEMBER 1, 2019 • BRENDA VACA

SCRIPTURE OVERVIEW: Advent is a season for turning our minds to the coming arrival of the Christ child. Isaiah looks forward to a future day when peace will reign in Jerusalem. All nations will come to hear the wisdom of the Lord. The psalmist rejoices in going up to Jerusalem in his own day. Jerusalem is a center of peace and a place for righteous judgment among the nations. Both readings inform Jewish expectations of a bright future with the arrival of the Messiah. Paul tells the Romans that part of receiving the reality of the Messiah is self-preparation. We should put aside immoral living and put on the Lord Jesus Christ. Matthew looks forward to the future return of the Son of God, which will happen at an unexpected time.

QUESTIONS AND SUGGESTIONS FOR REFLECTION

- Read Isaiah 2:1-5. How do you look to the Bible's stories, prayer, and the Holy Spirit to help you work toward God's kingdom?
- Read Psalm 122. What does it mean for you to pray for peace?
- Read Romans 13:11-14. How do you stay awake to salvation's nearness?
- Read Matthew 24:36-44. Who in your life lives as though they expect the Son of Man? What does it look like to be ready to meet Christ?

Pastor of Nueva Vida Ministries in San Francisco, California.

MONDAY, NOVEMBER 25 ~ *Read Isaiah 2:1-5*

I remember my father pulling out the *Thomas Guide* whenever we were going on a trip. This dusty book seemed to be the key to many far-off places and, indeed, it was. But things change over time. I now have a GPS navigator on my cell phone. I even used it once when I was at a conference in Arizona with clergy friends to get us to the Grand Canyon. We did not have a map, but this GPS navigator somehow pinpointed our current location. I just had to type in "Grand Canyon," and *voila!* Instant directions to one of the Seven Wonders of the World!

I wish I could tell you that we have a fabulous device with GPS for the Christian path. No church or denomination has a GPS navigator for keying in your current location to get clear instructions on how to arrive safely at your desired location. Instead, we have a magnificent set of stories in our sacred scripture that point in the direction we need to be headed. And, thankfully, we have prayer and the Holy Spirit to help guide us on the journey. But there is no manual or *Thomas Guide* to give us the exact steps as we trudge along the road. Instead, God asks us to pay close attention to God's teachings so that we may follow in God's paths.

We will know that we have finally arrived at the mountain of the Lord when we see swords turned into plowshares and spears into pruning hooks! War no more! This is what it means to walk in the light. This is what it means to live in God's house.

Loving God, as I try to live and walk in this Christian journey, help me to follow in your paths so that I can know your ways all the days of my life. Amen.

TUESDAY, NOVEMBER 26 ~ *Read Romans 13:11-14*

My brother John is a heavy sleeper and always has been. We grew up in Los Angeles in a time when it seemed like there was a major earthquake twice a year. Inevitably earthquakes occur at ungodly hours, three or four in the morning. Each time, as our family scrambled to squeeze between thresholds or under tables, someone would ask, "Where's John?" Eventually my brother would emerge (usually after the quake had subsided), rubbing his eyes, asking, "What time is it?"

In his letter to the Romans, Paul is eager to remind his friends: "Salvation is nearer now than when we first believed" (NIV). Perhaps Paul writes of a chronological time that he believes will actually arrive at any moment. But let us consider our salvation as John Wesley did: as a journey.

There was a time in our faith journeys where we were not aware of the love of God. During this time, God watched over us with prevenient grace—the grace of God that arrives before we are even conscious of it. Then comes justifying grace—it comes when we realize we believe—the moment we first open our eyes to God's reality because of Jesus' teachings. The rest of the journey is sanctification—or as Paul would identify it, our salvation coming "nearer."

Once we are awake to God's loving grace, we cannot go back to sleep. We cannot pretend that it does not exist or push the pause button while we have our good time. We cannot afford to doze off in this grace because to do so would mean living in spiritual darkness. And if we are living in this spiritually dark place, how can we possibly recognize the light when it greets us in the morning?

God of life and light, help me to be like Jesus, who clothed himself in light and lived his life out loud in praise to your holy ways. Amen.

WEDNESDAY, NOVEMBER 27 ~ *Read Psalm 122:1*

In countless churches across the United States, and probably around the world, this verse greets churchgoers every Sunday as they enter the sanctuary, "I rejoiced with those who said to me, 'Let us go to the house of the LORD'" (NIV). Every time I visit a new church or attend a committee meeting, I stop at the entrance of the sanctuary to get a first impression and more often than not I find these words.

We have to admit that these words are powerful and joyful. They signify a group of people being glad to go to a familiar place, the house of the Lord. But what of those who feel they are not invited? What of those children of God who do not know where the house of the Lord is?

During this season of Advent—this season of eager anticipation and of radical hospitality—I have to stop and ask with whom are we to rejoice? Who is being left out? I know a day laborer in San Francisco who lives under the freeway near my home and church. I am constantly inviting him to church or social gatherings. Often he admits to me that he does not dare enter the church or the parsonage for fear of being judged—judged for what he is wearing or because he has not been able to take a shower for the week. Unfortunately this has been his experience of "church" many times over.

We must realize that we are living in a different time. Some people can no longer assume that church is a safe and welcoming place. We must be willing to be the ones who say, "Let's go," as Jesus so often said to friends and strangers. We must be willing, especially during this season, to be a loving people who go and seek those on the outside.

Gracious God, you welcome me and love me. Help me to be the arms and heart of Christ in my corner of the world. Amen.

THURSDAY, NOVEMBER 28 ~ *Read Romans 13:11*

Thanksgiving Day, USA

Today is Thanksgiving, a day when many gather around tables to celebrate family and to give thanks to God for the blessings of the past year. Yet it can be a difficult time for many, filled with unpleasant memories of past wrongs or painful reminders of isolation and loneliness. Holidays have a way of dredging up old feelings, no matter how much we anticipate the goodness of the day. Sometimes holidays are more than we can bear.

I know some people who ignore special occasions of all kinds—birthdays, weddings, Thanksgiving, Christmas, New Year's. Hurt at some time in the past, they have convinced themselves that they are better off without the big hoopla of celebrations. They are essentially asleep to the possibilities of positive experiences with loved ones or even strangers. But cutting ourselves off from experiences and relationships is no way to live our lives. After all, this is real life.

Paul urges his friends in Rome, "Wake up!" Wake up to what? And why wake up now? These words call us to live in the light of Jesus' teachings. And *now* is the time because we do not know exactly when salvation will come . . . because salvation is not something that we possess. Salvation is something that possesses us.

And, yes, being awake to this love and sharing this love with others means that we are putting our hearts on the line. Yet, there is salvation and power in this kind of vulnerability—the power of love to overcome all obstacles. It is the same power that quickens the coming of our Savior.

Jesus, as I break bread with loved ones or strangers today, awaken in me your divine love. Let me know that I am yours. Amen.

FRIDAY, NOVEMBER 29 ~ *Read Matthew 24:42*

When I ordered internet service at my new home, the sales person gave me a four-hour window of time during which the technician would come to install my cable service. I hated it. The same is true when you order other kinds of utility services or use UPS or FedEx. The dreaded four-hour window: 8:00 a.m. until noon, or 1:00 p.m. until 5:00 p.m. No matter how you slice it, it is a chunk of your day when you'd rather be doing something else.

As twenty-first century people, especially Americans, we want things fast and we want them to arrive precisely at the expected time. Christians are not exempt. We don't like surprises, and we definitely don't like being caught off guard. Even the four-hour window is better than no window at all. We at least can prepare ourselves emotionally to expect when something is about to arrive. That way the house can be clean, the dog can be on her best behavior, and we can look our most presentable as you open the door.

Yet our scripture today urges us to stay on guard. To keep watch. To be alert. Because we do not know the appointed time. We will not get a four-hour window that will let us know "the coming of the Son of Man." What does this mean? It means that we must be ever conscious of the coming kingdom. It means staying connected to God and trusting in God for all things at all times.

God of all time and place, may I live today ever conscious of your presence in my life and in the world. Amen.

SATURDAY, NOVEMBER 30 ~ *Read Psalm 122*

There is a woman named Betty who prays for peace every Sunday. She has been doing this for as long as I have known her, and certainly since the wars in Iraq and Afghanistan began. She stands up every Sunday and raises up her prayer concerns for the week. She adds without fail, "And, as always, for peace."

I do not know Betty's political persuasions. I do not know if she believes in just war or if she believes that no war is ever just. I do know that Betty is faithful and that she believes week after week that she is responsible for praying peace into the world. She is absolutely convinced that she is responsible for praying for the "peace of Jerusalem" and for all those she knows and loves.

Betty reminds me that I cannot be apathetic to the violence and hatred happening around me. I am responsible for it. You are responsible for it. We are accountable to pray peace into this world for the sake of God's coming kingdom. No matter our political persuasions, our nationalities, our theology, our call at all times is to pray for peace. Praying for peace will indeed signify that we are living in the spiritual Jerusalem. It will be a sign that we stand at the gates of God's holy city and that we seek God's kingdom first. When we claim peace in Jesus' name, it will come.

Prince of Peace, guide and guard my heart as I pray and work for your kingdom. Amen.

SUNDAY, DECEMBER 1 ~ *Read Matthew 24:36-44*

First Sunday of Advent

There is a popular bumper sticker I see often in the San Francisco Bay Area, "Jesus is coming. Look busy." I imagine many people put this sticker on their car to poke fun at the Christian concept of the "last days." The underlying message of this bumper sticker seems to be *I'll just take my chances that if God does come, I can always manage to look Christian at the last minute.*

Our scripture passage likens the coming of Jesus to the story of Noah. Noah is a man who certainly keeps busy while the rest of the world's inhabitants go along their merry way, "eating and drinking, marrying and giving in marriage." Now, none of us would profess that these things are evil or sinful. Quite the opposite! We love to do these things.

But what if our lives become completely focused on these things alone? What happens if my whole life's purpose is looking for something good to eat, looking for the best bar in town, or searching for Mr. Right? Sooner or later, I will wake up and realize that I have lived my life only for myself.

Noah is a great example of Advent living. He has the communication lines open with God. He focuses on godly things. And he lives for others. Remember, he doesn't build that ark for himself or even for him and his loved ones. He brings every kind of creation onto that boat with him. What a feat! To live a life that matters means focusing on the things beyond our own survival and desires.

God of our salvation, help us to focus our lives on you. Help us walk this day in the way of Advent. Amen.

The Peaceable Kingdom

DECEMBER 2–8, 2019 • NAOMI YODER

SCRIPTURE OVERVIEW: The readings from the Hebrew scriptures look forward to the coming of the Messiah. Isaiah describes a root from the family of Jesse, that is the family of David, that will rule fairly and usher in an age of peace. The psalmist extols the virtues of a royal son who defends the poor and the oppressed and causes righteousness and peace to abound. Christians traditionally read these psalms as prophecies about Jesus Christ. Paul in Romans quotes several prophetic passages from the Hebrew scriptures, but he begins by emphasizing that those writings were given for our instruction. Christianity without the Hebrew scriptures lacks its foundations. Just as we prepare our hearts during Advent for the arrival of the Christ child, John the Baptist prepares the way for Jesus in Matthew.

QUESTIONS AND SUGGESTIONS FOR REFLECTION

- Read Isaiah 11:1-10. What appeals to you in Isaiah's vision for The Peaceable Kingdom? What challenges you?
- Read Psalm 72:1-7, 18-19. Consider the ways you lead in your church, community, or work. How do you nurture the life God has created in these environments? How can you better lead toward God's righteousness, justice, and peace?
- Read Romans 15:4-13. How can you welcome others as Christ has welcomed you?
- Read Matthew 3:1-12. How can you prepare yourself to accept a wild or risky proclamation of God's kingdom?

Pastor, East Goshen Mennonite Church (Mennonite Church USA) in Goshen, Indiana; enjoys hearing people's stories, traveling to visit family and friends, and exploring Goshen's many greenways and baked goods.

MONDAY, DECEMBER 2 ~ *Read Isaiah 11:1-10*

Do not let babies play with venomous snakes. It does not take parenting books, care guidelines, or child protection policies to teach us that; the thought of a chubby infant arm reaching into the den of a coiled, poisonous serpent is enough to send a shudder up even the stiffest spine. Yet Isaiah gives us precisely this image of defenseless flesh meeting deadly power as an image of the fulfillment of God's promise, of the very kingdom of God.

Isaiah's prophetic vision announces an ideal leader and a kingdom in which all creatures live in harmony with one another, in which the calf and the lion and the lamb all lie down together. Christians know this image, sometimes called the Peaceable Kingdom, so well that it can start to seem sweet and simple. These are, however, pictures of tremendous risk; the defenseless and the deadly dwell together. All boundaries of "safety" and "threat" have been transformed. The Peaceable Kingdom offers possibilities for relationship where before there was only risk.

Until the Peaceable Kingdom comes in its fullness, it is probably wise not to let children play with vipers and cobras. In this season of Advent, however, we look toward the transformative power of an infant who reaches toward the dangerous, deadly, venomous violence of the world. As followers of Christ called to live into the kingdom of God, we too may have encounters with people, situations, and hard truths that send a shudder up our spine. We may feel that our vulnerable flesh, our weakness, is exposed to deadly powers. Where might our ideas of danger and defense need to be transformed? Where might risk give way to relationship in our lives?

God, set my imagination alight so that I may catch a vision of your prophetic promises. Help me not to cling to safety but to reach out in confidence toward a vision of your wild and risky kingdom. Amen.

TUESDAY, DECEMBER 3 ~ *Read Isaiah 11:1-5*

Imagine an ideal political leader or Supreme Court justice. What skills would he or she possess? What characteristics might be her trademarks? What might he wear? A belt of righteousness or of faithfulness might not be the first thing that comes to mind. Judges using neither their eyes nor ears seem odder still; keen observation and clear vision are highly prized in leaders and decision-makers. Isaiah's descriptions of the sal vific figure in our passage, however, remind us that the "shoot" or new life of the Messiah we have come to identify as Jesus does not conform to the usual image of things. Out of the good roots of the Hebrew heritage, Jesus brings fresh ways of being. Those new patterns are the surprising Peaceable Kingdom, or the kingdom of heaven, throughout our texts this week.

In our Advent preparations to welcome in this new king, perhaps we should ask ourselves whether we are ready for a leader who wears garments of righteousness and faithfulness rather than designer labels or trendy fair trade apparel. Are we ready for a judge not swayed by finely spoken words or proper appearances? We speak with joy about the promise of Christ's birth, but we get caught up in the very things—what we see and hear—by which our Lord "shall not judge." We let gossip in the church bias us against one another or allow social media posts to lead us into all sorts of assumptions. We judge whether people "fit" our congregation by how they dress or speak. In this time of Advent, the new life of our Messiah calls us to new forms of judgment based not in what we can see and hear but in wisdom, understanding, and the knowledge and fear of the Lord.

Lord of all, grow your new life into my life. Help me not to judge by hearsay or appearances but by what is faithful, just, and loving. Amen.

WEDNESDAY, DECEMBER 4 ~ *Read Psalm 72:1-7, 18-19*

Although summer may seem like a distant memory and spring like a far-off promise during these early days of December in the global North, few things draw the mind as quickly to warmer weather as the smells of freshly mown grass and rain on warm dry earth. This imagery from Psalm 72:6 powerfully captures the visceral sense of growth. It testifies to the vibrancy of life and all that sustains it.

As with the passage from Isaiah, today's reading presents us with a picture of ideal leadership. Praying that the king will seek justice, care for the poor, and deliver the needy, the psalmist asks for God to guide their leader toward the good of all the people. The rain analogy affirms that compassionate, loving, and just leadership can be life-giving; like rain falling on mown grass and watering the earth, good leadership can seep into the world around it and nourish growth.

We too are welcomed into the type of leadership that Psalm 72 describes. As citizens of the kingdom of heaven, we are called to work toward God's righteousness, justice, and peace. Each one of us can nurture the growth of the kingdom. We must remember, though, that we are not the ones who create life or growth. As the final verse of this passage reminds us, God alone does wondrous things. By God's welcome and God's mercy, we can offer support and sustenance to the vibrant life around us, but only God can begin and truly sustain that life. We can pray to fall like rain on the earth, but God alone is the creator of heaven and earth.

God of the mighty and the weak, give us your justice and your righteousness. Help us to nourish the growth of your kingdom as we remember that only you can create and sustain life. Amen.

THURSDAY, DECEMBER 5 ~ *Read Romans 15:4-13*

Do God's promises offer lessons, or limits? The audience for this Romans passage, the early Christian community in Rome, is caught up in questions of identity and belonging; those from the Jewish faith and those of Gentile background are working to figure out how they all fit into the scriptures and stories of God's people. In the midst of these tensions, Paul proclaims God's expansive welcome. He tells the young church community that all that was written before is intended to teach, to encourage, and to offer hope—not only for the Jews, but for the Gentiles as well. For Paul, the Hebrew scriptures and tradition are not an exclusive boundary of God's action but an expansive, welcoming example of God's glory. God's promises are not limits but rather lessons of God's faithful, steadfast love.

Questions of belonging and identity neither begin nor end with the early Roman Christians. Such questions are alive and active in our communities today too. Paul's words invite us to ask whether we treat God's steadfastness and encouragement as restrictive or instructive. It is tempting to let the ways that we have experienced God's promises and faithfulness become benchmarks for success or boundaries for exclusion. We can start to use the rich legacies of our denominations or congregations as signs that we have the corner on God's blessings. We can start to see our own testimonies of God's goodness as measuring sticks against which to hold up the worthiness of others. Paul's words to the Romans remind us that our experiences of God's love and faithfulness are not for us alone; God's promises are not limits but rather lessons that we can share for the hope and healing of all creation.

God of hope, I want to learn from the steadfastness and encouragement of your word. Help me not to limit your promises but to welcome all people to glorify you as together we live into your will. Amen.

FRIDAY, DECEMBER 6 ~ *Read Romans 15:4-13*

Welcome can feel like a familiar and comforting word. It appears on airport signs and doormats. We hang it on our walls and read it on websites. "Welcome home!" "We welcome your business!"

Paul's words in this passage, however, remind us that real welcome is not always so easy. Truly welcoming one another as Christ has welcomed the people of God is a rather frightening prospect. Jesus' welcome makes him the object of ridicule and derision; he gets the reputation of one who spends his time with sinners. Jesus welcomes the rich and powerful and those whom society has declared unclean. Ultimately, Jesus Christ welcomes humanity and all of creation so fully that he enters into the vulnerability and danger of our violent world. He welcomes us in spite of our sins, welcomes the world that rejects him, and finally welcomes death for our redemption and forgiveness. That is a radical and risky welcome. That is the welcome of Christ. Paul invites the Roman church, and all followers of Christ, into that welcome.

Welcoming one another as Christ has welcomed us requires more than hanging a sign or putting out a doormat. It requires opening ourselves to one another and seeking one another's wholeness. Such a welcome involves risky vulnerability; we might get a reputation for welcoming the wrong sort of people. We might face rejection. We might even end up in danger. In all of those risks, though, we are offered a sense of certainty and hope; Christ has welcomed us. Our Savior has opened his arms wide in welcome, even unto death. As we seek to live in harmony with one another and welcome one another, we can find sustenance in Christ's sacrificial and eternal welcome.

Glorious God, grant me the courage to welcome others as Christ has welcomed me. Amen.

SATURDAY, DECEMBER 7 ~ *Read Matthew 3:7-12*

John the Baptist's words in verse 7 strike out at the Pharisees and Sadducees of Matthew's story with a quickness and venom fitting the snake imagery. Given only the scant background information that these religious elites are joining many going out to John to be baptized, John's rebuke may seem strong to us. "You brood of vipers!" he lashes out. "You descendants of snakes!" John's words become clearer and sharper as he continues, "Do not presume to say to yourselves, 'We have Abraham as our ancestor.'" In place of the honor and strength of calling themselves children of Abraham, John casts these Jewish religious leaders as children of snakes.

The painful sting of John's words can strike us too. Like the Sadducees and Pharisees, we might come to signs of confession and restoration with unspoken confidence that our backgrounds—our religious pedigrees—save us or make us superior. While our words might not be "We have Abraham as our ancestor," perhaps we too may feel our religious affiliation or family background, our education or church involvements give us the freedom to go through the motions of repentance without making real change. John's words can strike us painfully; all our perceived privilege is worthless. We might as well be children of snakes.

The beauty of this sharp critique, though, is that it still allows for transformation. God does not abandon the Pharisees and Sadducees to their arrogance. John offers them, and us, the chance to "bear fruit worthy of repentance." No one is outside God's possibilities of repentance and promises of redemption. We are all welcome to transform our lives. While we might sometimes be more akin to children of snakes than children of Abraham, our Advent passages remind us that even vipers and their offspring have a place in God's promised future.

God of Abraham and vipers, humble me. Help me to give up my false assurances and to bear fruit worthy of repentance. Amen.

SUNDAY, DECEMBER 8 ~ *Read Matthew 3:1-6*

SECOND SUNDAY OF ADVENT

A wild man in the wilderness probably does not come to mind for most of us when we think of preparing for Christmas. In the midst of hanging twinkling lights and carefully wrapping gifts, a camel-hair-clad impassioned prophetic preacher eating locusts and honey in the desert does not quite fit. Yet this Advent story offers us John the Baptist, whom our scriptures label as one who is "prepar[ing] the way of the Lord." This strange figure turns hearts and minds toward the coming of the kingdom of heaven we celebrate in the incarnational miracle of Jesus' birth.

This Advent time of reflection and anticipation is a chance to ask ourselves, *Are we ready to hear the voices proclaiming the reign of God, even when those voices might feel strange, shocking, or wild? Are we open to hearing from those outside our boundaries of what is comfortable? Can we hear the voices crying out in the religious or social wildernesses of our world?* God's kingdom brings peace, but it also brings disruption. It requires repentance, reorientation, and transformation. Preparing for the coming kingdom of God might mean getting outside ordinary patterns. Like camel hair on skin, the roughness of the kingdom can chafe against the soft and easy comfort of our lives. The strangeness of Christ's commandments can be hard to swallow. We can feel as though we are leaving the bustling patterns of what we know for the stark emptiness of the wilderness. If we are not willing to reach toward something new, though, how can we receive the new life of the kingdom of God? If we are not willing to turn toward something risky, how will we hear God's wide and wild welcome?

Ruler of Heaven, help me to hear the voices that proclaim your kingdom even when they come in ways that are unusual, uncomfortable, or untamed. Amen.

God's Coming Kingdom

DECEMBER 9–15, 2019 • TONY CAMPOLO

SCRIPTURE OVERVIEW: Isaiah anticipates a future time of total restoration. The desert will bloom, the blind will see, the lame will walk, and the people will return to Jerusalem with joy. Since ancient times, some have understood this as a description of the age of the Messiah. Luke records the song of Mary. After Elizabeth blesses her and her unborn child, Mary praises God for God's strength, mercy, and generosity. In the epistle, James encourages his audience to be patient as they await the second coming of the Lord. In the same way, we wait for the birth of the Messiah during Advent. An uncertain John the Baptist sends a message to Jesus to ask if he is the promised Messiah. Jesus responds by affirming that he fulfills the messianic expectations in the prophets.

QUESTIONS AND SUGGESTIONS FOR REFLECTION

- Read Isaiah 35:1-10. When has scripture strengthened you through personal or societal crises?
- Read Luke 1:47-55. Those with power interpret scripture differently than those who are oppressed. How can you make room for perspectives other than your own as you interpret scripture?
- Read James 5:7-10. When have you had to endure frustration with patience? How have you been strengthened by these experiences?
- Read Matthew 11:2-11. What does it mean to you to be greater than John the Baptist?

Professor Emeritus, Eastern University; Associate Pastor, Mt. Carmel Baptist Church, Philadelphia, Pennsylvania, American Baptist Churches, USA.

MONDAY, DECEMBER 9 ~ *Read Isaiah 35:1-10*

Jews and Christians have this in common: Both await a glorious future with the coming of God's Messiah. In Psalm 35 we get the good news that when that Messiah comes and establishes God's kingdom here on earth, it will be a time of celebration with songs of joy and gladness. Jesus likens his coming kingdom to a wedding celebration. (See Matthew 22:2-13.) When someone asks us what time it will be in this glorious future we'll shout back, "It's Party Time!"

Then all things will be as they should be. Environmentalists will be thrilled because the earth will be restored to what God willed for it to be when God created it. The desert will be watered and grass and flowers will blossom where once only desolation pervaded the land. The blind will gain sight. The deaf will hear. Persons once deemed unfit for Temple worship will be welcomed into the house of the Lord. The highway going to the Holy City will be safe, and we won't have to worry about foolish people who aren't always cautious of dangers when traveling.

We are not to be passive while waiting for this glorious future. God calls us to participate in making all things as they should be. All of creation waits for us to become co-laborers together with God as ecological activists and as God's agents to eliminate poverty, racism, sexism, and Islamophobia in making the highway to the new Jerusalem safe. Evangelism will not be confined to getting people ready for the next world but will emphasize recruiting people to join God's revolution in the here and now.

Lord, make us into joyous heralds and participants of the glorious future that you are creating. Amen.

If I believed, as some social scientists do, that people are nothing more than what their past experiences have conditioned them to be, I would have to give up on efforts to get my social work students at Eastern University to commit to trying to change people. If societal influences and the psychological experiences of persons' yesterdays predetermine who they will become, then hopes to redirect their lives into what God calls them to be are minimized. Instead, I tell my students that persons determine their lives more by the future they choose than by their past experiences.

The young woman hurt by molestation at the hands of adults she trusted is not necessarily doomed to a life of anger and hurt. The teenage boy whose father abandoned him is not predestined to being resentful forever. Everyone can be free because the future is open. We can become what we will to be, and God wants to participate in that decision.

Despite their many hardships, the ancient Jews maintain a sense of joy because they have a vision from their prophets of a bright and wonderful future. The words of today's scripture from Isaiah 35 keep them going even when they have reason to despair. In their dark times in Babylon, the people of Israel are assured by prophets that a glorious future is coming. We too can be future oriented.

In the midst of personal tragedy and injustice, we can still hope. When life is hard, we believe that someday and somehow all will be good.

From a societal standpoint, Isaiah 35 offers joyful assurance that a glorious future lies ahead for the whole world.

God, make us hopefully aware that whatever pain and troubles mark the present, you will lead us into a glorious future that we work together to create. Amen.

WEDNESDAY, DECEMBER 11 ~ *Read James 5:7-10*

A friend of mine told me how he almost quit his first pastorate. He found it hard to endure the seemingly petty complaints from his congregants. Members in the congregation threatened to leave if they didn't get their way. Some were overtly racist; others were opposed to women holding any roles of leadership in the church. He found it difficult to be patient, especially when people had their feelings hurt.

One evening, after a particularly contentious congregational business meeting, he felt he had reached the end of his rope and was seriously considering resigning as pastor. Discouraged and alone, he stood changing the lettering on the church bulletin board that announced the next Sunday's sermon title when a strange, disheveled, bearded, old man wearing a worn-out overcoat walked up to him and said, "You're the pastor here, aren't you?" "Yes, I am," my friend answered. "Well," the man said, "I stopped by to tell you not to be discouraged and to be patient. You're doing a good job! Things will get better. Just wait and see."

When my friend asked this stranger who he was, the man answered, "I'm Jesus."

My friend went home amazed by this surreal encounter. He told his wife about the weird man who had claimed to be Jesus and who had told him that he was doing a good job and to be patient.

His wife responded carefully, "Well? How do you know that he wasn't Jesus?"

In Galatians 6:9, Paul writes, "Let us not be weary in well doing: for in due season we shall reap, if we faint not" (KJV). In other words, "Hang in there!"

Jesus, thank you for being patient with us, and by your grace make us patient with others. Teach each of us to be more understanding of those who seem to establish barriers to our best laid plans and to treat them as you would. Amen.

THURSDAY, DECEMBER 12 ~ *Read James 5:7-10*

There's a story about a young minister who was not long into his first pastorate when he was visited by his bishop. The two of them talked over the affairs of the church. Then, the bishop asked the novice pastor if there was anything that he, the bishop, should pray about for this frustrated pastor and his church. The young preacher answered, "Pray that God would give me patience." He explained that as he began this position just out of seminary, he had been anxious to implement a host of new programs that seminary professors had inspired him to start. "I have plans and ideas," this young clergyman continued, "but the people in this church seem to want to hold me back. No matter what I suggest, I can expect someone to say, 'I'm not sure our people are ready for what you are suggesting,' or 'Give us some time to think over your suggestion, and we'll talk about it at the next church business meeting.'"

The two of them went up to the altar and knelt down. Then the bishop prayed, "Lord, bring troubles into this preacher's life. May his tribulations increase."

"Wait!" the young minister shouted. "Why would you pray for me to have troubles and difficulties? I asked you to pray for me to have patience!"

The bishop reminded the young minister of what Paul writes in Romans 5:3-4: "We glory in tribulations also: knowing that tribulation worketh patience; and patience, experience; and experience, hope" (KJV). There is more to patience than what we usually mean by that word. More recent translations of the passage the bishop quoted reveal the depth of what Paul means: endurance. When frustrations immobilize us, we can ask what we might gain by enduring them. God may be trying to slow us down, and God has given us the prophets as our example.

God, help us to learn to endure frustrations with patience as we wait for the coming of the Lord. Amen.

FRIDAY, DECEMBER 13 ~ *Read Luke 1:47-55*

Many years ago, I heard this passage from Luke's Gospel read from the pulpit of the African-American church where I have been a member for more than sixty years. It was the Sunday before Christmas, and our pastor chose to preach his sermon on these verses, which are commonly referred to as the "magnificat." They record Mary's response to the announcement that she will soon give birth to the long-awaited Messiah of Israel. She is stunned with this incredible news.

As the preacher read these verses in his loud and dignified manner and declared with authority that this coming Messiah would "bring down the mighty and exalt those of low degree," and that "the rich would be sent away empty," there were cries of affirmation from congregants across the sanctuary. Elderly African-American Christians who had been put down and humiliated and economically exploited by many of us in the white establishment seemed unable to contain themselves as they cried out, "Yes," and "Thank you, Jesus."

As a member of the mighty and the rich cohort called white middle-class America, I felt threatened by all of this. I always knew the scriptures needed to be interpreted through various contexts. But until that Sunday, I hadn't realized that powerful people interpret scriptures one way and that disenfranchised people interpret them another way.

Over the years, through education and hard work, our church people have gradually become middle class. But I wonder if they still get out of the reading of scripture the truths grasped sixty years ago.

God, sanctify our imaginations so that we might be able to read the scriptures through the eyes of the poor and oppressed, because it was for them that you brought good news. Amen.

SATURDAY, DECEMBER 14 ~ *Read Matthew 11:2-11*

According to Jesus, John the Baptist has a lot going for him. Jesus labels John the greatest of the prophets.

Crowds of people hikes out into the desert near the Dead Sea to hear John's message. John offers not sugar-coated platitudes but harsh words pointing out people's sins and calling them to repentance. His message clearly comes from God. His clothing of animal skins and diet of grasshoppers and honey make him strange. Nevertheless, people listen to what John has to say because he speaks with godly authority.

Despite John's credentials, Jesus tells his disciples that even "the least in the kingdom of heaven is greater" than John. That's because those of us who are heirs to the grace of God through Christ's sacrificial death have a direct relationship with God through the resurrected Christ. Living before the blessings that come from God following Pentecost, John knows only of the "works salvation" of the Hebrew scriptures. As post-Pentecost Christians, we are able to have a direct relationship with God that transcends what John preached.

John knew the God who could be encountered person to person only in the inner throne room of Jerusalem's Temple once a year on what the Bible calls "the Day of Atonement." Now, because of Christ, we all can have direct access to God through prayer without an earthly priest. Our intimacy is such that we can call God *Abba,* an intimate word for father. Not even John's status back then could top the relationship we now can have because of what Jesus has made available for us.

Jesus, thank you for the incredible and direct relationship we can have with God that you have made possible. Help us not to neglect this precious gift but to practice living in your presence daily. Amen.

Third Sunday of Advent

Mary seems thrilled with the announcement that she will give birth to Israel's long-awaited messiah. Listening to her, you would have to conclude that she couldn't be happier. I can't help but wonder, however, whether she would have felt so blessed if she knew what lay ahead for her baby Jesus.

Saint Ignatius, as one of his prescribed spiritual exercises for daily devotions, asked us when reading about one of the biblical personalities to imagine experiencing life from his or her point of view. Imagine being Mary.

Can she envision the incredible upset twelve-year-old Jesus will cause when she and Joseph cannot find him after traveling three days on their way home from Jerusalem? Can she imagine her frustration and confusion when, instead of apologizing, he tells her that he had to talk with the Temple rabbis in order to be about his Father's business?

Would Mary be joyous if she knew there would be further confusion when Jesus seemingly brushes aside her and his brothers to announce as he does in Matthew 2:50 that "whosoever shall do the will of my Father which is in heaven, the same is my brother, and sister and mother" (KJV)? I imagine it would prove most difficult for Mary to feel blessed if she could picture herself at the foot of her son's cross while Roman soldiers press down a crown of thorns on his head, drill nails into his hands and feet, and pierce his side with a spear. Might she then regret the joy she feels when an angel announces she will be the mother of the Son of God?

Christ, anoint our imaginations so that we feel what Mary and the disciples feel as they watch your passion on Calvary. Help us to feel their feelings; but most of all, help us to experience the fellowship of your suffering in both your life and death. Amen.

Covenant Keeping

DECEMBER 16–22, 2019 • LIB CAMPBELL

SCRIPTURE OVERVIEW: Isaiah is sent to the king of Judah to declare a prophecy of a future birth through a virgin. The boy will be called Immanuel, "God is with us." The psalmist cries out to God asking for an end to the suffering of the people. He believes that this will occur through a "son of man," an expression that Jesus later uses to describe himself. Paul's opening to Romans roots the gospel in the Hebrew scriptures. Jesus comes from the line of David and fulfills the things foretold. To understand Jesus, we must understand the Hebrew scriptures. Matthew recounts the visitation of an angel to Joseph to tell him of the coming birth of a son. Matthew interprets this birth as a fulfillment of this week's reading from Isaiah 7.

QUESTIONS AND SUGGESTIONS FOR REFLECTION

- Read Isaiah 7:10-16. How does Isaiah's prophecy continue to speak to you today? How do you hope for Christ's coming?
- Read Psalm 80:1-7, 17-19. Recall a time when you have relied on hope for God's restoration.
- Read Romans 1:1-7. What would it mean to add "servanthood" to your list of life goals?
- Read Matthew 1:18-25. How is your life different for having listened to God's call?

Retired elder, North Carolina Conference of the United Methodist Church; Pastor Emeritus of Spiritual Formation, Saint Mark's UMC, Raleigh, NC.

MONDAY, DECEMBER 16 ~ *Read Psalm 80:1-7, 17-19*

The psalmist knows the goodness of God in the world. God has led the people and cared for them as a shepherd cares for the sheep. But the people have fallen on hard times. Struggles mounting in the Northern Kingdom bring tears and sorrow. The community prays, laments loss, and offers petition. The light has gone out of their world. God, are you listening? A worshipful community prays and hopes the radiance of God will light the way. They speak a liturgical prayer: "Let your face shine, that we may be saved."

When life turns on us, when losses mount up and tears fall down, we may struggle to find hope, to know God with us. Consolation is illusive. Lament consumes us. Today we see people, whole communities, whose hope is tested. On every continent, in every country, on every street, hearts break and tears flow down with blood. Darkness permeates our world. Yet in this holy season, the psalmist leads us: "Restore us, O God of hosts; let your face shine, that we may be saved."

Give ear to your people, O God. Come close. Come in person if you can. Come to Bethlehem, to Jerusalem, London, Moscow and Mosul, to Raleigh and to everywhere in between. In ancient words and prayers of the faithful, restore your people. Let your light shine, that we may be saved.

God, are you listening? If that is the question, God's answer is on the horizon in the birth of a child, one who will fulfill a promise that justice will reign and a people will be restored. Lament and hope travel together in this psalm. Hurt and hope journey together in the world. However bad our circumstances, dawn will rise. Light will shine forth and God will be with us. Come, O come, Emmanuel.

Shine forth, O God, that we may see the light of your presence and know your salvation. Amen.

TUESDAY, DECEMBER 17 ~ *Read Isaiah 7:10-16*

The prophet Isaiah speaks to a situation of impending destruction of Judah in a time when the Northern Kingdom has been annexed by Assyria. King Ahaz of Judah struggles with alliances and apostasy, forgetting God's covenant with David. Judah is much beloved, and God keeps God's covenants.

The Gospel writers and Christians today confuse Isaiah's prophetic words to Ahaz with prediction. Isaiah's words are not a prediction about Jesus. Isaiah offers a vision of God's steadfast love and redeeming work that will soon be born as a child among them, a child already in the womb.

Isaiah knows well the messianic hope that a king from the house and lineage of David will sit upon the throne of Judah and bring peace and justice to the people. Isaiah shares that hope for a righteous king who will soon be born.

Prediction has an either/or outcome. When clouds gather, either it will rain or it won't. Isaiah does not look into a glass ball six centuries into the future to predict the birth of Christ. Isaiah offers a vision of the world where the potential for righteousness, justice, and peace will be born to set the world right for God.

Yet prophecy, unlike simple prediction, is more than either/or. Prophecy is the both/and of God's covenant love for all time: for Judah and for all people. The voice of the prophet continues to speak: A child will be born, one who will restore a broken kingdom. That voice speaks to us today as we await the birth of Christ into our own lives. As Christ is born, righteousness, justice, mercy, love, forgiveness, and grace bring hope that a weary world may once again be restored. We wait. We listen. We hope. Come, Lord Jesus!

O God, we hear the prophet's word. Fulfill your promise in our time. Amen.

WEDNESDAY, DECEMBER 18 ~ *Read Romans 1:1-7*

In my church's Sunday worship, following the Confession of Sin and the Assurance of Pardon, a leader invites the congregation to share signs of grace and peace: "As forgiven and reconciled people, let us offer signs of grace and peace to one another." What ensues is nothing short of an explosion of goodwill, grace, and peace. The rest of the service is put on hold as love breaks out among us.

Paul finishes his words of greeting to the Romans with the offer of grace and peace. The churches in Rome sit in the midst of a great pagan culture. Little gods (family gods, local gods, gods of the empire) permeate the hearts and homes of many. Grace and peace are not given or even asked for in the worship of little gods. Only Jesus the Christ brings the grace and peace of God. Paul offers grace and peace to the Romans through Christ.

Often, as I stand and watch the people of my congregation greet each other warmly and kindly with words of grace and peace, I wonder why we do not replicate this act outside the walls, down the street, into the marketplace, and around the world. What do we get so caught up in that we forget the grace and peace that breaks into the world in the birth and life of Jesus the Christ?

Soon we will gather in celebration of Jesus' birth. We will light candles and sing glory to God, raise alleluias to the highest heavens. Then we will go out into the dark, cold night. Exposure to grace and peace can change the way we greet the darkness of the world. Words of reconciliation, grace, and peace bear hope and open doors of possibility that through us the world will be healed.

May the grace and peace of Christ be offered to the world through me today and every day. Amen.

The Lord has a lot to say. God first speaks to Isaiah, and now God speaks to Ahaz, an ungodly king of Judah who seems bent on forming alliances that undermine Judah. But it seems that with Ahaz, God has talked enough; now God acts. God will send the world a child, who is God with us, a word that is heard from Sheol to the highest heavens: a baby who will be born as a sign of hope to a king in military crisis.

Isaiah's prophecy of a child is a prophecy of hope. Children by their very nature are a sign of hope, full of wonder and delight. In my congregation, the children leave the sanctuary after the reading of scripture to go to Children's Church. They come back into the sanctuary in time for Communion. The doors open and they skip in like a thundering herd of hope among us, eager to come forward with their little hands wide open to receive the Body of Christ.

Ahaz and all of us tremble in the threats that gather around us. Yet the Lord, even beyond Ahaz's reluctance to request a sign, sends one that fear has no place in God's world. Beyond fear, beyond hurt, beyond evil, there is goodness that is God with us.

In a world that is increasingly under siege, little children speak hope in the words of ancient liturgy: "The Lord be with you. And also with you. Lift up your hearts. We lift them up to the Lord." They know in these simple words that a little bit of Jesus will be given to them soon. As we await the birth of the child who is God with us, let us lift up our hearts and give our thanks and praise.

Lord, help me hope with the hope of a child. Help me learn to wait patiently. Amen.

FRIDAY, DECEMBER 20 ~ *Read Psalm 80:1-7, 17-19*

The community of Psalm 80 laments its losses while expressing its hope in the restorative power of God. This Advent, a small *lectio divina* community here in Raleigh, North Carolina, has that same hope.

Madeleine has been part of our *lectio divina* group since it began over ten years ago. For the past several years she has been slipping ever deeper into Alzheimer's. When Madeleine was diagnosed, we covenanted to journey with her through this illness. Although her capacities continually diminish, her faith does not. In fact, for the past few months, whenever she has spoken, she has said, "I am from Switzerland. I love the Lord. That's it."

For those two facts to be what remains is remarkable. She remembers an identity, and she remembers that she loves God. Psalm 80 preserves the same memories: identity and steadfast love of God.

A vine remains—a remnant people—broken, bruised, and fed with the bread of tears. They call on the Lord of Jacob for restoration. Alongside their lament comes a deep, unforgotten trust that is woven into their being. Even in their suffering, they remember. The One who sits at the right hand of God is strong and will save them. The people will never turn away; they will always turn to God.

God's steadfast love, which we know through Jesus the Christ, is imprinted on Madeleine. This memory is almost all that remains. Her face reflects the shining face of glory revealed in the Christ child, which remains bright even as all else is forgotten. Even as life fades, even as the vine withers, we will never turn back from you, O God. Give us life as we call on your name.

O Christ child, be born again in all of us. Whisper to us a love that restores and heals. Amen.

SATURDAY, DECEMBER 21 ~ *Read Romans 1:1-7*

In the opening sentence of Paul's greeting, he identifies himself as a servant of Christ. Few of us would likely identify ourselves as servants, given any other options. A disciple? Yes. A prophet? Maybe. But a servant? Really?

Reading the Romans text with twenty-first-century eyes, we may find that the idea of being a servant of Christ runs against the grain of our culture. "Servanthood" does not make it onto very many lists of life goals! Yet Paul employs it as his first self-reference. His identification with the lowliness of a servant speaks to his yielding himself in service to another, One greater than himself.

There is a show on television called *Undercover Boss*. Presidents or CEOs of large companies work among the least of the workforce: lower level managers, line workers, minimum wage people. The bosses hear all the complaints, struggles, and hopes of the staff as they work alongside their employees. They learn the effort, care, repetition, and tedium of the work many on the margins do. But few of us are interested in learning through such acts of lowliness.

The birth of Jesus represents a great reversal in the universe. In such reversal, the master becomes the servant and the servant becomes the teacher—and the last is first. In Christ, holiness, divinity, and glory hide under the cover of human flesh as Jesus comes with power from on high in the life of a little baby swaddled and held. Serving Christ and serving alongside Christ in the bearing of good news by offering grace and peace to the world is Paul's hope for the Romans.

In this Advent season often tainted in consumerism and greed, ask yourself, "Am I ready to be part of the great reversal the world is hoping for?"

Lord, make me a servant. Help me to be like you. Amen.

FOURTH SUNDAY OF ADVENT

Joseph must have gone to bed that night with a lot on his mind. His betrothed, Mary, is pregnant. He knows he has not contributed to this pregnancy. Out of goodness, he is concerned that Mary not be humiliated. He will "put her away quietly," so the scripture says. But this is not the end of the story.

Joseph dreams. In his dream an angel comes with news for this good man. Joseph's angel tells him not to be afraid. Joseph learns that he will be father to the One who is the fulfillment of the Davidic promise of his lineage.

Angels are extraordinary messengers, and dreams are amazing means of communication. Joseph is receptive to the message and the means of God's communication to him. He trusts what God asks him to do. He awakens to his call and his destiny as Mary's husband and designated parent of Jesus. He immediately becomes part of God's salvation story, that a child will be born who will be light and life, savior of the world.

What if Joseph had just rolled over, pulled the covers over his head, and slept away his calling? How different would the story of Jesus be? Is our sleep so deep, our awareness so dull, our listening so dim that we do not hear the messengers of God who come to us from all directions? Could our attention, our careful listening, and our trusting obedience change the story of God in our own time? Soon angels singing glory will fill the heavens. We will be called to come and see. Pay attention, you who sleep; do not discount the dream.

Holy God, open my ears to hear your call and awaken my listening. Help me to see, know, and trust enough to follow. Amen.

The Humility of God

DECEMBER 23–29, 2019 • RAY BUCKLEY

SCRIPTURE OVERVIEW: This week we celebrate the birth of Jesus! Isaiah reminds us that all that God does, including the sending of a Savior, flows from God's compassion and steadfast love. The psalmist declares that from the angels in heaven to the works of creation to all the kings and peoples of the earth, all should praise the exalted name of God. The "horn" is a metaphor used elsewhere in the Hebrew scriptures that is traditionally interpreted by Christians as a prophecy of the Messiah. The author of Hebrews emphasizes the humanity of Christ. Christ fully partakes of our human nature so that he would understand our weakness and fully execute his role as our high priest. Matthew interprets through prophecy the perilous early travels of the young Jesus.

QUESTIONS AND SUGGESTIONS FOR REFLECTION

- Read Isaiah 63:7-9. How has God's presence saved you?
- Read Psalm 148. How can you praise God for the glory of creation around you in your daily life?
- Read Hebrews 2:10-18. How does your relationship with the Child-of-God-Who-Is-Humble help you understand yourself as related to all other human beings?
- Read Matthew 2:13-23. How has your church or faith community made the choice to act in the best interest of the institution rather than to follow God's way of humility?

Lives in the Matanuska-Susitna Valley of Alaska.

MONDAY, DECEMBER 23 ~ *Read Psalm 148:1-6*

God is humble. A listening ear may find music in random sounds. All around us are the songs of animal composers, whale and bird, frog and cricket. Human composers gather and assemble sounds into a collective to invoke emotive response. Composing human music is mathematical, and there is music to mathematics. There is a rhythm to our hearts and the motion of the universe. The water in our soil, the roll of the tides, and the emotions of sentient beings are linked to the phases of the moon.

God is humble.

Spiritual grace surrounds those who examine the smallest facets of the universe and ask the hard question of traditions; spiritual grace surrounds those who work to interpret sacred texts. The faithfulness of God is in the asking and in the response to questions about God.

God is humble.

It is a remarkable gift to feel small within the universe. As we stand on snowy tundra beneath bright, undulating, curtain patterns of aurora borealis, the significance of our individual concerns falls into new perspective. In greens, reds, and purples, the aerial movement leaves us hushed as a quiescent participant in something larger than ourselves. The great bowl of bright stars seen from a Kenyan plain, fireflies in a July cornfield, and ravens surfing the snowy wind call us to see ourselves beyond our own conditions and imagined self-importance.

Perhaps God is not a seeker of praise, but a delighted-in-our-delight God—the Giver of good gifts, sometimes standing just out of reach, waiting for us to recognize glory and say, "Ah!"

God is humble, but humility is not quiescent.

O God-Who-Is-Humble, is it words of adoration you seek?
I cannot speak as eloquently as a leaf or sing like water.
While I search for words or ritual, you are already beside me,
Lover-of-My-Soul.

TUESDAY, DECEMBER 24 ~ *Read Luke 2:1-20*

CHRISTMAS EVE

Nothing that emanates from the character of God is static. Creativity that emanates from the person and presence of God still continues, changes, and grows. That spiritual process is renewed every moment of every day. All things do not shout of God, but all things speak of the character of God.

We are not always spiritually conscious of God's movement. We wonder why others seem to experience the movement of God in truly miraculous ways, while we, having done what is asked of us, wait for any sign. Where is I AM in my stable?

It is a night of miracles. The only word that the human experience knows to use is *glory*. God's glory, an awareness of the character of God, meant for the purpose of that moment. Glory is the light and the sacredness and the realization that all of a sudden you are in the middle of something foreign yet familiar. To the sheepherders gathered in the hills, the angel of the Lord appears, and they see a glimpse of the active, moving, creative character of God. It's done! It is for you! Here is a sign! And the sheepherders, who don't know they will be included in this night, become participants. And the sky fills with angels.

In Bethlehem, tending to her child, is the one person who has borne the greatest risk of all of humanity. She has not been with the sheepherders in the hills surrounded by the glory of God and the angels of heaven. The sheepherders will tell her.

The humbleness of a young girl meets the humility of the character of God in a stable in Bethlehem, and she keeps all of it in quiet, sacred space.

The stable,
Is not the beginning.
It is part of the movement
Of God.
Come to my stable, Lord.

WEDNESDAY, DECEMBER 25 ~ *Read Matthew 2:1-12*

CHRISTMAS DAY

There is no such thing in the universe as a one-person event. The story isn't about us alone. Even with our narrow focus, the narrative begins with me and the God-Who-Is-Humble.

My grandfather would remind us that the story of Jonah not only includes the sailors who rid themselves of Jonah, but the Great Fish, who, besides acting on behalf of God's plan, learns that the biggest things one swallows can also be spit out.

While we seek God, God is involved in the lives of all those around us, even those we perceive as hostile. Jesus teaches us that we are to love our enemies and pray for those who persecute us—not in a feigned act of holiness, but in humility. When the work of God is not about us alone, we can relinquish the ultimate outcome to the person of God.

In another part of the world from Bethlehem, scholars have been watching the sky. We do not know their tradition or when they first see the star. We do not know if they know one another or if seeing the star brings them together. We do not know when they leave or arrive, or how long their journey will be. We do know that the star is a sign to them and they believe. We know that their belief brings them toward Bethlehem. And they come to worship.

Not what they know, but what they do not, brings the scholars to Herod. Their dream leads them home another way. But Herod is not just a pawn. He too is given the gift of the star.

You-Who-Are-Truth,
Should I expect
That I alone have seen the star?
Should I be astonished
When you also give the light
To those who would hurt you?

THURSDAY, DECEMBER 26 ~ *Read Matthew 2:13-23*

There is a place I see often in my mind. In the summer heat, the grass is brown, but in the just-after-snow melt the green grass grows until it reaches high enough to wave in the wind. The winter is brutally cold. In this place several hundred people of all ages were killed. Their names are there. I often walk there. Sometimes I take off my shoes to feel the earth; when no one else is there, I lie down and listen for the grace of God.

In another place, I found a river stone shaped like a human foot. Then I found another. On them I painted a pair of moccasins. Two became a hundred, and then two hundred. I turned some stones to pairs of moccasins and some to bare feet. They became icons of footprints left by men, women, children, and even infants. Each set is different, as is each name. On the field of grass, I laid out hundreds of pairs of rocks. Whether painted with moccasins of differing colors or bare feet wrapped in cloth, it is the footprints of the babies that I remember the most.

Having seen the star, having been offered the grace, Herod the Great, the institution, makes a different choice.

Howard Thurman would remind us that all institutions will act in their own best interest, and that as queasy as it may make us, the church is also an institution. We face difficult moments where, when standing in the light of the character of God, we see within ourselves the calcification of our own spirits, spirits which have confused religious certainty with humility.

God leads Joseph, Mary, and the infant Jesus not through the institutional doors but out the back door in the dark of night, on a dead run, into a place of anonymity—until it is time.

Humble One,
Did the desert stones remember
That the footprints that led
Out of Egypt
Returned for a new reason?

FRIDAY, DECEMBER 27 ~ *Read Hebrews 2:10-18*

I find myself reaching back to remember once-familiar words or concepts now almost forgotten. I think to ask someone and then remember that those who might recall have entered another life and the words have not been remembered. For one such word I can only replace what once was a vital concept in a dying language with a hyphenated compilation of English words: something like, treating-a-representation-of-a-living-being-as-if-it-were-alive-and-related-to-you. It is a cultural commitment that enables spiritual formation of a sacred value.

Dolls are never left undressed, scattered, or thrown into a box. Toy horses or animals do not lie about or get left outside. At the end of play, certainly at the end of the day, everything, everybody, is cleaned, clothed, and put to rest, covered and warm. When children awake, they "awaken" the toys.

A toy, a learning tool, is treated as part of the family, so that from the time we can walk, we do not understand ourselves to be more important than those with whom we have relationship. There is nobody to whom we are not related. We participate in the relational care of all that God holds sacred.

The Word, this Child-of-the-God-Who-Is-Humble, our text today describes enters into the vulnerability of circumstance and human response by consenting to being born. This Child-of-the-God-Who-Is-Humble is the physical reality of the character of God. This Child-of-the-God-Who-Is-Humble is born related to everybody. When is the Incarnation? Is it the moment of birth? Or when the child assumes the loving relational care of all whom God holds sacred?

You-Who-Chose-and-Chooses to be family with your creation,
You did not think yourself
More important than those
With whom you have relationship.
You covered us and then crawled inside.

SATURDAY, DECEMBER 28 ~ *Read Isaiah 63:7-9*

One of the most beautiful gardens in Britain is at Highgrove. In a tucked-away portion of the garden stands a wall created of what appears to be broken pieces of stone carvings and architectural masonry. Some pieces are stone masonry samples; others broken or damaged works by student artisans. The assembly of disparate pieces of English limestone could grace a museum in any part of the world. As if pieces of cathedrals and halls of learning had leaped together, the wall is an act of grace, moss blending both edge and color. It is called The Wall of Gifts.

Between cornices, stone leaves, and rampant lions, rows of limestone in lapidary form bring the larger remnants home. The Wall of Gifts is not accidental art but the bringing together of hundreds of creative moments into a new expression. No one creative moment gets lost in the new. It is stone and fluidity, math and music. Beside and around the wall, shrubs grow and leaves fall.

You are mine. Not my possession; my beloved.

You are mine. I delight in you. I will restore you. I will not let you go. I will write your name upon my hand. You are mine. What I have begun in you, I will complete. I will be with you in times of trouble. You are mine. I am the Good Shepherd. I have called you by name. You will be like a stream whose waters never fail. You are mine. I will never leave you or forsake you. I am the bush which burns without consuming. Let us reason together. Taste me and see that I am good. You are mine.

Beloved, I am yours.

God of my heart,
You have taken what I thought was a mistake,
Broken.
Looking back, I see
You have built a place
For green things to grow.

SUNDAY, DECEMBER 29 ~ *Read Psalm 148:7-14*

We feel the sun; we see the moon, rain clouds, storm clouds, ice, snow, birds, great whales, and waves. We hear the sound of cicadas, thunder, and gulls. We look up at mountains, and our spirits turn outward. Our footprints are left in the sand-which-once-was-stone, but only for a time. We are part of the mathematics and the music. Both observer and participant, we are always impacted and impactful. God is humble.

To know God is to become increasingly aware of God's humility. To love God is to become increasingly aware of the love of God. That awareness seems to occur concurrently with the humility and love that God develops within us. God's humility confronts us; God's love surprises us. We are not asked to love without the love of God, nor are we urged to humility without the humility of God. Like the sheepherders in Bethlehem, we are overwhelmed by the glory of God. God is humble.

Alma Snell, a member of the Crow Nation (tribe) of Montana, had a profound spiritual presence to her daily life. She would suddenly and quietly say, *aho*, a word to express thanks and joy in the Crow language. It may have been in response to the sound of a bird or recognition of the presence of God. It was a vocal response to the spiritual moment of God-and-Alma. It was a delighted, grateful, you-are-here. *Aho* was enough and everything. That one simple word was like touching hands with God. There was not a moment in any day that Alma was inaccessible to God. Delighting in the creation around her, she lived the rhythms of the day as prayer. She listened for the heart of God. That was her praise.

Humility, Love, Faithfulness,
Glory, Delight.
My soul praises you,
Still astounded
Still awed.

As It Was in the Beginning . . .

DECEMBER 30–31, 2019 • ANNE BURKHOLDER

SCRIPTURE OVERVIEW: Jeremiah delivers happy news, a promise from the Lord of a brighter future day. God will bring back the scattered peoples from everywhere to their homeland, and their mourning will turn into joy. The psalmist encourages those in Jerusalem to praise God for all that God has done. God gives protection, peace, and the law to the children of Israel. The author of Ephesians encourages his readers with confidence in God's eternal plan. God's will was to send Christ and adopt us into God's family. We have been sealed with the Holy Spirit. The opening to John helps us understand the eternal scope of God's plan. From the beginning, the Word has been with God but then becomes flesh and lives among us to reveal divine glory.

QUESTIONS AND SUGGESTIONS FOR REFLECTION

- Read Jeremiah 31:7-14. Consider those who live in exile from their home or from their family relationships. How can you share Jeremiah's words of God's comfort?
- Read Ephesians 1:3-14. How can you live your daily life from the perspective of God's cosmic time? How will you praise God?

Associate dean of Methodist Studies at Candler School of Theology, Emory University; ordained elder in the Florida Conference of The United Methodist Church.

MONDAY, DECEMBER 30 ~ *Read Ephesians 1:3-14*

This week, endings and beginnings get jumbled together. The last month on the calendar coincides with the first season of the Christian year. The new year coincides with ending fiscal cycles. School semesters end and begin. We plan to relinquish poor habits and achieve new goals.

Today's reading frames God's relationship with Jesus-followers in cosmic time. All complicated temporal and spiritual cycles pale in importance compared to God's cosmic scheme, from "before the foundation of the world" to "the fullness of time." God's expectations and desires for the universe—and for us—are set between a time "in the beginning," prior to creation itself and when all will finally be gathered up in Christ.

As disciples of Jesus Christ, we are a redeemed people that exists for "the praise of the glory" of God. The Greek word for glory is *doxus*, the root of the word *doxology*. This term is familiar to many of us as something we sing during worship services: "Glory be to the Father, and to the Son, and to the Holy Ghost. . . ." But we cannot just praise God on Sunday mornings. As disciples, our whole lives are to be lived in praise of God's glory. How joyous, humbling, and overwhelming this can be!

Can you recall a time when you were consumed by efforts to complete a seemingly endless list of tasks to prevent a sense of personal failure or disappointment to others rather than by preparing for God's glorious gift—the gift of God's own Beloved? Let us commit this new year to reimagining our lives framed by praise for God's glorious grace and love and to living as redeemed people in the face of the challenges of our daily lives.

Holy God, thank you for the incredible gift of your Beloved, Jesus Christ. May my life always reflect my praise and gratitude for your grace and love. Amen.

TUESDAY, DECEMBER 31 ~ *Read Jeremiah 31:7-14*

My military family moved fifteen times before I left for college. I have used Google Earth and driven by former homes to see what they look like. I find myself asking, "Was that house really that small? Did we really play in those swampy woods?" Home, for me, was the community of my immediate family, not the domicile where we resided. My parents' love and support sustained me and helped me grow wherever we lived.

Jeremiah offers words of promise to an exiled remnant in Babylon. The remnant dreams of going home. But these dreams have been built on the memories of many who will not return. The people have been in exile for seventy years; two generations have already died. Those who came to Babylon are not the people who will "return." They are sustained in their journey by God's everlasting love. God assures them that their vulnerable members will not be left behind. They will be consoled, led to water, and provided with straight and level paths. Indeed, the blind, lame, children, and pregnant women will travel with ease.

As disciples of Jesus Christ, we are sustained by the love and grace of God that has come to us through Jesus Christ and the support of the Holy Spirit. Our home is the heart of God. In Jeremiah's words to the exiled Israelites we find the promise of a way home out of whatever exile—self-inflicted or inflicted by others—we experience.

No matter what exile has left you vulnerable, defeated, and separated from what you love, God will embrace and sustain you with everlasting love, console you, and lead you home.

Lord, lead me in your love and righteousness. Make your way plain and bring me safely home. Amen.

The Revised Common Lectionary* for 2019
Year C – Advent / Christmas Year A
(Disciplines Edition)

January 1–6

NEW YEAR'S DAY
Ecclesiastes 3:1-13
Psalm 8
Revelation 21:1-6a
Matthew 25:31-46

January 6

EPIPHANY
Isaiah 60:1-6
Psalm 72:1-7, 10-14
Ephesians 3:1-12
Matthew 2:1-12

January 7–13

BAPTISM OF THE LORD
Isaiah 43:1-7
Psalm 29
Acts 8:14-17
Luke 3:15-17, 21-22

January 14–20

Isaiah 62:1-5
Psalm 36:5-10
1 Corinthians 12:1-11
John 2:1-11

January 21–27

Nehemiah 8:1-3, 5-6, 8-10
Psalm 19
1 Corinthians 12:12-31a
Luke 4:14-21

January 28—February 3

Jeremiah 1:4-10
Psalm 71:1-6
1 Corinthians 13
Luke 4:21-30

February 4–10

Isaiah 6:1-13
Psalm 138
1 Corinthians 15:1-11
Luke 5:1-11

February 11–17

Jeremiah 17:5-10
Psalm 1
1 Corinthians 15:12-20
Luke 6:17-26

February 18–24

Genesis 45:3-11, 15
Psalm 37:1-11, 39-40
1 Corinthians 15:35-38, 42-50
Luke 6:27-38

February 25—March 3

TRANSFIGURATION
Exodus 34:29-35
Psalm 99
2 Corinthians 3:12–4:2
Luke 9:28-43

March 4–10
FIRST SUNDAY IN LENT
Deuteronomy 26:1-11
Psalm 91:2, 9-16
Romans 10:8b-13
Luke 4:1-13

March 6
ASH WEDNESDAY
Joel 2:1-2, 12-17 or
Isaiah 58:1-12
Psalm 51:1-17
2 Corinthians 5:20b–6:10
Matthew 6:1-6, 16-21

March 11–17
SECOND SUNDAY IN LENT
Genesis 15:1-12, 17-18
Psalm 27
Philippians 3:17–4:1
Luke 13:31-35

March 18–24
THIRD SUNDAY IN LENT
Isaiah 55:1-9
Psalm 63:1-8
1 Corinthians 10:1-13
Luke 13:1-9

March 25–31
FOURTH SUNDAY IN LENT
Joshua 5:9-12
Psalm 32
2 Corinthians 5:16-21
Luke 15:1-3, 11b-32

April 1–7
FIFTH SUNDAY IN LENT
Isaiah 43:16-21
Psalm 126
Philippians 3:4b-14
John 12:1-8

April 8–14
PALM/PASSION SUNDAY

Liturgy of the Palms
Psalm 118:1-2, 19-29
Luke 19:28-40

Liturgy of the Passion
Isaiah 50:4-9a
Psalm 31:9-16
Philippians 2:5-11
Luke 22:14–23:56

April 15–21
HOLY WEEK

Monday
Isaiah 42:1-9
Psalm 36:5-11
Hebrews 9:11-15
John 12:1-11

Tuesday
Isaiah 49:1-7
Psalm 71:1-14
1 Corinthians 1:18-31
John 12:20-36

Wednesday
Isaiah 50:4-9a
Psalm 70
Hebrews 12:1-3
John 13:21-32

Maundy Thursday
Exodus 12:1-14
Psalm 116:1-2, 12-19
1 Corinthians 11:23-26
John 13:1-17, 31b-35

Good Friday
Isaiah 52:13–53:12
Psalm 22
Hebrews 4:14-16; 5:7-9
John 18:1–19:42

Holy Saturday
Job 14:1-14
Psalm 31:1-4, 15-16
1 Peter 4:1-8
Matthew 27:57-66

Easter–April 21
Acts 10:34-43
Psalm 118:14-24
1 Corinthians 15:19-26
John 20:1-18

April 22–28
Acts 5:27-32
Psalm 150
Revelation 1:4-8
John 20:19-31

April 29—May 5
Acts 9:1-20
Psalm 30
Revelation 5:11-14
John 21:1-19

May 6–12
Acts 9:36-43
Psalm 23
Revelation 7:9-17
John 10:22-30

May 13–19
Acts 11:1-18
Psalm 148
Revelation 21:1-6
John 13:31-35

May 20–26
Acts 16:9-15
Psalm 67
Revelation 21:10, 22–22:5
John 14:23-29

May 27—June 2
Acts 16:16-34
Psalm 97
Revelation 22:12-14, 16-17, 20-21
John 17:20-26

May 30
Ascension Day
Acts 1:1-11
Psalm 47
Ephesians 1:15-23
Luke 24:44-53

June 3–9
Pentecost
Acts 2:1-21
Psalm 104:24-34, 35b
Romans 8:14-17
John 14:8-17, 25-27

June 10–16
Trinity Sunday
Proverbs 8:1-4, 22-31
Psalm 8
Romans 5:1-5
John 16:12-15

June 17–23
1 Kings 19:1-15a
Psalm 42
Galatians 3:23-29
Luke 8:26-39

June 24–30
2 Kings 2:1-2, 6-14
Psalm 16
Galatians 5:1, 13-25
Luke 9:51-62

July 1–7
2 Kings 5:1-14
Psalm 30
Galatians 6:1-16
Luke 10:1-11, 16-20

July 8–14
Amos 7:7-17
Psalm 82
Colossians 1:1-14
Luke 10:25-37

July 15–21
Amos 8:1-12
Psalm 52
Colossians 1:15-28
Luke 10:38-42

July 22–28
Hosea 1:2-10
Psalm 85
Colossians 2:6-19
Luke 11:1-13

July 29—August 4
Hosea 11:1-11
Psalm 107:1-9, 43
Colossians 3:1-11
Luke 12:13-21

August 5–11
Isaiah 1:1, 10-20
Psalm 50:1-8, 22-23
Hebrews 11:1-3, 8-16
Luke 12:32-40

August 12–18
Isaiah 5:1-7
Psalm 80:1-2, 8-19
Hebrews 11:29–12:2
Luke 12:49-56

August 19–25
Jeremiah 1:4-10
Psalm 71:1-6
Hebrews 12:18-29
Luke 13:10-17

August 26—September 1
Jeremiah 2:4-13
Psalm 81:1, 10-16
Hebrews 13:1-8, 15-16
Luke 14:1, 7-14

September 2–8
Jeremiah 18:1-11
Psalm 139:1-6, 13-18
Philemon 1-21
Luke 14:25-33

September 9–15
Jeremiah 4:11-12, 22-28
Psalm 14
1 Timothy 1:12-17
Luke 15:1-10

September 16–22
Jeremiah 8:18–9:1
Psalm 79:1-9
1 Timothy 2:1-7
Luke 16:1-13

September 23–29
Jeremiah 32:1-3a, 6-15
Psalm 91:1-6, 14-16
1 Timothy 6:6-19
Luke 16:19-31

September 30—October 6
Lamentations 1:1-6
Psalm 137
2 Timothy 1:1-14
Luke 17:5-10

October 7–13
Jeremiah 29:1, 4-7
Psalm 66:1-12
2 Timothy 2:8-15
Luke 17:11-19

October 14–20
Jeremiah 31:27-34
Psalm 119:97-104
2 Timothy 3:14–4:5
Luke 18:1-8

> **October 14**
> THANKSGIVING DAY, CANADA
> Deuteronomy 26:1-11
> Psalm 100
> Philippians 4:4-9
> John 6:25-35

October 21–27
Joel 2:23-32
Psalm 65
2 Timothy 4:6-8, 16-18
Luke 18:9-14

October 28—November 3
Habakkuk 1:1-4; 2:1-4
Psalm 119:137-144
2 Thessalonians 1:1-4, 11-12
Luke 19:1-10

> **November 1**
> ALL SAINTS DAY
> Daniel 7:1-3, 15-18
> Psalm 149
> Ephesians 1:11-23
> Luke 6:20-31

November 4–10
Haggai 1:15b–2:9
Psalm 145:1-5, 17-21
2 Thessalonians 2:1-5, 13-17
Luke 20:27-38

November 11–17
Isaiah 65:17-25
Isaiah 12
2 Thessalonians 3:6-13
Luke 21:5-19

November 18–24
THE REIGN OF CHRIST
Jeremiah 23:1-6
Luke 1:68-79
Colossians 1:11-20
Luke 23:33-43

November 25—December 1
FIRST SUNDAY OF ADVENT
Isaiah 2:1-5
Psalm 122
Romans 13:11-14
Matthew 24:36-44

> **November 28**
> THANKSGIVING DAY, USA
> Deuteronomy 26:1-11
> Psalm 100
> Philippians 4:4-9
> John 6:25-35

December 2–8
SECOND SUNDAY OF ADVENT
Isaiah 11:1-10
Psalm 72:1-7, 18-19
Romans 15:4-13
Matthew 3:1-12

December 9–15
THIRD SUNDAY OF ADVENT
Isaiah 35:1-10
Luke 1:47-55
James 5:7-10
Matthew 11:2-11

December 16–22
FOURTH SUNDAY OF ADVENT
Isaiah 7:10-16
Psalm 80:1-7, 17-19
Romans 1:1-7
Matthew 1:18-25

December 23–29
Isaiah 63:7-9
Psalm 148
Hebrews 2:10-18
Matthew 2:13-23

December 24
CHRISTMAS EVE
Isaiah 9:2-7
Psalm 96
Titus 2:11-14
Luke 2:1-20

December 25
CHRISTMAS DAY
Isaiah 52:7-10
Psalm 98
Hebrews 1:1-12
John 1:1-14

December 30–31
Jeremiah 31:7-14
Psalm 147:12-20
Ephesians 1:3-14
John 1:1-18

A Guide to Daily Prayer

These prayers imply worship time with a group; feel free to adapt the plural pronouns for personal use.

Morning Prayer

"In the morning, O Lord, you hear my voice;
    in the morning I lay my requests before you
    and wait in expectation."
        —Psalm 5:3

Gathering and Silence

Call to Praise and Prayer

God said: Let there be light; and there was light.
And God saw that the light was good.

Psalm 63:2-6

God, my God, you I crave;
my soul thirsts for you,
my body aches for you
like a dry and weary land.
    Let me gaze on you in your temple:
    a Vision of strength and glory
    Your love is better than life,
    my speech is full of praise.
    I give you a lifetime of worship,
    my hands raised in your name.
    I feast at a rich table
    my lips sing of your glory.

Prayer of Thanksgiving

We praise you with joy, loving God, for your grace is better than life itself. You have sustained us through the darkness: and you bless us with life in this new day. In the shadow of your wings we sing for joy and bless your holy name. Amen.

Scripture Reading

Silence

Prayers of the People

The Lord's Prayer (see Midday Prayer for text)

Blessing

May the light of your mercy shine brightly on all who walk in your presence today, O Lord.

Midday Prayer

"I will extol the Lord at all times;
God's praise will always be on my lips."
—Psalm 34:1

Gathering and Silence

Call to Praise and Prayer

O Lord, my Savior, teach me your ways.
My hope is in you all day long.

Prayer of Thanksgiving

God of mercy, we acknowledge this midday pause of refreshment as one of your many generous gifts. Look kindly upon our work this day; may it be made perfect in your time. May our purpose and prayers be pleasing to you. This we ask through Christ our Lord. Amen.

Scripture Reading

Silence

Prayers of the People

The Lord's Prayer (ecumenical text)

Our Father in heaven,
hallowed be your name,
your kingdom come,
your will be done,
on earth as in heaven.

Give us today our daily bread.
Forgive us our sins as we forgive
    those who sin against us.
Save us from the time of trial,
    and deliver us from evil.
For the kingdom, the power, and the glory
    are yours, now and forever. Amen.

Blessing

Strong is the love embracing us, faithful the Lord from morning to night.

"My soul finds rest in God alone;
my salvation comes from God."
—Psalm 62:1

Gathering and Silence

Call to Praise and Prayer

From the rising of the sun to its setting,
let the name of the Lord be praised.

Psalm 134

Bless the Lord,
all who serve in God's house,
who stand watch
throughout the night.

Lift up your hands
in the holy place
and bless the Lord.

And may God,
the maker of earth and sky,
bless you from Zion.

Prayer of Thanksgiving

Sovereign God, you have been our help during the day and you promise to be with us at night. Receive this prayer as a sign of our trust in you. Save us from all evil, keep us from all harm, and guide us in your way. We belong to you, Lord. Protect us by the power of your name. In Jesus Christ we pray. Amen.

Scripture Reading

Silence

Prayers of the People

The Lord's Prayer (see Midday Prayer for text)

Blessing

May your unfailing love rest upon us, O LORD,
even as we hope in you.

This Guide to Daily Prayer was compiled from scripture and other resources by Rueben P. Job and then adapted by the Pathways Center for Spiritual Leadership while under the direction of Marjorie J. Thompson.

the text this week
READ
STUDY
PRAY
WORSHIP
...ALL YEAR LONG
THE TEXT THIS WEEK IS YOUR LECTIONARY RESOURCE FOR PERSONAL AND COMMUNITY-WIDE ENGAGEMENT
DISCOVER NEW CONTENT EACH WEEK AT TEXTWEEK.COM